William F. Buckley Sr.

Also by John A. Adams Jr.

We Are the Aggies: History of the Association of Former Students, 1876–1979

Damming the Colorado: Rise of the Lower Colorado River Authority, 1933–1939
  (recipient of the 1991 T. R. Fehrenbach Book Award)

Softly Call the Muster: Mexican Banking and Investment in Transition

Keepers of the Spirit: The History of the Aggie Corps of Cadets

Bordering the Future: Impact of Mexico on the U.S. Economy

Texas Aggies Go to War: In the Service of Their Country (with Henry C. Dethloff)

Conflict and Commerce on the Rio Grande: Laredo, 1755–1955

Cyber Blackout: When the Lights Go Out

Warrior at Heart: Governor John Milton, King Cotton, and Civil War Florida

The Fightin' Texas Aggie Defenders of Bataan and Corregidor

*Murder and Intrigue on the Mexican Border: Governor Colquitt, President Wilson,
  and the Vergara Affair*

Over There in the Air: Texas Aggie Aviators in World War I, 1917–1918

My Duty Lies Here: Lawrence Sullivan Ross at the A&M College of Texas, 1891–1898

Standing Ready: The Golden Age of Football and the 12th Man Tradition

WILLIAM F. BUCKLEY SR.

WITNESS TO THE MEXICAN REVOLUTION, 1908–1922

JOHN A. ADAMS JR.

FOREWORD BY JAMES L. BUCKLEY

UNIVERSITY OF OKLAHOMA PRESS : NORMAN

Publication of this book is made possible through the generosity of Edith Kinney Gaylord.

Library of Congress Cataloging-in-Publication Data

Names: Adams, John A., Jr., 1951– author.
Title: William F. Buckley Sr. : witness to the Mexican revolution,
    1908–1922 / John A. Adams Jr. ; foreword by James L. Buckley.
Description: Norman : University of Oklahoma Press, [2023] | Includes
    bibliographical references and index. | Summary: "Tells how William
    F. Buckley Sr., father of the later-famous conservative commentator,
    left his native Texas as a young man in 1909 and built a fortune in the
    nascent oil industry while caught between revolution-racked Mexico
    and the United States"—Provided by publisher.
Identifiers: LCCN 2022041064 | ISBN 978-0-8061-9181-2 (hardcover) |
    ISBN 978-0-8061-9182-9 (paperback)
Subjects: LCSH: Buckley, William Frank, 1881–1958. | Petroleum
    industry and trade—Texas—Biography. | Petroleum industry and
    trade—Mexico—Biography. | Lawyers—Texas—Biography. |
    Mexico—History—Revolution, 1910–1920.
Classification: LCC HD9567.T3 A233 2023 | DDC 338.2/7280972—dc23/
    eng/20221125
LC record available at https://lccn.loc.gov/2022041064

The paper in this book meets the guidelines for permanence and durability of the Committee on Production Guidelines for Book Longevity of the Council on Library Resources, Inc. ∞

To John A. Adams III

Contents

Foreword, by James L. Buckley / ix
Acknowledgments / xiii

Introduction / 1
1. Revolution: Ojos Azules / 6
2. Huerta and Mr. X / 36
3. Tampico: Buckley and Buckley / 70
4. Church and State / 105
5. Buckley and the Fall Committee / 133
6. Lone Ranger from Texas / 170
   Epilogue: Legacy of an Adventurous Texan / 207

Appendixes
   A. Chronological Statement of Events
      in Mexico City / 211
   B. Embassy and Consul Staff, 1911–1919 / 217
   C. Pacto de la Ciudadela / 219
   D. Buckley Family Tree / 221
Notes / 223
Bibliography / 267
Index / 295

Foreword

SHORTLY AFTER I WAS BORN, my family moved from New York to a small village in the northwest corner of Connecticut. Sharon was idyllic because it was beyond commuting distance from anywhere, hence unaffected by the housing developments and the shopping malls and post-colonial architecture that have marred too many towns even in exurbia. Sharon was also tiny. In 1923, when we moved there, the sixty-square-mile town had a population of about sixteen hundred people. It has since exploded to around twenty-nine hundred.

Sharon is where I have spent most of my life, and it is where my heart has remained. But as my brothers and sisters and I were growing up, we were very conscious of being significantly different from our friends and neighbors. As our mother was from New Orleans and our father from South Texas, we were culturally southern. My mother would tell us tales of Con-federate heroism, and our meals tended to consist of such things as fried chicken, beans and rice, and corn bread, while our Yankee neighbors feasted on boiled potatoes, boiled beef, and soft store-bought bread.

But what distinguished us most deeply was Mexico. It had somehow per-meated our DNA. My father grew up in San Diego, Texas, of whose two thousand residents about eighteen hundred were Mexican-Texans whose ancestors had lived there for a century or two before the mostly Protestant Anglos arrived. So he grew up with a total command of Spanish, and as he was Catholic, he had especially close relationships with the Mexican com-munity, relationships that in time developed into a love affair with their former country.

And that is why, following graduation from law school, my father decided to move to Mexico and build a life there. It was in Mexico that he developed the skills and specialized knowledge that were essential to the rest of his life. And it was there that he had intended to live the rest of it . . . until he was expelled from the country for trying to save it from its worst aspects.

So it was hardly surprising that his children should have a Mexican nanny and grow up speaking Spanish as a second language. Or that we would spend the nine days before Christmas celebrating the Spanish posadas tracing Joseph and Mary's journey in search of an inn where she could give birth to Jesus. And as our family expanded (I was the fourth of ten children), so did our house in Sharon, and it did so in a rather startling way for a New England home. The two wings added to the house bordered a Mexican patio taken from the architect's plan for the house my father was about to build in Mexico City before his expulsion. So even our home had a highly Mexican favor to it.

To cap it all, there were the wonderful tales of Mexican adventures with which our father would entertain us at dinnertime when we were young. But very few of them dealt with the critical experiences that are the subject of this book. We did learn of his having declined the offer by the Woodrow Wilson administration of the civil governorship of Veracruz, but not the reasons why he would have been offered such a post. We also know he served as counsel to the Mexican delegation to a conference that was supposed to patch up the mess created by the American landings there—but again, not the reason why. And all of this while he was still in his thirties.

My father stopped telling us these tales when we were still young; and after his death, I kept kicking myself—and my brothers and sisters—for our collective failure to seek more than anecdotal information about his Mexican experiences. We knew that he had carved out a special role within the American community there, that he had established close relationships with key members of succeeding Mexican revolutionary governments, and that the United States Senate had invited him to testify on Mexican affairs. But we never inquired into the specific roles he was called upon to play, or the critical issues that were to be resolved.

And that is why I am so grateful to John Adams for providing the answers to all the questions my siblings and I failed to ask and for producing a book with such interesting insight into a most critical period of Mexican history, our own government's failures in dealing with it, and the roles our father came to play with respect to each. My great regret is that none of my brothers and sisters are alive to read this fascinating account.

James L. Buckley

Acknowledgments

MANY HAVE ASSISTED TO make this project possible. Years ago when I came across the William F. Buckley Sr. collection at the Benson Latin American Library in Austin, I had the same fleeting response of others who had reviewed the collection—that the voluminous papers were in a state of disarray. The reason for this chaos is covered in the introduction. While working on a book on the Vergara affair on the Mexican border during the Mexican Revolution, I dove into the first few boxes to find what I needed and made a note to return to this collection to do additional research on Buckley. Years later, I would like to thank the staff at the Benson Library, especially Adan Benavides and José Montelongo, for their timely assistance.

John A. Adams III, my son, provided tremendous assistance and many diligent long hours sorting through the boxes of documents at Benson as I set up individual files and drafted an outline and index to better deal with the jumbled materials. Without John's timely help and persistence, this project would not have been possible. John and I may be the only two researchers in the last one hundred years to review all of the Buckley collection.

A very special thanks is extended to Judge James L. Buckley, for providing timely information and feedback on the manuscript and contributing the foreword. I was further assisted with respect to family records and pictures by his nephews Cameron O. Smith in Sharon, Connecticut, and William Hunt Buckley in Mexico City.

Additional archival assistance that proved critical in developing the text was offered by the staffs at the Beineke Library at Yale University, the

DeGolyer Library at Southern Methodist University, the New Mexico State Archives, the Huntington Library, and the West Point archive. At the Cushing Memorial Archives at Texas A&M, ongoing research assistance and enduring patience was provided by Anton DuPlessis and Leslie Winter.

Critically important to the project was the review, feedback, and insight on the finer points of the manuscript provided by the late Henry C. Dethloff in College Station, John H. Keck in Laredo, J. Gilberto Quezada in San Antonio, Bill Page at the Evans Library at Texas A&M, and Jerry Thompson at Texas A&M International University in Laredo. Additional timely comments and suggestions were provided by Linda Hall at New Mexico and Stephen Andes at LSU.

Others who provided assistance include the late Allan Ashcraft, Anne Boykin, David Cardwell, Ollie Crinkelmeyer, the late Larry Hill, Jeff Jones, Andres Paxman, David Perez, and Memo Trevino, whose timely help brought this project to a conclusion.

Finally, for his skill, patience, and good humor, I want to thank copy editor Robert Fullilove, who has done a tremendous job; and at the University of Oklahoma Press, my thanks to Kent Calder, Steven Baker, and the entire staff.

And my wife, Sherry, as always, has been in steady support of all my projects.

John A. Adams Jr.

Introduction

WILLIAM F. BUCKLEY WAS raised in the sleepy frontier community of San Diego in South Texas. Ranching in the conservative, tradition-minded region dominated by Mexican families in the 1890s shaped Will's character and future as he departed for Austin in 1900 to attend the University of Texas. Upon graduation with a law degree in 1907, he moved to Mexico City, arriving on the eve of the revolution that forever changed his life and the course of Mexico for decades.

When the name Buckley or William F. Buckley is mentioned, most people immediately think of the ardent conservative commentator, writer, and founder of *National Review*—William F. Buckley Jr. Few are even aware of the dynamic career and impact of his father, William F. Buckley Sr. The roots of William junior's political leanings were greatly influenced by the family's conservative Catholic education and upbringing driven by his father. Like their father, the Buckley children were exposed to multiple cultures, political ideas, and languages. William Jr. and his nine successful siblings—all active in politics, book publishing, business—would in time be known in the popular press as simply "the Buckleys." This book is about the life and times of an inquisitive boy from San Diego, Texas, William F. Buckley Sr., who occupied a front-row seat to the Mexican Revolution and, following those events, embarked on a dynamic global business career that extended through the mid-1950s.

One of the higher-profile Americans in revolutionary Mexico, Will Buckley had routine contact with the local and national politicians (including Pancho Villa), diplomats, businessmen, oil well drillers, bandits, bankers, and rebel leaders who shaped the course and outcome of the violent, decade-long civil war that gripped Mexico. His story has not been fully told. The hubris and errors of President Woodrow Wilson a century ago in dealing with revolutionary Mexico and its leaders are outlined here in detail. Buckley documented his objections to the White House's often misinformed, heavy-handed policies and intervention in Mexico's complex social, economic, and political fabric.

The revolution in Mexico from 1910 to 1920 was the most tumultuous and violent period in Mexican history. More than 1 million Mexicans were killed, out of a population of 15 million. The era of revolt, carnage, and upheaval attracted international attention and concern and verged on open warfare with the United States. The American government weighed intervention options against the safety of its own citizens and the stability of Mexico necessary to return calm to the country. International tensions soon included the British, French, and German governments on the eve of World War I. Although the Mexican Revolution has been chronicled in scores of volumes, few studies have been based on first-person accounts—especially by non-Mexicans. Controversial American ambassador Henry Lane Wilson and the wife of the embassy chargé d'affaires, Edith O'Shaughnessy, each wrote and published, during the 1920s, memoirs from their diplomatic perspective in Mexico City. A rare volume is Consul Will B. Davis's memoirs, *Experiences and Observations of an American Consular Officer during the Recent Mexican Revolution*, privately published in 1917, covering the 1913–16 period. Recently published volumes, including *Murder and Counterrevolution in Mexico: The Eyewitness Account of German Ambassador Paul von Hintze* (2015), edited by Friedrich Schuler, and *Jenkins of Mexico* (2017) by Andrew Paxman, provide unique insights. If only Buckley had taken some time to draft a volume on his experiences!

William Buckley led a life of high adventure, often risky entrepreneurial business dealings, and occasional danger. After departing his South Texas ranch family home, he graduated with honors from the University of Texas, then cast his early career and future in Mexico. He was in routine contact with rebels, was captured by (and escaped from) bandits commissioned to murder him, and faced down snipers in the streets of Veracruz. He believed in self-reliance, was deeply independent, and distrusted government. He was a dedicated family man and was profoundly rooted and devout in his Catholic faith. He would cast a conservative influence on all his children, especially William Jr. Buckley Sr.'s son Reed captures the essence of the impact the Mexican Revolution had on his father: "Father's knowledge of Mexican history and his personal involvement with Mexico from 1908 to 1921 deepened his frontier suspicions of autocratic [leaders] (and big government in general), and this attitude dyes all his children strongly."

Only bits and pieces of the life and lore of William F. Buckley Sr. have previously been told in memoirs by family members and business associates. In pursuit of the bigger story, I interviewed Will's son, judge and former US senator James Buckley, as well as his nephews William Hunt Buckley and Cameron Smith. Their recollections were extremely insightful and valuable. But the full story could not be told without access to the extensive archival collection of personal documents, intelligence reports, biographical profiles of revolutionary personalities in the files of the Benson Latin America Library at the University of Texas in Austin, as well as data on business, especially the petroleum industry, and records of the Niagara (ABC) Conference of 1914. Together these sources provide an, as yet to be told, dramatic, extensive picture of the period.

The Buckley Papers collection in the Benson Archives is one of the most fascinating document collections I have seen over four decades of research. William Buckley, shortly after he was expelled from Mexico by the Obregón administration in late 1921, donated to the archives at the University of Texas some three dozen boxes of records, clippings, and reports from his offices in Mexico City and Tampico, as well as confidential files he accumulated at the Murray Hill Hotel in New York City in preparation for the US congressional hearings on "Mexican Affairs" in 1919–1920. They were received by Will's former history professor and librarian Eugene C. Barker and stored untouched for some three years. Buckley advised Barker to limit access to the collection as well as include additional sources of documents to complement the archive. Given that so few years had passed since the dramatic events in Mexico, Buckley expressed concern that the documents be handled in a confidential manner.

The documents remained in storage until mid-1925 when Barker received a request from the American-Mexican Special Claims Commission of the US State Department to obtain access to the Buckley files. With Buckley's approval, the documents were provided and proved to be critical to the commission's research and investigations to document and confirm arbitration cases and proceedings for redress of American citizens who suffered wrongs in Mexico. There was concern about the documents' safe handling and access, and after a few months of negotiations the boxes were shipped to Washington. The documents were not returned to Austin until mid-1929. Barker's concern over how the documents were handled seems well founded in retrospect, as the files were disheveled and folders misfiled, leaving no way to determine whether documents had been removed and not returned. Thus, it is no mystery why there has been no extensive research using this collection. In spite of significant efforts I made to clean up and refile the documents, no fewer than five different indexes to the collection were discovered and no two lists matched. Thus, for this study upwards of fifteen thousand documents in the Buckley Papers were examined.

I quickly realized why there had apparently, since the mid-1930s, been very little use of the documents, due to the collection's sheer volume and jumbled contents. I have found very few references in published works to this collection. The exceptions are limited use by Jonathan Brown, Charles Hale, Linda Hall, John Mason Hart, and Robert Quirk. Nonetheless, the Buckley collection along with Buckley's extensive Senator Albert B. Fall Foreign Relations Committee documents, comprising 3,381 pages of testimony on the "Investigation of Mexican Affairs" in 1919–1920, are a trove of in-person perspectives on the Mexican revolutionary period from scores of US expatriates from 1910 through 1919.

Accordingly, the history of William Buckley's dynamic and eventful early career, based largely on these documents, is the primary focus of this book. Additional primary sources and letters by W.F.B. were found at Yale University's Sterling Library Archives, the West Point archives, the DeGolyer Library at SMU in Dallas, the Huntington Library in San Marino, California, and the New Mexico State Archives in Santa Fe.

In addition to the Buckley Papers in Austin, Will and Aloise Buckley's children have completed a number of memoirs pertaining to their father and their family. Four (of more than three score published by the Buckley children) that stand out are the compilation of essays in *W.F.B.: An Appreciation by His Family and Friends*, edited and privately published by Priscilla L. Buckley and William F. Buckley Jr. (1959); *An American Family: The Buckleys* by Reid Buckley (2008); *Will Mrs. Major Go to Hell?* By Aloise Buckley Heath (1969); and *Gleanings from an Unplanned Life* by James L. Buckley (2006). Cameron O. Smith and James Buckley also made available the "Buckley Family Files," which were very timely.

For years, after Buckley's departure from Mexico in 1921, family and friends were regaled with stories, lore, and humor from the years of the Mexican Revolution. Youngest son Reid recalled, "I grew up without need for stories of adventure. The legends about Father's early years in Mexico sufficed. They were kept alive by visits from unusually short, swarthy, corpulent men, one of whom [at least] had risen from banditry to governorship, which is just about the same thing."

And in his own words, the story begins with young South Texas lawyer Will Buckley's first meeting with the grand master of Mexico, Don Porfirio Díaz, in 1909. In a small group of visitors to the presidential residence at Chapultepec, he was introduced to the formidable dictator. Will, who most likely impressed Díaz with his impeccable Spanish and soft Texas accent, listened as the president reviewed in detail the glories of the robust Mexican economy yet expressed his concern over the nation's literacy. After listening attentively to the flowing self-praise, Will, "with his Southwestern directness," asked, "That's marvelous, Your Excellency, but what will happen when you die?"

At family dinnertime gatherings decades later, Will was still amazed by his naivete and abruptness, noting that the reception hall "went stock still" as someone whispered into his ear, "His Excellency will never die!"[1]

Viva Mexico!

CHAPTER ONE

Revolution
Ojos Azules

Madero has unleashed a tiger. Now let's see if he can control it.
—Don Porfirio Díaz, May 1911

O N THE LATE AFTERNOON OF Sunday, February 16, 1913, Will Buckley rode in a darkened sedan from his home near the *Zócalo* to the American Embassy three blocks south of Paseo de la Reforma. The normally quick ride was slowed by a labyrinth of improvised barricades, hundreds of bloated dead bodies in the streets, and scattered fires. Live electric wires dangled and sparked uncontrollably. A week of door-to-door fighting and artillery barrages had resulted in a lingering smell of decay and gunpowder—a marked departure from the usual crisp cool evening air of Mexico City. The Mexican Revolution had entered a new and deadly juncture.

As artillery shells exploded in the distance, he turned onto the dark and empty Avenida de los Insurgentes and pulled up to the front of what seemed to be a dark and abandoned embassy. Entering, Will was ushered into the inner courtyard filled with scores of exiled Americans, Mexicans, and foreigners looking for a safe haven. From an open door, Ambassador Henry Lane Wilson waved as if to indicate all was under control.

William F. Buckley, a resident of Mexico City since 1908, was as shocked and concerned as those he stepped over at the scale of the violent wave that had swept the city. A confidant of the ambassador, the young Texas attorney served as an unofficial liaison between the embassy and American business interests in Mexico and with officials at the highest levels of the Mexican government. Will's law degree from the University of Texas and his impeccable Spanish allowed him to flourish in business circles as well as the local political cliques in the capital. Little did he know he would have a front-row seat to the Mexican Revolution.

Madero

Within days of entering the National Palace on November 6, 1911, President Francisco Ignacio Madero met opposition from armed splinter factions across the country with divergent goals for the revolution.[1] The "tiger" was quickly beyond the control of the idealistic new president. Additionally, landed hacendados, the business sector, and foreign financiers expressed concern with the new administration's reforms and its ability to govern. In addition to the political and armed opposition, the press attacked Madero mercilessly. The first to express grave discontent with the new regime was Emiliano Zapata in southern Mexico, followed by an uprising by Gen. Bernardo Reyes in the north along the US-Mexico border. Emilio Vasquez Gómez organized a third revolt in the state of Chihuahua following a proclamation by Pascual Orozco, who expressed concern with the path of social reform. However, the most formidable opposition came from Felix Díaz, the nephew of Don Porfirio. Until early 1913, opposition forces had failed to affect the Federal District. Madero had shown signs of curbing his opposition. Reyes and Díaz had been captured and imprisoned awaiting trial for their previous acts of treason to overthrow the government. Venustiano Carranza, in early February, seemingly modified his concern about his own position and sent a written pledge of support to Madero. Rather than have Reyes and Díaz executed as traitors, which was the usual custom in Mexico, Madero agreed that they be properly tried! This soon changed—his clemency toward avowed enemies got the better of his prudence.[2]

Thus, a violent period—known as the Decena Trágica (Ten Tragic Days)—erupted in Mexico City on Sunday, February 9, 1913. When negotiations among counterrevolutionary groups against the sitting president collapsed, Madero found himself quickly besieged as complicated political subterfuge ushered in the bloody ten days of fighting in the streets of the capital. As Buckley waited in Mexico City along with a nervous group of expats, President Madero hoped he could hold on to his administration with the assistance of a loyal Federal army commanded by Gen. Victoriano Huerta. The general was a dangerous opportunist, and this would prove in time to be a fatal mistake.[3]

The anti-Madero *golpe de estado* (coup d'état) forces in Mexico City were led by General Reyes, who, after being freed from the downtown prison along with Felix Díaz, rallied partisan troops to attack the National Palace.

Headstrong and aggressive, Reyes was killed in the first attack, and the rebel leadership passed to Felix Díaz. Most of the fighting in the Federal District was in the heart of the residential area of downtown between the Ciudadela and the palace. All activities in the city of some 450,000 inhabitants came to a halt. The US Embassy soon became a haven and a gathering place as Americans were driven from their homes.[4]

Madero, thirty-seven years old, was elected to the presidency in late 1911 after more than three decades of iron-fisted rule under then eighty-year-old Don Porfirio Díaz. Madero, a member of one of the five richest families in Mexico, did not command the same control or respect over the Federal army, political factions, and rural fiefdoms as did Díaz. Furthermore, Díaz had begun an open-door development policy that attracted a great deal of foreign investment in all sectors of the economy, from railroads and mining to ranching. In the process, however, he had done nothing to reduce the growing divide and frustration between the rich and the poor. Some 80 percent of the Mexican population, predominately rural, was illiterate, and half did not speak Spanish. Madero's idealistic vision of a reformed, more democratic Mexico did not conform with the scope and complexity of the sociopolitical structure in the country. A change of government at the top would not usher in change in decades of deeply seated dynamics that comprised early twentieth-century Mexico. Historian John Mason Hart concluded, "Madero's idea of American-style democracy failed to grasp the realities of class confrontation in the Mexico of 1911–13."[5]

At the heart of the class discontent was a harsh land policy that deprived *ejidos* (communities) of their property and limited opportunities for the restless peasant class in the already stagnant rural economy. Additionally, there was labor unrest, with strikes at Cananea Consolidated Copper Mines in Sonora and peasant uprisings against the sugar haciendas in the state of Morelos and in the textile industries. Workers in Veracruz demanded more pay, reduced work hours, and better working conditions. An undated memo in the Buckley Papers assessed the disruption: "The promotion of strikes for impossible increases of wages, instead of negotiating privately for moderate increases which could be no doubt obtained under pressure from the Government, results in making enemies of the employees because of the compulsion and open injustice of the Government organizing the strikes; in making enemies of the men because they do not get as much as they have been led to expect; and making enemies of the public in general because it is they who eventually have to pay the bill." Noted Mexican historian Michael C. Meyer concluded, "Porfirian capitalism shunned the masses, elections at all levels of government were a farce, and third, freedom of the press did not exist."[6]

Will Buckley was an active leader in the so-called community of expats in Mexico City, which included US and European commercial members that had business and investment interests throughout Mexico. Buckley worked with Porfirio Díaz as representative of a number of foreign firms, predominately in routine corporate work followed by a growing practice in the booming oil production areas in Tampico and Tuxpan. While accustomed to the heavy-handed demands and stable centralized control under Díaz, during the transition Will quickly became familiar with the new Madero government and his chief lieutenants. The business community was concerned that the policies of the old president would not continue. Madero's campaign pledge to institute land reform created concern among all foreign entities nationwide. Ambassador Wilson advised President Taft in 1911 that a state of anarchy existed, and the Madero government was not fulfilling its obligations to protect Americans and their property. The ambassador's close access to the new president provides a unique insight into the dynamics of the period: "President Madero, who succeeded to the presidency [in 1911], was a man of French education, with a tendency to chauvinism, and to look upon the United States as the archenemy of Mexico and to see unfriendliness in our every act. However, he was a good man, of the highest political probity. His honesty was indeed as apparent as his unfitness for government."[7]

Buckley was a quick study of people and observed, as did others, Madero's constant nervousness and inability to delegate responsibilities to capable subordinates. Madero was the antithesis of the macho Mexican cacique—a vegetarian with a high-pitched voice, he failed to command respect. Nepotism, fueled by the increasingly harsh role of his brother Gustavo, and a so-called inside political group, or *porra*, diminished the president's lofty goals and alienated key domestic and foreign business interests. Coupled with growing disenchantment in the ranks of the Federal army, political opposition, and major concerns from the landed aristocracy, this background set the stage for the revolutionary activities that began in early 1912. Reports of treasonous actions and some six organized armed revolts (including detailed plans by Carranza in the north, contradicting his repeated pledge to support Madero) were ignored and misgauged by the president. Rumors of counterrevolutionary groups organizing along the Rio Grande in South Texas soon attracted attention. Governor Oscar B. Colquitt of Texas sent the first documented warning to Washington after Capt. John B. Hughes of the Texas Rangers discovered the Bernardo Reyes plot in Laredo in 1912. The governor's disruption of the Reyes revolutionaries was greeted in Washington with what Colquitt noted as "jealousy" over Texas's enforcement of the federal Neutrality Laws, which the state undertook in response to inaction by federal authorities. As the months passed, the threats mounted, and Madero, bound to his quarters in Mexico City, felt any reports of organized rebel opposition to his administration were overblown and simply "incredible."[8]

The quixotic Madero seemed naive to the rumors of impending danger. In a prophetic meeting with Don Porfirio hours before the latter's departure into exile from Veracruz in the German steamer *Ypiranga*, the crusty old former president cautioned the new young president, "Senor, a man must be more than honest to govern Mexico." With these last words, as the ship steamed into the Gulf of Mexico, the viewing crowd responded with salutes of "Viva Mexico!"[9]

By Monday, February 17, the fighting in the streets of Mexico City had begun to wane. General Huerta abandoned Madero and outmaneuvered the rival rebel factions, captured the National Palace, and ordered the arrest of the president and his vice president, José María Pino Suárez. Declaring martial law, the general declared himself the "supreme commander." Representatives of the business community, including Buckley and members of the foreign diplomatic corps, gathered at the US Embassy to encourage a swift settlement to the violence between Felix Díaz and Huerta. A private meeting of Ambassador Wilson, Díaz, Huerta, and Wilson's embassy clerk Luis d'Antin convened at 10:00 p.m. and negotiated until sunrise. Wilson recalled that news of the meeting of the coup d'état's leaders was leaked and that a vast crowd surrounded the embassy, awaiting a decision. An agreement, or *pacto*, signed by all the parties and locked in the embassy safe, was brokered to name Huerta the "Provisional President," with Felix Díaz expected to assume the "regular presidency" through a nationwide election later in the year. The promised election never occurred, and the full details of the closed-door embassy meeting have never been revealed.[10] (See appendix B.)

General Victoriano Huerta. Author's Collection.

Thus, the Pacto de la Ciudadela sealed Madero's overthrow and fate, with the implied blessing of the United States ambassador and the capital's foreign diplomatic community. Ambassador Wilson, who most likely had advance knowledge of the plot, would be roundly criticized for endorsing a coup against the Madero government. However, as early as February 10, President Taft's secretary of state, Philander Knox, had cabled to support "anyone in *de facto* control at a given time" without "any semblance of recognition."[11] Knox's cable possibly was interpreted by the ambassador as support to seek a quick solution to ending the violent uprising in the capital. During a lull in the bombardment and looting, Wilson suggested that Madero resign to end the violence. "Support" but not "recognition" was the result of months of diplomatic correspondence between the United States and Mexico. Thus, there is strong evidence that without the implied support given by the American ambassador to the Huerta-Díaz coup, the betrayal of Madero would most likely have failed.[12]

General Huerta wasted no time. During the interim fifty-six-minute presidency of Pedro Lascuráin, Huerta was appointed secretary of the interior, making him the next in line of succession. Lascuráin resigned, and Huerta acceded to the presidency on a legal technicality. A cabinet was duly installed, and Huerta instructed the new secretary of the interior to draft an amnesty law designed to encourage all rebel factions to lay down their arms. Huerta then boldly declared in a telegram, transmitted outside diplomatic channels, to President William H. Taft: "I have the honor to inform you that I have overthrown this Government. The forces are with me, and from now on peace and prosperity will reign."[13]

To restore calm in the capital, Ambassador Wilson, the dean of the diplomatic corps, decided to continue with a scheduled public unveiling of a large monument on February 22. The white marble sculpture of George Washington at Glorieta Plaza Dinamarca was dedicated on the American president's birthday. Edith O'Shaughnessy noted in her memoirs, "President Huerta gave a short address and Mr. Wilson made one of his finest speeches—a happy combination of Stars and Stripes and the Eagle and Cactus." Following the Washington's Birthday reception at the American Embassy attended by Buckley and the newly installed President Huerta, a number of ministers in his new cabinet were formally presented to the diplomatic corps by Foreign Minister Francisco León de la Barra. By the evening of February 22, silence had fallen over Mexico City. All appeared calm.[14]

Concerned with ensuring a smooth transition, Ambassador Wilson, accompanied by the Spanish and German ministers, met with General Huerta to request assurance that Madero's life be spared and that he be safely exiled at once along with his family. Amid the excitement and celebrations, the new administration failed to honor the pledge to protect the diplomats. The former president and vice president, along with Col. Felipe Angeles, were placed in a guarded room in the National Palace. On the night of February 22, both Madero and Pino Suárez were removed from detention, driven to a dark street, and shot "attempting to escape." Such acts were permitted and sanctioned under Mexican law and known as *ley de fugas*, a mere euphemism for political murder. The murders destroyed Huerta's legitimacy to rule as well as any chance his government had to be recognized by the United States. As biographer Michael Meyer concludes, "The assassinations most assuredly changed the course of Mexican history."[15]

It has never been confirmed who gave the order to carry out Madero's murder, but Huerta continues to receive the lion's share of the blame. "The martyred Madero," Robert Quirk noted, "gained a popularity in death he had never achieved in life." Secretary of State Knox advised Ambassador Wilson, on February 24, that recognition would be considered "when the situation in Mexico City had settled down." However, the outgoing Taft administration decided to leave the complicated situation for the next president to deal with. The ambassador responded to Knox, "If the government can not be maintained, chaos must inevitably result and the demands and necessity for intervention could hardly be resisted." A key factor that immediately poisoned President-elect Woodrow Wilson's opinion against the general was his method of taking power. It would soon be the prime reason for the United States to oppose and refuse any efforts to grant

US ambassador to Mexico Henry Lane Wilson and Buckley were friends during the earliest days of the revolution. A strong supporter of American business, the ambassador was ostracized by the Wilson administration. After his recall he remained close friends with Buckley. Author's Collection.

official de facto recognition. Most historians have embraced the conclusion, as one observer noted, that "Madero's murder shook the country to the very roots"[16]—giving rise, according to John Womack, to "passions and impulses and organizations more radical than any since the crusade for Independence a hundred years before." And Edith O'Shaughnessy, wife of the American Embassy chargé d'affaires, in her 1916 memoir lamented, "It is a pity that the Embassy did not hide Madero behind its secure door."[17]

However, in an interesting clarification and footnote to history, William F. Buckley Sr. later put the Mexican use of "political assassination" in perspective: "A point might be made in connection with the assassination of Madero that I do not think has been made in any book on this revolutionary period. The assassination of Madero did not shock Mexicans of any class or political affiliation. The enemies admitted it was good politics, and that it was what they would have done to Huerta if conditions had been reversed. It was only when the Madero partisans found out to their surprise that the American people were shocked and that President Wilson was disposed to take a hand, that they decided to make political capital out of the normal Mexican political expedient."[18]

San Diego, Texas

Will Buckley's journey to Mexico started in rural South Texas. His grandparents, John and Elinor Doran Buckley, first emigrated from Ireland to Quebec, Canada, in 1845. They eventually settled in Hamilton, Ontario. Their first son, Will's father, John, married Mary Ann Langford. The family lore notes that due to health problems, the Buckleys and two children moved southward in 1874 to the rolling blacklands of Washington-on-the-Brazos, which had been the first capital of the Republic of Texas, some forty years earlier. William Frank Buckley was born on July 12, 1881, shortly before his father relocated the family to San Diego, in Duval County. Brother James recalls that their staunchly Irish grandmother refused to acknowledge that one of her children had been born on "Orangemen's Day," and so celebrated his birth a day earlier. This small ranching community was located on the Texas Mexican Railroad, fifty miles west of Corpus Christi and eighty miles east of Laredo.[19]

San Diego indelibly shaped Will's character during his formative years. The Buckleys settled on a ranch to raise sheep, surrounded by a rural community and small town with a population of about two thousand, 80 percent of whom were Mexican Americans. In the early 1880s, the county, part of the Nueces Strip, boasted that it had more sheep (deep in the heart of cow country) than any other county in the United States. Like the Buckleys, most of the Anglos were immigrants from Europe and other parts of the country, primarily the deep South. Will was the third of six children. Following the murder of his older brother John at age nineteen, his surviving siblings included Priscilla, Claude, Eleanor, and Edmund. All were well versed in literature, math, and music as well as detailed religious studies at the local Roman Catholic church in San Diego, led by parish priest John Pierre Bard from the Basque region of Spain. Their daily contact with Mexican culture, language, and influence—and Will's fluency in Spanish—was pivotal to their future pursuits. The early education of the Buckley family, like other Anglo settlers in South Texas, is aptly described by one observer: "They learned Spanish and acquainted themselves with Mexicans' psychology, traditions, and habits. In the process, they were themselves in a measure 'Mexicanized.' The whole relationship was natural and was not necessarily resented by those who submitted to it; most of them had never been used to anything else, either in Texas or in Mexico."[20]

Built around a central plaza like a typical village in Mexico, San Diego's most prominent feature on the square was the tiny Catholic Church of San Francisco de Paula, copied architecturally from Basque churches of Spain. As Claude recalled, we were "blessed with neither electricity, gas, telephone, running water, nor refrigeration." Water was delivered door-to-door by the traditional *barrilero*, a vendor with a wooden barrel mounted on a two-wheeled cart pulled by horses or mules. Amusements were Mexican in nature and included cockfighting, dancing, horse racing, and the occasional visit from a traveling circus. San Diego's celebrations were a mix of Texas frontier and indigenous traditions, such as a love for fiestas, highlighted by Christmas, Easter, New Year's, and Cinco de Mayo, along with the annual two-week-long celebration of Diez y Seis de Septiembre, the anniversary of Mexican independence from Spain in 1810.[21]

Relatives remembered Will's father as fearless and honest. He was elected sheriff and tax collector of Duval County in a hotly contested 1889 race, called only after a voter fraud lawsuit was settled against his opponent. Buckley was a devout practicing Catholic in a county where Protestants were outnumbered ten to one. The *Fort Worth Daily Gazette* noted his

Duval County Sheriff John Buckley *(left)* and an unknown deputy
in San Diego, Texas, in 1894. Buckley Family Collection.

strong relationships and congenial reputation with the local Mexican
ranchers: "Buckley was the only white man on the Mexican ticket [for sher-
iff] and he is politically king of the county." The well-respected and popular Sheriff Buckley, carrying only a Walker Colt .45, operated across the wild
Nueces Strip between the Nueces River and the Rio Grande, assisting law
enforcement throughout the region corralling cattle rustlers and capturing murderers and those who violated border neutrality laws. Claude
recalled, "The town itself and the county and the whole Southwest was wild
and woolly. They abounded in law breakers of all types and kinds. The worst
of these were the cow thieves and the smugglers, the latter were a mean
bunch who made a living by smuggling tequila from Mexico to San Antonio and other points in Texas—the direct route came right through San
Diego."[22]

This strong local Mexican following was a challenge to the Anglo-
Democratic political machine that worked to control all aspects of the

community. The target of numerous assassination attempts, John was indicted on trumped-up charges, arranged by opposition power brokers, that he had aided anti–Porfirio Díaz revolutionary leader Catarino Garza of Palito Blanco, Texas.

A coalition headed by local political boss Archie Parr voted John out of office in 1898. The charges soon evaporated. Following the defeat, John returned to buying and selling sheep at a time when the wool business was on its last leg due to drought and disease, until his death in 1904.[23]

After high school graduation, Will taught at the little rural school in La Mota de Olmos, near Benavides, Texas, for nearly two years. He enrolled in the University of Texas in the fall of 1900. Threatened by the financial loss following his father's death, Will's mother and four siblings moved to Austin to live with Will in a small house on the corner of Lavaca and Nineteenth Streets. Will, in his final years of undergraduate studies, was a Spanish instructor, earning $28.50 each month. With the strong recommendation of family friend and state senator Marshall Hick of San Antonio, both Will and sister Priscilla made steady incomes as translators of Spanish documents in the Texas General Land Office, a few blocks from the campus. His command of Spanish resulted in friends and sightseers hiring him to accompany them on visits south of the border. These tours gave Will his first look at Mexico. James L. Buckley recalls his father telling stories of selling soap in Mexico to pay for his travel and how, on one visit in 1906 or 1907, Will briefly served as Pancho Villa's interpreter. He completed his BS degree in 1904 and his LLB degree a year later. He joined the John C. Townes Law Society and Delta Tau Delta fraternity and was a founding member of the Catholic Church–sponsored Newman Club. Following a bout with typhoid that required hospitalization, in 1905–6 he was selected editor-in-chief of the university yearbook, *The Cactus*. Will received a license to practice law in Texas on June 6, 1906, worked for the American Surety Company for a year, and was admitted to the Texas Bar Association in 1909.[24]

Mexico City

After briefly practicing law in Austin, Will boldly moved to Mexico City. He and his brother Claude studied at the Escuela Nacional de Jurisprudencia, completed the required exams in Mexico's Napoleonic Code system of

The 1907 Delta Tau Delta chapter at the University of Texas included brother William and Claude H. Buckley, along with longtime friends Walter Garnett and Walter S. Pope. Buckley Family Collection.

law, passed the bar, and registered to practice throughout the country. Business throughout Mexico was hectic in the final years of the Porfirio Díaz regime. As President Díaz approached the end of his rule, he seemed to maintain control and the promise of a smooth transition; there was little warning of the upheaval soon to face Mexico. Tensions, however, were rising over landownership and access to farmland by the peasantry. Furthermore, many Mexicans believed their nation lacked control over the primary sectors of the economy, which were increasingly dominated by foreigners: public utilities, transportation, banking, as well as mining and the oil industry. Widely publicized comments that Díaz was "considering" retirement "smashed the floodgates for revolution, and shook the Díaz edifice to its foundation," as one biographer put it. As the Buckley brothers made plans to open a law office in Mexico City, numerous grassroots opposition movements organized in northern Mexico and South Texas, in what Robert Curley termed "a portentous moment for [Mexican] national politics." Nonetheless, the government and the business sector in Mexico City ignored the signals of civil unrest as the nation prepared for the grand national centennial celebration planned for 1910.[25]

During thirty-five years of the Porfiriato (Porfirio Díaz's rule), more than $3 billion of multinational foreign direct investment (FDI) and concessions by the government had greatly improved the country's once-backward infrastructure. The seaports were expanded, the banks were flush with reserves, new railroad lines connected the capital with Laredo, Texas, on the Rio Grande (an initial concession to American industrialist Jay Gould in 1881), and mining of silver, copper, and iron flourished. By 1900, American investors and engineers had built more than twelve thousand miles of railroad connecting Mexico with what John Mason Hart deemed was "the fundamental element in American power and influence." They soon expanded operations into all sectors of the Mexican economy. Under the direction of Finance Secretary José Yves Limantour, Mexico produced its first budget surplus since independence. Foreign investment, which grew under Díaz, controlled 97 percent of all mining. The big surprise that caught the immediate attention of the Buckley brothers was the oil boom in eastern Mexico that began in 1909. Soon brother Edmund, who graduated from law school at the University of Texas, joined the Mexico City firm, which allowed Will to open an office in the heart of the oil district in Tampico in 1911 on the Gulf of Mexico south of Brownsville, Texas. In addition to representing American, Mexican, and British oil companies, Will began to acquire land and oil leases. Worldwide industrial advances, such as companies and naval operations converting fuel sources from coal to oil, ushered in a skyrocketing demand and scramble to acquire petroleum leases, production, and shipping facilities.[26]

William Buckley maintained constant contact with local government officials, the president's office, and the US Embassy. The American community of expatriates in and around Mexico City totaled over twenty thousand, and nationwide about thirty thousand. Young Buckley and his brothers were active in the social scene. Will was just under six feet tall, dark haired, fair complected, and with blue eyes accented by wire rim pince-nez that made him look older than his twenty-seven years. The American expats—and especially the Texans—were keen to observe and celebrate any event deemed worthy, including parties for dignitaries and visitors from back home. Events at the Hotel Jardín, Hotel Regis, and Hotel de Geneve comprised receptions and dinners often followed by a dance. A former classmate from Austin, Amy Hopkins, visiting her parents in the capital recalled, "Will was a 'oiler' down there and was a beautiful dancer." The Buckley brothers hosted the Alumni Association of Texas at Will's home at Calle de San Francisco No. 18, in honor of Dr. W. F. Fulton, UT dean of education, and popular history professor Eugene C. Barker. During this period, Will was a frequent dinner guest and confidant of Ambassador Henry Lane Wilson. Mexico City was vibrant prior to the overthrow of Madero. Life was very relaxed, as the wealthy entertained and drank in private clubs, and the citizens imbibed in the choice cantinas, the abundant small corner taverns, or pulquerias—serving the fruit of the maguey plant, pulque. Overall, business was brisk, and the strong foreign presence of British, German, French, Dutch, Chinese, and Japanese interests ushered in a competitive and often cutthroat approach to business. That competition extended to legal services that worked to gain favor with the central government to obtain preferable concessions. Large landowners first sensed the tension beneath these good spirits in 1907, as a heightened call for land reform energized the opposition's political call for redress.[27]

Mexico, in the final years of Díaz's administration, was in an economic boom that was stymied by the depression of 1907. Despite fluctuation in the price of silver, the country's number one export for decades, the Mexican economy showed signs of improving. From 1900 to 1910, Mexico maintained a balanced budget and treasury surplus. The large amounts of foreign direct investment opened development of the country's vast untapped natural resource wealth.[28] Investors were focused on profits and on recovering the tremendous costs of investment in mining, real estate, railroads, sugar production, and petroleum exploration. While infrastructure improved—for example, in railroads, seaports, communications, and electrical services—as well as new jobs for Mexicans, the newfound wealth due to the FDI did not adequately trickle down to the mostly low-paid populace. Many statesmen and businessmen from the United States and Europe, as late as 1910, were lauding Don Porfirio's rule. William Jennings Bryan, during a seldom-remembered trip to Mexico in 1897, spoke of the aging leader in eulogistic terms, commending his "great work." As historian

Robert Smith concluded, "Any real attempt at redistribution or asserting national control over property would upset the status quo and adversely affect foreign property interests." Soon, the new jobs, the inflows of new investment, and rising incomes—the whole period of improved economic conditions prior to 1911—were virtually wiped out by the decade of the revolution.[29]

Despite the president's active role in governance and in courting foreign investors, political change was in the wind as Madero prepared to reenter Mexico from Texas. As Ambassador Henry L. Wilson noted, "At the time of President Díaz' overthrow, he was ill almost unto death [actually suffering a bad toothache], and that together with his age, had, I think, more to do with his surrender of power than anything else—the government of Díaz collapsed."[30]

Mary Ann Langford Buckley *(seated)*, mother of William F. Buckley Sr.,
surrounded by family in Austin, Texas, in 1908: *(from Mary's right, clockwise)*
Priscilla, Claude, Edmund, Eleanor, and William Sr. Their father,
Sheriff John Buckley of San Diego, had died in Rockport, Texas, in 1904.
Buckley Family Collection.

Huerta

The rise of Gen. Victoriano Huerta was not a shock to those who were close observers of the politics and maneuvering for power and position during the final years of the Porfiriato. Huerta was born in the small rural village of Ocotlán in Jalisco in southern Mexico and attended school at the local Catholic church. Short and broad-shouldered, as a teenager he was an aide to a federal general who secured him an appointment to the National Military Academy. He excelled as a cadet and was commissioned as a second lieutenant in the corps of engineers in 1876—the same year Porfirio Díaz assumed control of Mexico. Huerta rose through the ranks with both skill and political connections. At the time of the Madero revolution, he commanded the Federal army forces in Morelos against the rebel Zapatistas. Shrewd and strong, he was a man with many vices. Known for his hard drinking, he had a loyal following in the army. Although the pay was low, Díaz did maintain strong support for the military, spending nearly one-fourth of the annual budget on equipment and training. The military during the late 1800s was involved in the improvement of infrastructure across the nation, especially by installing a modern communication network. Huerta and most of the standing Federal army made the transition from Díaz to Madero. As a sign of trust, Huerta was selected to command the military escort by railcar of exiled President Díaz to Veracruz in May 1911.[31]

Huerta's "personal ambition" to seize the presidency was reported in diplomatic cables to the State Department as early as September 1912. This was no surprise to Buckley and the business sector in Mexico City. After the coup, most federal generals and state governors pledged support and allegiance to him. He was keen to fill the cabinet with skilled statesmen, the banks remained open, and the trains ran on time. However, there was opposition to the "villainous" coup. Within hours of Huerta's declaring his position as president, splinter rebel factions in the north and south of Mexico questioned his legitimacy.[32]

Two weeks after General Huerta occupied the National Palace, Woodrow Wilson, the former governor of New Jersey, was sworn in as the twenty-eighth president of the United States. His campaign had focused almost totally on domestic issues and priorities. In the final days of his administration, Taft decided to let the new president deal with Mexico. Little did Wilson know what awaited him. He remarked to a friend just before departing for Washington that "it would be the irony of fate if my administration had to deal chiefly with foreign affairs!"[33]

While more than a dozen nations recognized the new Mexican government, Woodrow Wilson was vehemently opposed to extending formal diplomatic recognition to Huerta. Wilson's idealism demanded "constitutional legitimacy," while other nations, and the United States itself prior to 1913, based recognition on traditional de facto governmental control. The British Foreign Office advised the new secretary of state, Williams Jennings Bryan, "His Majesty's government is recognizing the President [Huerta] ad interim of Mexico."[34] Unlike Wilson, who was primarily focused on the moral standard for Huerta and not the general norms of diplomatic recognition, the British, mindful of their growing direct investments in all segments of the Mexican economy, were undeterred by moral qualms about the Huerta regime. In the weeks after Huerta assumed office, and as Buckley watched from Tampico, foreign financiers and investors expressed concern with the ability of the Mexican treasury to honor periodic loan payments. Ambassador Wilson, a Taft administration appointee and vocal proponent of business-friendly "Dollar Diplomacy" to advance American interests in Mexico, was ostracized by President Wilson and Secretary Bryan. Neither man had any international diplomatic or business experience, but they determined nonetheless that the ambassador had "meddled shamelessly" in Mexico's internal affairs.[35]

With the advice of Will Buckley and the American business community, the ambassador maintained direct contact with General Huerta, who was aware that Ambassador Wilson had repeatedly advised Washington to recognize the new government. The primary aim of those in the foreign business sector, strongly supported by the ambassador, was government stability and legal consistency to protect profit and foster commerce. Ambassador Wilson gave this example of how he worked with Huerta: "I went to see him [Huerta] one morning regarding an American who was held as a spy and whom I had been informed would be shot the next morning. General Huerta had just received a cable saying that owing to the intervention of the government of the United States in Paris, the loan which he had hoped to get would not be floated. You can imagine that he was not in the best of humor. He received me courteously. I asked him if he would immediately telegraph to have the American in question sent to Mexico City for trial. After some minutes of silence he said, 'I will do it'—then he added, 'let's have a drink of brandy. There are only two good foreigners in Mexico—Hennessy and Martell.'"[36]

President Wilson, with his sanctimonious idealism and moralistic approach to the chaos south of the border, quickly spurred a debate in Washington and in major European capitals about US intentions. The president, as historian Kendrick Clements points out, "assumed that all issues troubling nations were essentially political in nature. The major objective of the foreign policy was self-determination for small nations of the developing world, and Wilson realized that a major obstacle was the quasicolonial, dependent status forced on such nations by their need of foreign capital that in turn often brings varying degrees of foreign control."[37] Speculation spread rapidly that the United States would forcibly intervene to secure peace and establish a government to its liking. In the fall of 1913, the British, despite numerous concerns by investors in the oil sector, remained perplexed by Wilson's actions, noting "the President is inexperienced in foreign policy, and sublimely confident is his own unaided sagacity." Shortly thereafter, Wilson famously quipped to a senior representative of the British embassy, "I am going to teach the South American republics to elect good men!"—democratic government should be decided with "ballots" rather than "bullets."[38]

This condescension was not well received by Huerta. The Wilson administration's presumption that it would tell Mexicans how to foster self-determination was uninformed and myopic, with little regard for the cultural dynamics of Latin America in general and Mexico in particular. By contrast, one observer of Buckley noted that those who worked with him in Mexico in business and knew him in private life testified that he was sincere and fearless "in his love for their country, his respect for its sovereignty, his friendship and esteem for its people." As Will noted in a letter to Colonel House, "There are few Americans in Mexico who associate more with Mexicans than I." And his strong Catholic faith and command of the language and culture provided the foundation for Buckley's lifelong connection with Mexico.[39]

Will increasingly became involved with foreign companies in Mexico, attempting to assess their investments and risk. He worked with the government and the US Embassy to calm clients concerned about the spread of the revolution. Ambassador Wilson sent numerous cables to Washington warning of the potential damage to American investment and expressing grave concern for the safety of American citizens. Some one hundred Americans had already been killed in random violence without any accounting for the circumstances of their deaths. The White House ignored Ambassador Wilson's repeated calls for recognition of the Huerta government as well as redress for the victims of violence. There were, however, those in Congress who were concerned with the violence in Mexico and Wilson's diplomacy. Senator Henry Cabot Lodge, Republican chairman of the Senate Foreign Relations Committee, who viewed the new idealist president as self-righteous and a "pompous prig," wrote to Sir Cecil Spring Rice at the British ministry in London shortly after the inauguration, "I hope they got a man now of the Porfirio Díaz type who will do sufficient throat-cutting to restore order. That seems an unpleasant thing to say but it is apparently impossible to maintain order or any approach to decent government in Mexico upon any other terms."[40]

The complicated environment of the revolution was further accented by foreign intrigue primarily by the British, Germans, and Japanese—and to a lesser degree, the French.[41] In addition to their diplomats and businessmen, each government dispatched intelligence agents. The meddling in the internal affairs of Mexico reached a heightened level. Will Buckley's primary contact with the various multinationals was through the Petroleum Club in downtown Mexico City. Over long lunches and in the private meeting rooms, business executives, bankers, and diplomats unofficially met to exchange information and hammer out contracts and loans. When possible, Huerta's purchasing agents solicited and received special support and terms for arms, munitions, and equipment from all these countries. The jockeying of Americans, British, and Germans for access to ample supplies of bunker fuel for their naval fleets was soon a critical area of competition.

As capital flight intensified, the Wilson administration tried to increase pressure on Huerta by placing a moratorium on foreign loans. European financiers, concerned with losing lucrative public and private financing arrangements, reacted with disgust and contempt. Many international loans were generally secured by customshouse receipts. Interestingly, the American ambassador to Germany cabled the State Department noting that while the Germans had commercial concerns in Mexico, they had "no political interests, that if we [Americans] intervene there will be a long and cruel war; that if we do not recognize Huerta he will fall, with resultant anarchy."[42] And from London, in a meeting with the foreign secretary,

Ambassador Walter Page summed up President Wilson's views noting, "I explained how we could not consider financial interests except as secondary to moral interests!" Regardless, the legal and commercial services of Buckley and Buckley made the firm well known and profitable.[43]

To combat the growing rebel activity, primarily in northern Mexico, President Huerta increased the size of the Federal army from 50,000 to more than 250,000 troops—some ten times the size of the Porfirian army when the revolution began and three times the size of the US Army (see table 1). The British conducted a significant amount of intelligence work among senior US commanders to determine the aims of the Americans. Both Gen. Leonard Wood and Gen. Tinker Bliss were much "perturbed" by the small size and underequipped nature of the US Army. Following a visit to Mexico City, visiting British admiral Sir Christopher F. Cradock, commander of the fleet in the Gulf of Mexico, and his officers made a port of call at Galveston in early March 1914. They conducted an onshore reconnaissance across Texas, provided a detailed assessment of American troop strength, readiness, equipment, and attitude toward nonintervention. General Wood described the attitude of the American army and people as one of "unqualified disgust" toward the Mexico situation. Referring to Mexico, Buckley expressed concern that a large standing Federal army had mixed blessings. As the quality of the troops in the Mexican Federal army declined due to poor training and shortage of equipment, the cost to fund the army

Table 1
Strength of the US Army, June 30, 1913

Units	Authorized	Actual
General officers	21	19
Staff corps	3,316	3,339
Engineers	2,167	1,850
Cavalry	14,949	14,473
Field artillery	5,765	5,025
Coastal artillery	19,646	17,376
Infantry	35,218	31,674
Miscellaneous	8,476	62,230
Total regular army	89,558	79,986

Source: "Peace and War Strengths of the Army," April 20, 1914, BFA, 311.

Note: Both British and German intelligence in Mexico and the United States kept close watch on US Army and Navy strengths and deployments.

became unsustainable. As the pressure increased on Huerta to maint.
power, he became increasingly dictatorial and impetuous. His primary
threat, however, was a rebel offensive from "the Men of the North";[44] while
unofficial, this was a formal name for Villa's army, which took on the name
"Constitutionalist Army of the North" as several armies merged.

The First Chief

The major challenge to the Huerta government came from the governor of
Coahuila, Venustiano Carranza, a tough and often pompous fifty-three-
year-old hacendado with flowing white whiskers and blue-tinted specta-
cles. An early supporter of the Madero faction, he chose not to recognize
the new Huerta regime, declaring his revolution by claiming that his only
objects were to avenge Madero and to defend the Mexican constitution.[45]
Carranza telegrammed all northern leaders to follow suit. Only two agreed:
Alberto Terrazas in Chihuahua and Alvaro Obregón in Sonora provided
strong support along with the governor's armed jefes, Pascual Orozco
and Pancho Villa. The three northern Mexico revolutionary factions agreed
in late March 1913 to draft the Plan of Guadalupe.[46] The plan, a call to
arms, concluded with formal withdrawal of recognition from Huerta and
named Carranza Primer Jefe (First Chief) of the newly formed Constitutionalist Army of the North. The document was narrowly focused and
included none of the social and land reforms touted by Madero, but it
did contain a statement that the interim president would be Carranza
or someone he designated upon Huerta's removal. Ambassador Wilson
secretly cabled the American consul in Saltillo, John R. Silliman: "Call on
Governor Carranza and tell him that he is in open rebellion against a
legally constituted government strongly entrenched on the confidence of
the people. Tell him his downfall is inevitable. Put this matter strongly to
him and as solemn warning." Carranza rejected all such demands and was
quick to remind his correspondents of what he felt was interference by US
representatives. These events soon had a tremendous impact on the business and safety of the Buckleys and their clients in Tampico.[47]

Carranza's declaration of opposition against Huerta attracted the attention and support of the White House. Public relations in the United
States became critical. Cloaked in such terms as "constitutional" and
"self-government," the opposition to Huerta launched a PR campaign to

ican public opinion by dwelling on the violent "murder" ich gradually proved an effective tactic. The view from ferent, however. Buckley recounted what he considered the e of the Constitutionalists in a memo for Senator Fall's hearing outlining his assessment of Lic. Luis Cabrera, whom Buckley termed the "intellectual director of the revolution." Cabrera, Buckley wrote, believed that the Mexican people were "incapable of self-government." Cabrera's own proposed reforms, which would be "beneficial to the people," needed to be "forced upon them by himself and his associates." Madero's failure, to Cabrera, was his "endeavor to introduce such reforms by constitutional methods." According to Buckley, Cabrera was fond of repeating that "no reform . . . no real progress" was ever made "except by force of arms." The "constitutional machinery must be held in abeyance and the revolutionary program be forced through by a dictator supported by an army." This was, of course, quite different from what revolutionary leaders and Ambassador Wilson were telling Americans.[48]

Little did President Wilson know that years of death and destruction were forthcoming, fomented by the First Chief and his followers. The White House manufactured public sympathies in opposition to Huerta, and Carranza with his agents in Washington fueled them. According to Buckley, "Carranza realized his opportunity and proclaimed loudly that his purpose in revolting was to avenge the shameful murder of his beloved chief." Most Americans had little or no knowledge of what was happening in Mexico or of the country's history and culture. Two series of events began to catch the attention of the news media and the American public. First was the increasing number of stories and rumors of Americans killed in Mexico and along the border. Second, US border state governors and law enforcement had little recourse but to address the violence. Their requests to Washington for military assistance were generally ignored except for the deployment of a small number of army units to Texas.[49]

In May 1913, the Constitutionalists intensified the revolution's violence on a decree by the First Chief declaring that all captured Federal soldiers would be summarily executed. The indiscriminate murder of local elected officials, businessmen, low-level bureaucrats, and citizens across Mexico compounded the pronouncement's effect. Proximity to the United States was a key element to revolutionaries who had access to arms, a market for stolen cattle, and a convenient sanctuary to plan and recruit. Most of these developments were generally unreported in the news media north of the border. The unbridled use of political assassinations by all factions in the bloody revolution soon broke down the rule of law. This wanton violence had a direct impact on the Buckleys, their staff, clients, and local officials in the Tampico region. As Carranza's and Villa's forces, both official and paramilitary bandits, fanned out to steal cattle, extort bribes, and commit kidnappings, no one was safe, and there was no recognized legal authority to curb the attacks on civilians.[50]

President Wilson and Secretary of State Bryan continued to ignore recommendations from the ambassador in Mexico City, sending Henry Lane Wilson a brief note that they were "not ready to consider recognition." By demanding Huerta's resignation, President Wilson left no room for negotiation, and thus, the old general had no incentive to cooperate. Concerned with the lingering influence of the diplomatic staff from the previous Taft administration, the leading State Department expert on Mexico, John Bassett Moore, suggested strongly that the provisional government be recognized. Wilson was not impressed, and Moore was unceremoniously transferred to Belgium. The seasoned diplomat had presented two clear options that did not fit the narrative espoused by the White House and were roundly rejected. His recommendations were, first, to nominate a new ambassador, who could present his letters in due course; and, second, to identify Carranza as merely a rebel opposing the central government and not the head of any rival Mexican government. The president's rejection of the advice from both Moore and the ambassador for a new government was confirmed in the secret notice Ambassador Wilson gave Carranza on March 3, 1913. Clearly President Wilson was unmoved by decades of traditional diplomatic means of transition, recognition, or protocol.[51]

Wilson's new presidential cabinet was also of little assistance. Handpicked by Colonel Edward House, a seasoned political operative from Texas, the members included four Texans: Albert S. Burleson, David Houston, Thomas W. Gregory, and Thomas B. Love. These men offered little insight and few solutions that would help direct the president's Mexico policy. To circumvent normal US State Department and intelligence channels, the president created a plan to send his chosen personal representatives or "confidential agents" that were friendly to the White House and paid by a slush fund managed by Colonel House. The influence of the colonel, a close friend and neighbor of Buckley's from their time in Austin, would grow during the Wilson administration, as the British ambassador soon reported to the London Foreign Office: "This trusted adviser . . . , though very unobtrusive in his methods, is in fact 'the power behind the throne,' and is, perhaps, the only man who really influences the President's policy." Wilson soon dispatched a series of amateurish and inept nongovernment agents to Mexico over an eighteen-month period to report back directly to him about the situation inside the country. Agriculture Secretary Houston, who was previously president of the University of Texas (when Will Buckley graduated), concluded at a cabinet meeting, "Mexico loomed as an ugly problem."[52]

As the president's confidential agents arrived with no advance notice or introduction to the American Embassy and only a vague letter to the Mexican government, confusion reigned. Ambassador Wilson learned of the first agent, William B. Hale, from a newspaper reporter. None of the agents could speak Spanish, nor did they possess any knowledge of the culture or any understanding of the dynamics of the revolution, and its various combatants, that had raged for nearly four years. One of Hale's implied assignments, while posing as a newspaperman, was to collect and forward damaging information, mainly rumors and gossip, on Ambassador Wilson. Rumors surfaced that the ambassador had armed US citizens in the capital to promote an atmosphere of hysteria that would help trigger an intervention. Further gossip indicated that there was a spy in the American Embassy who compromised all its communications. In an interview with Senator Fall's subcommittee on Mexico in January 1920, former consul Felix Sommerfeld disclosed the allegation (confirmed by two sources) that "Luis d'Antin, confidential clerk and interpreter at the American Embassy gave the Mexican Government a copy of every telegram, even in code, sent by Ambassador H. L. Wilson to the State Department and to President Wilson." This same secret information was illegally passed to *Harper's Weekly* reporter, Robert H. Murray, who wrote a controversial article, "The Two Wilsons and Huerta."[53] The full extent of this damaging leak is unknown, yet clearly at the time it put both the US Embassy and the White House at a marked disadvantage.[54]

The manager of the Mexican Bureau of the International News Service, N. A. Jennings, in a letter to his boss, William Randolph Hearst, revealed the nature of d'Antin's clandestine activities: "I am informed that Louis D'Antin, clerk and interpreter at the American embassy, has been carrying messages back and forth between the revolutionary junta here (in the suburb of Culiacan) and John Lind. . . . D'Antin is very thick with Lind and has made several trips to Veracruz to see him. D'Antin . . . has been getting a great deal of money lately, accounting for it by saying that he was speculating in French *rentes* [government bonds], which I know to be untrue."[55]

The American business community, and bankers who wanted stability and the rule of law, strongly favored recognition of the Carranza regime. Hale told the president what he wanted to hear. His reports concluded that Huerta's government was not legitimate and supported the president's wish to depose Huerta, even going so far as to characterize "the general as a drunk 'ape-like' Indian." If this report issued from the embassy cable room—manned by d'Antin—then Huerta was well aware of the tone, slander, and attitude of the president's special agent. In Washington the president privately stated, "I will not recognize a government of butchers."[56]

Recalled

In the summer of 1913, despite detailed endorsements from the American business community and diplomatic officials in Mexico City, Ambassador Wilson was abruptly recalled to Washington, DC. The president selected no replacement because he did not want to take any official action that implied recognition of Huerta. Seasoned diplomat Nelson O'Shaughnessy, a close personal friend of Will Buckley, assumed the leading diplomatic role as chargé d'affaires at the US Embassy. Yet he was kept uninformed of the function, instructions to, or number of White House "confidential agents" roaming Mexico. In close contact with Huerta and the American business community, O'Shaughnessy was routinely undercut by each new agent the White House sent. Designating a successor to follow "agent" Hale, the president, in early August 1913, personally typed instructions in his second-floor study. He bypassed the State Department, sending the confidential message to John Lind, a former governor of Minnesota.[57]

In an extraordinary departure from diplomatic norms, Lind "was chosen, so Washington informed the American people, because he knew nothing about Mexico and, consequently, was not prejudiced."[58] His credentials were addressed "To Whom it May Concern." Lind's dispatches to the White House were inaccurate, misleading, and often filled with gratuitous "anti-Indian" and anti-Catholic language. Will Buckley, a devout Catholic, noted that Lind was "bitterly anti-Catholic," advancing "in public" his belief "that until the Mexican people were converted to Protestantism there was no hope for them." In Mexico, Lind was seen as interfering in the internal affairs of the country and soon became persona non grata. As Buckley noted in a letter to Senator Fall, Lind had "placed President Wilson's will above the will of the Mexican people." Not surprisingly, Lind's proposals to Huerta's representatives were indignantly rejected, and his naive approach was quickly attacked in the local newspapers. He was paranoid he was being followed by Mexican security agents (he was). Fear kept Lind indoors at the US consulate in Veracruz, which led reporter James Creelman to call him "Mr. Wilson's cloistered agent." Furthermore, the Mexican government was insulted by these amateur representatives who arrived with demands, yet who had no authority officially to represent the United States. Buckley and numerous experienced business representatives of the American colony in Mexico City were equally insulted by Lind's ineptitude.[59]

American business executives were vocal at the time of the crisis and during the US congressional hearings. Michael J. Slattery, a large owner of mining operations in Mexico, recalled the general attitude toward Wilson's so-called "confidential agents": "The president certainly picked a lot of lemons. You know John Lind's visit to Mexico City was a joke, and if it were not so serious it would be a comic opera. He came down there with his chest thrown out, and he was coming down there to show those Mexicans how to do things!"[60] Following Lind's return to Washington to report on his failure to sway Huerta into following Wilson's plans, the president went before a joint session of Congress on August 27, 1913, to outline his position on the crisis in Mexico. In addition to restating his demands on Huerta, he advised that all Americans leave Mexico for their safety. Any doubt of the president's idealistic approach to foreign relations falls away in light of his concluding remarks on Capitol Hill: "The steady pressure of moral force will before many days break the barriers of pride and prejudice down, and we shall triumph as Mexico's friends sooner than we could triumph as her enemies."[61]

Will Buckley and his brothers witnessed the confusion of Wilson's agents and the Mexican government's reaction to their undiplomatic approach. Even after the president abruptly announced that all Americans should leave Mexico at once, Buckley told the *Austin Statesman*, "It is my judgment that Americans in Mexico will not heed the president's advice and will remain in the Southern Republic." In the coming weeks, Buckley spent time in Mexico City, Veracruz, and Tampico protecting his business interests and supporting his clients, who were highly concerned with the lawlessness sweeping the country. Buckley's concern for his own safety arose only through an encounter with the rebels.[62]

Pancho Villa

The Constitutional forces roamed northern Mexico attacking Huerta's Federal garrisons, robbing mining camps, commandeering trains, and rustling cattle to be smuggled into Texas in exchange for arms. Concerned with the investments and safety of their clients, Will and Claude took a direct role in assisting them. The rising violence placed Will Buckley face-to-face with the most flamboyant and controversial rebel leader, Francisco "Pancho" Villa (born José Doroteo Arango in 1878 at Hacienda de Rio Grande, San Juan del Río, Durango). Buckley recounted his experience in a story—which some people termed a myth—told at family gatherings and captured by his son Reid in *An American Family* (2008):

> Father's meeting with Pancho Villa took place when he was riding a train, his mission being to deliver the payroll of a big US company [and client].
>
> It was a hot day in summer. Dust, coal smoke, and cinders blew in through the open windows, stinging eyes, covering the passengers—who protected mouths and nostrils with handkerchiefs, which grew grimmer with every mile of track. Pancho Villa had been regularly raiding and robbing and killing in the area, causing Will to wonder where he could hide the payroll should Villa, exalted by revolution to the status of patriot, have got wind of the loot. This was in the form of gold coins, rolled tightly in paper. After thinking hard on the problem, he got up from his seat and heavy satchel in hand, walked toward the back of the car, where the evil-smelling men's room was located.
>
> Once inside, curtain drawn, he looked around him; and, satisfying himself that the chamber was empty, began to drop the rolls of

coins one by one into the wide, dish-shaped mouths of the cuspidors. Should Villa's brigands board and search the train, surely they would never think of the cuspidors.

Satisfied with his stratagem, he washed his hands, stepped out of the rest room, and took his seat up the aisle. He had fallen half asleep when pistol and rifle shots rang out, people shouted and screamed, and the thundering of horses' hooves burst upon his ears.

The locomotive's brakes screeched and sizzled, and with a series of jolting stops that knocked people half out of their seats, the three cars of the train ground to a halt.

In poured the bandits, Villa at their head—unmistakably Pancho Villa—shouting, cursing, pistol smoking, strutting up and down the aisle demanding wallets, gold watches, women's cameos, bracelets, wedding rings, and hat pins, whatever of value anyone carried. Suitcases were torn from the overhead racks and tossed to the floor, where they were broached. Will's empty satchel was yanked down, opened, peered in, flung to the floor. "Where is it?" demanded Villa, his temper rising as gunmen who were ransacking the other cars reported that they had found nothing.

Some spy in the home office [in Tampico] had tipped Villa off, it became plain, because he shouted, "I know the gold is here, where is it?" He turned on the terrified conductor, who was dragged toward him by two of the bandits, "You—where is the gold, tell me!" And he drew his pistol, placing its long barrel flat against the poor man's brow.

"But there is no gold!" cried the conductor, falling on his knees, wringing his hands.

"Don't lie to me!" shouted Villa, furious. "We know the gold is on this train. Do not lie to Pancho Villa. Be quick, tell me, or you are a dead man."

As the conductor continued miserably pleading ignorance, there came a shout from the back of the railway car, and two of the bandits burst out of the men's room, declaring they had found the gold, they (or the train's hard stopping) had knocked over one of the cuspidors, and the coins, bursting their rolls, rolled out.

At this, Villa's face darkened with anger, and he raised his pistol, cocking the hammer, pointing it at the conductor's skull, but Will had meantime got up from his seat near the back of the car and now called out in loud voice, in Spanish, "Don't hurt that man. I hid the gold. He knew nothing about it."

"Who are you?"

"My name is Guillermo Buckley. I was bringing the payroll for the company, and I hid it without this man's knowledge."

"Oh, thank you, thank you," the conductor cried at these words, writhing on the floor in his wretchedness.

"Shut up, you disgusting worm," said Villa. "I am going to shoot you anyhow."

At this, the conductor began blubbering of his wife and multiple children, begging for pity. Will had come to within a few feet of Villa, whose face was black with disgust—saying, "I know you won't shoot that miserable man."

"Who are you to say that, *Ojos Azules* [blue eyes]? You will be fortunate if I do not kill you, too."

"Because you are too great a man to shoot a wretch like the conductor. Pancho Villa has become famous in Mexico. Children all over the country are being taught to respect and revere his name. Pancho Villa stands for justice to the poor. You would never waste your reputation on such a wretch as this."

He continued shamelessly in this fashion, speaking of Pancho Villa's fair fame. At first the bandit was stony, but he liked what he heard, maybe especially from this American, and when henchmen grabbed my father to pull him away, he said no, let the gringo speak, this *Ojos Azules* was telling the truth. He swelled visibly with gratification at father's continued extolling his reputation, and Villa began glancing down at the conductor benevolently.

"Get up, get up!" he said at last. "Don't grovel. I have no intention of hurting you. Are we through here *caballeros*?" he shouted at his men, who indicated they had pried the last gold tooth out of the last mouth and were ready to go.

"Good. And you, Guillermo Buckley, come see me at a better time. I respect Courage. I might even have use for you."[63]

And this would not be the last encounter between Guillermo " Ojos Azules" and Pancho!

CHAPTER TWO

Huerta and Mr. X

*The present policy of the Government of the United States is to isolate
General Huerta entirely; to cut him off from foreign sympathy and aid
and from domestic credit, whether moral or material, and to force him out.
If Huerta does not retire by force of circumstances it will become the duty
of the US to use less peaceful means to put him out.*
—William Jennings Bryan, secretary of state, November 13, 1913

*The so-called Tampico flag incident was a comedy of errors, a tragic comedy
in a way, a veritable tempest in a teapot. Woodrow Wilson transformed
a very minor event into an "affair of honor."*
—Lon Tinkle

THE WILSON ADMINISTRATION in late December 1913 concluded
that there were only two possible ways to exert influence over the chaos
in Mexico and oust General Huerta, whose regime the president characterized as a "mere military despotism." The first, rapidly developing option
was to strongly support Venustiano Carranza and the Constitutionalists
in northern Mexico. The second was direct military intervention. Confirmation of US policy and options was provided by Secretary of State Bryan
to Chargé d'affaires O'Shaughnessy in Mexico City: isolate Huerta or we
will use less peaceful means. In the meantime, President Wilson, following a conference with John Lind on January 2, 1914, aboard the USS *Chester*, off Gulfport, Mississippi, stated that his policy would be to watch and
wait to determine any further actions, a policy the news media quickly
dubbed "watchful waiting." In so doing, the president pressed his "confidential agents" to establish better links with Carranza and determine a
means to unseat Huerta. To assist the rebels in the north, Wilson considered arming and supplying the troops. As Buckley waited in Tampico to
gauge the impact of Wilson's moves on the oil industry, Carranza appealed
directly to President Wilson to permit the importation of arms for the

Constitutionalists "without difficulties being made by the United States authorities."[1] In contrast, German and Japanese arms agents, with the implicit approval of their governments, actively supplied arms and munitions to Huerta. Often arms delivered by the Germans were purchased in the United States and transshipped via Hamburg to Tampico or Veracruz. The Japanese sold directly to the Federal government and dropshipped to the port of Mazatlán on the Pacific coast. The supplying of the rebels by smugglers along the Rio Grande border with Texas was more clandestine.[2]

For more than a decade the United States had a strict arms embargo law to prevent upstart groups from launching and supplying filibustering actions into Mexico. This law was selectively enforced. The seeds of the Mexican Revolution of 1910 were planted and germinated from the United States, which allowed various rebel groups to raise money, recruit, train, publish newspapers, and arm themselves. The smuggling of arms was not a violation of US neutrality law along the border with Mexico until the passage of the Arms Embargo Law of 1912. The embargo of arms naturally aided the government in Mexico City and was intended to hamper the rebels. Notwithstanding, the border was a sieve of arms trafficking with little or no control. US federal requirements to monitor border activities and cross-border shipments proved fruitless, given the understaffed border patrol and paucity of customs agents and immigration officials. The southbound flow of arms was no secret to those living on the border; a vast number of local merchants and citizens engaged in the trade. The 1,951-mile-long border was porous and ripe for smuggling. Thus, a vast amount of arms and munitions crossed through the twin-city ports along the border under the eyes of those tasked with intercepting contraband.[3]

In addition to the smuggling of arms and contraband at remote locations on the Rio Grande, there was a brisk flow of smuggled contraband in the downtown area of each border town. In Laredo, the railroad from San Antonio and Dallas would routinely deliver a casket for "general delivery" to the International and Great Northern RR (I&GN) dock five blocks from the border. The casket would have no name, only instructions for interment. It would be reverently handled and picked up late at night by unknown parties—its contents not a body, but Winchester rifles. The Mexican embassy in Washington protested to the State Department "that the American authorities at Naco, Arizona, continue to protect the rebels, that cross the boundary-line with impunity carrying provisions and ammunition without being molested by the [US] authorities." In El Paso, women simpatico with the revolution were so active smuggling cases of ammunition under their clothing to Ciudad Juárez that the Customs Service hired female border agents to handle body searches. Watermelons were hollowed out in Del Rio to hold handguns and ammunition. The currency for these transactions was either gold, due to the worthless value of Mexican paper money, or cattle confiscated from ranches in northern Mexico and driven across low-water crossings to be sold in Texas.[4]

Many of the clients represented by Buckley and Buckley as well as employees transporting equipment needed by Will Buckley for his oil company and other foreign industries were caught in the constant cross fire between those demanding arms for the revolution and industries trying to maintain operations in spite of the civil war.[5] By late 1913, Generals Villa and Obregón were in near total control of the railroads in northern Mexico, further limiting the flow of much needed industrial equipment and food into the Mexican interior. The prime rebel objective in the new year was to overrun Huertista garrisons at the strategic border crossings to limit Huerta and the Federal army from obtaining supplies from Texas. A full-scale operation was launched by the Constitutionalists along the Rio Grande on New Year's Eve 1913–14. Frontal attacks were planned for Nuevo Laredo across from Laredo, Texas; Ojinaga across from Presidio, Texas; and an added effort around Ciudad Juárez, across from El Paso, Texas. The purpose was to drive out the Federal garrisons and occupy these key locations. The Nuevo Laredo garrison stayed strong and repelled a massive forty-eight-hour attack. The Ojinaga Federal garrison repulsed the first attack, only to be overrun by a second wave launched by Pancho Villa, who took personal charge of the assault. In Ciudad Juárez, the attacks waned and a stalemate, which had lasted for some two years, continued.[6]

Will Buckley, in a confidential memo to the State Department, included the following regarding Pancho Villa and his operations:

Decision and courage are stamped upon the swarthy face of the Constitutionalists' general. His squared shoulders, his brisk gait, his open manner, all in a way portray the man with a single purpose. His men idolize him.

Shortly after the battle [at Ojinaga] I received a letter from one of his aides which told how the general led the charge that day. It was at half past six in the evening. They were eager to try again—the leader shouted these words to be passed along the line:

"There is Ojinaga. Here are we. It is half past six. At half past seven any man who is on this side of those fortifications will be shot. If I am on this side, you shoot me! Come on. Boys."

The works were carried and the Federals fled in terror across the Rio Grande [into Texas]. Everyone of Villa's men remembers this incident of the battle which was not specifically reported at that time in the newspapers. It was just twenty minutes after seven o'clock when the last man who was able to run or walk pulled himself over the barricades.[7]

The American public had little understanding of the revolution south of the border, yet the situation was captured in a sensational series of syndicated articles by John Kenneth Turner and released in book form as *Barbarous Mexico* (1911).[8] During this period, the American news media made Pancho Villa nearly a household name and dubbed him the "Mexican Robin Hood." The Mutual Film Company paid Villa $25,000, plus a 50 percent royalty on earnings, in exchange for the exclusive rights to film the general and his Army of the North in combat.[9] Villa was colorful and crude of speech—a rebel with a swagger who murdered at will. The *New York Times* published a full-page article on how this convicted bandit leader, age thirty-five, might someday become the president of Mexico, and a full-length silent movie, *The Life of General Villa*, premiered in New York City on May 9. In the weeks to come, Woodrow Wilson, who detested Huerta, became increasingly frustrated with Carranza, and so the president considered Villa as the potential new leader of Mexico! There is little wonder that there was such confusion and misunderstanding of the revolution from the White House to Main Street with headlines like these:

Villa, Bandit and Brute, May Be Mexican President
The Conqueror of Chihuahua and Taker of Juarez Has a Lifelong
Record of Murder, Pillage, and Cruelty—Compared to This
Presidential Possibility, Huerta Is Mild and Innocent[10]

Rebellious factions controlled the railroads throughout the
Mexican Revolution. Buckley's first encounter with General Pancho Villa—
a face-to-face meeting—occurred on a trip to Tampico. Soldiers routinely
guarded trains and supplies. Author's Collection.

Dollarless Diplomacy

Woodrow Wilson entered office with the intention of championing progressive reform of American foreign policy that had been dominated by big
business and fully repudiating the previous Republican era of "Dollar
Diplomacy." The president wanted to craft a new policy to be based on
morality and justice, not global corporate investments, and he deemed
Huerta to be the highly immoral extension of decades of abuse and plun-
der in Mexico. Former ambassador Henry Lane Wilson, who, after his
recall, did not retire quietly, called attention to the unreasonableness of this
policy and to the application of prior tradition and norms of diplomatic
protocols: "the policy transmitted into effect meant simply that no government established in Mexico by revolution would be recognized by the

American government, if, according to our estimate, the revolution was unjustified. We thus constituted ourselves the judges of the laws and the facts, and the dictum amounted to a subversion of the sovereignty of Mexico and a threat against all Latin American governments established by revolution."[11]

In a confidential letter to his old Austin, Texas, friend and neighbor Colonel Edward House, Buckley detailed for Wilson's chief presidential adviser a lengthy sixteen-page assessment of conditions and attitudes in Mexico, in which he stated:

We all believe here that there is but one solution of this difficulty, and that is American intervention. I venture to say that when the first revolution broke out, ninety per cent of the American residents in Mexico were opposed to intervention in any form. They have been converted to this policy, not because they desire to see a conflict between the United States and Mexico, but because they believe that it is the only solution of the problem, due to the lack of patriotism and courage of the Mexican people, and that it will be necessary to conserve American prestige in this country and prevent the domination here of European influence.[12]

A major component of the Wilson administration's plan to isolate Huerta was to disrupt and stop the flow of financial support for his pro-British and pro-German regime. Revenue for the government had three primary sources: first, funding generated from taxation, railroad profits, and duties from the customhouses; second, loans and bank guarantees from domestic banks; third, and most critical, long-term loans and debt financing from foreign financial institutions, primarily in France and Great Britain and to a lesser degree in Germany and the United States. The *Cologne Gazette* saw Huerta as "the man of the hour for Mexico," noting, "Huerta is all in all, the man whom Mexico needs and must have if she is not to be swallowed up by the United States." This was confirmed by Buckley at the 1919 congressional hearings, where he stated, "Mexicans favored Huerta, principally because they were anxious for peace and order." By February 1914, the overwhelming drain on the treasury was the funding of the Federal army, which had grown to more than 250,000, and the purchase of supplies and maintenance of the infrastructure, primarily the railroads (gross

RR earnings in 1913 declined $4,077,000), to move and supply the army. The lifting of the arms embargo on February 3, 1914, was a key step in promoting success for the rebels.[13]

The Thorn in My Side

When Porfirio Díaz was deposed in 1911, the Mexican treasury had a balance above $70 million (at today's value more than $800 million) and a robust inflow of revenues from customhouses, mining fees, and taxes. European bank funding depended on a requirement that Mexico be fully recognized by the United States. Early 1914 was the first time since 1885 that foreign direct investment declined, and the value of outstanding bonds was discounted. Inflation of the money supply soon resulted in larger and larger quantities of worthless paper money owing in part to rebels in the northern states printing their own currency. This, combined with the loss of revenue from the railroads, the drop in the export price of silver, and the mounting damage to foreign mining operations, quickly placed Huerta in a critical position to fund day-to-day operations needed to sustain his government and the military—in effect, a "form of financial starvation, a variety of dollarless diplomacy," favored by the White House. In February 1914, Huerta ordered that all interest and bond payments to foreign creditors be halted. One of the first reactions from the European lenders was to establish an arrangement, which was undercut by Washington, to set up collection agents at the customhouses to collect revenue to satisfy the payment demands. This had been a proven method endorsed by the United States in other Latin American countries, such as Nicaragua, Haiti, Cuba, and the Dominican Republic, and fully the norm and purview of nations to intervene to facilitate bankers collecting debts.[14]

Mexico was unwittingly caught in a geopolitical struggle among the major nations over two looming items: first, the growing demand for petroleum needed by these industrial nations; and second, a simmering diplomatic and commercial conflict between the United States and Great Britain over usage and rates at the new transisthmian Panama Canal, scheduled to be opened in August 1914. The United States opposed British demands to submit the canal tolls dispute to arbitration. There was some concern that the British would ink an agreement with Nicaragua to construct a rival canal along the San Juan River and through the isthmus there. While the revolutionary factions in Mexico had little or no concern about the canal, they did see an opportunity to extract bribes and control by attacking both American and British oil companies and their operations. Notwithstanding the canal toll issue, the British wanted stability in Mexico and had recognized Huerta to preserve and enhance their critical petroleum interests in Tampico and Tuxpan, which had an indirect impact on Buckley's petroleum export operations.[15]

Only eleven months into his presidential term, the steady avalanche of problems, mostly in foreign policy, had become severely taxing on Wilson. In a most interesting and revealing letter to old friend Mary Allen Hulbert, he provided a view into the dynamics of his presidency:

> The thorn in my side is of course Mexico. I have a sneaking admiration for at least the indomitable, dogged determination of Huerta. No doubt it is founded in large part on ignorance, but it is as firm as a rock. It makes the task of smoking him out so much more interesting. He seems to hate me venomously (shall we blame him?), but I have no personal feeling about him whatever. His insults do not disturb me in the least: they are only an evidence of how things are going with him, and how successfully I made myself his insuperable stumbling block. But the problem is most puzzling because I must keep the men in Europe quiet to whom he is not paying the interest on his debt at the same time that I steer our own public opinion in the right path. . . . I fancy a man grows old fast at this business. . . . *I am now paying the price of having told other people what they ought to do when I never had the slightest idea that I should ever be thrust into their place.*[16]

Vergara and Benton

The increasing violence between the rebels and Huertistas soon involved more and more bystanders, particularly foreigners. Villa's troops alone had driven hundreds of Chinese, Spaniards, Italians, and Germans out of Chihuahua to El Paso, compelled "under penalty of death."[17] To excite a growing nationalistic fervor, crowds were encouraged to chant, "Muerte a los gachupines!" (Death to the Spaniards). By early February 1914, unofficially more than one hundred American citizens had been killed, and no one had been brought to justice. The revolution proved a good cover to those committing random crimes. Two high-profile murders were soon to involve the highest levels of the American and British governments. On Valentine's Day, 1914, nine days after President Wilson revoked the arms embargo, South Texas rancher and US citizen Clemente Vergara was lured across the Rio Grande near Laredo in a dispute over the ownership of horses. In the small Mexican village of Hidalgo, across from San José de Palafox, Texas, he was seized by Federal soldiers, beaten, held overnight, and then shot. His body was left hanging from a tree on the outskirts of town. His family sent an alarm to Laredo and to the American consul in Nuevo Laredo, Dr. Alonzo Garrett. The consul immediately cabled the State Department and the American Embassy to contact representatives in the Huerta government to address the kidnapping and murder. President Wilson was notified, and a cabinet meeting was called to review the incident. Governor of Texas Oscar B. Colquitt contacted the White House for a response, indicating he would "send the [Texas] Rangers across the Rio Grande in pursuit of the lawless element." Yet, no official action was taken as the local Mexican Federal authorities claimed, first, that Vergara had been transferred to the garrison at Piedras Negras, and second, that he had escaped to join the rebels. The secretary of foreign affairs in Mexico City released a statement that no one knew "officially that such a man as Vergara ever existed or been killed."[18] Neither report was true.

A week after the Vergara abduction, a British citizen and landed hacendado in Chihuahua, northern Mexico, William S. Benton, had a heated confrontation at Gen. Pancho Villa's headquarters over the ongoing theft of cattle from his multimillion-dollar ranch, Los Remédios. As insults were exchanged, Benton was accused of trying to take a shot at Villa (or his bodyguard Rodolfo Fierro), who responded by having him executed after a "quick trial." Benton was buried in a shallow grave along the railroad track, and when asked, Villa expressed no knowledge of the incident. The twin cold-blooded murders quickly increased pressure on the White House to take action. An immediate demand for redress came first from Governor Colquitt, who had lodged dozens of complaints with Washington on the border violence to no avail. He indicated that if Wilson would not act at once, he would send the Texas Rangers into Mexico to bring Vergara's murderers to justice. News of the governor's threat to send the Rangers was greeted as front-page news in Mexico City's *El Imparcial*, which declared the fiery Mr. Colquitt had "Mexican fobo." Secretary Bryan quickly telegraphed the governor saying it was illegal for the Rangers to cross the border.[19]

Carranza's key Constitutionalist staff members, including Francisco Urguizo, Isidro Fabela, and Luis Cabrera, realized quickly that the death of a leading British citizen in Mexico at the hands of their primary general could have major ramifications. The Buckley Papers contain unpublished memos and public relations articles that the First Chief and his staff drafted claiming self-defense and due process of law to quell media attention and to hopefully calm both British and American officials demanding immediate answers:

By order of the First Chief

Nogales, Feb 23, 1914

Referring to your message of the twenty-first to the First Chief William Benton attempted to assassinate Gen. Villa, who personally was able to disarm him, owing to the quickness with which the general defended himself. Gen. Villa did not administer justice by his own hand, but only, proceeding fairly, delivered him to the competent military tribunal. The court which judged Benton sentenced him to death in accordance to the law. There is no question, then, of an act of vengeance by Gen. Villa or any of his subordinates toward Benton. The unfortunate occurrence was only a consequence of Benton's conduct and the application of the military law. The First Chief of the Constitutionalist Army, Don Venustiano Carranza, is confident that the foreign nations interested in this affair, as well as the press everywhere, will place the true estimate on the case.

Isidro Fabela, Acting Sec. Foreign Affairs[20]

The primary source of pressure came from the British Foreign Office, which demanded a full accounting of the circumstances of the Benton murder. Months earlier, to keep the British out of Mexican affairs as Washington dealt with Huerta, President Wilson had pledged to protect "whenever feasible, all foreigners" in Mexico, and especially British citizens.[21] British indignation did not impress the American ambassador in London: "Kill an Englishman at home," wrote Ambassador W. H. Page, "and there is no undue excitement. But kill one abroad and gunboats and armies and reparation are at once thought about." Of the more than one thousand foreigners killed or murdered in Mexico during the revolution, the Vergara and Benton cases would be the only two individual incidents that would attract extensive worldwide news coverage and directly involve both the American and British governments at the highest level (not to minimize the deaths of more than a dozen Americans at Culabra Tunnel, the murder of engineers at San Ysidro, or the raid on Columbus, New Mexico). Members of Congress began to lobby the White House in favor of armed intervention to stop the violence, especially against Americans. And the British government, which was backed by extensive oil interests, and which had previously recognized Huerta in February 1913, further complicated the situation by issuing an official statement it would never recognize Carranza (the preferred candidate of President Wilson).[22]

The Buckley Papers contain a confidential document not found in the State Department files: a copy of a private memo from Nelson O'Shaughnessy concerning a private conversation with General Huerta at Chapultepec Castle, a year to the day after he assumed the presidency. The chargé had become a friend, and maybe a confidant, of Huerta, and he found himself in his official position at the American Embassy having to negotiate with Huerta on behalf of a White House that abhorred the general and entertained no compromise. O'Shaughnessy wrote:

> General Huerta asked me to sit down alone with him and proceeded to talk to me regarding matters for a long time. I beg to herewith submit a synopsis as near as possible of what he said to me at Chapultepec on the evening of February 18th [1914]. He said the relations between himself and the United States were a matter of regret and concern to him. . . . He recognized the attitude of the President with regard to the non-recognition of Governments which arose by coup d'état was the right one and that he did not desire to criticize but rather to say to me that, in his opinion, the present policy of the United States towards Mexico, if it defeats him in pacifying the country, will force the United States to assume the difficult and unthankful task of armed intervention in the affairs of Mexico.[23]

The Wilson administration's policy of "watchful waiting" continued, regardless of the increased clamor for some form of intervention in Mexico by Senator Albert Fall and other members of Congress, Governor Colquitt (who still lodged complaints about US border agents not stopping the smuggling of arms and munitions into Mexico), and numerous business executives. These appeals for action followed the extensive media coverage of the murders of Vergara and Benton (as well as numerous other incidents). In January 1914 plans for an armed invasion of Mexico were secretly prepared by the president, Secretary Bryan, and members of Wilson's cabinet (it is not known precisely by whom). They considered how such "incidents" or events might provoke direct American military intervention. However, unsure where these high-profile murders were leading, Wilson wrote Colonel House, "The Benton case down in Mexico gives us a great deal of uneasiness." Following a notice by Carranza that he would become the prime contact to investigate General Villa and the Benton incident, the First Chief (primarily to placate the British) appointed a commission, chaired by Gen. Ramón Fraustro, to look into the deaths.[24]

Carranza managed to squelch—or as Will Buckley termed it, "turn back"—all attempts to bring Villa to account for Benton's death or any other incidents. Weeks of investigation, diplomatic exchanges of cables, and misinformation from Wilson's agents in Mexico did little to bring about change. No action was taken, and those responsible were never brought to justice. Governor Colquitt, unaware of the administration's planning for potential intervention, sent strong reminders to the White House urging that American casualties and property losses not be neglected by Washington. He blamed the administration's inaction primarily on the insufficient number of federal troops and agents along the Rio Grande. In fact, the US Army had quietly staged some twenty-four thousand troops at Texas City, along with an extensive stockpile of arms and supplies. By April, a new incident would occur to put an end to the policy of "watchful waiting." In the meantime, the British, more concerned with their oil interests, did not press the issue, and the murders slowly faded from the news.[25]

Tampico

The calm of late March 1914 soon faded. In a briefing paper prepared by Buckley for Senator Fall, he provided a first-person account of the incident at Tampico that would change the course of the revolution: "The most serious phase of the Mexican situation for the U.S. was reached on April 9, when a launch from the U.S. gunboat *Dolphin* carrying the paymaster and a small detachment of Marines landed [unannounced] at Tampico. They came for a supply of gasoline, were unarmed though in uniform, while the launch flew the American flag. The detachment was placed under arrest by the Mexican commander and paraded through the streets of Tampico and were detained for a time."[26]

The American sailors and marines inadvertently entered a restricted area of the port unannounced. The Federal commander had been on high alert for rebel attacks, and there were no clear lines or clear identification of combatants. Local oil companies and citizens were in an elevated state of fear, and the Constitutionalists were carrying out hit-and-run operations and raids. Recent rebel raids had left oil tanks and buildings ablaze. Banks had sent their specie to the German cruiser *Dresden* offshore for safekeeping, and more than five hundred Americans and Europeans had taken refuge aboard foreign warships in the harbor. Once the American naval crew were identified and the misunderstanding about their visit was explained, they were immediately released, unharmed. There *was* no incident, only the routine precautions of the Federal army in a combat zone. The commanding Mexican general asked the crew to convey his "regrets" to their commanding officer for being briefly detained. Buckley recorded the American naval commander's response: "Admiral Mayo, in command of the American naval force at Tampico, protested at the 'treatment' of his men and demanded of the Mexicans a salute of 21 guns as reparation for the insult to the American flag."[27]

Admiral Mayo, at the time of his demand on the Mexican commander at Tampico for a twenty-one-gun salute, had not made any contact with either the War Department or the State Department in Washington. In 1914, communications from the Gulf coast of Mexico took eight to twelve hours to reach Washington depending on radio transmission connections and atmospheric conditions. The admiral's unilateral demand placed the honor of both the United States and Mexico at a confrontation point. Was the landing of the US naval launch a provocation planned by the Americans? Was it a means to create an incident against "the flag" being flown over foreign soil during an unauthorized visit? Had Wilson (under constant pressure from Senators Albert B. Fall and William A. Smith) finally run

The oil fields of Tampico and Veracruz were constantly the target
of rebel factions hoping to disrupt business and cut off supplies of oil
to the federal government. Attacks by rebels, as well as well-head accidents,
were not uncommon. Here, the Potrero de Llano, a large well
near Tampico, burns. Author's Collection.

out of patience with the Mexicans' failure to remove Huerta? And was this
incident to be the catalyst to authorize armed intervention? John Lind, who
had left Mexico to consult with the president in Washington, was advised
by Consul William Canada that "anti-American feelings" were increasing
across the country, and that all awaited the response to the Tampico "incident." And what was needed was an incident.[28]

President Wilson was informed of the situation in Tampico eighteen
hours after it happened. He had secretly gone to the Greenbrier Hotel in
White Sulphur Springs, West Virginia, to obtain medical treatment for his
wife, who was terminally ill. In a telegram to Secretary of the Navy Josephus Daniels, he expressed agreement with Admiral Mayo's response and
the demand for a salute. No investigation was made, and the reaction was
driven purely by emotion and hubris. Historian Robert Quirk, in *An Affair
of Honor*, has the best description of the president's frame of mind, referring to "Wilson's almost perverse conviction that he, himself, was perpetually right," and acknowledging: "He did not seek advice. Other men's
opinions did not really concern him, unless they should happen to coincide

with his."[29] Wilson exploited the incident to foster a showdown that would appear to justify intervention. This was the provocation he had been looking for. Lind, just returned from Mexico, urged the president "to force the issue." From Mexico City, Nelson O'Shaughnessy advised Bryan by cable that when the "old Indian" (Huerta) was briefed on Wilson's demands, the general responded that he would issue a formal apology. However, in a blunt message to O'Shaughnessy, Huerta expressed the "positive refusal of Mexican Government" to provide a twenty-one-gun salute. Mexico's national honor and pride was not to be violated for such a trivial incident, especially for the flag of a nation that had refused to recognize his regime.[30]

The seemingly minor events at Tampico soon turned into a major international confrontation, and Buckley curtailed his travel in light of the unsettled situation. Days passed without resolution, and on Monday afternoon, April 20, President Wilson addressed a joint session of Congress. His rambling presentation seemed to contradict the aims of the administration: "The people of Mexico are entitled to settle their own domestic affairs in their own way, and we sincerely desire to respect their right. The present situation need have none of the grave complicating interference if we deal with it promptly, firmly, and wisely." Citing minor slights and what the president termed "subsequent incidents," the House of Representatives agreed by a vote of 337 to 37 to allow Wilson to use force against Huerta and Mexico. The Senate was locked in a debate and set an ex post facto hearing on the resolution for April 22. The US Navy had prepositioned battle and troop ships (nine total), and many assumed they would be ordered simply to occupy a Mexican port. With the bulk of American naval forces located off Tampico, Admiral Mayo had apparently drafted plans for taking Tampico on April 22 or 23. Lind assured the president that the marines would be greeted with friendly, open, and welcoming arms.[31]

Veracruz and Snipers

Surprisingly, in the midst of the final planning, Consul Canada in Veracruz cabled the State Department on April 20 with urgent news that the German steamer *Ypiranga* was inbound and scheduled to land on April 21 with what was believed to be one of the largest cargoes of arms and munitions for Huerta.[32] How the consul learned of the contents of the *Ypiranga*, still on the high seas, is unknown.

Telegram to Department

Veracruz, April 20, 9:00 P.M. 1914

Department's ferky [*sic*]. Steamer's name Ypiranga. Owned by Hamburg-American Line. Will arrive tomorrow morning and go to pier four. Will start discharging at ten-thirty. There will be thirty cars on pier to load the munitions direct from steamer. Trains of ten cars each will be sent over the Mexican Railroad as loaded, making three trains in all. Ward Line agent will keep steamer Mexico at pier foer [*sic*] as long as possible to delay discharging Ypiranga unless otherwise directed by Admiral Fletcher.

The General in command here states will not fight, but will leave with all soldiers and all rolling stock tomorrow tearing up track behind him.[33]

Secretary Daniels at 1:00 a.m. sent orders to warn all American merchant vessels to leave Veracruz and Tampico and then woke the president with a call at 2:00 a.m. Officials quickly decided to use force to prevent the arms from landing, otherwise abandoning plans for Tampico, and to focus immediately on blocking the port and landing at Veracruz to intercept the arms shipment. The salute of the flag was completely forgotten. The American naval force at Veracruz under the command of Admiral Frank F. Fletcher consisted of two battleships, the USS *Florida* and USS *Utah*, and an old gunboat, the *Prairie*, which carried a detachment of US marines. Backed up by the largest concentration of American warships to date, the 420 marines under the command of Maj. Smedley D. Butler had been transferred from duty in Panama and prepositioned offshore at Veracruz in mid-January 1914.[34]

A very important historical note: the arms aboard the *Ypiranga* were only a pretext for the invasion. President Wilson and his administration had full knowledge of the cargo of the ship well in advance and provided authorization for the intervention prior to the ship's departure from New York City (not from Hamburg, Germany, as some reported) on April 17. If the US Navy had wanted to stop the ship, it could have boarded the vessel at sea (despite the obvious violation of neutrality and the diplomatic precedent set by the Trent Affair of 1861), thus avoiding an incident and confrontation at Veracruz that could be interpreted as an act of war.[35]

Nevertheless, the Port of Veracruz presented a great number of advantages over Tampico. Its harbor was the best on the east coast of Mexico, and it would be a strategic location connected by first-class railroads to supply an advance into Mexico (as it had in 1847). The US consul in Tampico, Clarence Miller, expressed fear that a rapid shifting of all operations southward would result in the exposure of American lives and property due to the prevailing rebel activity and growing anti-American sentiment. Buckley made plans to move from Tampico south to Veracruz, unaware, according to Henry Cabot Lodge, that President Wilson was so focused on removing Huerta that he was no longer concerned for the safety of Americans; Buckley quipped, "Americans in Mexico must take their chances or leave." In a memo to Senator Fall, Buckley stressed, as a prominent business and civic leader in Tampico, that "no arrangements were made by the American government or Mayo for the protection of Americans" in the city. Concerned with the escalation of the so-called Tampico "flag salute" incident, Buckley further noted, "In a conference held in Washington, between Secretary of the Navy Daniels and a committee of Tampico oil men, the former stated that such arrangements had been made, and on being pressed, admitted that was not the case." The rush to take action with the warships of four nations in Mexican coastal waters could have escalated into a larger confrontation. To interdict the arms on the *Ypiranga* intended for General Huerta legally, a blockade should have been declared, and any action toward a blockade, under international law, was an act of war. When advised by the legal staff at the State Department of the potential violation, Wilson was not deterred. The landing, executed prior to US Senate consent, was scheduled for Veracruz on April 21. (Coincidentally, this was the same day Hernán Cortés landed in Mexico in 1519.) Neither Gen. Leonard Wood, army chief of staff, nor Rear Adm. Bradley Fiske, chief of naval operations, was consulted. Fiske recalled, "We had worked out a joint [operations] plan, but it was never used or even asked for." President Wilson expected the landing to be peaceful and unopposed by Mexico. This expectation was based on the president's own misinformed idea that the Mexicans would welcome the Americans; possibly, in addition, it was based on Consul Canada's cable that the Federals in Veracruz "would not fight."[36]

On the afternoon of the American landing, Senator Fall took to the floor of the Senate during the debate on the resolution of war, noting as he spoke that the Associated Press had reported that US marines and Mexicans were dying in combat in the streets of Veracruz. Consul Canada's cable to the State Department, forwarded to Secretary Daniels, implied there would be no resistance to the American landing. Fall announced the fighting had begun with a eulogy for the fallen: "Peace to the families of the American Marines, peace to those writhing in their wounds, peace to the dead Mexicans, peace to those yet to die!"[37]

Will Buckley recalled how the American naval forces "seized the Customs House with a force of 1,000. In the fighting that followed the landing of the Americans, nineteen men were killed and dozens wounded. On April 30 a brigade of US Army regulars under the command of General Frederick Funston landed and relieved the naval and marine force." The assumed friendly landing had quickly turned violent. President Wilson, intending to humiliate Huerta and depose him, narrowly averted an

Brigadier General Frederick Funston, who commanded US military forces
at Veracruz in 1914–1915, encouraged Buckley to take an active role
in the American administration of the US occupation,
which Buckley declined. Author's Collection.

expanded war. The detailed plans to move inland toward Mexico City were taken off the table once the extent of anti-American outcry from across Mexico was reported to the White House. Days after the landing, Buckley noted, "Navy and army officers are extremely bitter in their denunciation of the Department in Washington and state that Mr. Bryan and the President are responsible for the many casualties that occurred in the taking of Veracruz."[38]

Family and friends recall Will being apprehensive about Wilson's invasion of Veracruz. Presumably Buckley was in Tampico during early April and was briefly in Mexico City before traveling to Veracruz during the American landing. His son Reid recalls he did not harbor grudges but, when needed, did not hesitate to take action. Reid wrote, "When he was apprised [by a friend] that Mexican snipers hidden on the rooftop cisterns of buildings (in Veracruz) were shooting down American Marines, he walked out into the middle of the street yelling obscene insults in his perfect Spanish at the rooftops, where the snipers were skulking, so that they popped up in fury to blast away at him—thus offering targets for Marine sharpshooters. I don't know how often he repeated this act of bravado, but I gather it was several times"; Reid conjectured further that his father "held Mexican marksmanship in Texas contempt."[39]

Quite possibly Buckley's active presence defending the marines in the streets of Veracruz and the prominence gained as an American practicing law in Mexico may account for the offer from the Wilson administration—which he quickly rejected—to be appointed the "civilian governor" of the city during the American occupation. To accept would have ended his credibility and damaged his reputation in Mexico. While he viewed most of President Wilson's representatives as amateur opportunists, he was appointed by Admiral Fletcher as an adviser to the committee, along with Captain Burnside and visiting Chicago attorney Robert Kerr, charged with drafting for the civil governor the proclamation of martial law. The US Navy issued a press release before Buckley could decline either appointment. Newspaper articles in Austin, Houston, and Dallas resulted in numerous letters of congratulations for a post he never permanently filled.[40] Buckley's short service on the drafting committee was based on an ulterior motive to secure a larger role with the US Army if it proceeded to Mexico City. "I can serve the American government, and I can serve the Mexican by curtailing the activity of the carpet baggers . . . and floor flushers" that follow the army. In spite of conflicting rumors, however, the army did not proceed to Mexico City.[41]

The events at Veracruz further confirmed and jelled Will's core values and his views on political realities that he strongly felt the idealistic Wilson misunderstood. First, he believed it was wrong for the United States to impose its "republican standards" on Mexico, which had never had the remotest experience with full and free democratic government. These views Buckley expressed in a series of detailed letters to Secretary of War L. M. Garrison during the months of the Veracruz occupation. Factors having an impact on this course of Mexican history included, for example, decades of dictatorial strongmen, low literacy levels, and stagnated economic development following the Panic of 1906–7. A second reality was the mantra that newly arrived investment in Mexico should excuse the graft and opportunism of foreign investors who came to the country motivated solely by pillage and profit. The revolution itself, and resulting Article 27 of the new Constitution of 1917, would in time address the issue of Mexico's sovereignty by proclaiming the government had the rights to own and transfer any of the lands within the boundaries of the nation. And third, and most disturbing, was the heavy-handed means by which the United States interfered in the internal affairs of Mexico. Reid Buckley concluded, "Apart from the violence done to international law, was a mortal transgression against Father's Southwestern doctrine of isolationism. Mexico dyed our father's politics indelibly and bred in his children distrust of populist charmers of whatever ideological hue."[42]

Backlash

News of the American landing at Veracruz spread fast. The response across Mexico was one of hostility from all factions. Riots, numbering in the thousands of protesters, broke out across Mexico City. The bronze bust of George Washington, dedicated only a year before by the American business community in the city, was torn down by a mob chanting, "Death to the Gringos!" The bust of Washington was paraded around the city and thrown at the foot of the Juárez Memorial, and it was replaced with a statue of Father Miguel Hidalgo. American businesses and tourists as well as the offices of the English-language *Mexican Herald* and Sanborns Drugstore were stoned. The American Embassy, where dozens of Americans flocked for safety, was attacked but not breached. In the hours just before the embassy was ordered to close, General Huerta visited in-person twice to check on the safety of the staff and status of any further American response. Confronting the O'Shaughnessys, Huerta was more perplexed than bitter. Edith, the chargé's wife, recalled their exchange, "You have seized our port. *Su Excelencia el Senor Presidente* Wilson has declared war unnecessarily, on a people that ask only to be left alone, to follow out their evolution in their own way, though it may not seem to you a good way."[43] After a mob stoned the embassy and tore the United States shield from its outer gates, Huerta ordered a twenty-four-hour guard by one hundred of the capital's best mounted gendarmes to patrol the streets around the official residence. During the final hours, the Brazilian minister in Mexico City, José M. Cardoso de Oliveira, agreed to represent the interests of the US consular agents who remained at their posts in more than a dozen cities across Mexico with little or no authority or protection. Thus, the American Embassy in Mexico City was abandoned and shuttered shortly before midnight on April 23.[44]

In advance of the Veracruz landing, US special operations agents had reconnoitered a complete survey of the approaches to Mexico City and the location of Mexican troops and fortifications. As of April 23, no official decision to move inland had been made. Buckley was concerned that any aggressive action or major counterattack by Mexican troops could trigger a full-scale invasion. When O'Shaughnessy left the embassy, Luis d'Antin remained at the legation. It is not clear whether he was ordered to stay, or if he took it upon himself to remain behind. Surrounded by what one reporter called a "drunken half-crazy mob," d'Antin set up machine guns (that had been hidden in the basement) on the second floor. When W. K. Burns, a friend, called from the railroad station to inform him the last refugee train to Veracruz was about to leave, d'Antin's last words were: "They've got to kill me before I go!" Apparently, no shots were fired, and the embassy was not breached. Mexican secret police issued an arrest warrant for d'Antin, after he took refuge in the Brazilian embassy, for his role in promoting "Carranza war propaganda." His capture was averted when the embassy declared d'Antin an employee of the legation, thus giving him "diplomatic" protection. News of this appeared in only a few papers and was confirmed by the US State Department and German intelligence.[45]

Nelson O'Shaughnessy and his family arrived in Veracruz by special train, accompanied by Will Buckley and under the protection of the US Marines and Navy. The town was quickly occupied and all fighting halted. While the military awaited instructions from Washington, the officers and diplomats lunched together to muse over their next steps. Will and the guests were welcomed and dined aboard the moored American and British warships in the harbor. In one of the more interesting footnotes to history, the *Ypiranga*—the ship supposedly at the center of the controversy—was itself anchored offshore, sitting idle beyond the harbor. On April 29, Captain Bonath hosted a dinner party for the O'Shaughnessys, Adm. John Cradock, and German diplomats on board the ship. The guests dined at length in the captain's stateroom, which was located directly above the ship's cargo hole containing the arms and ammunition that had been prevented from landing. Buckley learned only later of the volatile cargo.[46]

Presidential Shock

Reports poured into the State Department and White House from official consular posts and unofficial news sources of the mounting anti-American attacks across Mexico. President Wilson acted shocked at such a response. The consular offices in Saltillo, San Luis Potosí, Mazatlán, and Monterrey were sacked, including a public display targeting every American flag for burning. Three US consul generals and staff were taken as prisoners and jailed: Philip Hanna in Monterrey, John Silliman in Saltillo, and Wilbert Bonney in San Luis Potosí.[47] All were released unharmed, yet the American government took no official notice nor made any demands for apologies or redress for these hostilities. Consul Will Davis in Guadalajara reported that the consulate there was attacked with repeated cries of "Muera el Consul Americano—more distinctly heard by me because uttered especially for my ears!" Rumors along the US-Mexico border warned of retaliatory raids. As Consul Henry Miller in Tampico forewarned, the city with the second-largest concentration of Americans had the worst outbreak of anti-American attacks on persons and property. Federal forces under Gen. Morelos Zaragoza were helpless against the mobs. Adm. Henry T. Mayo considered landing troops but was able to broker a ceasefire with the assistance of German and British naval captains in the harbor. This

ceasefire resulted in the evacuation of hundreds of Americans and foreigners who wished to leave. Consul Miller proved exceedingly calm and
gallant and was the last to board a departing ship.[48]

The most vocal protest of the American landing, however, came from
the rebel leaders led by Carranza. The landing was considered an outright
"hostile" invasion of Mexico's national sovereignty and an infringement of
Mexicans' right to self-determination. Instead of praising President Wilson
for taking action, they issued a list of denouncements for the US actions in
Veracruz. Carranza made clear that the Constitutionalists would join forces
with all the other rebel groups *and* Huerta's Federals if American forces did
not withdraw at once. Villa, always unpredictable, was a bit more philo-
sophical in a meeting with Special Agent G. C. Carothers. He believed that
Veracruz was a mistake but not worth a "war which neither side desired,"
and the "little drunkard" Huerta was not going to draw him into a war
with the United States![49] Wilson was shocked by the vitriol of the vigorous
Mexican opposition. Having been deluded into expecting to be greeted
with welcoming arms, he was further shocked at the number of American and Mexican casualties. His actions had grave consequences beyond
his moralistic judgments of the revolution. And as one recent observer
noted in retrospect, "The president allowed missionary fervor to supplant
hard-boiled diplomacy."[50]

The president's shock can be directly attributed to the slanted misinformation supplied by his handpicked "confidential agents," which was prejudiced, often inaccurate, and sought to feed the president's ego.[51] The most
corrupt was John Lind. Wilson's notions of what the Mexican people wanted
was determined largely by Lind's misguided moralistic views and highly
biased reporting. Lind failed to entertain hard data from experts and
anticipated no resistance or bloodshed. Detailed periodic reports on the
complex social, business, and political conditions from a score of seasoned
consul generals in cities across Mexico were ignored by the president and
the State Department. Numerous US consuls viewed the president's use of
confidential agents as evidence that his State Department had chosen to
ignore the seasoned diplomats and discount the veracity of their daily
efforts. George A. Chamberlain, consul general in Mexico City prior to 1919,
spoke up and informed Congress, echoing Buckley's early 1914 assessment
that there was "no [US] policy whatever in Mexico—there was no protection for life and property."[52] (See appendix B.)

In the final hours before Americans departed their embassy, General Huerta visited again, as Edith recalled. He put his hand on Nelson's shoulder and said, "I hold no rancor towards President Wilson—he has not understood."[53]

Niagara Falls—ABC

While there have been numerous studies of the ABC Conference of 1914, none seem to have made use of the Buckley Papers in the Benson Collection at the University of Texas at Austin. The diplomatic and political impasse created by the armed actions at Veracruz was first addressed by an offer from several Latin American countries. The shocked president, according to Henry Cabot Lodge, "looked for an escape," which was provided four days after the invasion by the "good offices" of the plenipotentiaries from Argentina, Brazil, and Chile—hence, *ABC*. Historian Samuel F. Bemis noted the ABC offer of "good offices" was a way "of getting out of an ugly situation." This mediation and facilitation of negotiations helped prevent a larger war between Mexico and the United States and was reluctantly agreed to by the two countries. In advance of the mediation conference, President Wilson traveled to the Brooklyn Naval Yard on May 11 to address the gathering honoring the returned dead soldiers and sailors killed at Veracruz. In a rambling speech, he justified his actions by saying, "We have gone down to Mexico to serve mankind." Publicly for the rest of his life, Buckley harshly criticized the invasion at Veracruz and the president's gratuitous remarks at the memorial ceremony: "I do not imagine that the families of the boys that were killed in this affair felt compensated for this price of gross negligence and criminal ignorance by the graciousness of the President in coming to New York and delivering an oration over the biers of the men who were killed, where he took advantage of the occasion to deliver a eulogy on himself."[54]

The first meeting was scheduled to convene on May 18, 1914, at Niagara Falls, Ontario, Canada but was postponed by Carranza. This date coincides with the Constitutionalists' refusal to suspend hostilities until after they captured the Port of Tampico and with the Wilson administration's orders to customs officials in Galveston, Texas, to permit arms shipments by sea to Tampico and Veracruz only after the interception of the *Ypiranga*. The German ship, after floating around off the coast, eventually offloaded its enormous cargo of arms at Puerto Mexico (south of Veracruz on the Isthmus of Tehuantepec) on about May 25. In the end, the chain of events hardly matched the diplomatic intrigue and saber-rattling that had surrounded it. If the reason for the occupation of Veracruz was to prevent the landing of the *Ypiranga*, "the operation was hopelessly bungled." The US government was embarrassed to discover the arms were not German, but American-made.[55]

Shortly thereafter, the German carrier the *Bavaria* offloaded 1 million rounds of ammunition for the Federals. Throughout the Niagara Falls—ABC conference, shiploads of munitions sent by Huerta supporters arrived at Mexican ports from the United States and Germany. A blockade by a foreign nation to seal off a port could not be imposed because it may have been viewed as an act of war. When the Navy Department was asked for a clarification, officials avoided all inquiries. The shipment of arms was a blatant aid to Carranza. By refusing to attend the mediation conference or agree to an armistice, Carranza doomed any chance of a peaceful settlement and transfer of power, proclaiming in late June that he had no intention of dealing with Huerta "except on the battlefield."[56]

Following conversations at Niagara Falls, Mexican negotiator Emilio Rabasa informed Buckley, "The rebels want to obtain their triumph by force of arms, so as to achieve it unconditionally and to establish a dictatorship of conquerors until they consider that they have purified Mexican society in accordance with their infallible moral creed." Thus, given his fragile control of the revolution, the First Chief had no intention whatsoever of leaving Mexico for the conference in Canada. The ABC conference lasted several weeks but ended with no conclusive results. The mediation attempt accomplished little more than a stalemate and a delay.[57]

The conference was "conceived in bad faith," noted Buckley. Not only did Carranza fail to attend; he refused to send representatives to Niagara Falls. Yet throughout this period the rebels had nearly a dozen agents and paid lobbyists representing the First Chief's views in Washington, DC. For his part, Huerta accepted the mediation offer only "in principle" and selected Rabasa as chief of the delegation along with Agustin Rodriquez and Luis Elguero. Huerta aimed to capitalize on the invasion to strengthen his position, remove the Americans from Veracruz, and shift official American attention away from Washington's fixation on Carranza and the Constitutionalists. The behind-the-scenes representation of Huerta was led by William Buckley in Washington, and the documentation of his low-key participation has been all but lost in the Buckley Papers (but found and utilized in this study), which contain coded messages and secret correspondence on the negotiations. Interestingly, Rabasa, who recommended Buckley, was unaware of his friend's strident recommendation to Colonel House in November demanding intervention to solve the Mexican "problem."[58]

The fact that the Mexican delegation had an American lawyer on its payroll was a well-kept secret at the time and did not become public information until congressional hearings in 1919 investigating President Wilson's handling of the Mexico situation. Held in high regard by the Huerta government, Buckley was retained as its chief legal consultant. His restrained approach, aided tremendously by his command of Spanish, came close to reaching a deal with all parties, including an obstinate Carranza. In characteristic fashion, however, Wilson vetoed the progress made by his own appointed representatives.[59]

In Washington, Wilson, Bryan, and Daniels had already predetermined to undercut Huerta and promote Carranza even despite his many vocal anti-American protests. This vague policy included false representations at the negotiations in Niagara Falls, secret assistance to expedite arms to the Constitutionalists, and insistence "that Huerta surrender absolutely to Carranza." The First Chief would cooperate with Washington only on his own terms. Buckley, known in coded documents as "Mr. X," through back-channel conversations with the State Department surfaced and confirmed Wilson's true intentions. The president and Bryan used the ABC meeting only as cover, to mask their lack of commitment to a negotiated settlement. Apparently the president or Bryan, or both, delegated former University of Texas president and secretary of agriculture David F. Houston to negotiate, in Washington, with Huerta's representative(s)—Mr. X—shortly after the Veracruz landing:

> Before entering the conference the Huerta delegation made agreement with President Wilson to the effect that they would induce Huerta to resign and Wilson would support neutral government in Mexico. The A.B.C. intermediaries, after conferring with the American government, advised the Huerta delegation that the American government was willing to enter into this agreement. The agreement was concluded on the following day through Mr. X, representing the

Mexican delegation, and Dr. D. F. Houston, representing the President. Later, when Mr. X pressed Mr. Bryan for compliance with the agreement, Mr. Bryan admitted that such a compact had been made, but stated that the American government could not fulfill it. He insisted that Carranza must be made provisional and permanent President of Mexico, and stated that the purpose of the Niagara conference was not to settle differences between Huerta and the American government, as Huerta thought, and not to treat of the insult to the American flag, but to "transfer in a peaceful manner the government to Carranza."[60]

In still another misrepresentation by Wilson, the US government agreed with the Huerta delegation that an embargo would be enforced and no arms or ammunition should be shipped to Mexico. This was done despite the knowledge of American officials that ships loaded with arms and munitions were in fact leaving New York on the Ward Line. Bryan defended their action by claiming the government could do nothing about a ship on the high seas.[61] When confronted by Buckley, "Mr. Bryan admitted to Mr. X and the others that, after making the above agreements with the Huerta delegation, he advised the Carranza revolutionary Junta to bill the ammunition 'for delivery' to Cuba and then divert the course of boats to Mexico." Furthermore, if there was any question of their intentions, "The American government [US Navy] refused to stop this shipment [to Carranza], and threatened to sink Huerta's gunboats if the latter refused to allow the shipment to land at Tampico."[62]

The Buckley Papers include detailed copies of arms purchase orders processed by Mexican Consul Francisco Urquidi, stationed at 17 Battery Place, New York City. Years later, in the Albert Fall congressional investigation on Mexico, Sherburne G. Hopkins, "*consultor legal*" and lobbyist for the Constitutionalist junta, testified that John Lind had informed Carranza through him on how to evade US Neutrality Acts. British intelligence intercepted letters from Hopkins to Carranza, one of which stated: "Lind told me you should arrange to export such needed [arms] from some port on the Gulf, preferably Mobile or Pensacola, in small vessels to Cuba, which might alter their course to the mouth of the Rio Bravo [Rio Grande]. Lind assured me very positively that there *would be no interference whatsoever.*" It is unknown how much Wilson knew of these dealings, but given his focus

on eliminating Huerta, he was possibly involved in all aspects of this volatile period. As time passed, Huerta's position in Mexico became even more
untenable.[63]

With flamboyant speeches and pronouncements, the Niagara Falls Conference was a massive farce. As Robert Quirk noted, it "resembled nothing so
much as an elaborate quadrille from *Alice in Wonderland*," ending in
stalemate. However, it did help avoid an expanded war between the United
States and Mexico. The Latin American representatives who attempted
to be honest brokers were dictated to by a self-righteous Wilson who had
but one aim—to remove Huerta. Ambassador Michael Small in a recent
monograph reviewing the 1914 mediation at Niagara concluded: "Once it
became evident that Huerta delegates were not going to agree at the table
to an unconditional surrender, and that the Constitutionalists were not prepared to let the United States continue to represent them, the possibility of
mediating the internal conflict at Niagara Falls disappeared." This charade
continued until the fall of Huerta in mid-July 1914. The general collected
as much cash as possible, packed up his family, and traveled to Puerto Mexico, south of Veracruz, to board the German naval cruiser SMS *Dresden*,
which carried them into exile in Europe.[64]

In the scramble for control of power in Mexico following the departure
of Huerta, Buckley wrote a letter to Secretary of War Garrison echoing the
continued frustration of those in Mexico regarding the course of the revolution and the overarching role of the United States:

It is the belief that Carranza owes his success to the support of the
United States and that he will be the agent and puppet of the Americans. The capture of Veracruz, the open violation of neutrality laws, the
refusal to stop the shipment of arms to the rebels during mediation,
the valuable advice of Mr. Lind as to how to evade such laws as
existed in the matter and his counsel not to agree to an armistice, and,
now, the sending of Silliman as a traveling companion with Carranza,
and the proposed negotiations of the American government directly
with the Zapatistas and other disturbing elements,—are continually
being quoted by the Mexicans. In fact, they call the Constitutionalists "Los Hijos de la Intervención."

I hope no one in the United States harbors the delusion that
the Carranzistas are grateful to the American government for her

sympathy and aid; quite the contrary; the Constitutionalists is [*sic*] typical of the Mexican who hates the "gringo," and they have, in addition to their natural feelings, a feeling of contempt for the United States.[65]

Thus, the revolution, with no clear leadership (Francisco Carbajal was Huerta's replacement and acting president for less than a month), now entered a new and bloody militant stage. Secretary Bryan was quick to announce that in support of the new interim government, the United States would "refuse to recognize as legal any acts performed by the Huerta government subsequent to October 10, 1913." This refusal covered all concessions granted and all foreign loans. "Mexico is apparently no nearer a solution of her tragical troubles than she was when the revolution was first kindled . . . she has been swept by civil war as if by fire," was Wilson's piqued response. By August 1914, Wilson and Bryan, frustrated with Carranza and eager to find a new leader, considered switching their backing to Villa. The illiterate rebel, they concluded, better understood the need for agrarian reforms, something he had only a small interest in, and seemed to prefer only to continue the fight. During a meeting with a group of Tampico oilmen at the White House shortly after the landing at Veracruz, the president assured them that "Villa is the safest man in Mexico to tie to." The Wilson administration was totally blinded by the sentiments of the popular news media that the "Robin Hood of the North" had the backing of American public opinion and thus was the obvious selection.[66]

During much of 1914, Buckley expressed grave concerns about Wilson's handling of the Mexican intervention and ongoing meddling in the country's internal affairs. Nonetheless, "Mr. X" proved effective during the Niagara Falls mediation in developing a back channel to the State Department (and presumably to the White House). Doug Reed, a British business associate, noted: "after Niagara Falls W.F.B. became William Jennings Bryan's closest 'outside' adviser on Mexican affairs as long as Bryan remained Wilson's Secretary of State." Additionally, Buckley was no stranger to many of the key politicians in Washington. For more than a decade, he had known Secretary Houston from his university days in Austin as well as other cabinet members from Texas, including Watt Gregory, attorney general; Albert Burleson, postmaster general (and former congressman from the Austin district); and Colonel House, of Houston and Austin, the president's chief adviser. Buckley's most direct contacts that developed during weeks in Washington, however, were with Bryan—the one who needed the most accurate information on the complicated situation in Mexico—and with Secretary of War Garrison. Buckley was never dubbed an agent, a title he would have abhorred and avoided at any cost. Yet, beginning upon his return to Mexico in the fall of 1914, he began to send, generally weekly, a briefing paper to Bryan.

The details and content of Buckley's letters and reports, given the fact the American Embassy in Mexico City was closed, were extensive and timely; they kept abreast of the fast-moving events across the country. In addition to a balanced look at the political jockeying among the leading rebel chieftains, Will provided thorough information on infrastructure conditions (the railroads were in shambles) and on the viability of Mexican currency. A major concern and an unaddressed issue he correctly noted was the growing shortage of food and the damage to the crop-producing capacity. Those farmers that tilled the land had been summarily drafted into one of the rebel groups or the Federal army. Livestock, especially most plowing oxen, had been confiscated. Seed corn and grain were also in short supply. Hard currency in the form of silver coins had disappeared from circulation. All currency policies enacted by Huerta were declared null and void, leaving in circulation worthless paper currency. Thus, there was very little foreign exchange or available cash (and no loans or lines of credit) to pay for imports or foodstuffs.[67]

Mexico City Sacked

The Mexican Revolution had only briefly brought Mexico City under attack during the February 1913 Madero coup and rise of Huerta. Therefore, the city was in a state of shock when Carranza's Constitutionalist Army boldly entered the capital. Following three days of pillaging, which the troops "say they were promised for their support," there continued a steady wave of looting, killings, and mass lawlessness. Thousands of Huertista followers, Federal soldiers, priests and nuns, and bureaucrats fled the city to Veracruz, preferring to take their chances with the occupation of the US Marines. And still, police shot scores of citizens in cold blood, government officials were killed, and dozens were wounded. All city services, health care, sanitation, and local policing came to a halt. The greatest spectacle was the near constant parading of hundreds of stolen "motors" (automobiles) through the streets. Will Buckley was an eyewitness to the violent occupation of the capital: "The Carranza army, upon its entry into Mexico City, did not show the restraint that Mr. Lind speaks about. The armies committed all manner of excesses and the officers distributed among themselves the finest dwellings in Mexico City, where they held orgies for several months and which they eventually looted. It is notorious that what Mr. Lind states is not true, and his statement is merely the statement of a Carranza propagandist." During the Fall Committee hearings in 1919, Lind was defensive in his comments about the sacking of Mexico City, concluding, "I have no doubt that there were excesses."[68]

Buckley in a letter on September 2, 1914, chronicled conditions in Mexico City, stating that "the situation is beyond words" and concluding:

> No President. No cabinet. No Congress or Senate. No law; no constitution; no law courts or tribunals. For several days last week, no police in town. No Banks—no transactions. No newspapers, except official sheets, and these working only to keep us in the dark. On the other hand, perfect freedom on the part of officials to do and decree what they think fit, or suits them. More than a hundred of the most magnificent houses, with all their furniture and belongings, and about four hundred automobiles, in the hands of the conquerors, all taken without any other reason but their good will. Over and above this, persecution to Catholic priests and nuns.[69]

The *New York World* reported that "army leaders swarmed like locusts upon the real property of the aristocrats, former *Científicos*, and former members of the Díaz and Huerta regimes" as well as of some former Madero officials. While Carranza quartered himself at Chapultepec Castle, scores of homes were seized, among them the residences of Joaquín Casasús, Díaz's ambassador to Washington; Enrique Creel, a hated member of the *Científicos*; Pedro Lascuráin, Madero's former foreign minister; and the home of Díaz treasury minister José Yves Limantour. General Obregón commandeered the home of the widow Senora Thomas Braniff, an American citizen. Prime targets were the numerous homes of President Huerta. Before departing the city, he sold all his properties—which were rumored to have been bought at a discount with Federal Treasury money—to the government "at inflated figures and collected in cash." All industry and business came to a near standstill. Shops were closed, food was in short supply, and hard money vanished almost entirely as the Constitutionalists printed millions of worthless pesos. Will recalled, "The entire Republic of Mexico was then given over to a state of anarchy," with three different rebel factions in three different cities claiming to be the legitimate government of Mexico. As Villa and Zapata and their combined armies approached Mexico City, Carranza withdrew in late November to Veracruz, arriving only hours after the last US soldiers and marines withdrew from Mexico. While touting a return to peace, Villa during a few days in the city executed more than twenty-five ex-Federals, either personal enemies or those directly concerned with the "Ciudadela" affair. What followed was a momentous meeting of the rebel leaders in *la capital*.[70]

"Come See Me Sometime"

The year 1914 for Will Buckley had been a whirlwind. Close attention to his business and investments occupied much of his schedule as he worked to set Pantepec Oil Company on a solid footing. Harassment by rebels and bandits posing as rebels took a toll on all those in the Tampico area. Buckley traversed Mexico, from Tampico, to Mexico City, to Veracruz during the most eventful months. Following the Veracruz landing, he spent nearly three months in Washington, DC, and New York City representing the Huerta regime during the Niagara Falls mediation. After returning to Mexico in September 1914, he faced deteriorating business conditions as the civil war became even more violent. Drilling camps were routinely being raided. Oil company staff and workers were robbed and kidnapped, cattle were stolen, and hard currency was in short supply. Of greatest concern were the local ranchers he worked with along the eastern coast from Veracruz to Tampico. Tensions were at an all-time high as there was no clear governing authority.

In early December 1914, a complete break in trust and cooperation occurred between Pancho Villa and Emiliano Zapata, on the one hand, and

Carranza, on the other. Unwilling to heed any further dictates, Villa and Zapata rode triumphantly at the head of some thirty thousand troops into Mexico City. At the zenith of their power, the two legendary warrior-rebel leaders agreed to a grand celebration in the ancient Aztec gardens of Xochimilco. The picture of the two rebel leaders sitting side by side at the head table is one of the most iconic images of the revolution. Leon J. Canova, retained by Secretary Bryan to work with Carothers to gain better relations with the rebel factions, was witness to the gathering, noting that "Zapata greeted Villa warmly," yet once in the meeting hall they "sat in an embarrassed silence, occasionally broken by insignificant remarks, like two sweethearts." Soon the ice was broken. The huge table was in a squared U shape, and all participants—still well armed with a pistol by each plate—were laughing, joking, and drinking, except for Villa, who did not drink. The raucous dinner was primarily a victory celebration and an attempt to smooth hard feelings among the competing combatants. There seems not to have been a high level of security, other than the armed rebels, and visitors and onlookers had easy access.[71]

The facts of Guillermo Buckley's next encounter with Pancho Villa are a compilation of the memories of Cecilio Velasco and Reid Buckley. No one seems to know exactly what triggered the face-off, but Buckley was angry that Villa's guerrillas had repeatedly raided, stolen, and harmed workers on his ranch outside of Tampico. According to Velasco, who was present, he saw Buckley suddenly approach the head table straight toward Villa. The dialog is provided by Reid:

> Villa glanced up at Will and said, "Ah, Senor *Ojos Azules*, what brings you here? What can I do for you?"
>
> "You can keep your men off my property," Will answered.
>
> Villa, Senor Velasco recalled, smiled—but his eyes flicked toward Zapata, on his left, whose eyebrows had cocked. What—Pancho Villa was asking himself—would Zapata be thinking of the presumptuous attitude by a gringo?
>
> He said, "And why should I do that, Guillermo Buckley? Just what will you do if my men trespass on your property?"
>
> In the often told story, it is best recalled that Will answered something on the order of: "Because the next time one of your men puts his foot on my property, he will be shot."

Velasco recounted to Reid he watched as Pancho Villa's cronies at the head table grew still and the hall became silent and the *Dorados* or "Golden Ones"—Villa's handpicked warriors [bodyguards]— placed their hands on their pistols, gazing at their chief.

There ensued moments of extreme tension; and then Pancho Villa laughed, saying something like, "My men won't be bothering you, Senor *Ojos Azules*, I promise you."

Villa laughed again, "Come see me sometime."[72]

government in secrecy. All business and investment activities as well as permitting and adjudication generated at the local level were ultimately approved in Mexico City at the federal level. Many times, the established law did not matter. As one observer concluded, Americans were allowed to function as "an aristocratic caste above the law of Mexico." Often, industrial materials for foreign operations were imported duty-free and were exempt from taxation. Mexican officials were routinely granted stock, appointed as legal consultants, and often given outright "gifts." In addition, preferential treatment by the Mexican court system was often slanted generously toward the foreign investors.[1]

In the voluminous Buckley private papers and collection there are numerous items, reports, memos, and draft comments that include analysis and perspective on the challenges and tribulations of Mexico in the years prior to the explosion of the 1910 revolution and continuing through the fall of Huerta. Buckley was knowledgeable about Mexico's historical past and often expressed his irritation at greedy foreign investors, diplomats, and so-called experts, like President Wilson's band of "confidential agents," that had no affinity for the political, cultural, and social dynamics of Mexico. A draft document of the revolution's objectives that was prepared prior to publication by Carranza confidant and aide Luis Cabrera, the key spokesman for the Constitutionalists in Washington and a delegate to the Niagara Falls mediation, is one such document in the Buckley Papers. It details a stunning and candid assessment of the underbelly of the revolution wrapped in the impact of unchecked foreign investment and preferential treatment:

> The lack of Mexican capital is the reason that mining and other Mexican industries have not been developed save by foreign capital. . . . This system of privileges and monopoly comprised not only the mining, petroleum and water power industries, but all kinds of industries and manufactures, commerce and banking. . . . The problem for Mexico is to find the way in which foreign money and immigrants can come freely to Mexico and contribute to her progress without becoming a privileged class. Instead of becoming a menace to the sovereignty of Mexico, they should contribute to the consolidation of her sovereignty and her independence as a nation."[2]

Given the presence of this draft in Buckley's possession and files, prior to its publication in a leading American journal, one wonders if Will was a contributor to the content, language, and presentation of the document. In the coming years, Cabrera would repeatedly publicly deny knowing William Buckley. Cabrera's clear concern was for Mexico to be competitive and profitable among the behemoth international oil concerns as they jockeyed for an ever larger slice of Mexico's petroleum reserves. Furthermore, he, without stating so by name, argued for a strict adherence to the Calvo Doctrine, which stated that foreigners must obey the laws of the government in which they are domiciled or under which they do business. This became an ongoing matter of contention as the foreign oil companies lobbied to maintain their subsoil rights, tax exemptions, and privileges. Cabrera would evolve as the leading anti-American voice of the revolutionary era.[3] A contemporary would pen in 1916 an apt characterization of Cabrera:

> In Mexico, of those that appear to have the fortune of their country in the hollow of their hands, we see most frequently the name of Luis Cabrera. The First Chief's right hand man is socialistic, involved, and impractical; but he has an alert, clever mind and as lobbyist has few equals in or out of Mexico. He and Carranza are responsible for the nightmare of *bilimbiques*, which perhaps may be charged more to ignorance than to dishonesty. He is a lawyer by profession and an intriguer by nature.[4]

By late July 1914, Carranza struggled to gain control of Mexico against Villa and Zapata and to seat his handpicked cabinet. Buckley, in a letter to Secretary of War Garrison, was able to provide firsthand impressions of most of the rising new operatives in the Constitutionalist faction, noting,

> Lic. Cabrera is certainly one of the most brilliant men in the Constitutionalist party; he is a man who has a the . . . . he was my Professor of Civil Law for over a year in the National University in this city, and, while I have the greatest affection for him, I have always regarded him as being *dangerously theoretical*. Like most intellectual men, he has the most unbounded confidence in the infallibility of his own conclusions.

Buckley further noted that Cabrera, having no real-world business or financial experience, might "prove dangerous" if charged with the nation's financial policy at this critical period of transition. Buckley closed his letter with a disclaimer: "I have not that broad grasp of finances that would make my opinion of much value; I asked permission to take this matter up with Dr. Houston [secretary of agriculture], who, as you know, was my professor of Economics at the University of Texas some ten years ago and who is a shark on financial problems." Clearly Buckley had many excellent contacts.[5]

Black Gold

The importance of Will's fluency in Spanish cannot be overstated. He set up his first small law office and practice near the Zócalo in the old section of the capital. He partnered with what he called a "powerful" attorney who proved to be a "crook." He quit after eight months and established a private practice. Fees he earned in the early years in Mexico City were sent home to help pay for university tuition and expenses for brothers Claude and Edmund, who, upon finishing their law degrees at the University of Texas, joined William in Mexico. The Buckley and Buckley firm's assistance to the existing foreign nationals and new investors in Mexico was in high demand. From 1909 to mid-1911, the business grew into an internationally recognized firm. Located at Calle de San Francisco No. 10 at the Zócalo, together with the law practice of Emilio Rabasa and his partner, Nicanor Gurría Urgell, the Buckleys were joined by Martin C. Ruiz, Modesto Aguirre, and José A. García. Records indicate that Will remained the lead counsel in most of the dealings with businesses and the government, while his brothers provided invaluable in-house support and a backstop to the expansion of the firm. As Will traveled with clients to the Gulf Coast of Mexico, it become increasingly apparent that Mexico's petroleum sector was on the verge of opening new and profitable opportunities. The oil business demanded a great deal of familiarity with the Mexican legal system. Buckley and Buckley focused on this opportunity as well as their seemingly unlimited contacts to invest and participate in new ventures. However, due to the hushed rumors of revolution engulfing the country in the final months of the Porfiriato, Will determined after numerous activities in Tampico that "times were getting hard in the interim and I thought I saw a big opening in the oil fields."[6]

Buckley was one of the first American businessmen to translate oil and gas legal documents from English into Spanish. This expertise was most valuable and critically necessary to operate in Mexico. Perfecting titles to lands and leases for exploration required a constant vigilance to the new regulations placed on the industry by the government. As the oil industry grew, companies were increasingly tempted to use their influence to get around rules that they deemed unnecessary or too costly. Close adherence to the rule of law was seen as impractical in this frontier atmosphere. Graft was an ever-present unwritten means to encourage cooperation by Mexican officials. Buckley was candid in his observation regarding daily means to expedite business operations: "[Bribery] has become customary that the Carrancista officials demand it and feel no gratitude toward the companies when they get it; they feel that the companies pay it to them because they are afraid of them and not because they like them, which is of course the truth."[7]

The epicenter of the coming oil boom in Mexico from 1910 to 1920 was the land stretching along the coast from Tampico sixty miles south and thirty miles inland to the adjacent Tuxpan region, also known as the Huasteca region of the northern state of Veracruz and to newly arrived oilmen as the "Golden Lane." The city of Tampico was built ten miles inland on the northern bank of the Pánuco River. Initial oil production began in 1901 with a couple of uncontrollable gushers (the Cerro Azul gusher broke the world record with 200,000 barrels of daily production). By 1910, following the introduction of technology and capital, Mexico had risen to be one of the largest producers of "black gold." The inducement to invest in the growing demand for oil and gas brought the country international attention and investment. The small tropical town of Tampico, which had 17,500 inhabitants in 1900, grew to over 23,000 by 1910. The town had all the trappings of a Wild West town. It boasted seventy-seven liquor stores, thirty-four bars, nine watchmakers, twelve tailors, scores of brothels, nine Chinese laundries, a dozen law firms, bakeries, a baseball field, seven professional photographers, and yet no active church.[8]

The town grew yearly with the continuous dredging of the river that added new land for homes and businesses. Will and brother Edmund acquired a charter from the federal government to incorporate La Compañia Terminal la Isleta, S.A., to dredge an area of marshland on the eastern tip of Tampico, creating a 1,324-acre site for homes and businesses. Taxed by the city as one contiguous unit of land, the property was divided into lots with improved roads, electricity, and sewage service. The brothers retained seven La Isleta lots, often referred to as "Buckley Island," and sold the balance by late 1920. The dusty streets of Tampico were some of the first paved in Mexico with Edward Doheny asphalt. The first commercial airport in the country was opened on the narrow island of Moralillo. By 1920, more than sixty oil companies maintained headquarters for field and shipping operations as the population jumped to some seventy-five thousand. Routinely concerned with the threat of hurricanes and the strong Gulf currents that piled up sand that constantly blocked access to the river, Tampico would become famous as the oil capital of Mexico, popularized with corridos (ballads) such as Samuel Lozano's "El Puerto del Oro Negro" (The port of black gold).[9]

Eres gran puerto de fama,
unico en el mundo entero,
por eso Samuel le llama,
"El Puerto del Oro Negro."

From Swamp to Oil Giant

Mexico's mining laws and regulations, dating from 1884, vested unlimited ownership of subsoil rights to the owner holding title to the surface. As Buckley noted, "The law made it very clear that the state asserted no claim to any interest in mineral oils."[10] Land, much of it sold by the government from the country's public domain, was traded at very inexpensive prices with no restrictions; few parcels if any were taxed, and the new owner held near feudal control. An additional dynamic was the rush primarily of British and American corporate investors to acquire or lease as much land as possible for exploration. By 1910, the American share of FDI in Mexico was 38 percent, valued about $1.3 billion. British holdings followed with 29 percent of FDI. The rush to drill was driven by the worldwide conversion from coal to oil in industrial plants, on railroads, and by naval ships. Another contributing factor that accelerated oil exploration was the development of new technology: geological mapping as well as improvements in storage, refining, and shipping. By 1918, Mexico was a leading international petroleum producer, second only to the United States.[11]

The boom and bust of Texas oilmen along the Gulf of Mexico near the Spindletop field at Beaumont and the growing news stories of oil in the Tampico region were major attractions to Texas companies and investors. Everyone sought a piece of the profits enjoyed by the big oil companies. These included major participants in the British concern Mexican Eagle Oil Company, owned by Sir Weetman Pearson (Lord Cowdray); the Waters-Peters Oil Company interests; and the American-owned Standard Oil of New Jersey. By 1912, Tampico had grown to a sprawling population above thirty thousand. Railroads soon connected the oil field with Monterrey and Ciudad Victoria in the north and Mexico City via San Luis Potosí in the south. Production reports indicate that "prominent" operators estimated a 250 percent increase in production in 1911–12. A vast array of storage tanks soon lined the Pánuco River, connecting pipelines and a new refinery. Eager to expand international operations, in 1911 the Texas Company (forerunner of Texaco), Gulf Oil, and Magnolia Oil made their first investments in Tampico.[12]

The Texas Company formed in 1902 after the bonanza at Spindletop as a joint venture between the Hogg-Swayne Syndicate and Joseph S. Cullinan land company in the Rio Grande Valley. The Texas Company with Cullinan as president competed directly with Standard Oil's operations in Texas. The founding investors comprised a "who's who" of powerful business and political leaders in Texas with links to financiers on the East Coast. Shareholders included members of the House family of Houston; former governor of Texas James Hogg and his son Will; state attorney general Thomas W. Gregory (later attorney general in the Wilson administration); East Texas lumber magnates J. S. Rice and John H. Kirby; and Walter B. Sharp, cofounder of the Hughes Tool Company. By 1905, the company began a land-acquisition strategy and oil-exploration survey of key sites in Mexico. A new group of well-connected investors, fully aware of the Texas Company's aggressive entry into Mexico, included defeated Democratic presidential candidate (and future secretary of state) William Jennings Bryan; San Antonio rancher and future US consul at Piedras Blancas John Blocker; and James Stillman, president of National City Bank (which also had extensive investments in mining). National City Bank provided financing for the Texas Company.[13]

With the acquisition of land in Tamulipas and Coahuila, Will Hogg and Richard Brooks, mayor of Houston and Texas Company director, accumulated more than 4.5 million acres in northeastern Mexico. Mexican operations and headquarters in Tampico were led by Henry House, with technical support, exploration, and field development headed by technical genius Walter Sharp and legal affairs headed by William F. Buckley. To streamline operations, a subsidiary company, the Mexico Company, was established and colocated with the Texas Company offices in downtown Houston. The new group expanded land purchases and leases to more than 2 million acres in the states of Sonora, Veracruz, and Chihuahua. Following the Panic of 1906–7 and the rapid decline in silver prices, the financially strapped government was assisted in receiving $25 million in gold bonds from Stillman's National City Bank and Speyer Bank "for irrigation" projects. By 1909, Buckley and Buckley was active as the lead counsel with oil companies who hired the firm to secure permits and licenses with the Díaz regime. Thus, by 1910, at least a dozen of Texas's elite investors and politicians had an extensive financial stake in the success and political stability of Mexico.[14]

In 1911, it was apparent to the Buckleys that establishing a second office in Tampico would be a timely move. Leaving his brothers in Mexico City, Will opened the operation in the booming backwater oil port. Claude, who eventually moved to Tampico, told nephew Reid in later years, "Buckley & Buckley set up office catty-corner from the Greek revival customs house, on the second floor above a saloon, reaching their offices every morning by stepping over the bodies of soused clients sleeping it off on the rickety outdoors staircase." They were the only American lawyers in town who could speak Spanish, and the demand for legal services in Tampico by foreign firms swamped the firm, requiring the addition of new staff. Chief among the new additions was soon to be lifelong friend and associate Cecilio Velasco, who Will claimed was the "bravest man he had ever known."[15]

As the leading oil and gas law firm in Tampico with an office in Mexico City, Buckley and Buckley became the lead legal counsel for the Texas Company in Mexico. Edmund remained in the Mexico City office, and Claude managed in Tampico. To the incoming corporate executives and government officials, image was important; hence Will was motivated to borrow and spend extravagant sums, estimated at $7,000, to decorate the law office. He recalled, "I realized that either we or the other people were going to get the big business and the other firm the small business." The Buckleys got the "big business." Their first year in Tampico, the brothers earned $70,000, and by the second year profits exceeded $200,000.[16]

After locating an office in Tampico, Buckley continued to engage in the civil and social activities of the booming port town. To address a housing shortage, he contracted a firm to dredge a sandbar in the Pánuco River to create an elevated area that became the first major housing development in the community. Efforts to develop the property were contested by land thieves who attempted to manipulate the title to the property, but he prevailed, and the site became the location of his home. Additionally, he was a founding investor and major depositor of the Petroleum Banking and Trust Company, managed by his friend George L. Rihl. The port and commercial district of Tampico soon became the second-most populous city of Americans after Mexico City. Regular sea service to New Orleans, Havana, and Miami competed with the older Port of Veracruz, and by 1911, Tampico was a routine port of call for the navies of the United States, Great Britain, Germany, and France.[17]

The oil business in Tampico had a dramatic impact on Will and his brothers. As family members recall, the brothers loved to gamble, in what Will referred to in his confidential letter to Walter Pope as the "game." Reid Buckley noted this penchant for gambling was "the competitive pitting of his intelligence and foresight and determination against these same three attributes in others." While they had established a profitable legal practice, the real money to be made was in land and oil. Will's daughter Priscilla noted, "In business, it was never the discovery of oil that excited him, but the chase for it, and even more than that, the techniques and tactics that enabled him to keep his small companies in the field without so much as a by-your-leave to the mastodons that sought to devour him." The purchase of land and oil leases for their own benefit would soon lead to Buckley stepping back from the legal practice to concentrate on the oil business. Each brother would take similar and profitable paths investing in the oil sector. Edmond bought thousands of acres to develop over a four-decade career in the Tampico region.[18]

Will Buckley entered the oil business full-time in 1912 as president of the Mexican Investment Company (MIC). This enterprise primarily bought and sold leases, as well as representing other new start-up companies in Mexico. In 1913, he sold his interest in MIC and founded, with brother Edmond, the Pantepec Oil Company. The early era of the Mexican oil field

rush was rife with gamblers, spies, entrepreneurs, and opportunists looking to stake a claim and get rich fast, all amidst a nationwide revolution.
Buckley's eldest son and future president of the family's corporate oil
empire, John, recalled, "By almost all of the commonly held norms, Father
should have been a cataclysmic failure. Where the rule book says that
one should be cautious, he was a reckless plunger. Where mores of business
conduct thought the corporate assets should be carefully conserved, he
would commit all of the assets in sight, a lot not in sight, to some wild, hare-
brained scheme that had a way of making millions." With this mindset,
Buckley in 1912–13 fit in easily with the landmen, wildcatters, and hustlers
in the emerging the Tampico oil fields. With his business contacts, reputation, and knowledge of the oil fields, Will soon became one of the primary
leaders of the US business and expatriate communities in Tampico.[19]

The change of Mexican governments from Díaz to Madero to Huerta
brought corresponding changes in the interpretation of taxation of oil properties and production. Until early 1913, the oil companies compromised
with the government on levels of new taxes with the trade-off of cooperating with and not meddling in Mexican politics. As the revolution expanded
and Huerta became short of cash, he began to consider new presidential
decrees to extract what the companies termed an "extraordinary" tax revenue. To intercede, the foreign oil companies approached Ambassador
Henry Wilson. Wilson, who had toured the oil region to consult with major
American producers, pledged to protect them from unreasonable assess-
ments. The ambassador recalled, "The independent oil companies, which
were represented at the meeting by William F. Buckley, who afterward
played such an active part in the defense of American rights, staunchly took
the position that if the companies desired to receive protection, they must
ask for it as American citizens."[20]

Jugos de la Tierra

Prior to 1911, the leading foreign investments in Mexico were in mining and
smelting, cattle and agriculture, and infrastructure improvements, primarily railways and communications. As Luis Cabrera noted earlier, foreign
investors enjoyed a protective haven that allowed them to extract profits
with little overriding controls from the Mexican government. During the
Porfirio Díaz regime, the open policy aimed at attracting FDI did in fact

transform Mexico, although at a cost of a growing uneasiness with the dominance of foreigners. Prior to the oil boom that began in 1910–11, the three key concerns in negotiations with the central government over foreign investment were (1) access to additional investment opportunities, (2) concerns with the imposition of any new taxes, and (3) labor problems. Firms other than oil concerns, such as the Cananea Consolidated Copper Company, the Guggenheim smelting operations, railroad companies, and large-scale sugar and *henequen* (agave plant fibers) operations in southern Mexico, grew steadily. The emerging market for petroleum soon attracted the lion's share of new FDI.[21]

Prior to 1900, there was no commercial value to bituminous deposits of coal and oil. Dating from the period of Spanish rule, owners of surface land grants in New Spain were required to obtain permission to explore the subsoil for mineral deposits. Colonial-era subsoil exploration was primarily for metalliferous deposits, as memorialized in the Mining Ordinances of Phillip II in 1563. Grants to mine, known as a special franchise or concession, were freely given to native citizens as well as foreigners, subject to the payment of royalties. The Spanish Crown was only interested in mineral deposits that were of commercial value. Petroleum did not fall into this class. For decades, oil that was known to seep to the surface in lakes and streams was considered a nuisance. American Indians used the thick tar to seal baskets, caulk boats, and in some cases as a cure for persistent ailments. They were compelled to set fire to the petroleum, calling it *chapapotli*, to keep their horses and cattle from bogging down in the *jugos de la tierra*—literally, "juices of the earth." Upon Mexico's independence in 1821, the Spanish mining laws continued unchanged until the first formal Mexican mining code in 1884. That code, which followed a court case on the ownership and subsoil rights to mine coal, specifically declared that the subsurface minerals, including coal and petroleum, were the exclusive property of the owner of the surface land. This would be the law, with some slight modifications not materially affecting petroleum, until the Querétaro Convention and the implementation of the Constitution of 1917.[22]

As early as the mid-1860s, small quantities of crude oil and asphalt were mined in the Pánuco region and the northern part of the state of Veracruz. By the late 1880s, commercial-grade quantities were produced in Tabasco, with some exploration by the Mexican Petroleum and Liquid Fuel Company financed by Cecil Rhodes. The first sustainable oil exploration in

Mexico was in 1901. Edward L. Doheny, A. P. McGinnis, and C. A. Canfield purchased their first tract of 283,000 acres with a hacienda west of Tampico in 1900 for $325,000. They then organized the Mexican Petroleum Company (MPC). US Ambassador Powell Clayton arranged a meeting with President Díaz, who welcomed the investment but strongly requested that Doheny, who had been very successful in oil prospecting in California, promise not to sell to the Standard Oil Company without prior notice to the Mexican government. After drilling dozens of dry holes (referred to as "dead men") and low-producing wells, MPC hit a gusher in 1904, thirty-five miles west of Tampico at El Ébano. There was no infrastructure to capture, store, or ship the oil, and more importantly, there was no market for the oil. In the short term, MPC opened a paving subsidiary to successfully sell "asphaltum pavement" for streets to Mexico City, Durango, Chihuahua, Guadalajara, and Puebla. Doheny's first major commercial contract was assisting the Mexican Central Railroad to convert locomotives from coal to oil; he signed a fifteen-year contract to supply bunker fuel (i.e., diesel). H. Clay Pierce headed exploration for Standard Oil in Mexico. There was, however, a growing interest by foreign investors, particularly the British and Sir Weetman Pearson in the Compañía Mexicana de Petróleo El Águila, to gain a foothold in the region. The primary British drilling operations were on the Isthmus of Tehuantepec and at Huasteca. The rise of the automobile and the conversion of large industry, railroads, and naval fleet fuel supplies to oil drastically shifted the attention of industrialists, investors, and nations to gain access to Mexican petroleum. Oil production in 1901 reached 10,345 barrels a day and grew steadily to over 1 million barrels in 1907. By 1910, production had more than tripled to over 3.7 million barrels, yet Mexico still imported refined oil products to satisfy domestic demand. At the time that Will Buckley formed the Pantepec Oil Company, neither he nor the competition knew of the extent of the vast oil reserves in Mexico.[23]

Unrest in the Oil Fields

Buckley returned to Mexico from Washington, DC, in the fall of 1914 after the ABC mediation conference in Niagara Falls to near total chaos in the oil fields. Up until April 1914, Huerta's federalists had provided protection, controlling the Gulf Coast from Matamoros on the border to Tampico, and continuing on to Veracruz. Shortly after the US landing at Veracruz in late April 1914, the Constitutionalists occupied most of Tampico and Tuxpan, with the American forces holding Veracruz until November when it was occupied by Carranza. US Consul Miller in Tampico cabled the secretary of state a detailed message highlighting problems with the Constitutionalist troops and the "lawless conditions [that] prevail throughout this consular district." Destruction of petroleum operations was primarily of a hit-and-run nature by both organized groups. The bandits, acting like troops, preyed on the drilling camps and supply lines and targeted any chance to hijack a company payroll. Various means were taken to hide payrolls until they reached the camps, with some recalling money being hidden in the flue of a boiler, in kegs of nails, or inside an automobile tire.[24]

The occupation of the Tampico and Tuxpan region by the Constitutionalists raised concerns among the oil companies that wells, pipelines, and storage facilities might be sabotaged. In spite of US efforts to communicate with the Carranza interim government, hostile statements from key Constitutionalist advisers complicated the political transition. The mistreatment of the petroleum industry was a cause for concern. Luis Cabrera, now the head of Hacienda (secretary of the treasury), made bombastic statements that "Mexico was for Mexicans" and demanded all foreigners leave the country. In response, US Secretary of State Bryan on April 28, 1914, cabled Agent Carothers to secure a written agreement to designate

Table 2
Foreign Investment in Mexico, 1911

	(percentage by country)			
	USA	Britain	France	Germany
Public debt	4.7	8.3	36.1	3.0
Banks	2.6	1.8	11.0	18.3
Railroads	41.3	40.6	12.8	28.4
Public services	1.0	21.4	1.1	—
Mining	38.6	11.8	19.8	—
Real estate	6.3	9.2	1.8	9.0
Industry	1.7	1.1	7.9	41.3
Commerce	0.7	—	8.8	—
Petroleum	3.1	5.8	0.7	—

Source: Cosío Villegas, Historia Moderna de México, vol. 2, 1155.

the oil fields a "neutralization zone." Within this broad zone were many American, Mexican, British, and Dutch "foreign producers" concerned for the safety of their employees, families, and facilities. In requesting immediate measures to protect the region, Bryan contacted Ambassador Cecil Spring Rice to ensure agreement and cooperation with the British.[25] Carothers was successful in obtaining "in writing" a reply and agreement from Carranza, that he was concerned about the oil fields and the employees, many of them Mexicans, stating with some reservation: "Regarding the neutralization of the zones that the Secretary of State requests please inform him that this is not necessary because the region is now dominated by our forces; moreover in the lamentable event of a Huertista invasion it would not be possible to agree to his request in order to hinder military operations." This was the exact hostile situation and fallout Bryan and the British wanted to prevent.[26]

Secretary Bryan and the British Foreign Office stayed in close contact and advised one another of their naval forces moored off Tampico to be vigilant of any hostile activity. British naval commander Sir Charles Cradock, in light of the reaction to the US Veracruz landing, was skeptical of the Constitutionalists' "peaceful" intentions given their forced occupation of Tampico and control of the port facilities. He stated: "From conditions known to me and judging by my own experience I think it would be rash if American citizens relied too implicitly on Mexican assurances and returned now to the oil fields. Their return might be misunderstood, and a situation might arise which would imperil all foreign interests."[27] A few days after the British assessment, Consul Miller in Tampico wired a cautionary message to Bryan on the possible Huertista response: "Oil industry has been temporarily checked by the capture of Tampico by revolutionists but present situation complicated as federal force which evacuated Tampico is now in Pánuco District and it is generally believed prepared to destroy all oil wells if attempt is made to drive them out."[28]

Concern for the safety and security of the massive oil fields around and south of Tampico had indeed reached a critical point. Daily life in the oil region was dangerous. During much of June and July 1914, hundreds of oil field workers fled the operations for safety in Tampico or departed for Cuba or the United States until the situation improved. Carranza and his immediate staff of advisers were well aware of the magnitude and importance of the oil fields. To provide a show of force, the Primer Jefe, accompanied by newly designated confidential agent John Silliman and Washington lawyer and lobbyist Sherbourne G. Hopkins, traveled from their provisional capital in Saltillo to Tampico at the end of July. Buckley, concerned along with the dozens of oil field operators in the region, advised Secretary of War Garrison that Carranza "received the coolest reception I have ever seen accorded to any public man in Mexico," and even with the show of marching bands and parading soldiers, "the people here were sullen—applause was scattering and mild." Surrounded by dozens of principals and managers of the oil companies, Carranza seemed to ignore their presence and held two open meetings, the first with a group from the state of Veracruz vocally requesting immediate steps for the redistribution of land. Responding to Carranza's lack of concern, Buckley noted that the group was "very indignant when they were rejected." The second group wanted housing rental fees in Tampico reduced. They too were quickly declined. When notified that interim president Francisco Carbajal and his representatives, traveling from Mexico City, were en route via Tampico, the Constitutionalists quickly ended conversations and returned to Saltillo. However, prior to departing, Buckley pointedly noted, "Carranza, while here, thoughtfully decreed a new tax on oil of thirty cents gold a ton, making a total of about ten cents gold a barrel. Since the burden of this tax falls almost exclusively on Americans he thinks he may levy and collect the same with impunity." Alarm about the radical moves of the new government against the oil industry was seemingly confirmed by Buckley: "They are convinced of one thing, and continually give utterance to the belief, that the present administration regards all capital as immoral and all business men as criminals whose appeals for protection will be of no avail. It is not difficult to convince men that they are martyrs."[29]

Agent John Silliman

There was no clear dominant political force in Mexico. The transition of the new Carranza government-in-waiting and the obvious overreach of the US government and President Wilson to force a solution became even more disconcerting. Infighting between factions led by Villa, Zapata, and Obregón left the outcome in question. Nonetheless, Wilson, in dictating the negative outcome of the Niagara Falls mediation, was now committed to Carranza. One result of this was a new echelon of "confidential agents" dispatched by the president to Mexico to craft some form of organization and legitimacy out of the Constitutionalists. To deal with Carranza, Wilson again employed a friend, John Silliman, a fellow member of the Princeton class of 1879. In the mid-1890s, Silliman, no stranger to Mexico, had moved from his home in Alabama to Coahuila to engage in farming and dairying. In 1907, he was appointed vice consul at Saltillo and befriended Carranza, then governor of the state. Their relationship was cordial and allowed Silliman to establish close contact with Isidro Fabela, who would become Carranza's foreign minister. Following his harrowing three-week imprisonment incommunicado at the hands of the Huertistas after the Veracruz invasion, Silliman returned to Washington. There he was recruited by Wilson and Bryan and assigned to shadow and advise the First Chief at his headquarters.[30]

Thus, on his return to Mexico in early July, Silliman, fifty-nine years old, was named the full consul at Saltillo, but more importantly, his primary role would be as the president's newest confidential agent. Buckley and other observers, including Consul Will Davis in Guadalajara, witnessed as Silliman escorted Carranza in his travels as well as participated in many key meetings and contacts with political groups around northern Mexico. Speaking for the large foreign business contingent in Tampico, Buckley informed Garrison: "They regret to see Silliman traveling with Carranza, and think that possibly a more discreet method might have been found to accomplish the purpose of the administration, and one which would certainly be less embarrassing to Carranza. Such open participation in the direction of the internal affairs of Mexico is only making the task more difficult for the 'new president.'" The concerns of the business sector were for a stable and safe environment and a level of transparency of new laws, taxes, or decrees. Also of prime concern was the response by the other rebel combatants to the overt actions of the United States and Silliman in support of Carranza. As Buckley testified to Senator Fall's foreign relations subcommittee, "Silliman became so subservient to Carranza that he referred to the Carranza cause as 'our cause' and the Carrancistas as 'we.'"[31]

The July–August 1914 period was yet another milestone in the revolution. The departure of Huerta had left unanswered questions and chaos on the battlefield as well as in political circles regarding attempts to consolidate power. The role of Wilson's special operatives, in the absence of an ambassador in Mexico City, was expanded to include informal diplomatic efforts. Buckley recalled that the president "discarded the methods usually employed in international matters and sent a swarm of [new] personal representatives into Mexico." To manage the rebel relationships, Silliman was joined by agents Leon Canova and John W. Belt, who assisted as a translator. In Torreón, agent George Carothers kept in close contact with Pancho Villa, and Obregón was assisted by agents Paul Fuller and Zack Cobb. In the south, agents Duval West and Hubert L. Hall were in contact with Zapata. Buckley, discounting the value of these agents, told the Fall Committee hearing in December 1919, "These gentlemen, almost without exception, became ardent admirers and advocates of the cause of the particular faction to which they were accredited."[32]

Following their occupation of Tampico and the oil region, the Constitutionalists began a policy of issuing decrees that were viewed as increasingly anti-American and antibusiness "in sentiment and purpose." More than eighty oil companies had investments in the area to expand oil production. As these decrees became more frequent, the expatriate community enlisted Will Buckley to draft a letter to President Wilson for redress. The secretary of state appealed directly to Carranza and requested suspension of decrees on forfeiture and property rights, to no avail. Buckley completed the detailed letter that was signed by eighty-four Tampico oilmen. It outlined their concerns ranging from new rules to prevent Americans from acquiring new land, and to prevent those who presently owned land and leases from legally transferring their property to other foreigners. A bimonthly inspection fee of $300, payable in Mexican gold, for all oil-producing locations was required beginning June 1. Carranza and Cabrera wanted to control not just the oil fields but also the oil field workers' wages, so they ordered that payrolls be paid in daily devalued Mexican currency, at an arbitrary value fixed by the government. This was constantly updated "regardless of the commercial value of this paper money as regulated by supply and demand."[33]

The confused efforts by official Washington to execute the proper course of action were reflected in a confidential letter from Secretary Garrison to Buckley. "The greatest difficulty that one finds in the Mexican situation," Garrison wrote, "is that what seems to be a proper remedy one day, based upon existing conditions, ceases to have applicability the next day because conditions have changed."[34] Impromptu actions by the Constitutionalists confirmed Garrison's conclusions. The Carranza decree of January 7, 1915, created an uproar across the oil industry in Mexico, as the First Chief declared that action was needed "to prevent the continuation of unauthorized explorations and exploitation":

Constitutionalists' Oil Decree: January 7, 1915

No. 1   From this date, and until new laws determining the judicial condition of the oil derivates shall be issued, all work and construction on piping, drilling of wells and any other building connected with the exploitation of oil, shall be suspended.

No. 2   For no reason may work be continued, though already begun, not even provisional permission of legitimate authorities, without having first obtained express permission from this Government.

No. 3   The oil concerns and their managers will be held responsible for any infraction of this decree, and for the damages caused by work undertaken, which will make it impossible to have the property returned intact to its former state. The Constitutionalist Government can destroy any works which are undertaken in violation of this decree. The expense of destruction in this case will be charged to the concerns that built them or to the manager or person responsible for said works.

No. 4   Oil wells which might spring up as a result of violations of this decree will be considered as national property.[35]

Special Agent James Rodgers informed the State Department that Treasury Secretary Cabrera's intent was to shift oil taxation revenue from the states to the federal government. Revenue in 1916 was estimated at $2 million per annum. With the implementation of a new ad valorem taxation plan, revenue would be increased to an estimated $3 million. Any disregard of the new decrees and tax requirements would result in the military authorities' arbitrary imprisonment of violators, annulment of contracts, and property confiscation, especially that belonging to Americans. The only response and alternative given by the rebels was for Americans who did not wish to recognize the validity of the decrees in question to leave Mexico. Thus, the oilmen wrote to President Wilson demanding that Washington address this issue with the de facto government. They claimed the decrees violated existing Mexican law and argued that it was in Mexico's best interest to allow a transparent and equitable business environment. Interestingly, there was no mention of the increased demand for oil for the European war. Constitutionalist authorities were well aware of Buckley's role and leadership in crafting the letter, yet there seemed to have been no immediate repercussions for him.[36]

Overall conditions in Mexico by mid-1916 were not improving. Carranza controlled, at most, only about half the country and was unable to stabilize the economy. Oil investment and revenue, primarily in the state of Veracruz, was one of the few bright spots. Special Representative Rodgers provided the State Department with a remarkable assessment in June 1916 of the "general résumé [of] conditions" in Mexico: "Financial chaos threatened and impending, graft principally through army rampant, executive inefficiency pronounced, beneficial coordination [of] departments lacking, foreign treaty rights through ignorance or design being disregarded, State Government usurping Federal authority, aggression against property and vested privileges prevalent, public confidence almost disappearing, food supply insufficient and precarious, bandits operating boldly and successfully and political antagonism to general Government gaining strength. Every allegation can be proven by many evidences and instances. Indefinite prolongation [of] general condition the present seems impossible."[37]

The oil companies understood the Carranza decrees were a major change in their way of doing business in Mexico. The primary concerns for Buckley's clients were the security of their operations and leases in Mexico as well as the cost of doing business that was being modified monthly due to new taxes, security costs, and administrative fees. The initial response of the companies in Tampico was to ignore the decrees and to lobby to have them rescinded or modified. Shortly after the drafting of the Buckley letter to the president, the oil companies organized the Association of Foreign Oil Producers in Mexico. A second organization, the National Association for the Protection of American Rights in Mexico, was chartered to lobby for the business interests of mining, banking, and railway investors. The goals and leadership of these two groups overlapped and were dominated by oilmen and their financiers. These included Harold Walker of Huasteca Oil, Amos L. Beaty of the Texas Company, E. L. Doheny of Pan American Oil, Chester Swain of Standard Oil of New Jersey, Will Buckley of Isleta Oil, and Tom Lamont of J. P. Morgan Bank. Legal counsel and chief adviser in Mexico for both groups was the firm of Buckley and Buckley. While they were concerned about increased taxes on operations and production, they acknowledged that modest increases were warranted. However, the prime objective was the coordination of oil companies' response to the Mexicans that all contracts acquired prior to May 1, 1917, were firm and absolutely valid. Thus, to ensure protection of their investments, the associations began an aggressive campaign in Washington and London to encourage each government to intervene with the leaders of the de facto Mexican government. The associations knew from the outset they would have little support from the White House; thus they concentrated on the US Congress, the State Department, and newspapers for redress.[38]

The Great War

Little has been written about Mexico's role during World War I. In public government statements, Mexico pledged neutrality, while debate behind the scenes in Mexico City as early as June 1915 speculated on America's entry into the European war. This occurred regardless of rumors of German intrigue both in Mexico and along the border, and of active German agents on duty in the country reporting back to Berlin. There seems to have been no noticeable enemy espionage. Notably, there was no reported sabotage in the Tampico or Tuxpan oil fields. While Carranza was consistently pro-German, he fully appreciated that any commission of sabotage in the Tampico-Tuxpan oil fields could trigger an immediate US military intervention. Thus, Mexican-German relations remained a major national security dilemma for the United States. Eighteen months earlier, former president Huerta, after returning from a brief exile in Spain, was arrested in New Mexico by US federal agents and charged with conspiracy—with German operatives—to violate neutrality laws.[39] Little did the agents realize how the bombshell planning by German politicians would soon define the US-Mexico relationship during the war.[40]

The Zimmermann Cable

William Buckley's papers contain extensive information on the famed Zimmermann cable from Berlin to Mexico City (dated January 19, 1917, and made public March 1, 1917). This communication raised the specter that

Mexico was diplomatically and possibly militarily aligning with Germany and Japan. The Zimmermann telegram is one of the most fascinating historical documents involving Mexico and the United States. Written in Germany at the highest level of the government, it was intended to invoke further tension in a century-old conflict and edgy coexistence between the two nations. While at first the cable was relegated to a hoax, German foreign secretary Arthur Zimmermann publicly disclosed he had sent the message, written in the early heady days of the war when it seemed not only that Germany's army would sweep across Europe but that its navy, with its expanded U-boat campaign, would take control of the Atlantic Ocean and force the capitulation of Great Britain. The telegram detailed that if Mexico cooperated, at the end of the war it would "reconquer the lost territory" in the southwestern states of Texas, New Mexico, and Arizona ceded under the 1848 Treaty of Guadalupe Hidalgo. Given the total disarray of the Constitutionalists, this German intrigue surely was confounding in an already turbulent time. The matter of German meddling and espionage in Mexico that could threaten the entire United States was soon confirmed. Presidential adviser Colonel House told Wilson, "I am not surprised at the German proposal to Mexico . . . they have plans to stir up all the trouble they could in order to occupy our attention in case of hostilities." This errant top-secret communication had the effect of putting the United States on notice and heightened alert. This resulted in Carranza (who clearly sympathized with Germany and claimed ignorance of the Zimmermann cable) quickly declaring Mexico "would maintain 'strict and rigorous neutrality.'"[41]

Berlin, January 19, 1917

To His Excellency, The Imperial
German Minister to Mexico

On the first of February we intend to begin unrestricted submarine warfare. In spite of this, it is our intention to endeavour to keep the United States of America neutral.

If this attempt is not successful, we propose an alliance on the following basis with Mexico: That we shall make war together and together make peace. We shall give general financial support, and it is understood that Mexico is to reconquer the lost territory in New Mexico, Texas and Arizona. The details are left to you for settlement.

You are instructed to inform the President of Mexico of the above in the greatest confidence as soon as it is certain that there will be an outbreak of war with the United States, and suggest that the President of Mexico on his own initiative, should communicate with Japan suggesting adherence at once to this plan. At the same time offer to mediate between Germany and Japan.

Please call to the attention of the President of Mexico that the employment of ruthless submarine warfare now promises to compel England to make peace within a few months.

Zimmermann[42]

All plans for oil field expansion were temporarily interrupted with the outbreak of World War I. The immediate needs of both the American and British navies resulted in the commandeering of the only four oil tankers of the British-owned Mexican Eagle Oil Company. All four were eventually torpedoed and sunk by German U-boats in the North Atlantic. Also, all pending oil tanker orders, due to naval demands, were canceled. With the loss of the tankers, the oil companies gradually increased sales in war-torn Mexico. The Mexican railroad consumed only 5.2 percent of the total domestic production. The leading oil companies remained competitive by opening limited refining in Mexico and raising the price of gasoline. However, their main market was the shipping of crude oil to the United States for refining. Lord Cowdray, concerned with the loss of the tankers, secretly traveled to New Jersey to meet with Standard Oil to sell his Mexican crude at below market pricing (still highly profitable), for the balance of the war. Thus, significant supplies of neutral Mexican oil were crucial to the Allied victory.[43]

Edward Doheny and MPC were better prepared to meet wartime demand. The major Allied powers rushed to convert from coal-burning to oil-burning engines. For the first time, modern warfare was enormously dependent on a steady supply of petroleum. On the eve of the war, *Fuel Oil Journal* estimated the British navy consumed annually 200,000 long tons of oil fuel. Doheny saw not only profits but also a possible opening to marginalize his British competition in Mexico as MPC increased production, added new pipelines, and expanded storage tanks on the docks at Tampico to fill its fleet of oil tankers. At the wartime peak, MPC and Huasteca were shipping 100,000 barrels of oil per day by tanker.[44]

In return, Doheny and all the oil producers in Mexico made it clear to the Wilson administration that supplies of oil and improvement of facilities could not be accomplished unless interference from the Carrancistas was checked. Disregarding a call for cooperation, Carranza issued a new, detailed petroleum taxation decree on April 13, 1917, to be effective on May 1. Presidential confidant Bernard Baruch advised Wilson not to hesitate to seize the Mexican oil fields if there was any possibility of disruption of production.[45]

American hesitation to intervene in the Mexican oil fields became more problematic as both the Mexican federal government and the governor of Veracruz issued new oil decrees claiming they were complying with Article 27 of the new Constitution of 1917. The oil fields were in constant threat of disruption from Carranza's forces and by what Tampico consul Dawson, a close acquaintance of Buckley, called Gen. Manuel Peláez's "scattered bands with little opposition, using guerrilla warfare tactics."[46] Secretary of State Lansing responded to Ambassador Fletcher to advise officials in the Mexican government that no disruption would be tolerated and that, pursuant to the pledge and assurances given by President Carranza on August 2, 1917, no properties or assets were to be confiscated, impounded, or unduly taxed. Lansing's sole focus was to maintain a state of relative calm (without threatening intervention) in order to ensure a smooth and steady flow of oil to the Allies in Europe. He noted: "Oil interests assess new decree will wreck companies operating in Tampico oil fields, and seriously interfere with Allied naval operations. Advise what action, if any, you take [i.e., recommend]."[47]

Fletcher responded by reminding Lansing that Mexico had a poor means of collecting revenue and that the decrees and new laws were vague as to the means and timing of tax collection. Furthermore, he advised that an official response from Washington be drafted, insisting (1) that implementation of the decree be postponed; (2) that all Allied oil interests in Mexico "adopt identical attitude and response"; and (3) that all legal remedies and injunctions (*amparos*) be exhausted, noting the decree is "obscure and ambiguous." The ambassador emphasized that the immediate threat to Allied oil shipments was that Mexican officials might "resort to a refusal of clearance to oil ships in order to compel [tax] payment."[48] His recommendations were followed, and an amended oil decree gave an extension, while notifying the oil companies the duties would eventually have to be paid under Mexican law. Once the government published the American protest and the amended guidelines in the *Diário Oficial*, the newspaper

Pueblo responded with the headline: "President Wilson Threatens Mexico." Not to be outdone, the *Democratas* headlined in red ink: "The Gringos of the United States Threaten to Intervene If Its Pretensions Are Not Satisfied." Nonetheless, the legal process ensued, and a new oil decree was released in July 1918. In the meantime, no ships were blocked from sailing, and oil production and exports to the Allies increased monthly.[49]

In a confidential report for the Anglo Mexican Petroleum Company, noted geologist Everett DeGolyer concluded that Mexican petroleum products had four significant impacts: (1) they did indeed supply major amounts of bunker oil to the Allied navy and military; (2) they provided the oil critical for the operation of essential war industries in neutral countries; (3) they relieved the burden of Allied nations from supplying fuel to fellow Allies; and (4) most importantly, Mexican petroleum products were a major source of additional fuel to support the vast war industries in the United States. Once the Mexican-German controversy settled down, oil production quickly increased, due in large part to the invention by Howard Hughes of Houston of a rotary rock drill, which replaced the fishtail bit. The United States was the largest single market for Mexican petroleum, absorbing 65.9 percent of the country's entire production, only limited by available storage and transportation facilities. Between 1914 and 1917, despite the disorder and violence in Mexico, oil production there more than doubled. Production in 1917 was 55,292,779 barrels (of 42 gallons each), an increase of 14,782,058 barrels or 36.3 percent over the previous year. At the conclusion of the war, Lord Curzon, the British foreign secretary, proclaimed, "The Allies floated to victory on a sea of oil." By the end of the war, the place of oil at the center of all geopolitical-military considerations was firmly established.[50]

Aloise

Will Buckley routinely sailed on the direct ocean liner from Tampico to New Orleans to visit clients, bankers, and industrial suppliers for Pantepec. These periodic trips usually included a train trip either to Austin to visit his mother and older sister, Priscilla, or to New York City to consult with the headquarters of the large oil companies. James Buckley recalled, "My father's brother Edmund had met one of my mother's sisters in Mexico, where she was visiting a cousin whose father had moved there after the Civil

ESTA CASA SE ENCARGA DE T
CLASE DE TRABAJOS EN MAR
Ó EN PIEDRA, PARA TODO PANT
DE LOS DE MEXICO, Ó PARA
A CUALQUIER ES═ DE LA REPUB

Aloise Steiner Buckley, shortly after her wedding, arriving at the train station in Tampico, Mexico, 1918. Buckley Family Collection.

War rather than take an oath of allegiance to the United States. He learned that there was a bevy of attractive Steiner sisters in New Orleans and suggested my father call on them on a forthcoming trip to the city. So he did." In late 1917, Will, then thirty-six years old, met Aloise Josephine Antonia Steiner, twenty-two, daughter of an established New Orleans sugar industry family, later classified by her son Reid as "petite bourgeoisie." Her ancestors had arrived from Switzerland in 1845, and for a brief period, she attended Sophie Newcomb College, an affiliate of Tulane University, in New Orleans. After a whirlwind courtship lasting a few weeks, Will proposed marriage, and following a brief waiting period, her father agreed. A devout Catholic and well-born southern lady, nostalgic for the Old South, she liked to describe herself as a "daughter of the Confederacy." While in Monterrey, Mexico, Will wrote Mr. and Mrs. Steiner on October 21, 1917, a letter that he presented as "therefore of rather a formal nature," suggesting a wedding between Christmas and New Year's Day. Shortly after the wedding, Aloise and Will moved to Mexico. The Port of Tampico was a far cry from the glamour and ambience of the Crescent City. In 1918, Aloise (or Allie), their first child, was born, then John in 1920, and eight additional children followed. Adapting quickly to her new surroundings, as son William Jr. recalled, Aloise "spoke fluent French and Spanish." In Tampico the family faced a shortage of housing, poor water supply, malaria, and few amenities—the hallmarks of a booming oil town. While the environs were generally safe in town, the surrounding region and oil fields would soon succumb to the growing violence of the revolution.[51]

Postwar Violence

The Great War ended in November 1918, yet turmoil in the Mexican oil fields continued unchecked. A more serious problem emerged as the Carrancistas in the Tampico-Tuxpan region kept up their attacks on oil field workers, camps, and paymasters with deadly results. The occupying soldiers, who had announced they would help protect the region, included bandits who continued a wave of killing, robbery, and extortion, although the absence of real sabotage of oil facilities reduced the possibility of US occupation. These postwar threats of violence once again fueled the cry for US intervention to protect workers and facilities. While they seemed random, they were in fact targeted attacks. Numerous times traveling between Mexico City and Tampico, Buckley had to take refuge in Puebla or Veracruz until hostility waned. In addition to general harassment that often turned violent, oil company payrolls were targeted by thieves. During the yearlong period prior to the end of the war, there were nine murders of oil workers and more than thirty were wounded in attacks.[52] (See table 3.)

Land man, geologist, and close Buckley friend Charles W. Hamilton, of the Mexican Eagle Oil Company, was an eyewitness to the chaos and banditry. With Mexican currency near worthless, oil field workers accepted only gold or silver coin in payment. Safe transit to the oil camps through bandit-infested areas was risky business. Hamilton recalled:

All sorts of devious ways of transporting payrolls from terminal to camp were resorted to by the oil companies to foil the bandits. Coin packed in kegs of red lead, in cylinder heads of oil field pumps, in bales of cotton waste, in pipe, in stoves and in available heavy container being shipped to the fields on barges. Payrolls were carried by

Table 3
Bandit Attacks and Holdups in the Tampico Oil Fields
August 1917 to August 1918

	Location	Wounded	Killed	Theft (US$)
East Coast Oil				
Aug 15	camp A	2	—	725
Sept 1	pipeline	—	—	100
Nov 17	camp A	—	—	587
Jan 28	camp TB	2	—	0
Feb 8	camp A	—	—	10,000
Aquila Company				
Sept 4	pump station	—	—	199
Sept 29	launch	—	—	23,406 (P)
Oct 6	camp	—	—	350
Dec 27	launch	1	—	40,710 (P)
Feb 6	camp	—	—	3,000
Mar 1	camp	—	—	1,075
Mar 7	camp	—	—	1,700
Mar 28	camp	—	—	3,300
Apr 23	camp	—	—	1,359
Apr 25	pump stat.	—	—	300
Mexican Gulf Oil				
Nov 24	camp	—	—	1,423 (P)
Apr 15	plant	—	facilities shut down due to bandits	
May 6	cantina	1	—	machete attack
May 22	horseback	—	—	1,040 (P)
June 24	storage area	—	tanks with 150,000 barrels of oil set afire	
June 29	camp	1	5	5,562
Aug 1	launch	—	—	6,440 (P)
Texas Company				
Feb 12	launch	2	—	failed robbery
Feb 21	launch	4	1*	7,000 (P)
Feb 22	camp	—	—	1,300
Mar 15	train	—	—	500
Apr 6–7	camp	—	—	3,000
Apr 18	launch	—	—	2,000 (P)
May 16	launch	—	—	15,000 (P)
Metropolitana				
Feb 19	launch	—	—	failed robbery
Feb 21	launch	2	—	failed robbery
Mar 5	camp	—	—	1,341
Apr 12	camp	3	—	1,100

Table 3
(continued)

	Location	Wounded	Killed	Theft (US$)
Freeport Fuel Oil				
Mar 15	camp	—	2	1,000
Cortez Oil Co.				
Mar 28	launch	—	—	12,007 (P)
Apr 14	camp	drilling stopped due to deadly threats		
May 16	launch	—	—	10,547 (P)
July 22	camp	—	1	0
Aug 16	camp	12	—	0
La Corona Co.				
Apr 4	camp	—	—	3,050 (P)
Apr 26–27	camp	—	—	950
May 18	camp	—	—	300
June 8	camp	—	—	2,000 (P)
International Oil				
Apr 13	camp	6	—	1,000
Totals		36	9	

Note: "P": payroll

*Edgar House killed

Source: "Summary of Bandit Outrages and Holdups throughout the Tampico Oil Fields for the Year 1918," File 152, Buckley Papers; Dawson to State, 312.115/341 and 681, August 5, 1918, FRUS 1918; "Mexican Bandits in the Oil Fields," *New York Times*, October 20, 1918.

speed boats, sometimes in gasoline drums and sometimes concealed in bilge water beneath the floor boards; payrolls were sent overland by car in heavy tool boxes or packed in tires, and coins were transported in packs on burro backs or in saddle bags by horsemen. In due course, the bandits got wise to all these tricks and consequently, the risk became increasingly greater. Pay masters did not stay long on the job. They were either killed from bandit ambush or wounded so badly that they quit.[53]

The Cost of Doing Business

As the Carranza and Villa armies operated closer to the oil fields along with various paramilitary bandits, many deserters from the ranks of both armies created an atmosphere of growing violence. The attacks were checked by local strongman Gen. Manuel Peláez, whom other revolutionaries gave the sobriquet "The Rebel of the Huastecas." A large and powerful local land-owner and political leader in the Huasteca region, Peláez first demanded payment from the British El Aguila Company that had maintained oil camps and extensive drilling operations on his haciendas at Tierra Ama-rilla and Cerro Viejo. This agreement was in return for protection of their employees and facilities. The general, aware of the increased attacks against other oil companies, drafted a decree to all the oil producers in the region that he was neither Villista nor Carrancista and that if they wanted safety from the two factions and their renegade bandits, they each would begin paying between $10,000 and $40,000 per month. During the revolution many interests questioned the aims of the general's relationship with the major oil companies. The protection he provided did in fact provide timely safe operations in oil fields throughout the region. To receive protection, the companies willingly paid tribute akin to a "war tax" to equip a well-armed network of loyal regional generals and troops, numbering over thirty thousand, under the sole command of General Peláez.[54]

It is no surprise, given his extensive contacts throughout the state of Veracruz, that Will Buckley knew and consulted with General Peláez. Their acquaintance was one of mutual respect. While Buckley had at one time or another represented nearly all the oil companies in Mexico, he was always suspicious of the larger US and British companies that dominated the small firms. Friend and confidant Cecilio Velasco recalled, "They maintained very good relations and on some occasions W.F.B. gave Peláez sound advice concerning the convenient and practical way to conduct himself with the oil companies without neglecting the dignity and patriotism due his government and nation." Concerned that Buckley was too close with the general, the oil companies often blamed him for their problems with the upstart greedy Carrancistas and the demands of Peláez. The oil executives' ill feelings would later spill over to the Obregón presidency and mistakenly form part of the reason Buckley was expelled from Mexico as an undesirable foreigner.[55]

While there were random attacks on camps, pipelines, and paymasters, the fact remains that the petroleum industry experienced far less destruction and disruption than did mining operations in northern Mexico or the railroads, which faced constant attacks and damages. During the Fall Foreign Relations Committee hearings, Buckley noted when questioned about the role of the general: "Peláez has given Americans and their property and Mexicans and their property, every protection. During the war when

Carranza was pro-German and trying to drive Peláez out of the fields with arms and ammunition obtained in the United States with the consent of the American government, he was pro-Ally, and was protecting the oil fields for the Americans," and thus, this timely protection was "the only thing that has stood in the way of actual confiscation of the oil fields." The increased oil production noted by DeGolyer between 1914 and 1917 would not have been possible without such protection. The ransom payments to Peláez were viewed as "taxes"—a cost of doing business—that were diverted away from the Constitutionalists' coffers. Above the general's signature, once arrangements were made with each oil company, appeared the motto "Law, Morality, and Justice."[56]

Will Buckley was no stranger to violence and banditry in Mexico. In addition to two armed face-to-face encounters with Pancho Villa, hired gunmen doggedly stalked him, and a disgruntled rebel general swore, with a "Latin flourish," "If I don't live to kill Will Buckley and his sons, my sons will live to do it." Buckley and his partner Senor Velasco were the victims of kidnapping in early 1919. Oil field crime included murder for hire to end a dispute, a tactic Reid recalled was "swifter and more certain than pursuing one's end through the courts." In later years, the Buckley family was entertained by Will and his many visitors to Great Elm, their family home in Connecticut, who recounted stories of the oil days in Mexico. While Buckley was a well-known leader and businessman in the Tampico-Tuxpan area, he, too, had made enemies both known and unknown. With no organized effective local law enforcement, victims were grabbed and taken to the inland jungle, where many disappeared without a trace. There was no investigation or recourse. Buckley and Cecilio Velasco succeeded in evading capture at gunpoint by bandits near Vercrizana by crossing the Pantepec River to safety. Velasco, in a second incident, was held in the mountainous region of Huasteca. After being captured by rogue bandits, he was taken into the mountains through heavy rains. The deeper the kidnappers escaped into the jungle, the less likely the prisoners were to be held for ransom. James Buckley recalls Cecilio's account. During the first night the bandits drank tequila and feasted on a roasted goat, amusing themselves by executing one of their captives at random. Not wanting to risk a third night, Velasco found a piece of paper and scribbled some words on it. Then, after the bandits in the encampment had gone to sleep, he presented the paper to the sentry and advised him it was a pass that the leader had given him on the assumption that the sentries were often illiterate but would not admit it. He was, and he didn't. Velasco convinced the guard to let the prisoners "stretch their legs" since there was nowhere to go in the remote nighttime jungle. Once away from camp and into the dense jungle, Velasco made his escape. Aloise recalled the fear and thought that Will and Cecilio had been murdered. Yet, after a few days both men, bruised and scratched, survived to tell the story and return to work. There is no indication they added any security guards or additional protection in the years that followed their harrowing experience.[57]

The US news media were kept busy conveying to the American public the magnitude and dynamics of the Mexican Revolution. Cartoons such as this in the *Evening Journal* in 1919 depicted the uneasy situation in Mexico and the oversight of Uncle Sam. Author's Collection.

Postwar Oil Production

In spite of the bandits and violence, the Mexican oil industry continued to produce more oil each year. In 1919, Edward Doheny testified before the Senate Committee on Foreign Relations that he bought and developed his first oil well in 1900 and was an active advocate for the contribution and impact of foreign investment in the Mexican oil industry and economy. His argument was based on the level of investment, the resulting success, and a clear focus on the underlying laws that attracted and encouraged petroleum development in Mexico:

> Many millions of dollars' worth of oil-well machinery, supplies, engines, boilers, and pipe have been brought into this region from the United States to be used in the development of these oil-containing lands. Other millions have been paid out in wages to American and Mexican employees, mostly Mexican. Still other millions have been paid in taxes on petroleum and increased valuations of property to the various governments in Mexico. Wells have been drilled that, conservatively estimated, may be said to have a potential capacity of more than a million barrels per day (which is greater than that of the United States). All of this change was brought about through the enterprise and energy of Americans who were stimulated by American pioneer spirit of development and encouraged by the kindly feeling evinced and promises of help and protection made by the Mexican government under President Díaz and renewed by the late lamented President Madero. During 17 years American and other foreign money has poured into this region in Mexico for the purchase of lands, establishment of camps, and carrying on of oil-well development and production, with no objection from any governmental authority or suggestion of interference until 1917.[58]

Doheny's success was based on years of experience in the California oil fields. In Mexico, however, an old wildcatter like Doheny became even more successful as a new breed of geologist helped explore the jungles of the Golden Lane of Huasteca for some of the most productive wells in history. Ralph Arnold, a renowned geologist from Stanford University and a frequent visitor to the oil fields of Mexico, spent a decade compiling data and

Table 4
Comparison of Petroleum Production, 1920

	United States	Mexico
Proven producing area (sq. mi.)	4,500	25
Oil production in 1920 (bbl)	443,402,000	185,000,000
Number of producing wells	258,600	200
Average daily production per well (bbl)	4.9	2,600
Proven oil reserves (est.; bbl)	5–6 billion	300–400 million

Source: "Introductory Address of Ralph Arnold, American Institute of Mining and Metallurgical Engineering," February 16, 1921, File 153.4, Buckley Papers.

appraising possible oil formations. In 1906, the Mexican oil fields produced, for the first time, over 1 million barrels of crude, an amount that exceeded the total production from 1901 to 1905. Arnold was joined by Everett DeGolyer, Willard Hayes, and V. R. Garfias. Arnold provided comparative data on the growth of the Mexican oil industry by 1920 in support of Doheny's comments (see table 4).

Mexico Situation Reports

During the period of the Niagara Falls mediation and Washington visits, a new level of contacts and information was opened for Will Buckley. Connections from his college days at the University of Texas, along with other Texas political contacts in the nation's capital, proved highly useful. These friends and associates reached to the White House with his friend and fellow Texan Colonel Edward House, a former neighbor in downtown Austin. Furthermore, Buckley's law firm represented the Texas Oil Company in Tampico, which was managed by Colonel House's cousin Henry. These contacts and working relationships, many in Mexico, as well as his expertise in the language and nuances of cultural and political dynamics, proved to be invaluable. While working closely with the Wilson State Department and agencies to facilitate the ABC Conference, he also took the time to visit with several Republican senators, primarily Albert B. Fall, on the status of conditions in Mexico, especially as they related to US companies with large investments south of the border. In addition to a steady flow of letters and reports to Bryan, Garrison, and Fall, Buckley remained in increasingly frequent contact with oil company representatives and investors in New York and Texas. He worked with each successive Mexican regime from Díaz to Carranza and appeared to have been careful not to prefer any particular leader or political party. While such political contacts in Mexico were impossible to avoid, Buckley and his brothers focused on their legal business and then on their growing interest and investments in real estate and in the petroleum industry.[59]

Will was able to maintain offices in Mexico City and Tampico throughout the period of the Mexican Revolution. Furthermore, even with the rebel actions and disruptions, he was able to travel freely around the country. Writing to Secretary Garrison in late August 1914, he noted, "I left Tampico about three weeks ago for Monterrey" looking to meet with representatives of the Constitutionalists, but they "moved offices to Saltillo, San Luis Potosí, Querétaro, Tlalnepantla, and then to Mexico City, before I caught them."[60] The ability to travel and meet with government and business leaders gave Buckley a unique perspective on the constantly changing political and economic landscape. One primary means of tracking events and revolution-era personalities was the maintenance by his office of scrapbooks of newspaper clippings from a dozen Mexican and US newspapers covering all aspects of the struggle. These documents comprised a chronicle of day-to-day activities and formed a tremendous historical source on Mexico. This resource, along with incoming letters and observations from friends, diplomats, politicians, customs agents, bankers, and clients across Mexico, would gradually grow into an extensive historical archive.[61]

One key long-term associate in Mexico City was attorney and scholar Emilio Rabasa, whom Buckley referred to as "my consulting attorney in the City." Author of the landmark book *La Constitución y la Dictadura: Estudio sobre la Organización Política de México* (1912), Rabasa was recognized as one of Mexico's leading political historians and constitutional theorists, or as Charles A. Hale notes, "a true national *pensador* [thinker]." The distinguished jurist and senator (1894–1913), while awaiting an appointment as Huerta's Mexican ambassador to the United States (predicated on the recognition of Huerta's government), recruited Will as special counsel to the Mexican delegation at the Niagara Falls Conference. He, like Buckley, quickly saw through the backhanded subterfuge by Wilson (in cooperation with Lind, Cabrera, and Arredondo) and realized that Washington was not looking for a solution at Niagara Falls but only a delaying action. Buckley strongly encouraged Rabasa to write a history of the conference and advised him to be prepared to return to Mexico. However, when Huerta departed, Rabasa, now a bitter man marked by the Constitutionalists, settled into exile in New York City. After his longtime law partner Nicanor Gurría Urgell was arrested in Mexico City by the Carranza regime, Rabasa asked Buckley to take care of their Mexico City law office and work to free Gurría.[62]

The revolution continued to rage unchecked across the country. The de facto recognition of Carranza by Wilson in 1917 did little to calm regional jefes who allowed their forces and local bandits to prey on the people. Attacks on clerics soon expanded. Will Buckley, while mostly concerned with business and political activities, soon experienced attacks that would involve him in active participation in the defense of the Catholic Church.

CHAPTER FOUR

Church and State

Nothing will shock the civilized world more than punitive or vindictive
action toward priests or ministers of any church, whether Catholic or Protestant;
and the Government of the United States ventures most respectfully
but most earnestly to caution leaders of the Mexican people
on this delicate and vital matter.
—William Jennings Bryan, July 23, 1914

I am not trying to abolish the Church entirely. Religion is a good thing,
but it cannot be successful if it interferes with affairs of state and politics.
—Pancho Villa, July 25, 1914

I think the anti-clericalism has a traditional basis, and comes from the days
of the clerical domination and participation in civil affairs of the country.
It is also anti-Christian, and not only anti-Catholic.
—Nelson O'Shaughnessy, May 3, 1920

THE TREATMENT OF THE Catholic Church during the Mexican
Revolution from the perspective of William Buckley's observations
and reactions, as a staunch Catholic and avowed protector of the Church,
are critical to an understanding of the man. Buckley was at the crossroads
of many aspects of the revolution and attempted to remain apolitical in
a hyperpolitical environment. He was a firsthand observer of the attacks
on the Church and the political efforts to undercut its power and shackle
its influence. His observations, along with materials from the US State
Department, British Foreign Office, and the Biblioteca de Mexico, provide a
wealth of primary information. His defense of the Catholic Church was an
important contributing reason President Obregón expelled William Buckley from Mexico in November 1921.[1]

The growing power of the Church, whether real or perceived, exercised
a tremendous influence over secular norms and provoked anti-Catholic

liberals in Mexico. At the heart of the breach of trust was a divide between the orthodox foundations of the Church and the views of secular liberal progressives who in their revolutionary quest believed they were the champions to win the hearts and minds of the Mexican people. Additionally, the rebels were led to believe by their leaders that the Church was very wealthy. Their attitude toward the Church was expressed well by one observer: "It held the wealth and the learning, and the priest *preyed* upon the people as well as *prayed* for them. They were taxed to the utmost, and 'pay or pray' was the motto affixed to the cross by the priests." Thus, the revolutionary factions determined the privileged position of the Catholic Church had become a barrier to Mexican progress and the institution needed to be marginalized for Mexico to become a modern nation. Furthermore, gradually during the first decade of the twentieth century, it become apparent that Mexico needed reform and the Church became a convenient target. Buckley was well versed in the history of the Church.

The Roman Catholic Church in Mexico has been one of the most enduring institutions of the country's society, politics, and culture. Throughout four centuries since the arrival of Cortés and the conquistadors, the Church in New Spain coexisted with the state with a firm record of supporting the conservative state authorities. Cooperation with the agents of the royal colony to maintain the status quo proved lucrative for the Church as it amassed vast wealth. Seldom mentioned in conjunction with the Mexican Revolution of 1910, more than five hundred Jesuit priests were expelled from Mexico in 1767 after Charles III declared they had gained too much influence and wealth. Notwithstanding, the subsequent years of conservative political leaning and monopoly of religious activities through the mid-1800s would become a major liability when the revolution began. A number of historical privileges, including exclusivity in all religious matters, broad powers to raise and spend tribute, extensive landownership, tax exemptions, and seemingly undemocratic judicial practices (e.g., canon law trials), resulted in the privileged clerics' power and influence being viewed as a fundamental threat by the revolutionaries.[2]

The Church would certainly lose a great deal of power and wealth should it be displaced from the mainstream of the Mexican society. Efforts to reduce the control of the Church date from Benito Juárez's movement and the drafting of the Constitution of 1857. This new national document better defined the role of the government over several functions previously dominated by the Church. Juárez's aims were to secularize critical functions deemed civil responsibilities. These included issuance of marriage licenses, are of cemeteries, and the disposition of land. Reforms resulted in the confiscation of some Church properties, prohibition of priests from wearing clerical dress in public, and subordination of Church courts to civilian authorities. Church landownership was brought into question yet generally properties were "surreptitiously recovered" undisturbed with the rise of Porfirio Díaz as president in 1876. Díaz, though not a practicing Catholic, kept the Church in check by allying himself with the Catholic oligarchy, a dynamic in which Buckley was well versed dating from his earliest days in Mexico in 1908. This cooperation was critical to his political base of support throughout his more than thirty years as president. Carmen, his wife and a devout Catholic, acted as a mediator between the Church hierarchy and her husband.[3]

Thus, Díaz, in what can best be described as benign neglect, practiced a policy of toleration that did not limit the religious orders, which tripled in size during the Porfiriato. He also allowed anticlerical laws to fall into desuetude, leaving the Church to recover much of its temporal power. The foreign capitalists and financiers Díaz attracted to Mexico aided in the nation's stability and peace, but all the gain passed to a select few, including the Church. Wealth accumulation by the Church during the Díaz regime was estimated at more than 800 million pesos. However, with the departure of Don Porfirio and the rise of Madero, the Church felt threatened by the latter's idealistic plans, which, however, were never fully articulated or implemented due to his overthrow in February 1913. Thus, Catholic traditionalists were generally pleased with the Huerta coup and hoped the Church would again receive the preferred treatment it had enjoyed under Díaz.[4]

Scholars have conducted more than a century of research, analysis, and publication on the role, impact, and transformation of the Catholic Church during and since the revolution. In his key work *The Mexican Revolution and the Catholic Church 1910–1929* (1973), Robert Quirk notes that the conflict between the Church and the Mexican revolutionary government has drawn attention of researchers from both inside and outside of Mexico, with all writers "partisans of either the Church or State" endeavoring to define the decade-long "struggle for the souls of the Mexican people."

The support of Huerta's *golpe de estado* and rumors of the Church's collusion with Madero's removal would result in a decade of backlash from the liberal rebel factions that opposed the role and power of the Church. The Church would accept the rule of a strong man if it ensured peace and the Church's historical position of authority. The radicals among the rebels were violently anticlerical. As historian Enrique Krauze notes, "the Carrancistas gloried in acts of premeditated and jubilant sacrilege." The Church's support of Huerta proved to be a rallying cry by the rebels to debase all aspects of the Church. To support this argument, Luis Cabrera rushed into publication an anti-Catholic booklet, *The Religious Question in Mexico*, which attacked the anti-Constitutionalist actions of the Church. The already violent and divisive civil war became still more complex with the interjection of the struggle over the role of the Church. Carranza and the Constitutionalists set the tone during the days following Huerta's ouster, indicating that the party's religious objective was "to correct and chastise . . . such members of the Roman Catholic Church as may have lent moral or physical support to the usurper, Victoriano Huerta."[5]

Huerta and the Clergy

The clergy reluctantly backed Huerta in the hope that their role and influence would not be diminished. The backing of the Church, to include sympathetic Porfiristas, proved a strange, though critical, ally of General Huerta, given his hard tactics. Edith O'Shaughnessy, who spent considerable time with the president, indicated that while Huerta was not a religious man by nature, he recognized the value of the Catholic Church to the rural indigenous people: "To him the church was as an integral part of Mexico as her seasons, her rainfall and her drought. He was mostly respectful and conciliatory to the ministers of religion, doubtless recognizing the church as one of the few available rocks on which to build his state." This position would bring him in direct conflict with the liberal rebel factions. Further allegations that the Church provided money, arms, and political support are generally true. As historian Charles Cumberland confirmed, "Repeated condemnations of the Constitutionalist movement by priests from the pulpit and by lay Catholic leaders in the newspapers did much to convince Constitutionalist leaders that the Church was in league with Huerta." This relationship is reflected in the fact that when Huerta dissolved the congressional Chamber of Deputies in 1913, he did not arrest any sitting members of the Catholic Party. "They are," Huerta concluded, "after all is said and done, the conservative, peace-wishing element in Mexico."[6]

First Chief Carranza made it clear to his followers that their fight was against the Huerta-Catholic coalition. The clerical opposition to liberalism and secular practices had to be reversed. The Church was seen as anathema to their nationalist aims and a possible impediment to any additional reforms the Constitutionalists might pursue. President Wilson's refusal to sell arms to Huerta or to allow financing from European banks actually gained the dictator support from both the business sector and the Church. As a known representative of the president, John Lind found it damaging to be espousing publicly in Mexico and in reports to Wilson his strong anti-Catholic rhetoric. Buckley expressed his concern with the pompous Lind's attacks on the Church with Veracruz vice consul Canada. Apparently, President Wilson accepted these misleading reports at face value, and Carranza's agents in Washington worked to support the attack against Huerta and the Church. Wilson's dogged insistence that Huerta resign left no room to negotiate, nor did it give the proud Mexican president any incentive to cooperate. Huerta's departure in mid-July 1914 did produced neither peace nor improvement in the daily plight of Mexicans as the factions under Villa, Obregón, and Zapata rebelled and stymied the Constitutionalists' efforts to unify the country.[7]

The high-minded idealistic statements by Carranza and the Constitutionalists did not mirror the growing disillusionment of Mexicans as the revolution turned into a civil war. A confidential report from William Blocker, a longtime resident of Mexico and vice consul at Piedras Negras, captured the magnitude of the crisis:

> Among the working people in whose minds the revolution meant a change of conditions materially for the better in their general prosperity, there is a great disillusionment; they find that the promised betterments do not exist, and never before in the past quarter of a century has there been such distress and misery among them as at present. There is a constant unwillingness among them to serve in the army in marked contrast to their enthusiasm at the beginning of the struggle when their only desire was to shoulder a rifle and march to the firing lines; but now the majority of them realize that they are

now killing one another for mere questions of personal ambitions and jealousies, and that right and justice for them with a fairer division of the fruits of their labors is as far away as ever; while their superiors in education and position are using them as stepping stones in their race for wealth and power, quite regardless of the true interests of the country as a whole. This feeling of deep, but quiet discontent with the present state of affairs is rapidly spreading and may yet make itself felt as an aid to bringing peace. Although any open demonstration of disapproval places the persons who express it in danger of being executed by a firing squad without even a trial.[8]

Mexico for Mexicans

Within days of Huerta's departure into exile, the admonition by Carranza "to correct and chastise" members of the Church and their supporters who backed "the usurper" triggered a deadly wave of violence across the country. The Catholic Church and anyone affiliated with its activities were considered enemies of the revolution. Pancho Villa and his soldados were in the vanguard of harassment and extortion demands of clerics and Church staff across northern Mexico. Beginning with the occupation of Ciudad Juárez and Chihuahua City in December 1913, the general's troops assaulted Catholic seminaries, churches, and schools. Villa had a special hatred for Jesuits and Spaniards in general and Spanish priests in particular. Following a meeting with the foreign consuls, Villa ordered the expulsion of all Spaniards, or else they would be shot. Once the churches were closed, the rebels demanded increasing sums as ransom. For example, unable to collect a demand for 5,000 pesos, the friars went door-to-door begging and were able to collect only $3,327. This pattern of extortion, harassment, and deportation was carried out in each of the towns occupied by Villa or the other Constitutionalist armies. In Juárez, upon receiving a receipt, a dozen priests, two convents of nuns, and an assortment of teachers were herded together with 470 Spaniards, marched to the depot, and loaded on cattle cars. A witness noted, "Before the train left the station Villa entered, laughing and jeering at the Spaniards. Then meeting the fathers, he said to one of them: 'Are you a Spaniard?' He answered, 'I am. What is the matter with my being a Spaniard?' 'We are going to have only Mexican priests.' 'You will be pleased then, Senor Villa?'"[9]

Urgent telegrams from US consuls throughout Mexico, as well as French, Italian, and Spanish diplomats, began to pour into the US State Department with reports of attacks on Church officials. Consul John Silliman in Tampico confirmed reports from the French ambassador that his citizens and especially clerics were being attacked, and the consul routinely supplied Buckley with copies of his confidential dispatches to Washington. The intensity of the acts against the clergy depended on the disposition and vitriol of the leader in command. The Brothers of the Christian Schools in Zacatecas were ordered by Villistas to pay a ransom of 500,000 pesos for the release of nineteen brothers, but the ridiculous demand was made only to scare them. In the scuffle two French friars, Messrs. Astru and Gillis, were shot on Villa's order. Villa had long been antiforeign, which should have come as no surprise to Secretary Bryan. Silliman cabled Bryan that "the attitude of the revolutionist toward the Catholic priesthood, especially Jesuits, and also to many teachers in the schools of faith . . . is regarded as having been almost unanimously enemies of the ideals of the Revolution and perniciously active in their interference in secular affairs." French Ambassador Jean Jules Jusserland in Washington advised Bryan, "Colonel Rodolfo Fierro [Villa's right-hand man known as the "Butcher"] simulated executions of the French priests, called out separately, in order to induce other captives to pay a million peso ransom." Violent attacks on the Church and Mexicans assisting the clerics, which included Church-sponsored hospitals, continued unchecked in Durango, Tlaquepaque, Guadalajara, Santa Ysabel, San Luis Potosí, and Tlaltizapán.

In Aguascalientes, the Church of San Antonio was converted into a legislative hall; in Querétaro, the Church of San José was made into a public library; in Nuevo Laredo, the church building was turned into a horse stable; and at the Church of Santo Domingo in Mexico City, the Carrancistas pretended to say Mass and seated themselves to take confessions. They then publicly mocked the unexpecting parishioners. The nearly four-hundred-year-old Jesuit college at Tepotzotlán, as well as Catholic colleges at Saltillo, Guadalajara, Puebla, and Michoacán, were sacked and the priests deported. In Yucatán, where the alliance of the hacendados and the Church was particularly close, the violence and the pillaging of the cathedrals was particularly savage. Salvador Alvarado, Carranza's governor in Yucatán, had a free rein in Mérida to publish harsh anti-Church decrees: "Let us remember that RELIGION IS IGNORANCE and that, as the REVOLUTION triumphs, GOD goes down. You must destroy all FANATICISM; everything that constitutes a hindrance to Progress; an impediment to education, an obstacle to science and LIBERTY, and a stupifying [sic] cloud upon the representatives of the MAYA race." Constitutionalists, to justify their authority, developed a systematic legal justification for anticlerical acts under these often hastily issued decrees. Constitutionalists followed by claiming ownership of church property as a matter of "law." Alarmed by growing violence, Agent Silliman advised Washington that it would be prudent to advise the diplomatic representatives of Spain, France, Belgium, and Italy, which were engaged in efforts to assist the Church in Mexico, "to retire from the country."[10]

Will Buckley, a devoted Catholic, was actively assisting the clergy under attack. Sheltering as many as possible, he, along with a number of Catholic laypersons, helped numerous clergy escape to safety. His firsthand knowledge of events is reflected in the details of his testimony before the US Senate Foreign Relations Committee in 1919, one of his few public appearances. He blamed the wanton violence against the clergy in Mexico City on Gen. Alvaro Obregón, the commander of the vanguard of the Constitutionalists' army that entered the capital. Buckley's comments before the Fall Committee in 1919 created a great deal of political uproar in Mexico on the eve of the presidential election. Furthermore, it was the first time that Buckley, who had long maintained a low political profile, had interjected his views.[11]

These openly expressed sentiments would eventually result in his forced expulsion from Mexico. The following are details presented by Buckley:

Obregón had entered Mexico City flying the black flag of anarchy. To get the rabble started he sent his troops to lead them in looting a prominent church in the very center of the city, the Church of Santa Brigida, and also the adjoining parochial school. After the soldiers had started the looting the rabble went in and took the tapestry off the walls and also took out the flooring. Some Americans and Mexicans became so indignant at the sight that they seized clubs and dispersed the mob. When Obregón heard of this, he dispatched troops to the church, not to punish the mob for looting but to protect it against those who had interfered with the looting. The soldiers pursued the small number of Americans and Mexicans to the America

Club, where they barricaded the doors and protected themselves against Obregón's soldiers until the Brazilian Minister de Oliveiro [*sic*] could arrive at the club and persuade the soldiers to desist. When the populace started to demonstrate against such outrageous treatment [of priests], he had his troops fire into them, killing several people and stopping the public manifestation. Obregón then took these unfortunate priests, put them in box cars and cattle cars and shipped them down to Veracruz.[12]

Baffled

British intelligence and the Foreign Office continued to be baffled by the lack of response from Washington to the violence against Catholics in Mexico City and the killing spree across northern Mexico by Pancho Villa and his followers. Following the brutal murder of eleven Spaniards in Torreón, no official response was forthcoming from the White House. Shortly after this incident, Ambassador Spring Rice in Washington informed London, "Villa was, as the President himself said to me, *the sword of the revolution*, the bold soldier who was the incarnation of the rightful struggle to be free of the oppressed population of Mexico." Wilson in his determination to oust Huerta had been led, "within nine months, into an intimate alliance with the most notorious bandit in Mexico."[13]

One primary reason for the slow and confused response by Wilson and the State Department was the fact there was a shuttered embassy and no official senior American representative in Mexico City. The Constitutionalists, knowing the individual US consuls were powerless, used the absence of a recognized American ambassador to their advantage. In the interim, Brazilian Minister de Oliveira, who was in ill health throughout this period, represented the United States to the best of his ability. Often matters were handled by a young clerk with no authority. De Oliveira warned the State Department of the violent persecution and extortion of the Catholic clergy across Mexico, many of whom sought refuge in the capital and assistance from the minister. The Jesuits were encouraged to hide and only come out in disguise to avoid arrest. Secretary Bryan responded by sending a note to Consul Hanna in Monterrey for delivery to Carranza, expressing the "hope he will order full protection" to all persons and property of all religious organizations. Although all religious organizations were under attack,

Catholics were singled out for the bulk of assaults. The warnings from Washington to halt the violence had little or no impact.[14]

The archbishops of Guadalajara and Monterrey increased their calls to Minister de Oliveira for "benevolent consideration" as killings, ransom demands, and forced imprisonments became commonplace. No place was safe as clergymen were forcibly dragged out of the American Consulate in Monterrey and the Spanish Consulate in Querétaro. The minister continued to cable information to Washington, but no action was taken until senior American Catholic representatives lodged complaints. Appeals from Catholic organizations were forwarded to the State Department by J. C. Gibbons, archbishop of Baltimore; Monsignor Francis C. Kelley, president of the Catholic Extension Society and editor of *Extension*, a monthly Catholic magazine; and Rev. Richard H. Tierney, chairman of the Committee of the Federation of Catholic Societies in New York. Tierney was among the first to submit graphic and detailed charges of crimes committed by the revolutionaries. These appeals were followed by detailed letters from Kelley challenging the anti-Catholic comments of Lind and his strong ties to and conflicts of interest with the Constitutionalists.[15]

At the White House, President Wilson responded with less than a resounding interest in the depredations, replying to Archbishop Gibbons, "For the present, apparently, we shall have to wait the subsidence of the passions which have been generated by the unhappy condition of the country." To gain more attention for the plight of Catholics in Mexico, Theodore Roosevelt wrote an article for the *New York Times* calling into question three years of missteps and idealism: "Mr. Wilson's elocution and Mr. Wilson's action are in flat contradiction. His elocution is that of a Byzantine logothete—and Byzantine logothetes were not men of action." However, it must be remembered that the political and business sectors in the United States at the turn of the century were dominated by the Protestant establishment. "The caste line drawn at the elite level" precluded Catholics from most high-level positions in government and industry.[16] It was not until January 14, 1915, that Bryan took action and requested all US consuls in Mexico report on attacks and incidents involving the clergy since January 1, 1914—to which he received more than fifteen detailed responses.[17]

Following the reluctance on the part of the United States government to support polices openly to limit attacks on the Church in Mexico, Msgr. Kelley took action and became the primary representative of the Roman

Catholic Church in America to defend and lobby for the clergy in Mexico. In addition to active political engagement in Washington, Kelley was in routine contact with Will Buckley. One concern Kelley worked to overcome was the impression, advanced by Carranza's agents in America and by Constitutionalist-controlled newspapers, that Americans in general were opposed to Catholicism in Mexico. This was totally false, with Kelley noting "their discovery of the tolerance and general attitude toward the Church in this country has given them an entirely new knowledge of and appreciation for the American point of view." To counter Constitutionalist propaganda, Kelley responded with the publication of a detailed booklet chronicling the anticlerical violence, *El Libro de Rojo y Amarillo: Una Historia de Sangre y Cobardía*. In fact, most Americans had little or no knowledge of the dynamics of the revolution in general and surely did not understand Mexican Catholic issues in particular.[18]

Articles in newspapers nationwide expressed concern with conditions in Mexico, yet except for a limited campaign to a number of outlets there was no grassroots response. Buckley continued to lodge complaints with Consuls Stillman and Canada. Other than a couple of diplomatic notes from Secretary Bryan requesting fair treatment of the Catholic Church, the US government did nothing to advance any relief for the plight of Catholics in Mexico. In the months prior to the Fall Committee hearings in late 1919, Kelley went to Paris to lobby for redress of the treatment of the Church in Mexico. He also expressed strong opposition that the disgraced Carranza government was not being allowed to enter the League of Nations, and lobbied for provisions to be added to the covenants of the Paris Peace Conference making religious liberty one of the qualifications for membership. Kelley's efforts did not curb the attacks on the Catholic Church in Mexico.[19]

Within days, Silliman cabled Washington with additional details on the declared limitations and restrictions on the Church imposed by local military chieftains, such as Antonio I. Villarreal, governor and military commander of the state of Nuevo León. One bishop referred to Villarreal as "the most clerophobe among the Constitutionalists." Villarreal issued a sweeping decree that in effect limited access to all churches and their schools and prescribed punishment for violations.[20] Buckley's business agents, consular officers, and Mexican friends sent him detailed reports of attacks on the Church. Churches in Monterrey were sacked with confessionals, furniture, extensive research libraries, and art stacked in the street and publicly burned. Vestments and sacred vessels were defiled, and churches were turned into barracks. The archbishop's residence was occupied by the Carrancistas, and the rectory archives were searched for scandalous material to publish in the anticlerical rebel newspaper *El Bonete*. None of the Nuevo León clergy suffered death, no nuns were violated, and the archbishop escaped to Mexico City and was ordered to leave the country. "In the Catholic schools," Villareal opined, "the truth is perverted; the pure white soul of childhood, the idealistic burning spirit of youth is deformed."[21]

General Villa telegraphed his approval of the new decree and Gen. Cándido Aguilar in Veracruz—whom Consul Canada, in an urgent message to Washington, characterized as "a Mexican socialist whose radical ideas border on anarchy"—issued his own decree of "General Rules." These local decrees and local actions from the Villistas and Constitutionalist commanders foreshadowed future constitutional deliberations in late 1916 at Querétaro, which included, for example, the following:

All foreign Catholic priests (friars) and Jesuits are expelled immediately.
Churches will open daily from 6 a.m. to 1 p.m. with approved priests.
Confessions and confirmations are prohibited.
The public is not permitted to enter the Sacristy.
Church bells will not be allowed to ring except on Constitutionalist holidays.
All school instruction will be limited to only academic studies.
Clergy cannot occupy elected office.
All Church property is subject to control by the state.
Infractions will be punished by fines, or imprisonment, or expulsion.[22]

Across northern Mexico, the Church was under fierce attack. In Tamaulipas, Catholic priests were expelled to Texas but left the churches open. US Consul William Canada reported in Veracruz that all foreign priests were expelled, and only one native Mexican priest was allowed for each ten thousand inhabitants. Reports of atrocities continued to be confirmed: four Christian brothers were killed near Zacatecas by order of General Chao; fourteen were banished to Santa Fe, New Mexico and forced to pay $5,000 ransom; and twenty-two priests were threatened with death, forced to pay 100,000 pesos, and exiled to El Paso. Beyond harassment and ransom threats, often masquerading as taxation, the desecration of churches and holy objects was justified by Constitutionalist general Salvador Alvarado thus, "It was for the deliberate purpose of showing the Indians that lightning would not strike—that the rebels were not the enemies of God as priests had told them, that generals rode their horses into churches and publicly smashed the statues of the venerated saints."[23]

Details of the "horrible state of distress" continued to be cabled to the State Department by America's representative in Mexico City, Brazilian minister de Oliveira, as well as through reports from US consuls Bonney in San Luis Potosí and Canada in Veracruz. In response, Secretary Bryan sent a second warning of concern to Carranza via special agent Silliman—to little affect. The chaos within the Constitutionalist movement, the infighting among the generals in northern Mexico, the lack of a formal US ambassador, the void of a functional government and rule of law—these conditions combined make one wonder why things were not worse. The capital was in a harsh condition with no rule of law, a growing shortage of food and water, and a steady exodus of citizens to avoid the wave of rebels sacking the city. General Obregón, Buckley noted, "was not satisfied to starve the population of Mexico City, he decided to outrage their religious sentiments, and arrested over 150 priests." Many took refuge in Veracruz in the hope of escaping to Cuba or the United States. Only a year earlier, Wilson's special agent Lind, an opinionated anti-Catholic, vocal in his public remarks, characterized the Church and clergy as "little more than agents of repression." Any and all goodwill on the part of the Wilson administration was lost with the release of a remarkable dispatch to the State Department, in which the pompous agent fully discounted the role and future of the Church, suggesting in writing that the United States take an option on the iconic National Cathedral at the Zócalo as a future site for a new embassy.[24]

Buckley versus Lind

The extent of John Lind's subterfuge, in his role as a special agent in Mexico for President Wilson, was not fully known and made public until the Fall Committee hearings in 1919–1920. The attacks on the Catholic Church in Mexico and the ambivalent response by the Wilson administration were directly linked to the comments and actions of Lind. From the time Lind landed in Veracruz in 1913, he alienated most of his contacts. Given his instructions, which were typed by the president himself, Lind approached General Huerta with a predetermined list of nonnegotiable demands. Buckley and many in the American business sector, as well as diplomats in Mexico and government officials, were quickly at odds with Lind's approach. Foreign Minister Francisco Gamboa was so disgusted he formally mocked him, referring to the messenger only as "Mr. Confidential Agent" in diplomatic communiques. Members of the business sector were concerned that Lind's unprofessional mixed messages and ignorance about Mexico would damage US-Mexico relations further. And among the most irritated with the embarrassing sham was Will Buckley.[25]

The hearings exposed the behind-the-scenes operations of the Wilson administration that were conducted to support the Constitutionalists and Carranza. In the White House's panic after the disastrous landing at Veracruz in April 1914, a group of the very countries in Latin America whose domestic path to internal rule Wilson intended to decide formed the ABC group to hold negotiations and prevent a war. The mediation proved to be a farce as Lind worked to circumvent export laws and neutrality to smuggle guns and ammunition into Mexico. In Washington, Buckley had a clear view of these efforts to undercut Huerta. During the Senate hearings, John Lind was asked if he knew Buckley and he replied, "I think I met him once, I recollect the name." The questioning of Lind followed Buckley's testimony that provided details of Lind advising Secretary Bryan (and possibly the president) on how to circumvent the law, while conducting a disingenuous delaying action with regard to the ongoing talks in Niagara Falls, with the purpose of shipping tons of munitions and arms to Tampico. Using false documents consigning ships to Havana, Cuba, the schooners *Antilla*, *Sunshine*, *Grampus*, and *Susan* made six round trips from Galveston to Tampico. When questioned about how they failed to land at Havana, their captains reported the occurrence of bad weather and being "blown of course to Tampico."[26]

Lind's ineptness and prejudice were most evident in his vehement attacks on the Catholic Church. As his biographer, George M. Stephenson, has noted, Lind believed that to have "reforms [in Mexico] along the social, economic, and political lines, the power of the church had to be curbed." The historical records are extensive in this regard and detail his blind support of Carranza, regardless of the Mexican leader's anti-American statements and attacks on foreign business and Church clerics. Buckley testified that during the mediation facilitated by the ABC group, Lind was advised that the Pan-American conference might not recognize Carranza, to which he responded, "My God, poor Mexico will fall back into the clutches of the Catholic Church."[27] Casting doubt on Lind's claim not to remember that conversation, Buckley continued in testimony, "In private conversation Mr. Lind attributed all the ills of Mexico to the influence of the Catholic Church and argued that this institution in Mexico must be destroyed." Asked during the hearings about the anti-Catholic statements, Nelson O'Shaughnessy confirmed Lind's comments that "the more Catholic priests they killed in Mexico the better it suits him"—"I regret very much to say that Mr. Lind did make that statement."

The prime concern with these remarks was that Lind was the one confidential agent who had the most direct access and personal contact with both Wilson and Bryan. Lind's repeated anti-Catholic opinions seem to have agreed with Wilson's view of the administration's policy and treatment of the revolution. Buckley had met with Lind in Mexico and Washington several times and possibly in New York City during the Niagara Falls mediation in mid-1914. Buckley was one of the first to identify publicly Lind's questionable activities and strong support of Carranza. Lind was the direct connection between Carranza's agents in Washington (e.g., Cabrera, Arredondo) and President Wilson. Claims that Lind was being paid $25,000 by Carranza's agents were rumored by numerous sources, including the First Chief's legal counsel and chief lobbyist in Washington, and for months Lind worked full-time for the Constitutionalists in Washington lobbying for the de facto diplomatic recognition in October 1916.[28]

The White House faced a critical dilemma in regard to its response to attacks on the Catholic Church. President Wilson and Secretary Bryan seemed to view the reports from Mexico and the incessant pressure from the Catholic Church for protection as merely a byproduct of the revolution. Without a recognized government, there could be no law and order. All demands for redress were met with polite evasion that religious liberty would soon be provided by a new government. Former chargé d'affaires O'Shaughnessy, when asked by the Fall Committee if John Lind, who advised the president during this turmoil, was shocked by the fact that the

Carrancistas had killed priests, responded, "No, I do not think it shocked him. The Carranza people evidently thought that these atrocities were not unpleasing to the American government." Privately it appears that Wilson shared with Lind a disdain for all the pressure, noting to Bryan that the anticlericalism had "too much Mexican history" behind it for there to be much hope of curbing the short-term abuse of clerics and churches. Historian Kendrick Clements bluntly concludes, "Wilson realized and accepted as a necessary fact that the success of the revolution meant a measure of religious persecution and expropriation."[29]

De Facto Recognition

By late 1915, President Wilson assumed that Carranza would emerge (with Washington's diplomatic and financial endorsement) as the strongest leader to form a new government and end the civil war. Confidential agents, customs officers, and military intelligence agents had tracked the movements and strengths of the key revolutionary generals. Special Agent J. W. Belt had conducted several visits with the First Chief to determine if he could command the country. Carranza gradually began to give a consistent set of "acceptable" answers to the administration and news media that he would reduce violence and foster the protection of foreigners and their property. In the case of the Catholic Church, he gave a weak response to Belt, stating that "only Catholics that have meddled in politics have been punished. All religious toleration in Mexico will prevail as in the past." Clearly this was not the case, given more than two years of undisputed attacks on the Church and clergy. At the White House, there was a rising level of attention to the war in Europe, and Wilson had no desire to become more embroiled in Mexico after four years of confrontation. German agitators would have liked nothing better than a continuation of the civil war in Mexico, which could potentially draw America across the Rio Grande into a full-scale military intervention and disrupt oil production. However, American policy toward Mexico was quickly subordinated to an increased focus on Europe. Despite Carranza's many anti-American policies and his failure to curb violence against the Church, the ongoing conflict worked to his advantage. On October 19, 1915, in Washington, Secretary of State Lansing informed the Constitutionalists' special agent Eliseo Arredondo that President Wilson would extend de facto recognition to the interim government of Mexico, of which Venustiano Carranza was the chief executive.[30]

Protest among American Catholics against recognition of Carranza was immediate. The Holy Name Society in Brooklyn issued a vehement remonstrance to President Wilson and the White House spokesman, Joseph P. Tumulty. They accused Tumulty of being an "apologist" for the First Chief: "Carranza and his subordinate officers have been guilty of the most revolting crimes and have avowed their determination to persevere in a career of lust and blood unparalleled in history." Tumulty, caught off guard by the heated response to this disingenuous remark, countered with a strange reference drawing attention to the historic recognition of President Benito Juárez by the Buchanan administration. This had followed the "bloodiest of all civil wars ever waged in Mexico" marked by "all the bitterness and cruelties of a religious war." Wilson's dismissal of the violence disregarded the detailed diplomatic note sent by the secretary of state, drafted with his assistance at the White House on July 22, 1914. This transpired shortly after the departure of General Huerta, in which a major part of the cipher regarded the treatment of the Roman Catholic Church and those who represent it. Tumulty should have reflected on the words of Bryan, who noted, "Nothing will shake the civilized world more than degrading or vindictive action towards priests or ministers of any church whether Catholic or Protestant . . . on this delicate and vital mater. The treatment already said to have been accorded priests has had a most unfortunate effect upon opinion outside of Mexico." The White House had placed itself in a corner to support Carranza regardless of the reports of violence from Mexico.[31]

Luis Cabrera and the Constitutionalists' special agents in Washington, pleased with the bland response from the White House, issued a number of responses to the press. To counter this Constitutionalist propaganda, Buckley repeatedly warned Secretary Bryan of Cabrera's duplicitous assault on the Church. These releases countered the objections by declaring that the "radical" Catholic bishops in Mexico were fully responsible for inciting the revolution and unrest. This claim was accompanied by paid editorial placements that included a statement by Carranza proclaiming commitment to a "free exercise of all religions" and protection of "the persons of native and foreign clergymen, who do not mix in the political life of the country."[32] Few in America understood the degree of chaos occurring in Mexico. Buckley expressed his concern to Reverend Tierney that the recognition of Carranza "will justify in the minds of this faction their past conduct towards the Catholic Church and will further stimulate them to destroy this institution in Mexico."[33]

Chaos and Violence

If immediate calm was expected in Mexico, there did not seem to be any groundswell of approval over the de facto recognition of Carranza. There was no permanent government, Mexico City was in a crisis over the shortage of food and water, there was no law and order, the courts were closed, the peso was deemed near worthless, and rebel groups were once again being placed on the defensive or directed to withdraw and curb their activities. One rebel was quickly hostile to the announcement from Washington. Special Agent Carothers, who had spent weeks embedded with Pancho Villa, referred to President Wilson as an "evangelistic professor of philosophy," and his staff reported in a carefully worded cable that the general was "very indignant and defiant" and would continue the fight, "also [on] Americans if necessary."[34]

In late October, Wilson ordered a suspension of aid and arms for Villa's army and redirected the war supplies to General Obregón. Villa's pledge to attack Americans was not a hollow threat, as evidenced by a rapid increase in incidents of violence, climaxing in the slaughter of eighteen American mining engineers pulled from a train and shot in early January at Santa Ysabel, Chihuahua. This atrocity was followed by the infamous March 1916 cross-border raid into New Mexico that killed nineteen US citizens in the small town of Columbus.[35] The US Army gave chase and soon claimed to have killed or captured a score of the Villistas. Within hours, the incident that the White House did not need or want resulted in President Wilson ordering Gen. John "Black Jack" Pershing, with eight thousand troops supported by the first military use of airplanes, to cross the border with the "single purpose" of capturing General Villa. The First Chief of the Constitutionalists distanced himself from Villa's raids by informing the State Department that he "sincerely lament[ed] the occurrence," although Carranza was more concerned with General Pershing's "Columbus Expedition," which he said violated the sovereignty of Mexico. Given the anti-American attitude of the population in northern Mexico, expectations were slim that Villa would be caught or even found. Any question about Mexicans' attitude, or at least of those in northern Mexico—in favor of Pancho Villa and against the "invading gringos"— was answered in the clash at Carrizal and Parral between US troops and Mexican soldiers and civilians.[36]

Presidential Campaign, 1915–1916

In late 1915, Will Buckley began an active correspondence with Charles D. Hilles, chairman of the Republican National Committee (RNC) in New York. Will indicated he felt the "real facts" about Mexico would discredit the Wilson administration. The chronicling of these facts would be a "splendid opportunity for the Republican Party" and political fodder for the 1916 campaign.[37] In a series of letters to members of the RNC, including Thomas W. Streeter in Boston as well as Senators Boise Penrose and Henry Cabot Lodge, Buckley identified groups and issues that would work to secure the needed facts to attack the political opposition. His prime intent was to demonstrate the hubris of Wilson in his dealings with Carranza. Buckley's collection of sources comprised a broad cross-section of groups and individuals: (1) the American Publicity Committee of Mexico City: data and affidavits of outrages across Mexico; (2) the former *Científicos*: technocratic advisers of Porfirio Díaz; (3) the Huerta delegation to the Niagara Falls Peace Conference: documentation of the US government's bad-faith actions during the negotiations; (4) the ABC diplomats: concerning the Pan-American conference when the recognition of Carranza was "forced on the delegates by a veiled threat to intervene in Mexico if this step was not taken"; (5) the Catholic Church: extensive information concerning attacks on the Church; and (6) the Red Cross: provided data "that would startle the American people" and reported how the organization was reprimanded by President Wilson for supporting the plight of Mexicans. Buckley indicated he would provide additional information and encouraged that "a few Mexican and American" detectives be retained to investigate corruption.[38]

During the fall of 1916, considerable attention was on the US presidential campaign, which pit Republican Charles Evans Hughes against Wilson. The Catholic Church rhetorically attacked the White House while business executives supported by Buckley demanded intervention in Mexico. Representatives of both the Church and private business lobbied with little success to influence the American public to care about the violence and civil war south of the border. In the weeks prior to the election, Carranza, who generally believed "the clergy shared responsibility for many of Mexico's historical misfortunes," issued a decree to halt the confiscation of Church property by making the Ministry of Finance responsible for enforcing ecclesiastical law. Notwithstanding, the war in Europe attracted extensive media attention. Wilson ignored all criticism regarding his Mexico policy as he campaigned across the country on steadfast neutrality and the slogan "He Kept Us Out of War." This primary message carried him to reelection.[39]

In Mexico, Carranza faced formidable challenges. He found it easier to destroy the old government than to form and lead a new one. The First Chief was unable to corral some three dozen local generals, jefes, and their followers. Consul Canada informed Washington, "Carranza now holds little territory away from the railroads and large towns." One potential challenger, Gen. Alvaro Obregón, who only weeks earlier had been declared killed in the Battle of León, was alive and well and pledged his support to the First Chief.[40]

Each factional leader commanded his small slice of Mexico, with no clear cohesion or allegiance among them. US military intelligence agent Dr. Paul Bernardo Altendorf, a Pole, operated in Mexico under cover as a German citizen; "I traveled as a German; for no one but a German is safe in Mexico," he recalled. At times he acted as a merchant, a dentist, and an officer in the Carrancista army. In addition to reporting on the chaos and violence, Altendorf questioned the legitimacy of Carranza's government:

> No real government exists south of the Rio Grande except such authority as a thug with a gun exercises over an unarmed victim. Mexico is nothing more than an agglomeration of anarchist gangs who kill and plunder with no restraint but their own caprices. To discriminate between Carranzistas and other banditti is to make a distinction without a difference. All alike live by plunder. Of these rebels and banditti there are 100,000 men operating in gangs of 40 to 4,000, under 37 known leaders of importance who hunt in definite territories. In addition there is an unknown number of smaller fry who operate independently at times and again assert allegiance to some larger gang when they need protection.[41]

Carranza had agreed to the US intervention behind closed doors—in reports from the president's special agents—but in public the First Chief vehemently denounced the wanton invasion of Mexican soil by the gringos. Villista and rebel raids, by groups identified by agent Altendorf, soon intensified with increasing frequency across the border at Nuevo Laredo, Eagle Pass, San Ygnacio, Nogales, Glenn Springs, and the Brite Ranch in the Big Bend region as hundreds of Americans fled Mexico.[42] There was little prospect that Villa would be apprehended as both his soldiers and Carranza's officers had stated openly they would aid the general's escape and not allow Americans to capture him. "Viva Villa and death to the gringos!" was the war cry across northern Mexico. As Wilford Callcott concluded, "The military were entirely too powerful for the good of the country and too often the old *ley fuga* was applied to opponents." The violence would continue throughout 1916, and General Pershing's expedition accomplished very little, save serving as a significant propaganda tool for Carranza. The civil war raged as Villistas personally commanded by General Villa entered Torreón on Christmas Eve, killing sixty Chinese and more than eighty Carranza sympathizers. The American Expeditionary Force returned to the border in early 1917. Despite little success against Villa, the troops of the AEF performed a major, yet little noticed, humanitarian mission by escorting 489 Chinese refugees (who had been accosted for monopolizing the grocery stores and laundries across the northern state) from the Torreón region to Columbus, New Mexico, and San Antonio, Texas. In Mexico, through the recognized government, Wilson hoped to influence the civil war; toward this end, the first formal steps were taken by establishing constitutional order and rule of law at Querétaro.[43]

In a rushed, staccato decoded cablegram to the State Department, Consul Canada provided an assessment of conditions and unrest in the Veracruz region, not unlike the chaos in northern Mexico:

Marauding bands are numerous and daring. No cohesion among the de facto officers. Growing unrest of organized labor. New paper money rapidly depreciating. Banks practically closed, exports less, business depressed. Food except fruits scarce marauders have hampered agriculture. Most cattle have been seized by soldiers stolen or slaughtered for hides. Hunger throughout State. Many beggars. Hundreds homeless sleep in open air. Many unemployed. Higienic [*sic*] conditions bad. Mines this district shut down. Every week one or more trains blown up. General attitude authorities and populace toward foreign interest growing worse."[44]

The Constitution of 1917

The fighting and jockeying for political control that followed the departure of Huerta in July 1914 continued until early 1917, leaving the country in near ruin. Not until Carranza (or someone) finally obtained a degree of control did there seem to be possible an end to the raging civil war. The attacks on the Church and the clergy had gained scant attention in the world media. Protests from the US State Department, the British Foreign Office, and the Vatican fell on deaf ears in Mexico City. Their churches destroyed and sacked, the clergy fled over the United States border by the hundreds. The Constitutionalist convention called at Querétaro, which opened on December 1, 1916, would forever change the role of the Church in Mexico. The First Chief presided over the opening session, presenting a model constitution for discussion and consideration, yet he soon realized he and his small group of dedicated supporters, the *bloqué renovador*, did not have control over the proceedings. In historian Robert Quirk's interpretation, "There would be no Porfiristas or Huertistas, no Catholics, no Zapatistas, no Villistas—it actually only heralded the radical social revolution." As the radical anticlerics took control of the debate, the convention exceeded many of Carranza's proposals for the Church. As debate ended and the Constitution of 1917 attained the convention's approval, it became clear that the document would have an unprecedented impact on church-state relations in Mexico. The framers of the new constitution undertook to avoid future domination of the country by either foreign capital or any ecclesiastical institution. Msgr. Francis Kelley, when quizzed by the Fall Committee regarding why the Church was persecuted, responded, "The first reason was the adoption, by the politicians of the principles of the French Revolution. That revolution was decidedly anti-religious, and as the Catholic Church was the only church they knew anything about its sympathizers vented their hatred for her."[45]

The debate among the many rebel factions and inexperienced delegates was often led by those without battlefield experience and was at times hostile, rancorous, and vindictive. The delegates, most of whom were political novices, were bound to a major change in the country's political future based on secular principles and centralized control. Anticlerical debate did not connote any pro-Protestant leanings or special attention. The role of the Church in education led to a great deal of debate on the content and emphasis of the instruction to be provided. The Laws of Reform and new constitutional provisions were crafted over a hasty six-week period in large part by the victorious "Men of the North." These reforms aimed to curb centuries of influence of the Catholic Church and private property rights, and thus were sweeping in their language to limit the power of the Church and to establish a managed state. The new constitution included, among other measures:

Article 3 redefined free education as a secular function of the state.
Article 5 prohibited monastic orders.
Article 24 banned worship in public locations outside of churches.
Article 27 nationalized all Church real estate and control over all property and Church buildings.
Article 33 established that the executive has the exclusive right to expel any foreigner from the country.
Article 37 allowed that citizenship could be withdrawn for disobedience of the constitution.
Article 130 denied the Church legal existence.
Article 130 allowed only native-born clergy on Mexican soil.[46]

With the approval of the new constitution, the Carrancista revolutionaries exercised a systematic anticlerical policy and laicization of the Church. While Article 3 declared independence from the Church in favor of sweeping secular reforms, clearly the details of Article 130 represented the most anticlerical section of the Constitution of 1917. The Church in Mexico, lacking "legal existence," now had no recourse to address grievances. The power to control who could be eligible to be a priest resulted in complete regulatory power to monitor the clergy's activities. Furthermore, priests and nuns were not allowed to speak publicly on political issues, and clerics of any creed were banned from holding elective office and were prohibited from voting. All clerics, including Baptist and Methodist ministers and missionaries, were required by the new law to "be Mexican by birth." Mormon colonists who had won the favor of Porfirio Díaz and Huerta for their colonizing genius and industriousness had begun their exodus from Mexico as early as 1912, yet did not avoid attacks. All churches, regardless of faith, needed permission from the Department of Interior (Gobernación) before dedicating any new facility. No Church body or political group was permitted to have an official spokesman in the legislature. Marriage was established as a civil contract, and no minister of any religious creed could inherit any real property. And there was no recourse or appeal to the Vatican without first going through the federal government. Rev. Erwin Brown of Puebla, a Baptist minister, concluded shortly after being expelled as a "pernicious foreigner" that "Mexico and Mexican people avowed above and beyond no need of any religion." A keen knowledge of these historical dynamics would prove critical in Buckley's briefing of the Fall Committee.[47]

The new constitution not only directly attacked the Catholic Church but also took a parallel tack with all foreign investment and oil interests, which included, principally, years of concessions held by Americans.[48] Buckley, in his memo to Senator Fall titled "The New Anti-American Constitution of Mexico," detailed decades of prior protests and efforts to redress of the new laws that had impacted investment and current operations.[49]

Carranza

Carranza was elected president of Mexico under the new Constitution of 1917 in April against virtually no opposition. Alvaro Obregón and Pablo González expressed interest in the presidency. At last it was determined that the First Chief, after years of fighting, would forgo his long-held role as the leader of the preconstitutional period to become the revolutionary Mexico's first legal president on May 1. Ambassadors were formally exchanged between the United States and Mexico for the first time in nearly four years. As Carranza entered office, the country remained in chaos. Interestingly, he did not fully endorse the constitution he had signed, and which had authorized his election. Thus, while not in full agreement with all parts of the new constitution, he was inclined to selectively enforce and advance the items he felt were best for Mexico and play down any others. Quirk notes that the radicals at Querétaro who demanded extensive changes were stalled in their efforts at sweeping reform and had "perhaps gained a hollow victory against the supporters of the First Chief."[50]

Despite the fact that he signed the new constitution, Carranza felt no particular obligation to enforce it, especially the articles on the Catholic Church, education, and land reform that offended him. One main reason there was no overriding central authority to enforce the new constitution was its requirement that the articles had to be reviewed by the new Congress. This ensured delay by factional disputes, credentials fights, and basic unfamiliarity with prudent parliamentary procedures. These matters were further complicated by the responsibility of the Congress to fix procedures and penalties for offenses. Furthermore, Carranza, with his government, was in control in title only. Villa was still in rebellion in the north and Zapata in the south; moreover, a number of generals still operated as independent jefes harassing the Church, confiscating property, invoking martial law and random justice. Notwithstanding, American ambassador Henry P. Fletcher was directed on September 27, 1917, to present formal de jure recognition to the Carranza government. Unable to control all factions, Carranza turned his attention to education and religion.[51]

When confronted by lay members of the Catholic Church, led by several committees of ladies, on the harsh treatment and limits on religious activities and access to education, Carranza replied that they themselves should deal with the state governors and officials. With no clear guidelines from Congress, governors had to trust their own interpretations of the articles in the constitution. Across Mexico, exiled priests and bishops had secretly returned, slipping across the border in disguise. The revolutionaries continued to hound all clerics, yet there seemed to be some relaxation of harsh treatment by early 1918. Governor Manuel M. Diéguez allowed some smaller parishes to reopen, but the main cathedrals in Guadalajara remained closed. Bent on control, the governor continued to harass Catholics, Quirk recounts: "On Ash Wednesday of 1918 Diéguez stationed guards at the doors of the churches in Guadalajara where services were held. Soldiers stopped each person leaving the church with ashes on his forehead and advised him to remove them. If it was not done, they took them to the police station where the spot was wiped off by force and a fine levied. The government announced that it would put an end to this "dirty custom," for the law forbade all "outward signs of religious faith."[52]

Governor Diéguez, an ardent anticleric, realized that he would be unable to control the rising wave of organization among Catholic laity and underground groups of believers flouting the rules. In July 1918, the governor

approved a new decree, most likely unconstitutional, that limited the number of churches and priests, allowing only one priest for each five thousand inhabitants in the state. Priests would be required to register with the
government in each town to prove they were Mexican citizens by birth.
The local bishops, who were determined to resist the law, began working
quietly to reorganize each diocese. The government quickly expelled
many bishops, only to have the *Damas Católicas* and other lay groups initi-
ate public protests. Aloise Buckley allowed priests to hold Mass secretly at
her home in Tampico and regularly assisted clergy and smuggled Church
artifacts to New Orleans for safekeeping. Following a number of strikes
and boycotts organized by pro-Church advocates in early 1919, conditions
gradually improved, which allowed some bishops and priests to return to
Mexico—albeit only after they proved their citizenship.[53]

Education

A major byproduct of the civil war and anti-Catholic excesses was the stag-
nation of social services and the disruption of education. The central
question that would have a lingering long-term impact on Mexico was who
the country's chief executive would be and who would control education
for its citizens. Historically, education had been one of the lowest-funded
items in both national and local budgets in Mexico. This was, in large part,
because of the role the Catholic Church had played in providing resources
for instruction and teachers at the local level. The radical government leadership and the bitter debates during the drafting of the new constitution
resulted in the Article 3 demand for a secular and "free" approach to education. Fervent radical anti-Catholics contended that no schooling at all
was better than education in Catholic schools. Given the fact that some
72 percent of the citizens in 1920 were illiterate (down from an estimated
80 percent in 1900) and that there was no funding or programs to begin
public education, Mexico would struggle for years to attain adequate levels of education. Further, the country had a shortage of certified teachers.
Luis Cabrera claimed in early 1917 that the Catholic Church was a "failure
as an educator," thus blaming it for Mexicans' low levels of access to education. The improving literacy rate is surprising given the fact that the public schools across Mexico were mostly closed for more than five years and
did not reopen on an extended schedule until March 1916. Following the

decrees of the Constitution of 1917, the education system experienced even more disruption.[54]

Because the damage done to educational programs across the nation was not fully realized, the government's optimistic plans to reopen public schools on a national level failed. The system was underfunded and short of professional staff and teachers. Carranza therefore abolished the post of minister of public education and referred all aspects of education relating to the reinstating of schools to the local town governments. While these plans were well intended to encourage local control, they too brought disastrous results. Most local governments had no ability to organize or fund the needed schools. A memo prepared for Will Buckley prior to the congressional hearings paints a bleak picture: "The primary schools are about as bad as you would ever be able to conceive or imagine. They are dominated by the injurious element in the revolution, native and alien, whose principal object is to take possession of all public instruction in Mexico. They have succeeded to this extent that no Catholic laymen, much less a priest or other clerical, is permitted." Local schools had little to work with, as demands on local municipal services drained away all funding from education. General conditions grew worse across the country as travel was unsafe, bandits were in control, corruption was rampant at all levels of government, and the communications and railroad systems were in total disrepair. In many areas of Mexico, all religious activities were outlawed on threat of jail and firing squad.[55]

An example of the near total displacement of the education system was the massive teachers' strike in Mexico City in May 1919. The federal government under Carranza and Treasury Secretary Cabrera abruptly stopped paying teachers and referred them to the municipalities, which had no funds. Expected to work without pay, the teachers walked out on strike after being told their salaries were going to the troops in the army to pay for "expenditures demanded by the pacification of the country." Very soon the government authorities found themselves under attack by hundreds of women teachers. Buckley notes, "There were disorders in the streets and some persons wounded in an exchange of shots between police and strikers. Women strikers attempted to interfere with the street car service and threw themselves in front of the cars and a policeman threatened to shoot a woman if she did not arise." El Universal and Excelsior newspapers had extensive coverage following a blackout of news to the United States. Fire departments were used to disperse strikers, all saloons in the city were closed, and two regiments of cavalry were brought in from Texcoco to patrol the streets of the capital. To end the strike, Cabrera and the mayor of Mexico City agreed to pay the teachers two-thirds of their pay, reduce the number of schools to eighty (down from more than two hundred), and then increase the number to 120 by July; they also appealed to the "parents to support private schools."[56]

Sowing the Wind

As reports of continued violence and incidents like the events in Guadalajara and Mexico City were sent to Washington, still there was no formal response from the US State Department. Buckley's protest as well as numerous consul reports went unnoticed or ignored. Addressing a party of visiting Mexican newspaper editors in early June, Wilson made no mention of the anticlerical depredations or the reported rise of Bolshevism, instead stressing his concern about German espionage in Mexico. Fully focused on the war in Europe, the president informed the visitors very matter-of-factly: "The influence of the United States is somewhat pervasive in the affairs of the world, and I believe that it is pervasive because the nations of the world which are less powerful than some of the greatest nations are coming to believe that our sincere desire is to disinterested service." Interestingly, this was the first official statement by Wilson of his view of America's role following the war. Secretary of the Navy Daniels confirmed that Wilson was "severely criticized" for his wavering Mexico policy. Clearly affairs in Mexico were a very low priority.[57]

By mid-1919, it was clear that the enforcement of the Constitution of 1917 would involve a continued denial of religious liberty in Mexico and an inability to provide Mexican children with educational instruction. Nonetheless, the Catholic Church, while weakened after a decade of civil war and persecution, still wielded strong historical ideological influence over all classes of Mexicans. The attack on the Church beyond the turmoil of the revolution caused William Buckley to reassess his active role to defend the faith. Wilson's "missionary diplomacy" began and ended with a Mexican regime seeking American recognition. Paradoxically, those whom Wilson presumably sought to assist were the ones who suffered the most; he sowed the wind, and the people of Mexico reaped the whirlwind.[58]

CHAPTER FIVE

Buckley and the Fall Committee

The confiscation of oil properties is provided for in the Constitution
of 1917. The other interesting effect of the new constitution relates to foreigners.
The expulsion of the Americans in Mexico has always been known
to the initiated as one of the prime objects of the revolution—
stemming the tide of American influence in Mexico.
—William F. Buckley Sr., Fall Committee Hearing, December 6, 1919

He was lucky. For he had indeed materially aided a counterrevolution
movement. The fact the counter revolutionists were decent men, and those
in power barbarians, does not alter the political reality, which is that it
is a very dangerous business indeed to back an unsuccessful insurrection:
and he knew it, and barely escaped with his skin.
—William F. Buckley Jr., *National Review*, October 25, 1958

I N THE MONTHS FOLLOWING the November 1918 Armistice, which
ended a tragic war in Europe, the major nations were crafting peace
negotiations to shape the future. Mexico was not a party to the postwar
peace process and intended to remain neutral. This did not lessen the revolutionary chaos surrounding the Carranza government. Over 1 million
Mexicans had been killed in a decade of civil war. A stable federal government languished in disputes, corruption, and an absence of law and
order. The Mexican economy was in shambles. Mining operations in the
northern states were damaged, the railroad system was in "utter ruin," disrepair, and debt. The educational system was in chaos. Factories were
wrecked and looted, and the banking system attempted to reestablish a
stable currency. Food was in short supply, and the once profitable Yucatán
henequen industry (a coarse fiber used to make rope and twine) was a
mess. The once thriving domestic sugar industry in the states of Morelos
and Puebla was in complete ruin. The great textile mills were shut down, and
owners were selling the machinery at "paltry prices as junk."[1]

Only the petroleum sector had seen steady growth—despite the bandit attacks, new government decrees, and aging infrastructure. New foreign investment was cautious as the central government in Mexico City extended a steady stream of taxation decrees. The potential expropriation of all foreign operations remained an ongoing threat. Article 27 of the Constitution of 1917 implied sweeping regulations for the oil industry. The continued near unanimous pushback by foreign investors only delayed the inevitable, as articulated by Buckley, "In the acquisition of real estate, of mining and oil properties, an American citizen must waive his right to the diplomatic protection of the American Government. The penalty for a mere appeal for protection was the forfeiture of the property involved. Title to all lands acquired from co-owners, tribes, settlements, and hamlets existing since the law of June 23, 1856, was declared void."[2]

The preoccupation of the White House and US State Department with the end of the war and the president's intensive efforts to shape the Paris Peace Conference during 1919 relegated Mexico and all of Latin America to a low priority. While attacks on the Catholic Church and clergy had waned, critics of the Wilson administration's lack of a postwar Mexico policy surfaced with vocal demands for normalcy from corporate business, political opponents, and Americans in Mexico. Critical issues regarding the scope of regulations and oil industry ownership and taxation were in a state of flux. With President Wilson and the secretary of state in Paris, a group of midlevel administration officials attempted to maintain the status quo as friction with Mexico mounted. One bright spot was the appointment of Henry P. Fletcher as ambassador to Mexico City. A seasoned diplomat who had served in Peking, Havana, and as the first US ambassador in Chile, Fletcher quickly grasped the magnitude of the situation and the need to recast the administration's failed policy. His first year in Mexico City, until the Armistice in November 1918, was spent monitoring the pro-German Carranza administration. At the request of Secretary of State Lansing, he drafted a detailed memorandum covering the diplomatic options available to the president on March 1, 1919. President Wilson, totally immersed in the talks in Paris, did not read the memo until August 4, 1919, and then only asked if anything had changed. Fletcher, on the eve of the upcoming Senate Foreign Relations Committee hearings and the heightened corporate demands for action, calmly warned that a sudden emergency or incident might force US intervention. Several days later, after receiving no response from Wilson, Fletcher submitted his resignation, only to be persuaded that he should remain and take a leading hand in readjusting US policy toward Mexico on a sounder footing.[3]

The Pershing Expedition failed in its original intent as Pancho Villa resupplied and formed an army of seven thousand strong to threaten the border. These bandits became emboldened to attack and pillage north of the Rio Grande. By mid-1919, the Wilson administration staged more than sixty thousand US troops, a squadron of airplanes, and a battalion of tanks (fresh from duty in France) along the border in the event of expanded hostilities. If the US Army had not responded in force in El Paso, Ciudad Juárez would have been recaptured by Villa and would have become a strategic rebel stronghold. In Wilson's absence, his cabinet, in addition to increasing military forces on the border, reinstated the arms embargo, and over the complaints of the Mexican government, the US Army again sanctioned "hot pursuit" of bandits south of the Rio Grande. Dozens of cases of Americans being killed or kidnapped went unsolved, contrary to Carranza's claims that all were safe. Carranza continued to have trouble controlling all of Mexico as rebel groups under Felix Díaz, the "Felicistas," organized to present an alternative to the waning authority of the Carranza government. The continued vacillation over oil rights and multiple taxation decrees from Mexico City led to heightened calls for an active US policy to alleviate an already volatile situation.[4]

In Washington during the immediate postwar period, the Wilson administration was preoccupied with the final treaty arrangements with the Allies and the implementation of the League of Nations. Thus, very little attention was given to the situation in Mexico. In this shifting geopolitical power structure, one significant outcome of the world war was that the United States would dominate Latin American affairs for years to come. The result marginalized the commercial and political influence of both the British and the Germans. Anti-American propaganda in Mexico, fomented by Carranza, who claimed to be a "worthy follower of Simón Bolivar," called on Latin America to snub all Americans. Mexico viewed its opinion of the United States and its hemispheric policies as the touchstone for the rest of Latin America to follow. In spite of the fact that he was unable to stabilize his own government in Mexico, Carranza encouraged Luis Cabrera to visit and extend overtures and assistance to Central American countries to reject US influence. The scheme hatched among the Constitutionalists was to

train, arm, and finance expeditions launched from Veracruz, Quintana
Roo, and British Honduras (now Belize). This plot was designed to simultaneously attack and overthrow the existing legal governments in Guatemala, Nicaragua, and Honduras (all of which were friendly with the United
States). Once in control, the plan was to establish a revolutionary leader as
president. Carranza arranged funding for the operation, known as the
Marazan Plan, with assistance and clandestine funding from Ambassador
Baron von Eckhardt and the German embassy in Mexico City. The principal agent of Carranza to create the new nation of Marazan was R. R. Villavicencio, the Mexican consul general in New Orleans, who negotiated the
final planning with Pedro Grave de Peralta, agent for the Central American revolutionary junta. The integral Central American plot never mate-
rialized. Such plans were encouraged by Carranza, Cabrera, and Obregón
and driven by boisterous anti-American rhetoric that helped divert
attention away from Mexico's deteriorating domestic front. In view of
Mexico's instability, American industrialists and policy makers in Washington concluded that a strong stance protecting their inalienable property rights and investments in Mexico would benefit future activities with
emerging business, industry, and investment opportunities in the wider
hemisphere.[5]

Will Buckley continued working with his oil company and land investments, and as counsel to the Buckley and Buckley firm, which was managed daily by his brothers. He remained an active defender of the Catholic
Church in Mexico, which by the fall of 1919 was on the record as being
against armed intervention. Additionally, he supported and helped fund a
number of associations formed to represent the interests of Americans in
Mexico. Key among these new organizations, which lobbied in both Washington and Mexico City, were the National Association for the Protection
of American Rights in Mexico (NAPARM), founded by Edward Doheny
in December 1918, and the Association of Foreign Oil Producers in Mexico. The common goals of these organizations included protecting the rights
of Americans, discrediting the Carranza administration, and, if necessary,
promoting the need for the United States to intervene in Mexico. As the
dissatisfaction with Carranza grew both in Mexico and America, counterrevolutionary political factions demanded a change. Weary of the decade-
long civil war, many in the country were ready for new leadership. Mindful

of the impact of the revolution, they also were focused on the return to a stable economy with law and order established nationwide.[6]

The backlash over the antibusiness interpretation of Article 27 of the Constitution of 1917 resulted in American (and British) oil companies making increased demands on Washington to protect their rights and investments in Mexico. Wilson's preoccupation with Europe allowed Mexico to slowly institute its new policies. Concerned with their impact, industry leader Edward Doheny donated $100,000 to establish a foundation of researchers to investigate and catalog their concerns. The Doheny fund contracted twenty university professors and subject-matter experts for a year-long study. These professionals were given offices at the University of California at Berkeley. The lead researcher was Robert Glass Cleland. The clear objective of this project was to counter the Carranza government and the antibusiness articles in the new Mexican constitution—and, if necessary, to create a propaganda machine to promote and justify US intervention. However, the research team was not inclined to endorse military intervention in Mexico. The main propaganda arm was NAPARM with a dozen paid journalists instructed to produce pamphlets, as well as distribute articles in nationwide publications. The board of NAPARM included not just representatives from the petroleum sector, but also active board members from mining, rubber, agriculture, and financial services. Dan La Botz noted that one of the association's public relations releases, titled "Bread—Bolshevism—Binder Twine," argued that the revolution in the Yucatán henequen plantations was forcing up the price of "binder twine" for American farmers. This was probably the only time in history that the "rising cost of string was used to justify a foreign war."[7]

A number of Republican senators were aware and were supportive of the association's goals, but none was more focused on the situation in Mexico than Senator Albert Fall. The New Mexico senator was no stranger to Mexico, having worked south of the border for nearly four decades in mining, industrial development, and ranching. Upon statehood in 1912 and subsequent to his serving in the first New Mexico legislature, Fall was elected as US senator in 1913. Concerned with the deteriorating conditions in Mexico, the rampant killings, and the degradation of the Catholic Church, Fall—a leading critic of the White House's "watchful waiting" policy—lay all the problems in Mexico at the feet of President Wilson. Fall criticized what he viewed as Wilson's inept and misguided policies. Furthermore, Fall had publicly harbored interventionist sentiments (influenced by Hearst, Doheny, and William C. Greene) since early 1913, and in late 1916, before the United States entered the war in Europe, Senator Fall wanted 500,000 troops to be organized and immediately staged on the US-Mexico border.[8]

Convening a congressional hearing in Washington, DC, proved to be an effective and public means of highlighting the problems in Mexico. The resulting media attention alone surfaced Wilson's failed polices and the unstable situation in Mexico. As a member of the Senate Foreign Relations Committee, Fall secured approval on August 8, 1919, to "investigate" the Mexican problems and violence toward Americans and their property. The "said committee shall further investigate and report to the Senate what if any, measures should be taken to prevent a recurrence of such outrages." The chairman of the Foreign Relations Committee, Senator Henry Cabot Lodge of Massachusetts, stressed that Fall was the best man to "put Mexico into a proper relationship with the US." A three-member subcommittee was formed, composed of Fall and Senators Frank B. Brandegee of Connecticut and Marcus Smith of Arizona. Formation of this subcommittee was the political fruition of months of effort by all of those with a vested stake in intervention and stability in Mexico. The former US assistant attorney general Francis J. Kearful served as committee clerk, with the staff of Dan Jackson, legal counsel; Henry O. Flipper, translator and interpreter; Senior Capt. W. M. Hanson of the Texas Rangers, chief investigator; Gus T. Jones of the Department of Justice; and Capt. George E. Hyde, US Army, of the War Department. Given the subcommittee's charge, there is little doubt that the Senate hearing from its inception was very partisan and was used to embarrass the Wilson administration's handling of Mexican affairs.[9]

Unlike today's more open-ended investigations, the Senate committee set forth a specific detailed process for the investigative work and the terms under which the special committee was empowered:

1. The relations, economic, political and military, of the Government of the United States with the republic of Mexico from the year 1910 until the date of the report to be made.

2. The conditions and incidents leading up to, concerned in, or responsible for such relations.

3. The economic, political, and physical treatment accorded to American and other foreign citizens in Mexico and elsewhere, as to their lives and properties in the Republic of Mexico, subsequent to 1910.

4. The extent to which the Government of the United States, through Ministerial assurances to foreign Governments or otherwise, has obligated the people of the United States for the collection, payment, or liquidation of public or private claims against the Government or people of the Republic of Mexico.

5. The policy and activity of the Government of the United States, in presenting and pressing claims of American citizens for loss of life and property by violence, confiscation, retroactive legislation, or government activity, in seeming violation of the norms of international law, since 1910, including measures taken and representations made to the Government of Mexico in efforts to forestall the inimical effects of such acts or measure of the Mexican Government.

6. The individual and factional responsibilities for robbery, maltreatment, and murder of American citizens in the republic of Mexico and on American territory contiguous thereto.

7. The special committee is empowered to meet anywhere in this country or in Mexico, and is authorized to summon any Cabinet officer, employees of Government departments, and of the Consular Service, and officers and men of the army and navy. Any person who "in any manner obstructs or hinders" the committee by refusal to attend or to produce records, or who makes "any disturbance" while the committee is sitting, may be arrested and brought before the Congress for contempt.[10]

Suite 420, Murray Hill Hotel

Will Buckley was a longtime friend and associate of Senator Fall. They shared views on the issues in Mexico and concerns about what they determined was a weak and problematic approach by Woodrow Wilson and the

State Department. For most of early 1919, Buckley and a vocal group was formed that included Edward L. Doheny, oil magnate; Msgr. Francis Kelley; William R. Hearst, publisher; George Carnahan, president of International Rubber Company; Charles Swain, Standard Oil executive; William C. Greene, mining impresario; and Henry Lane Wilson, former ambassador to Mexico. This group demanded that action be taken to address the increased antibusiness policies against Americans in Mexico, attacks on the Catholic Church, and (perhaps the largest issue), the treatment of the multimillion-dollar foreign-owned oil investments and property in Mexico that were routinely attacked by Carranza and the new Constitution of 1917.[11]

With more than a decade of personal experience in Mexico and experience participating in the dynamics of the revolution with various government and leaders, Buckley became the prime source of information and provided Senator Fall with a detailed "Outline of Topics to be brought out," for those who would testify before the committee. He also served as a liaison with interested business and Church organizations both in Mexico and the United States. In early July 1919, Buckley moved into Suite #420 of the Murray Hill Hotel in New York City. He brought with him his extensive collection of records, reports, and potential witness interviews regarding the Mexican situation. A staff of seven, "all Americans, who have lived in Mexico for a number of years," assisted in the compilation of "a mass of material on every phase of the Mexican situation." This material included economic conditions in Mexico, including the status of railroads, the status of henequen in Yucatán, and mining and oil data; and information regarding the Carranza government, such as its methods, outrages on American citizens, attacks on the Catholic Church, and confiscation of American property. A key component of Buckley's papers were his detailed records and profiles on key Mexicans and Americans. The files included dozens of detailed first-person reports on conditions in Mexico. New York City was chosen as a location due to the large number of exiled Mexican business leaders, politicians, and clergy living there. In addition, New York served as the headquarters for many of the leading American petroleum companies and financial institutions that maintained operations and investments in Mexico. An added benefit for Buckley was the proximity of the capital, only a two-hour train ride away.[12]

The variety of witnesses and scope of the Fall Committee was extensive. Over 300 witnesses were considered and vetted by Buckley's and the Senate staff, with over 250 summoned to testify. Investigating teams traveled thousands of miles nationwide and on confidential trips to Mexico, to secure documentary evidence and interview witnesses. Concerned with the political and public relations ramifications of the highly publicized hearings, Carranza forbade Mexicans to give testimony, and he refused to grant an entry visa to any American who gave testimony. However, some Mexican citizens residing in Mexico did testify in executive closed sessions to avoid reprisals by the Carranza government. The hearings began on September 8, 1919, in the Senate Office Building in Washington, with additional hearings held over an eight-month period in New York City, as well as Laredo, El Paso, and San Antonio, Texas; Nogales and Tucson, Arizona; and Los Angeles and San Diego, California. The witness testimonies fell into those for or against intervention, as well as a large group, with a vast and varied perspective, who were undecided on the best policy to pursue. Concern was expressed confidentially to Buckley by Felix Sommerfeld that possibly Ambassador Wilson should not be called to testify because he "would find it very hard to explain his conduct before, during and after the "*Cuartelazo*" (military coup). The ambassador did appear before the committee and provided compelling information. All who testified were vocal, sharing stories and observations on the course of events and the administration's response, or lack thereof, to what many viewed as a crisis in Mexico. Interventionist proponents received a surprising boost in October 1919.[13]

The Jenkins Affair

The safety of Americans was the centerpiece of concern regarding the unchecked violence and extortion in Mexico. As the Senate hearings proceeded, US-Mexico tensions were further strained by the kidnapping of US Consular Agent William O. Jenkins in Puebla on October 19, 1919.[14] The incident became very complicated, controversial, and a main cause of the diplomatic impasse between the two nations. Jenkins, a popular rancher and wealthy textile manufacturer, also served as the credentialed US consul. During 1919, splinter rebel groups in Mexico led by former and current military officers hoped to take advantage of the seemingly weak

Carranza government by creating a provocation that could result in intervention by the United States. The scope of their actions suggested a high level of planning and organization. One such action was reportedly encouraged by Manuel Peláez in Tampico, who advised local jefe Federico Córdoba in Puebla to strengthen his rebel faction by kidnapping prominent officials. Interviewed in early December 1919, Córdoba confirmed that his rebels attacked Jenkins's office, emptied the safe of an estimated 50,000 Mexican pesos in gold, and took the consul captive. The kidnappers left word with Jenkins's wife that the kidnapping was not an act of banditry but certain proof that "my [Córdoba's] objective was to prove that Carranza is incapable of furnishing guarantees either to natives or foreigners." Trying to remain low-key and avoid undue attention, the US State Department cabled Chargé d'affaires George Summerlin in Mexico City to "take effective steps to obtain his release unharmed." This understated approach failed and quickly resulted in a major diplomatic impasse.[15]

Inquiries by friends and embassy officials in Mexico City of the local government in Puebla were referred to the capital. Rebels demanded a ransom of 300,000 pesos, but the Mexican government refused to deal with them. Throughout 1919, and long before the Jenkins kidnapping occurred, there was an ongoing concern that Americans and their property were continually subject to attack largely because Carranza refused to negotiate and did not have the authority or backing to govern effectively. Furthermore, evidence surfaced exposing the extent of the pro-German sympathy that had existed during the war, which further strained diplomatic relations. Before adequate information could be gathered for a response by the US Embassy to these events, Senator Henry L. Myers of Montana hastily introduced a resolution on the Senate floor demanding immediate action and urging the president to "use all the armed forces and power of the United States" to "recover Jenkins alive or his abductors dead." The Fall Committee hearings were temporarily recessed as officials in Washington grappled with a response to this new crisis in Mexico.[16]

While his captors reported he was safe, rumors planted in Mexican newspapers alleged that Jenkins had collaborated with Córdoba and the rebels to stage a fake "self-kidnapping" incident. A small portion of the ransom demanded at the end of October was arranged. The partial ransom was paid with funds collected by Jenkins's friends, and he was released after two weeks living in a remote cave, sick and weakened, yet alive. Jenkins returned to Puebla and was hospitalized for shock and exposure. Senator Myers withdrew his motion, and the diplomatic incident seemingly ended. However, the political implications of the rumored staged abduction heightened tensions as the governor of Puebla, Alfonso Cabrera (brother of Luis), demanded an inquiry. Orders to arrest Jenkins coincided with Cabrera making anti-American statements against the American Embassy and the United States. Jenkins vehemently denied all allegations. After a week recovering in the Puebla hospital, Jenkins was arrested on charges that he actively assisted in his kidnapping in exchange for a scheme to pay an additional ransom of $150,000 for rebel arms and ammunition. Secretary of State Robert Lansing was well versed in the Mexico situation and demanded the case be closed at once. Yet Mexico responded, erroneously, that consular agents were not subject to diplomatic immunity—which, in fact, they generally were. There is no known documented connection between Jenkins and Buckley, but given the small community of expatriates, it is reasonable to assume they knew each other.[17]

With President Wilson preoccupied with Paris and unavailable, Lansing made policy changes without consulting Wilson. At the strong urging of Lansing, Ambassador Fletcher considered severing all diplomatic relations with Mexico. By late November, communications became increasingly heated, bordering on a call for intervention, with such headlines in the *New York American* as "Intervention Certain If Carranza Fails to Release Jenkins." At this point, it was recommended that the ABC powers once again step in to mediate. Historian Charles Cumberland noted of the perilous situation, "National pride, political exigencies, and a deep animosity toward the policy of the United States demanded that Carranza refuse to bow to the demands made by the state department." Sentiment in favor of intervention gained a sudden boost.[18]

The Jenkins affair hit at a bad time for the State Department, which, at the urging of the American drillers, was in the middle of sensitive land-ownership talks with Mexico City officials about oil rights and Article 27. The recalcitrant US Congress (dominated by Republicans) was testy. Senator Lodge, chairman of the Foreign Relations Committee, orchestrated increased pressure on all the administration's foreign policy actions. Concerned with the possibility of additional damaging incidents, Secretary Lansing wrote a letter on November 18, 1919, to Buckley and a dozen American-owned oil companies with investments in Mexico urging them

not to take drastic action in response to threats of confiscation and informing them he was working to protect their vested rights and toward a settlement of the petroleum question.[19]

At White House presidential cabinet meetings on November 18, 25, and
26 (which Wilson was unable to attend due to his massive stroke), Mexican oil and Jenkins were the primary topics, yet no consensus or best course
of action was decided. Reports surfaced that the relations between the two
countries were "more strained today than at any time since the overthrow
of Porfirio Díaz." Mexico responded that Washington's actions were "inexplicable." Additional pressure came from Great Britain when it was confirmed that British consul William Hardaker in Puebla was also targeted
for kidnapping, but was in Mexico City when Jenkins was taken. All indications pointed to there being a major plan in the works. Others targeted
for high-profile kidnapping included the American consul in Guadalajara,
the Spanish consul in Puebla, and the US chargé d'affaires in Mexico City.
Summerlin was followed for ten days by rebel Bernardo Reyes, who failed
"to grab" him.[20] On November 28, following a very heated meeting between
Lansing and the Mexican ambassador, Ignacio Bonillas, who said he
had been "severely talked to and grossly insulted," President Wilson at last
became directly involved. However, further complicating the situation,
beginning in early October the president had suffered another paralyzing
stroke triggered by the exhausting trip across the country campaigning to
save the Versailles Treaty.[21] After attempting to sell the accord to "the
people" prior to a vote in the US Senate, Wilson remained bedridden in
the White House for weeks as his health rapidly failed. Senator Fall, in El
Paso holding a committee hearing, was recalled to Washington in antici-
pation of pending action on the Jenkins case. The State Department, the
oil industry, and many in the Senate pushed for action and possible intervention, while Wilson continued both physically and politically debilitated
over the failure of his campaign for the League of Nations. In advance of
any abrupt action in the Senate, Senator Lodge encouraged a meeting with
the president. Senator Fall visited the White House on December 5 for a
meeting held in the second-floor bedroom attended by the president's wife,
Edith; his private physician, Dr. Cary Grayson; and his private secretary,
Joseph Tumulty. The president appeared to be alert and vigorous while
briefed on the situation in Mexico. He emphasized he would not approve
any intervention. Wilson's abrupt statement, coupled with the release of

Jenkins from jail in Puebla on the same day as the White House meeting, momentarily calmed the rush to intervene. Tumulty, the day prior to the Wilson-Fall meeting, bluntly told Lansing, "If there is war, let the Reps [Republicans] do it!" And thus, there was no war with Mexico.[22]

In early December, Buckley traveled to Washington to brief the Senate staff on possible witnesses and to prepare for his committee presentation. Additionally, he met at length with Senator Fall on the ramifications of the White House meeting with the president, and with other Republican senators regarding any further action related to the Jenkins affair. The Buckley files compiled in New York City contain an extensive amount of background reports, interviews, and back-channel investigations in Mexico by his private agents. Prior to departing Murray Hill, his staff packed his final reports and notes into a detailed briefing file, known as the Shoreham Papers, named for the Washington hotel Buckley stayed in. The extensive material covered the background of Jenkins's kidnapping and the reaction of American and Mexican authorities to the affair as well as options to assist the State Department in addressing the volatile incident. Buckley's primary operative, known only as "No. 16," and other assistants were aggressive in compiling the facts, biographical profiles on key potential witnesses, and notes on political dynamics surrounding the Jenkins kidnapping and subsequent imprisonment. As Buckley worked with Secretary Lansing at the State Department, who received reports from the staff at the US Embassy, tensions mounted between those who wanted immediate intervention and a second group, backed by the president, that wanted a more studied but swift peaceful solution. At no time during this crisis did Buckley advocate intervention. Yet he directed attention to his old friend Luis Cabrera, whom he described to the senators as blatantly anti-American. Buckley, realizing there were those in the opposition who were totally disingenuous, stressed, "Again the old *Científico* ghost has been dragged in," adding that Cabrera's activities and comments to the press outside of diplomatic channels "were entirely gratuitous."[23]

By late 1919, Buckley had changed the hard-line position presented in his long letter to Colonel House in November 1913. Prior to the landing of troops at Veracruz, he revised his strong stance that insisted armed intervention by the United States should be avoided. Such armed intervention had not worked at Veracruz, nor had the Pershing Expedition in northern Mexico. He believed that any efforts to enter Mexico by force would only inflame the already tenuous relations and accomplish nothing but to extend conflict for years. Buckley publicly testified to the Fall Committee on December 6, only hours after the Wilson-Fall meeting at the White House, outlining this nonconfrontational view. Buckley not only provided the most detailed remarks and overview of the current situation in Mexico but also supplied the committee with an extensive political and historical perspective of US-Mexico relations that few had ever heard. Much of his new position for avoiding intervention was based on a century of Mexico's failed efforts to stabilize the country due to repeated foreign incursions in the nation's political and economic sphere. Clearly his views ran in opposition to those of his friend Senator Fall, many in the interventionist oil lobby, and dozens of companies Buckley and Buckley represented in Mexico and New York City.[24]

More concerning at the time of Buckley's testimony on Capitol Hill was that the US government and Mexican officials had not resolved the Jenkins affair. An escalation of misinformation and media coverage or an additional incident (e.g., the sudden death of Jenkins) was feared in both countries, which might precipitate a call for military intervention. One indication of the fragile situation—a handwritten confidential memo drafted by agent "No. 16"—is found in the Buckley Papers, but not in the State Department foreign relations files. After "politely declining to officially discuss the Jenkins case," Emiliano Lopez Figueroa observed that:

> all the newspapers in town were full of stories about intervention, the possibility of U.S. withdrawing their recognition from President Carranza etc, etc. This situation was rather delicate and extremely dangerous for Mexico. He even intimated that personally he didn't care what could happen to Pres. Carranza but that he was very anxious to try to help Mexico in avoiding what he considered would be a disaster for Mexico. He explained there was one way out of the "hole" & that was to have *somebody, it did not matter whom*, bail Jenkins out.[25]

Lansing and Fletcher realized the controversy should be defused and advised Fall to delay any swift response, such as a concurrent resolution mandating some level of action, in the Senate. Numerous cables continued to be exchanged until mid-December when the Carranza government decided to move the Jenkins case out of Puebla to the Federal Supreme

Court in Mexico City.[26] Jenkins was freed on bail (paid by an anonymous source), which, according to the *New York Times*, was arranged by Luis Cabrera. This was apparently done with the full intention of defusing the situation and having the charges modified from conspiracy to perjury. Historian and Jenkins biographer Andrew Paxman notes, "Jenkins was livid to learn that his freedom did not signal a removal of all charges." Furthermore, Jenkins stated in an interview with the *New York World*, "I wish to deny vigorously the local insinuation that my alleged action was to promote intervention. I do not favor intervention. For one reason, it would damage my business."[27] The Mexican courts allowed the case to languish, and formalities were carried out to cancel Jenkins's official diplomatic credentials. Further resolution was complicated by the dysfunction of the Mexican court system, which was poorly funded and understaffed. Outcomes were often the result of fraud, as the *New York Times* reported: "It is very possible to secure the most illegal action if you are willing to pay the price."[28] Concerned that the release of Jenkins was "fixed," the Fall Senate subcommittee explored the possibility of subpoenas for Mexicans involved with the case. The Wilson administration was satisfied with the release of Jenkins and did not want to pursue the case further. Jenkins was fully exonerated by a Mexican court in December 1920. However, the full story may never be known. At the time of the kidnapping, Jenkins was a multimillionaire; thus, his participating in a "self-kidnapping" scheme seemed both unlikely and very dangerous. Gerald Brandon, a reporter for the *Los Angeles Times*, was one of the few in 1919 to interview the attorneys and judge in Puebla and obtain access to court records. He concluded, "The supporting proof that figures in the testimony that has been compiled against Jenkins have [*sic*] proven unworthy of credit."[29]

The embarrassing inability of Mexican officials to protect key diplomats and citizens was a convenient means used against his opponents by the deeply unpopular Governor Cabrera. While a ransom was never paid to Mexican authorities, and Jenkins also never recouped his loss in a complaint for $285,000 filed with the bilateral American-Mexican Claims Com-

investments. In contrast, the president was convinced, after having already intervened twice in Mexico to no avail, that further intervention should not and would not happen.[30]

With the Jenkins affair under control and the president clearly on the record that he would not endorse any further intervention consideration, the Fall Committee continued its deliberations into early January 1920. In his testimony, Buckley provided a number of options and a detailed review of the negative impact of a possible US intervention. Following his letter to Colonel House, Will tempered his interventionist stance. The issues that would preoccupy the hearings would include the safety of Americans in Mexico (more than a dozen were killed or abducted in January alone with no recourse), the continued concern with foreign investment rights, and new political undercurrents in Mexico regarding Carranza's reaction to the transition of presidential power.[31]

Areas controlled by various factions in Mexico, August 1919.
Source: US Army War College.

Undercover

The public revelations and graphic stories of witnesses before the Fall Committee, along with the confused Jenkins affair, greatly rattled Mexican officials in the Carranza administration as well as diplomats in both Mexico City and Washington, DC. Increasingly concerned that these events would be used to justify intervention, Mexican operatives conspired to aggressively attack and discredit all involved with the Fall Committee, especially the Association of Foreign Oil Producers and NAPARM. Buckley and his group of investigators and agents did the majority of the screening for the Fall hearings. No limits or restrictions were imposed on the collection of information, including over whom they spoke to, either as background subjects or as potential presenters before the committee. A key concern was whether former ambassador Henry Wilson should testify. Will Buckley's confidential files contain a briefing paper from a most unlikely source, Felix Sommerfeld, a double agent loyal to the German cause dating from the Madero presidency who possessed an interesting perspective on the ambassador's potential appearance. Operative "No. 16," whose identity remains unknown to this day, provided Buckley and Fall with the following note after interviewing Sommerfeld, who was still in the employ of the German government, at Murray Hill Hotel in New York City:

From: No. 16
Date: January 19, 1920
Subject: Henry Lane Wilson
Source: F. Sommerfeld

Sommerfeld claims that it would be unwise for the Committee to have Ambassador Wilson testify. He thinks the Ambassador played too much politics and if cross examined many things would come to light which would implicate him. (S. refers to Wilson's participation in the "Convencion de la Embajada," Madero's murder, etc.)

for his articles in *Harper's Weekly*, entitled "The Two Wilsons and Huerta."

S. also claims that H. L. Wilson would find it very hard to explain his conduct before, during and after the "Cuartelazo." it seems March 2d and 3d, 1913, he sent a telegram to the American consul at Saltillo saying some thing to this effect: "Call on Governor Carranza and tell him that he is in open rebellion against a legally constituted government strongly intrenched on the confidence of the people. Tell him that his (Carranza's) downfall is inevitable. Put this matter strongly to him and as a solemn warning. (Signed) Wilson."

It also seems that American Consulates in Mexico received a circular from the Embassy saying: "All foreign governments have recognized Huerta and the U.S. government will do so in a few days."

One of these was pasted on the door of the American Consulate at Monterrey and signed by Consul General Hanna.

It also seems that some Senators (Democrats) would be interested in seeing Wilson testify and possibly have a chance to bring charges against his testimony before the Committee. This they might be able to use for political purposes to discredit the work of the Committee.[32]

Sommerfeld failed to mention the Mexican efforts to target the Fall hearings—in particular, the principal leaders: Fall, Hanson, and Buckley. Knowledge of these plans and activities was discovered by undercover US federal agents. The primary agent was a newspaperman, Charles E. Jones, who served as an operative for the US Justice Department's Bureau of Investigation in late fall 1919. His efforts to penetrate a network of Mexican agents and diplomats in New York City, Washington, DC, and along the border uncovered numerous plots and indications of plans, if necessary, to assassinate Fall, Hanson, or Buckley.[33]

Jones had extensive experience working undercover operations in Central America, Mexico, and along the US-Mexico border. He tracked the activities of German spies and rebel propagandists, sending detailed reports directly to bureau chief A. Bruce Bielaski. Jones, whose code name was Cresse, was used to counter "innumerable leaks which went directly back to various Mexican factions." Jones, whose cover was as a newsman with the *Los Angeles Times*, was brought to the attention of Mexican operatives looking to hire someone to craft their message for the American public, aimed at "disgracing all the principal [anti-Mexican] parties implicated, and likewise create sympathy for the Mexican [Carranza] government." Jones was approached by attorney Adam Leckie, an American lawyer in Washington, DC, who in 1917 joined the Mexico City firm of González Roa (a close adviser to Carranza), Carbajal, and Leckie, to work for the Carranza government as its "publicity director." Jones, known for his extensive contacts in Mexico, was offered a salary of $20,000 per month. However, the primary aim of Jones's employment was to gain access to and purchase the treasure trove of counterrevolutionary documentation and sources of information from the Fall Committee that he collected and held. Sight unseen, Mexican agents offered $40,000 for the documents. Jones informed the bureau of the offer, and Chief Bielaski quickly determined that the documents could be used in negotiations as "bait" to penetrate the Mexican clandestine operations in the United States. He ordered Jones "under no circumstances allow the Mexican government to get hold of the papers and documents pertaining to the activities of their revolutionary enemies in the United States or elsewhere." Thus, Jones was to maintain the Mexicans' interest and collect more intelligence on planned activities, including the names and locations of key individuals involved.[34]

In time, Jones would penetrate a web of agents and diplomats ready to employ whatever means possible to protect Carranza and maintain formal diplomatic recognition by the United States. Simultaneously in the fall of 1919 and early 1920, a new wave of disgruntled counterrevolutionary groups was plotting to replace Carranza and his corrupt government. The chief Mexican government coordinator of Carranza's supporters in the United States was Ramón P. de Negri, consul general in New York City. Mexican ambassador Bonillas assigned Negri as the primary contact to avoid any political or diplomatic conflict. Bonillas was "tapped" by Carranza to become the next president of Mexico. Leckie sent a confidential letter to Bonillas confirming Jones's background and retainer. Thus, Negri managed an extensive web of agents and safehouses to acquire information and deliver money to drop sites on the East Coast and along the US-Mexico border.[35]

counterrevolutionary groups. By Christmas of 1919, no less than a dozen rebel groups were engaged in planning and fundraising. The most prominent opposition included Gen. Salvador Alvarado, governor of Yucatán, Gen. Luis Caballero in Tamaulipas, P. Elias Calles from Sonora, and Gen. Esteban Cantú in Baja California. However, the two individuals who were best positioned to challenge Carranza were Adolfo de la Huerta and the government's minister of war and marine, Gen. Alvaro Obregón. Both were fully aware of the splinter rebel groups and their ambitions and mixed allegiance to Carranza. The field was filled with prospective candidates who did not share Carranza's desire to handpick, or "tap," a successor. Confirming the uncertainty, Alvarado, who himself was secretly developing plans to become the next president, bluntly told Charles Jones, "It will make absolutely no difference at all whether Obregón starts a revolutionary

William Frank Buckley's photo in his 1918 US passport,
signed by Robert Lansing, secretary of state during the
Wilson administration, 1915–1920. Buckley Family Collection.

movement [to become president] or not. If he don't [*sic*], Calles will, de la Huerta will, or I will."[36]

On the eve of Buckley's testimony in Washington, undercover agent Jones was called to meet Consul Negri (noting that all future payments to Jones would be in cash so there would be no records) and was further instructed to "wait until plans are fully executed; and when they are the people of the United States will know that Mexico and Mexicans are not fools." Operatives from a safehouse at the Bender Hotel in Laredo, Texas, departed for Washington with a sealed letter of instructions. The messenger arrived at the consulate, complained about the anti-Mexican attitude of the American Association of Mexico and the Fall Committee, and said, "Fall and Hanson are going to get theirs very soon." A Mexican agent named Seguin bragged, "We have a man who has plenty of guts and who at the proper time will put Hanson and Fall out of the way." Jones notified the bureau of the plans to "bump off Fall and Hanson." Political assassination was all too common during the Mexican Revolution. For example, foul play was suspected in the death of former US Embassy employee Luis d'Antin, who, after leaving Mexico, was working for the Mexican embassy in Washington; when dispatched to Mexico City, he mysteriously "died" en route.[37] Captain Hanson was informed by Jones of the threat and contacted the Washington superintendent of police and US Capitol security, who assigned bodyguards to Senator Fall. Shortly after Fall was informed, "two young Mexicans were seen trying to enter the senator's hotel room," but were scared away and not apprehended.[38]

Ranger Hanson, in San Antonio to interview witnesses for the committee, telephoned agent Cresse, who was traveling to Laredo to check the source of the threats and could be found there at the Hamilton Hotel. On the evening of December 5, Hanson talked with Buckley at the Shoreham Hotel. Buckley, who was preparing for this appearance before the committee the next morning, warned Hanson of the plot that he had gotten wind of. Jones, still in New York City, was immediately called to Washington to meet with Ambassador Bonillas. He was handed $75 in cash and booked

given the news that Senator Fall planned to introduce a resolution in Congress demanding the withdrawal of recognition and urging intervention. Jones quickly learned that Senator Fall was the primary target of a hostile plot. The ambassador was disheveled and very nervous; as Jones recalled, "He trembled as though he had palsy. His customary poker face was lined deeply, and his mouth twitched." The ambassador asked Jones who his high-level contacts were in Washington and if he could get to members of the Foreign Relations Committee to stop Fall. Bonillas wanted Jones to use influence (which he did not have) and said, "Something must be done to discredit Fall." He was prepared to pay him $75,000 to actively "assault" (i.e., harass, not assassinate) the Fall Committee and the senator. If possible, the ambassador concluded, we have to get a message of concern to the president, who had changed his close advisers. A new clique close to Wilson included Bernard Baruch and Attorney General A. Mitchell Palmer. The ambassador told Jones that both Colonel House and Secretary of State Lansing (hard-liners against the ongoing chaos in Mexico) "had lost their influence with President Wilson, which was a most fortunate thing as far as Mexican affairs were concerned."[39]

Bonillas and Negri were not aware of Fall's meeting with the president on December 5, which resulted in Wilson declaring there would be no intervention. Continued recognition of Carranza was not discussed at the White House, but it was implied. The ambassador was informed by the State Department of the president's rebuff of Senators Fall and Lodge. Any attempt to assassinate Fall failed (or was abandoned). The attempt on Fall and Hanson was real, as Jones and Hanson confirmed. A paid assassin in the employ of the Mexican consul in New York City, Javier Favela, stalked both men in Washington and on trips to San Antonio and Los Angeles without success. Senator Fall withdrew his pending resolutions against Mexico. Buckley testified for more than three hours on December 6 outlining historical details of the Mexican situation, providing profiles of the key leaders, and giving a candid assessment of how the revolution had impacted Americans living in the country as well as answering extensive questions on options to consider to calm the violence south of the border. The Bureau of Investigation, not wanting to disclose the source of the intelligence it provided, urged Senator Fall, Will Buckley, and Captain Hanson to say nothing of Jones's activities, contacts, and warnings.[40]

In the wake of the events of December 1919, Consul Negri departed or was fired from his job and threw his efforts behind General Obregón. Quite possibly, Negri could have been influenced by Charles Jones ("Cresse"), who prepared a top secret report on "the next Mexican presidential elections" for the US Justice Department, correctly forecasting the future:

I am convinced of the fact from the constant observation I have had the opportunity to make during the last year that Obregón will win in next Mexican presidential elections. Feel sure of the fact that one way or the other Obregón, irrespective of any difficulties that may be placed in his way, will succeed Carranza. Furthermore, if Carranza resigns, or is forced out, or is assassinated before the next Mexican election, Obregón will immediately start the fight to succeed him."[41]

The Fall hearings, which had begun on September 9, 1919, ended on May 20, 1920, with chief committee investigator and Texas Ranger Capt. W. M. Hanson as the final witness. Within a week, the committee issued a detailed report to the Senate with three key suggestions: first, postpone the recognition of the Mexican president until evidence was given of the stability of the nation; second, authorities in Mexico needed to make it clear to the United States that the government would vigilantly safeguard the welfare of all Americans in Mexico; and last, demand that Mexico do everything possible to protect both lives and property. Clear warnings were outlined to protect all religious orders in Mexico. Recommendations included that Articles 3 and 130 of the Constitution of 1917 would not apply to American missionaries, preachers, and teachers, and that Article 27 would not apply to Church properties owned by Americans.

Furthermore, American citizens, under Article 33, would not be expelled until after due judicial proceedings. To address claims of outrage and damage to life and property, a joint American-Mexican Claims Commission should be established and its findings should be binding. The looming cri-

Revolution Weary

The pressure on the Carranza government brought by the Fall congressional hearings and the Jenkins affair was only compounded by growing discontent in Mexico, from the foreign oil companies, predictably, but also on the part of the people of Mexico themselves, who were weary after a decade of civil war. Thousands of Mexicans from the interior crossed into the United States to escape the revolution and avoid being "forced at the point of guns into Carranza's armies." As Alvarado concluded, "Mexico is not even safe for the Mexicans." As Carranza issued more decrees to tax, to suspend drilling permits, and to disrupt the petroleum industry, the oil companies refused to comply to register (or reregister) their properties with the government. Behind the scenes in Mexico City, Doheny and agents of the Association of Foreign Oil Producers in Mexico lobbied the legislature to curtail any actions that would nationalize or place strict controls on the industry or levy undue taxes. Despite constantly threatening to impose new petroleum regulations, in the end the Mexican Congress delayed all action to avoid a conflict with the United States. Mollified but not satisfied, the oil lobby wanted the Carranza government overthrown and the Constitution of 1917 revoked or amended to remove the harsh intentions of Article 27.[42]

In November 1919, Constitutionalist soldiers began to forcibly stop foreign oil companies from drilling due to lack of approved permits. These actions were seen as bad faith, so talks between the Mexican government and oil representatives were suspended. Buckley contacted Secretary Lansing to warn that any abrupt action could trigger a major disruption of critical oil exports from Tampico. Concerned to avert a major crisis, Lansing convened a conference of the major oil companies at the State Department in early January. Buckley, as a small independent producer, was not invited. Most who were invited were, unlike Buckley, absentee owners who demanded immediate action to protect their massive investments. They supported the sending of US warships to the Gulf of Mexico and more troops to the southern border. Lansing reconfirmed, over their boisterous demands, that President Wilson would not approve any military intervention or break in diplomatic relations. In the meantime, the Republican-controlled Senate—disgruntled with White House policy—succeeded in blocking the confirmation of Wilson's nominee, Hans Morgenthau, as the new ambassador to Mexico. Once again, the two

countries were faced with a crisis without senior US diplomatic representation in Mexico City.[43]

In the post–World War I geopolitical structure, the major Allied nations
soon realized that military and naval power and economic welfare increasingly were predicated on access to plentiful supplies of petroleum. The
steady supply of oil was critical for both industry and the maintenance of
large navies. Two unrelated events brought focus to the matter of who controlled access to Mexico's oil reserves. First, in January 1920 the US Bureau
of Mines released a detailed report addressed to the Army, Navy, and Shipping Board that concluded that, in addition to petroleum reserves in the
continental United States, "the United States needs and must have large
quantities of fuel oil for tankers and boiler purposes, and oil of this character
can most economically be supplied from Mexican crude. It is the duty of the
Government to protect that ownership as a matter of national welfare."
The second item was that American ally Great Britain (due to inroads in the
Middle East) and the British Admiralty had declared as a primary goal to
control the world's petroleum reserves and to "do what we like" to enhance
the British Empire's influence in all parts of the globe. Doheny, the largest
owner of foreign petroleum operations in Mexico, and small producers such
as Buckley used these two events to pressure the State Department and
Navy Department to dispatch additional destroyers off the coast at Tampico
and Veracruz, thereby sending a clear signal to both Mexico and the British
that the United States stood ready to protect its investments.[44]

By the spring of 1920, tensions among the rebelling factions resulted in
a split between Carranza and Sonoran general Alvaro Obregón, who, in
Mexican revolutionary fashion, endorsed an antigovernment declaration—
the Plan of Agua Prieta—which called for the removal of Carranza and the
appointment of a provisional president until an election could be held. Concerned with the upheaval in Mexico, Buckley wrote a lengthy memo to
Secretary of State Bainbridge Colby on the "Mexican Situation." He urged
extreme caution, reminding the secretary that "in the past he [Obregón]
has been intensely anti-American."[45]

in Mexico were expressed in a confidential letter to Judge Ireland Graves in Austin:

> I think we are near the end of our troubles in Mexico. None of us are falling for this pro-American propaganda of Obregón's, but we are all wishing him all manner of success in driving out Carranza. I doubt if Obregón will attain the presidency or if he does if he will remain there for any length of time. He has not the same qualities as Carranza; he is impetuous and not the type of nonentity that will be tolerated by strong generals as was the case with Carranza. I believe we are on the verge of a series of revolutions and counter-revolutions, and that Pablo González, Diéguez, Aguilar and Obregón will all aspire to the presidency and be entirely willing to fight for it. From this general situation there will come the chance of the cientificos or decent people, or intervention.[46]

The country was in chaos, and as historian Enrique Krauze has written, "much of the new political class was treating public office like private property." Still, Obregón, with his strong political and military support in northern Mexico, attempted to gain full control. The governor of Sonora, Adolfo de la Huerta, was allowed to become supreme chief of the army in the transitional government. The First Chief moved away from working with Obregón and selected an unknown, Ignacio Bonillas, as his choice for the next president. Carranza soon found himself powerless. Threats and rumors spread panic and chaos across Mexico City in late April 1920. Trying to consolidate his political power, he was determined to move his government to Veracruz, under the command of his loyal son-in-law Gen. Cándido Aguilar. The lumbering train departed Mexico City, stopping briefly in Guadalupe Hidalgo, where an observer noted, "I saw Carranza's patriarchal figure on the rear of the presidential car, leaning over the gilded grill-work, grandiloquently flinging coins to scrambling Indians." He departed the capital by train with about four thousand troops that he presumed loyal, and some $4 million in gold from the national treasury. His force quickly began to dwindle to a few hundred supporters and finally stalled near the Gulf Coast to camp in the small village of Tlaxcalantongo. On the night of May 21, 1920 (the day after the close of the Fall Committee hearings), Carranza and a number of his bodyguards were ambushed and killed. Rumors of who ordered the murders continue to this day. Obregón claimed he had offered to ensure the old president's life if he would halt his actions and admit the "cause" was lost. Attempting to avoid a potential transformation of Carranza's death into martyrdom, Obregón ordered Gen. Lázaro Cárdenas (a future president) to investigate the possibility that Carranza committed suicide. Some research suggests that Gen. Manuel Peláez, with possible support from oil interests, was behind the assassination. The subject soon evaporated as Obregón endorsed support for Adolfo de la Huerta as interim president and Sonoran general Plutarco Elías Calles for secretary of war. Interestingly, Luis Cabrera, the chief architect of many of the Constitutionalists' programs, propaganda, and policies, was in the village the night of the attack, but owing to his chameleon-like loyalties he escaped injury. To complete the transition to power, a presidential election was set for September 5, 1920, with Obregón's ascension to the presidency scheduled for December.[47]

Obregón the Usurper

In the spring of 1920, William Buckley returned to Mexico after nearly five months in New York and Washington assisting the Fall Committee. Brothers Edmond and Claude, together with Cecilio Velasco, had managed the family's business interests in Mexico during his absence. They were pleased to report that Pantepec's Well No. 2 in Chinampa was a success. However, returning to the chaotic environment in Tampico, Will, no supporter of Carranza, like many investors with large interests in Mexico, was faced with yet another radical change of government that was no improvement from the previous administration. Obregón, Calles, and de la Huerta (known as "the Sonoran triangle") were fully aware of the existing conflict with the petroleum industry and indicated that they sought an accommodation to reduce tensions. A strong suggestion floated among bankers and oil executives to avoid the threat of confiscation was the creation of a "finan-

leaders in the oil industry wanted immediate action. Secretary of the Navy Josephus Daniels recorded in his diary, "Doheny wishes intervention & speaks of adding 28 stars to our flag by adding Mexico."[48]

Doheny continued to pressure the US government for action, starting his own privately funded campaign to support counterrevolutionary factions against the government of President Obregón. There could be no US recognition of Obregón without protection for foreign oil interests in Mexico. Buckley was an increasingly hard-line advocate for reform and order in Mexico. In a confidential letter to Senator Fall, Will concluded, "Obregón is extremely ambitious and aspires to be the second Porfirio Díaz of Mexico, he has little respect for law, and is as anti-American as ever." Since returning from Washington, Buckley abandoned his discreet noninvolvement stance in Mexican politics after receiving reports that Obregón referred to the Catholic Church as a "cancerous tumor." Thus, he determined his primary objective was to prevent formal US recognition of Obregón. Much like the Constitutionalists' propaganda attacks to influence President Wilson against Huerta after the death of Madero, Buckley hoped to use the cold-blooded assassination of Carranza against Obregón. A year after the death of the First Chief, Buckley notified Ranger Hanson: "I was talking to General [Francisco] Murguia yesterday and he told me that Basave y Pina, who, you remember, sent a statement to the Supreme Court of Mexico in which he stated that he had transmitted the orders to kill Carranza from Obregón to [Rodolfo] Herrero, who was in Guatemala. It has occurred to me to have him come to New York from Guatemala to do some interesting articles for the *New York Times*. I believe this would be very beneficial in our work against recognition."[49]

It is not known if any one incident influenced Buckley to become an active partisan, as he abandoned his historically staunch position of political neutrality in Mexican politics. This change, which seemed to expose a festering resentment in the wake of the attacks on the Catholic Church, would have a lasting impact. The initial planning for a counterrevolution—to be led by the anti-Obregónista Col. Esteban Cantú, former governor of Baja California—foundered for months until early 1921. At that time, Buckley became directly involved with Doheny by enlisting the support of old friend and Tampico strongman Gen. Manuel Peláez to support Cantú. The loyalties of the counterrevolutionaries were quite mixed. Peláez feared he might be implicated in any attempted coup, and he quickly returned to

Mexico City to inform Obregón that Doheny and William Greene were secretly cooperating to engineer a counterrevolution. Concerned with the fledgling rebel groups launching new attacks from the United States, Washington assigned federal agents from the US Department of Justice to monitor a number of Mexican generals, as insurgent plans were rumored to be formulated in Laredo, San Antonio, Los Angeles, and New Orleans. Buckley was also followed by bureau agents. Federal agents compiled reports that were sent to headquarters in Washington with confidential copies to Senator Fall. As a participant in the schemes, Senator Fall in turn kept Doheny, Swain, Hearst, and Greene informed. Buckley's high-profile propaganda organization, the American Association of Mexico (AAM), along with the Association of Foreign Oil Producers in Mexico were very clear in their mission to confront the government of Mexico with demands to reduce taxes, preserve property rights, and repeal Article 27 of the Constitution of 1917. Buckley's activities in early 1921 can be traced back to the research activities, political contacts, and secret planning meetings at the Murray Hill Hotel in lower Manhattan. These associations did not constitute a cover operation but instead represented a fully organized and vocal extension of the public lobbying efforts, as published in the AAM *Bulletin*, made during the Fall Committee hearings and continuing in late 1920 and into 1921.[50]

Many of the federal agent reports can be found in the Fall documents at the Huntington Library in San Marino, California. The agents' goals were to track any new counterrevolutionary movements and related funding activities being organized north of the US-Mexico border in violation of US neutrality laws. There remained little doubt of Buckley's active role. The Bureau of Investigation's report, filed by Agent Kosterlitzky from the Los Angeles office, on August 12, 1921, noted that Will, on behalf of Doheny, "offered CANTU the sum of $50,000, with which to start immediately an attack on Mexicali, Lower California, and if successful, and once the town is in the possession of CANTU and his followers, inside of 48 hours BUCKLEY was to place at the disposal of CANTU $200,000, and negotiate at the same time recognition of belligerency for CANTU's party."[51]

against the Texas Legislature. Such resolutions were routinely sent to the Harding administration in Washington endorsing the recognition of Obregón. "As a result, the Texas State government is looked upon by Americans in Mexico as one of the several propaganda agencies in the United States of the Mexican government," noted Buckley.[52]

Will Buckley detailed how Obregón paid 15 million pesos in travel expenses for the governor of Texas and his staff to visit Mexico along with a delegation of "Texas excursionists" from the American Chamber of Commerce in Austin. He indicated that the promotional visit completely overlooked the ravages of a decade of civil war and the more than five hundred Americans killed during the revolution. Buckley focused on the disruption along the Texas-Mexico border and the extensive property destruction. He added the fact that most of the schools across Mexico had closed for lack of funds and that American Christian ministers were excluded from Mexico. He further noted the ongoing confiscation of mining and oil properties and the antibusiness features of the new constitution. Included in his statement was recognition of the real possibility that any American citizen might be expelled from the country at the discretion of the president of Mexico without cause and without trial. The antibusiness component of the Mexican constitution was confirmed in August 1921 when the Mexican Supreme Court (after conferring with President Obregón) ruled in the Texas Company case (*amparo*). The court decided that Article 27 of the Constitution of 1917—that "American interests at large which have held lands in Mexico under freehold title since before May 1, 1917"—was *not retroactive* for companies or individuals. The *amparo* was simply a ploy for recognition, according to Buckley, for "the prostitution of the Mexican Supreme Court," by Obregón, to "buy off the oil companies." A week following the publication of Buckley's article, copies were sent by train via Laredo to Mexico City and translated in *El Heraldo de México*. Buckley thanked the editor for the "courage" to publish his comments, concluding, "There are no secrets connected with my own opinions on Mexico or the policies of the American Association of Mexico." In Austin, a response refuting Buckley's claims was published by an Obregón partisan from San Antonio, C. E. Castaneda, who stated, "President Obregón's reforms have made Mexico quieter than it has been for a dozen years."[53]

In a matter of months, after years of a somewhat neutral stance in the expression of his views on the political situation and personalities in

Mexico, Buckley become an active, vocal supporter of anti-Obregón and counterrevolutionary activities—in action, financial support, and in print. Furthermore, Will Buckley's testimony before the Fall Committee in December 1919 graphically detailed the looting and killing of citizens in Mexico City in the fall of 1914. Such violent actions were under the command and orders of Gen. Alvaro Obregón. The general's forces entered the city, as Buckley testified at the Fall hearings, flying the "Black flag of anarchy" and "committed every outrage that his ingenuity could suggest." These statements joined the fact that there is reason to believe that President Obregón had seen some of the agents' reports, either provided to him by the US Embassy or coming directly from Washington. He saw or was briefed on the detailed article in *El Heraldo de México*. Buckley's connections with possible plots against Obregón and his increased role in promoting the activities of hard-line advocates at the AAM were fully exposed.[54]

Expulsion

In mid-November 1921 Buckley traveled to Mexico City both on personal business and to engage in lobbying efforts on behalf of the American Association of Mexico. Upon arrival, he was advised by Chargé d'affaires George T. Summerlin that the Mexican Foreign Office had orders dating from September 2 for Buckley's arrest and expulsion from Mexico. While no explanation was given for the delay in enforcing the order, the reason given for the order was that his activities in "connection with the American Association were obnoxious to the Mexican government." An article in the newspaper indicated there was an order for his arrest for revolutionary activities near Lower California and stated, "He will be captured and shot before daybreak." Buckley advised Summerlin that the association was organized solely to defend the rights of small property holders in Mexico. "My offense," he said, "is that since March I have been advocating the Mexican policy of the American government." No further mention was made in the official press of the details of his activities in northern Mexico with

The dream home William and Aloise Buckley designed and planned
to build in Coyoacán, a historic colonial section of Mexico City, in 1920.
Yet, as their daughter Priscilla noted, it never happened, because her father
was involved in "one too many revolutions" and expelled
from Mexico in 1921. Buckley Family Collection.

"passionately promoting revolution." Summerlin advised Buckley to remain
at the US Embassy while he investigated the circumstances of the expulsion order with the Foreign Office.[55]

Within hours of Buckley's arrival in Mexico City, events transpired that
may explain the swift action of the Mexican officials. A major engagement
was reported six miles south of Tijuana in which seventeen members of an
insurgent group led by former governor Esteban Cantú, whom Buckley had
secretly supported, were badly defeated by Mexican federal troops, leaving seventeen rebels killed. This first skirmish had been met with an overwhelming Obregónista federal force of five hundred troops and by closure
of the border to prevent any arms and munitions resupply. A second development was a major shift of American sentiments toward Mexico, owing
in large part to a reversal by William Randolph Hearst of his long-held

imperialist stance. In the cause of preventing US recognition of the Obregón government, Hearst had joined former Texas governor William P. Hobby on a month-long tour of the country. However, afterward Hearst declared, "I was for intervention, but when the Mexican administration is protecting Americans in their lives and liberties, I am for recognition of that competent and friendly administration." The response from Hearst, which led to a pro-Mexico stance by his newspapers across the United States, must have been a shock to Buckley, Doheny, Greene, and Senator Fall as well as the American associations fighting for redress in Mexico. There is no known response from Buckley.[56]

The chargé d'affaires informed the Mexican authorities that Buckley was in the American Embassy. The Americans' concerns were the manner and procedure of the expulsion and whether such an order was cause for an arrest. Buckley recalled a heated conversation with Luis Cabrera in Washington during the Niagara Falls negotiations. At those meetings, Cabrera had great sway in setting the tone of the Carranza government and declared that in "expelling the American(s) from Mexico the Constitutionalists would receive the sympathy of the American government—any protests from Washington were viewed as sincere and merely perfunctory." The charges against Buckley were confirmed by Summerlin, yet never in writing. Buckley sent a lengthy telegram to then Secretary of the Interior Albert Fall in the new Harding administration and "friends in Washington" advising them of his situation. His dispatch, highlighted in *Bulletin* No. 8 of the American Association of Mexico issued on November 3, bluntly predicted: "If the American government rules that an American citizen may be expelled from Mexico with impunity and does not insist on a repeal of the order of expulsion I will leave the embassy and submit to arrest." Authorities in Mexico City and Washington were well aware that Buckley was no ordinary citizen.[57]

Without mentioning the Cantú incident and Hearst article, the demands of federal officials for expulsion by edict of the Mexican government were adamant. They did not want a repeat of the events that swirled around

Adolfo de la Huerta, Mexican Minister of Finance, asking me if I would discontinue my efforts as president of the American Association of Mexico and dissolve the organization, in which event I would be permitted to remain in the country. This I refused to do. Although the official press in Mexico for a long time has termed me an interventionist, I do not favour such a move. I thought I had proved so to the *Carrancistas* in 1914 when I declined to become the American governor of Veracruz." Buckley's efforts received no encouraging response in either Mexico City or Washington.[58]

Buckley sent the following telegram "in code" to a friend in New York to forward to brother Edmund:

11/24/21

To: FURMAN

Following to Edmund from W.F.B. Order issued my arrest do not know whether charge activities American Association or complicity revolution. In any case think intentions eject me from country.

Am in American Embassy entirely safe and happy. American Charge will ascertain exact charges tomorrow Friday. He will undoubtedly keep State Department advised. You can probably get details there. STOP Am in no danger. Do not come here but suggest Edmund go to Washington and stay there. Please advise Fall (Secretary of Interior) Hudson (Paul) Smith (Sidney) and Streeter. Do not advise sister unless appears in papers or she hears otherwise. STOP If charge is activities American Association I will resist on ground American Government does not recognize right Mexican Government expel American citizens for such activities. Also will insist on written order of expulsion. Ask Fall see secretary of State and insist on these two points in communication to American Charge here. STOP Think will close deal with Thomas today. Will wire later.[59]

After a weeklong stay in the American Embassy, Summerlin advised Buckley it was time "to leave the country for his own safety." Tensions were already high in Mexico City as Ambassador Fletcher, considered a stumbling block, was at odds over negotiations for recognition, with some opponents predicting he was on the verge of being recalled to Washington. Furthermore, many Mexican politicians and representatives of the large foreign oil companies harbored a dim view of Buckley's long-standing relationship with General Peláez—blaming the two for their misfortunes. Years after Will's expulsion, Cecilio Velasco noted, "The treacherous, arbitrary, and frightful methods practiced by the oil companies, precipitated conflicts that gave rise to the nationalization of petroleum, and later to expropriation." In the interim, the chargé negotiated with Foreign Secretary Alberto Pani "safe conduct" for Buckley from the capital to the border at Laredo on November 27. The agreement, still not in writing, technically did not expel Buckley under Article 33, yet it was implied he would need the authority of the president of Mexico before he could return. This was in effect arbitrary expulsion without actual official enforcement.[60]

The secretary of foreign affairs wasted no time in agreeing with Summerlin to grant safe passage. The chargé escorted William to the train station with five copies of the following permit on the secretary's letterhead to travel to the border:

México, 27 de noviembre de 1921

Por la presente se suplica a las autoridades civiles y militares en la ruta México-Laredo, no pongan obstáculo al ciudadano americano William F. Buckley que se dirige a la frontera americana.

SUFRAGIO EFECTIVO. No REELECION

P. O. del Secretario El Jefe de Protocolo[61]

At the time of the abrupt expulsion, Will's wife, Aloise, was in Austin with their five-week-old baby, Priscilla, three-year-old Allie, and one-year-old John. Concerned that news might travel to Texas and alarm his wife and mother, he telegrammed Aloise: "Important business has kept me in Tampico. Will be several days longer. Love Will." His concern was justified, as the *Austin American* on November 27 ran a bold banner front-page headline; "AUSTIN MAN DRAWS WRATH OF OBREGÓN· W. F. Buck-

million dollars. His home in Tampico was abandoned. The official registration of the Pantepec Oil Company remained in place, however. Edmund and Claude, apparently not involved with their brother's activities, remained in Mexico. Buckley immediately appealed to the US State Department, but the department refused to intervene.[62]

Years of work, investments, and life in Mexico came to an immediate halt. Buckley would not return to Mexico for nearly a decade. James Buckley recalled that close friend and business partner Cecilio Velasco "covertly handled" some of Will's properties and assets in Mexico, providing funds to the family when assets were sold and collected.[63] Clearly, Will had been warned that his increasingly hostile actions against the Obregón government could place him in danger, regardless of his high-profile and wide professional reputation in Mexico. In a very interesting letter written in 1927, Buckley articulated why, with the change of government under President Calles, he should be allowed to return to Mexico. Buckley called this letter "a very rough draft and subject to correction and improvement." It is the best-known assessment of the background to his November 1921 expulsion from Mexico:

Mr. W. F. Buckley, an American citizen who resided in Mexico from 1908 until 1921 and has large holdings in that country was expelled by executive order in 1921. According to the correspondence that passed at that time between the Department of Foreign Affairs and the American chargé d'affaires Summerlin, Mr. Buckley was expelled for the reason that he was president of the American Association in Mexico, an American organization which opposed the recognition of the Obregón Government. At that time, at Mr. Buckley's request, the State Department refrained from asking the Obregón Government to re-consider its determination and permit Mr. Buckley to return to Mexico to look after his affairs. Upon the recognition of the Obregón Government the American Association disbanded, and Mr. Buckley has resided in New York and has spent part of each year in Venezuela.

Mr. Buckley's interests in Mexico have suffered greatly because of his inability to devote to them his personal attention, and he is extremely anxious to return to Mexico to look after them. The Department thought that in view of the fact that this American citizen's property interests in that country are so great, and considering that the reasons for his expulsion in 1921 had to do with his endeavor to influence the action of his own government, and to the further fact that even such activities ceased five years ago when the Obregón government was recognized by the American government, that under the circumstances the Mexican government would be entirely willing to remove the obstacle to Mr. Buckley's return to Mexico, if indeed any such obstacle now exists, and give him protection and guarantees.[64]

William F. Buckley's expulsion did not go unnoticed in Mexico. Friends, clients, Mexican politicians, and diplomats were surprised, given Obregón's attempts to calm negative press about the country and improve its image. In fact, Obregón (and Calles, who followed as president of Mexico) were products of the revolutionary era, steeped in the struggle for power and stability. While rumors of rebel activities persisted during the early years of the Obregón government, the talk of an American intervention in Mexico stopped, coincidentally, at the end of 1921 following the deportation of William Buckley. More than likely, the anti-imperialists at last were successful in sowing a division within America's political ranks that raised doubts about the wisdom or long-term strategic value of intervention. He filed a formal statement with the State Department on January 22, 1922, but still there was no official response.[65] Yet, Buckley's departure attracted attention. A headline in the leading newspaper in Mexico City, *Excelsior*, called into question the wisdom of Obregón administration officials, under Article 33 of the Constitution, to abruptly expel an individual without due process and a hearing and without concern for repercussions from the foreign government: "Un Error mas de Politica que de Diplomacia." This was followed by an editorial in the *San Antonio La Prensa*, widely circulated in Mexico, titled, "Un Error del General Obregón."[66]

These parting commentaries brought an abrupt close to Buckley's career in Mexico.

CHAPTER SIX

Lone Ranger from Texas

If oil one day should give way, among the other requirements of man,
to something else that comes out of the ground, the big operators
when they arrive on the scene will find the name of Buckley,
or one of the companies he organized on the claim-stakes already
planted, and he will be pegging claims somewhere else
outside the range of that moment's interest.
—Douglas Reed, business partner

Father carried on a love affair with oil all his adult life;
it was the perfect medium for his talents.
—John W. Buckley, son

THE ABRUPT DEPARTURE from Mexico was bittersweet. Will Buckley had invested his youth and energy in developing a home and profitable business for his family. The repercussions from the Fall Committee hearings on conditions in Mexico, his vocal defense of the Catholic Church, and his zealous support for the American Association of Mexico (AAM), which advocated blocking the formal recognition of the Obregón presidency, over time proved almost fatal. His expulsion in late 1921 was, in hindsight, a watershed for both Buckley's career and the Mexican petroleum industry. Foreign oil investors and producers in Mexico increasingly faced an uncertain antibusiness legal and tax environment, aging infrastructure, scarcity of supplies, rising global competition, and the intrusion of salt water into the Tampico-Tuxpan oil fields. The continued attacks by Carranza and Obregón on the existing petroleum and mining industries soon created an environment substantially opposed to foreign and new capital investment. These developments naturally caused international investors to look elsewhere for friendlier markets and regulatory climates as well as stable political regimes to enable them to open new businesses. The Mexican government miscalculated the looming threat to the

oil sector by failing to fully grasp the overall impact of the petroleum industry on the economy, which was estimated to exceed $1 billion in capital
investment by 1922. Any curtailment of oil production would result in a
severe decline in much needed revenue. Furthermore, those that invested
the most, namely foreign companies, were targeted for the highest tax assess-
ments and faced a continual threat of confiscation. In 1922, $606 million
was invested in Mexico by US companies and $355 million by the British.
Mexican-owned companies invested $11.5 million, a mere 1.1 percent of
the total.[1]

During the early 1920s, just as he and his brothers had been pioneers in
the boom days of the Tampico oil rush, Will turned his full attention to
the emerging petroleum opportunities in Venezuela. Buckley relocated his
family first to New Orleans, then to Austin, and subsequently to the Bronx,
in New York City. In 1923, eager to depart the big city, the Buckleys settled
in Sharon, Connecticut. There Will purchased and renovated an eighteenth-
century home on twenty acres. It was known to all in the region as Great
Elm, named for an impressive elm tree, Connecticut's largest and grand-
est, that dominated the property for more than two hundred years. The
country site allowed him to be a train ride away from business contacts and
financiers in New York City. However, the stuffy northeastern social environment, cold winters, and unpleasant business dealings in the city were
far different from the challenges of Mexico. This began a period of reas-
sessment of Will's business contacts and investment opportunities. He
quickly directed his attention to petitioning to recover his lost assets in
Mexico. And over the next few years, he continued his active and vocal
presidency of the AAM.[2]

The Big Five

During early 1922, Buckley worked to determine what forces were behind
his abrupt expulsion from Mexico. He also studied the likelihood of recovering or liquidating his assets in Mexico. The Petroleum Banking and

Aloise S. Buckley's photo in her 1921 US passport, taken after her
departure from Mexico and signed by Secretary of State
Charles Evans Hughes (1921–1925). Buckley Family Collection.

American-Mexican Claims Commission at the US State Department. At
the time the order was issued in Mexico City for his arrest in September 1921, the so-called Big Five oil companies were secretly negotiating
with President Obregón to draft an agreement to protect their interests
and investments in Mexico. This action would be clearly to the detriment
of independent oil firms and investors like Buckley's midsize Pantepec Oil
Company. The big oil companies sought this protection in exchange for
their pledge to suspend all antirecognition propaganda being spread daily
by the associations. The big oil firms also pledged to endorse recognition
of the Obregón government in Washington. The result was the Bucareli
Agreement. Drafted by Obregón, it suspended Carranza's decrees against
the oil industry and assured the Americans that Article 27 of the Constitution of 1917 would not be applied retroactively. Buckley informed confidant

Cecilio Velasco that information he obtained confirmed that "the large oil companies *arranged for my expulsion* from Mexico," in order to achieve this objective. His close business adviser, George S. Montgomery, stated, "His career in Mexico alone brought him powerful enemies who never relented in their malicious efforts to destroy him." Buckley (without any reference to his support of counterrevolutionary activities) was irritated and disappointed with Secretary of State Charles Evans Hughes and the State Department's failure to "secure protection for my properties in Mexico." In addition to Velasco, Buckley's former Mexico City law partner, Emilio Rabasa, who had recently returned from exile in New York, also concurred with Buckley's conclusions.[3]

The competitive conflicts, excessive use of government regulatory power, and opposition from the large oil companies would not end in Mexico. Buckley routinely encountered the heavy-handed actions of large oil companies—now the "Big Three"—in Venezuela. Standard Oil (Creole), Royal Dutch (Shell), and Mene Grande (Venezuela Oil Concessions, or VOC) continued to interfere with his actions for the balance of his career. His independent efforts and success in locating new oil fields for exploration and production opportunities, as well as being politically savvy in successfully dealing with foreign governments, perpetually irritated and confounded the multinational oil firms. John Buckley recalled, "He was generally distrusted and disliked by large and important segments of the oil industry. Father was a *force* in business. I think, fundamentally he felt *sorry* for people who were timid, or unimaginative, or disagreed with him, or controlled millions but wouldn't invest in his latest idea, or hated him, or were dull or stupid, or didn't enjoy life."[4]

To great success, Buckley applied in Venezuela the skills he learned in Mexico.

Venezuela Beckons

In terms of the oil industry, Venezuela in 1922 was a full decade behind the

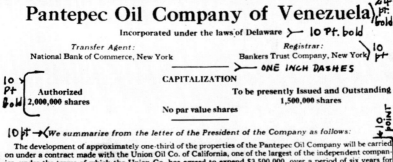

Instructions—Space 130 lines over 4 columns. Border 3 point and hairline. Text inside on 40 pica measure, 4 picas blank top, one and one-half picas bottom. All display in Caslon Bold. Balance in Bookman.

Pantepec Oil Company of Venezuela

Incorporated under the laws of Delaware

Transfer Agent:
National Bank of Commerce, New York

Registrar:
Bankers Trust Company, New York

CAPITALIZATION

Authorized
2,000,000 shares

To be presently Issued and Outstanding
1,500,000 shares

No par value shares

We summarize from the letter of the President of the Company as follows:

The development of approximately one-third of the properties of the Pantepec Oil Company will be carried on under a contract made with the Union Oil Co. of California, one of the largest of the independent companies, under the terms of which the Union Co. has agreed to expend $3,500,000, over a period of six years for development, drilling and other purposes and the Pantepec Company will share equally in the profits derived from oil produced. The proving up of any portion of the properties covered by this contract will also tend to prove up the remaining properties of the Pantepec Company which are contiguous and in which it has an undivided interest.

The Pantepec Company owns or has conditional contracts to acquire, or options on, oil concessions covering about 3,044,074 acres throughout Venezuela. Subsidiaries of the Dutch Shell, Standard Oil of New Jersey, Standard Oil of California, Atlantic Refining Co., Gulf, Sun and others are actively engaged in development in Venezuela, and large parts of the Pantepec properties lie close to fields which are now producing oil, or

After Buckley's departure from Mexico in 1921, he transferred the charter and incorporation of the Pantepec Oil Company to Venezuela. This is a copy of the draft stock certificate, made just prior to registration. It notes that the new company had oil concessions covering about 3,044,074 acres in Venezuela. Author's Collection.

begun to address regulations for concessions, oil exploration, pricing, and taxation. Initial investments in Venezuelan oil production were dedicated to supply local fuel oil use and asphalt for road construction, to address the country's poor infrastructure. The first measurable increase in oil production was followed by new exploration after the war and was spurred by declining Mexican production and logistical problems faced by Middle East suppliers.[5]

Given the growing demand worldwide for more petroleum and the publicity of the gusher Barroso No. 2, drilled on the shore of Lake Maracaibo in December 1922 (which flowed at a rate of 100,000 barrels per day), the major oil companies took immediate notice of the new opportunities for exploration and production. This resulted in a flood of contracts and drilling proposals submitted by British, Dutch, and American firms for Venezuelan cabinet approval. Overwhelmed by the interest, the government postponed all contracts with the aggressive foreign oil companies until the government could issue a set of regulations. Government officials in Caracas were certainly watching the events and regulatory decrees taking place in Mexico prior to drawing up their *Reglamento*. The new mining law was enacted in late 1922, separating the exploration of oil and gas from the balance of the mining sector. The 1922 petroleum law, with a few modifications, would regulate the Venezuelan oil industry for more than twenty-seven years and was generally lauded by investors as the best in Latin America. And he did as an eager young Texas lawyer in 1910, Buckley in 1922 worked with Henry O. Flipper to translate Venezuela's new petroleum laws into English and prepare the required applications and permits for new investors. While he no longer actively practiced law, Buckley knew, unlike the slow-moving corporate lawyers in New York City, what was required to be prepared for the coming wave of investment and how to deal with the bureaucrats in the Venezuelan government.[6]

Aware of the Mexican government's oil industry conflicts, Venezuela hoped to avoid a similar contentious situation and to maintain profitable opportunities for investors that would also benefit the government. The challenge, in order to avoid conflicts like those experienced in the Tampico-Tuxpan oil fields, was to balance the attraction of foreign direct investment with the need for corresponding tax revenues on an equitable basis. The Mexican Constitution of 1917 attacked foreign business and disrupted stability in the oil industry. Mexico rushed to tax and regulate all levels of ownership and production in a way that, as historian Jonathan Brown concluded, "increasingly marginalized the Mexican oil industry in the international market." This led the minister of development in Venezuela to conclude that lower taxes alone would not be the key, since taxes were not currently onerous, but that instead taxation needed to be balanced with the level of FDI and the enforcement of regulations. It was determined that in fact a reduction in taxes would not herald a rush of new investors, but would instead reduce production and lower government revenue. To sidestep the confusion experienced in Mexico, Venezuela avoided couching reve-

ministry addressing a major flaw in Mexico's law that required the government to tie contract modifications and adoption of its existing contracts to
any future changes in Venezuela's oil laws and decrees. In a memo to President Juan Vicente Gómez, the minister of oil advised: "Mexico, a disorga-
nized country, and in perpetual war, proceeds in a manner that increases
taxes which precipitates an ongoing crisis with companies who refuse to
expand production and the export of oil until taxation is stabilized."[7]

The political stability in Venezuela in the early 1920s, in comparison to
the decade of chaos in Mexico, resulted in a business-friendly environment. The overwhelming dynamic that marked the stable political environment was the development and regulation of the Venezuelan oil industry
under the strong rule of General Gómez. The president had come to power
in a bloodless coup d'état in December 1908, the same year Will Buckley
had started his legal career in Mexico City. During his twenty-seven years
as president, the general was the undisputed absolute ruler of Venezuela.
The nation was an active agricultural producer, especially a major leader
in the export of coffee, and by 1935 Venezuela would be the second-largest
oil producer in the world. Ambitious to improve the country, Gómez had
plans to expand the economy through the vested interests of his *gómecista*
family-owned concessionaires. Progress toward this goal slowed prior to
1920 due to the nation's poor infrastructure, low levels of foreign direct
investment, and the overall backward nature of the country. Foreign interests in mineral exploration from the United States, Germany, and Great
Britain vied for dominance; foreign companies held nearly all Venezuelan
oil concessions at the end of World War I. These companies gradually
assisted the country with new FDI and technology, which helped protect
Gómez politically. By 1922, the president began to realize that the expansion of the oil industry, while avoiding at all cost any friction with the
United States, could provide a dynamic and profitable means to raise
revenue for the government, create jobs, attract new investment, and
improve the overall economy.[8]

Muy Simpático

Buckley arrived in Venezuela in mid-1922 with the intent of exploring real
estate options and investment opportunities in the infant oil industry. He
began surveying the inland jungles and the coastline, following geologist

Ralph Arnold's survey of the Maracaibo basin in the 1910s, where the large oil companies had failed to explore prior to and during the war. He traveled across the country accompanied by his geologist, Henry Hinds, looking for the next bonanza with a group of oil scouts, many of whom followed him from Mexico. Always interested in a new challenge, Buckley reminded close friends that his competitive edge was that "the majority of the people in the oil business have no curiosity about unexplored areas—there is no oil anywhere until someone brings it to the surface." To carry out his Venezuelan investment program, Buckley depended on "land-man" Warren W. Smith and West Point engineer and linguist Henry Flipper. They performed day-to-day operations and interfaced with government officials for Pantepec Oil until 1930. In his memoirs, business associate Douglas Reed concluded that President Gómez instructed his secret police to perform a background assessment on the "*lone Ranger from Texas* and the lonely stranger from Tampico," and that "Buckley is too big a man to trifle with; either throw him out of the country or make a deal with him." John Buckley, who became president of Pantepec Oil in the late 1940s, traveled with his dad in Venezuela and recalled stories of the first meeting and conversation with General Gómez in the president's box at a Caracas cockfight:

> *General Gómez:* "Mr. Buckley, you have been in Caracas for over a month and you haven't come to see me. Why is that?"
> *Father:* "General, I didn't call on you because I knew how busy you were, and, as a matter of fact, I've been pretty busy myself."
> *The General:* "Mr. Buckley, it would be well if you were to remember this: I am never too busy to see you, and you are never too busy to see me."[9]

The two power brokers became fast friends—the president henceforth treated William as *muy simpático*—and would go on to interact in scores of business deals and partnerships until Gómez's death in December 1935. His ability to converse in Spanish with the president gave Buckley a sig-

of petroleum production with pipelines to coastal loading facilities, Buckley quickly promoted the imperative of expanding exports and developing oil export terminals, which were named in US Embassy dispatches sent to Washington as Buckley Port. Having been active in the development of the oil terminals at the Port of Tampico, Buckley formed the Pantepec Consolidated Company of Venezuela in 1924 to build a full-service deepwater port at Salinas Bay on the Paraguaná Peninsula.

The Gómez government was pleased with Buckley's detailed plans for centralizing commercial transshipment facilities, which would allow the government to better monitor for "royalty" enforcement (i.e., tax collection) the production and export amounts logged by the various oil companies. Will's oil field experience gained in Mexico were keys to his acceptance by the Ministries of Development and Public Works. Buckley established a joint venture with Compañía Maritima Paraguaná, C.A., to build the commercial port facilities; following formal registration in Caracas, the project was granted permission to proceed on June 24, 1924, to negotiate the contract following a private meeting with President Gómez. Buckley actively promoted his new project in Venezuela in a feature article in the *Journal of Commerce* titled "Oil Producers May Abandon Mexico," in which he noted: "The title to oil is secure in Venezuela, the outlet to Venezuelan oil has not yet been solved, nor have the American companies invested large sums in that country's pipelines and oil terminals. Venezuela has a stable government that respects and makes others respect property rights."[10]

No sooner was the ink dry than vocal protests and diplomatic complaints arose from several major multinational oil companies. According to James Buckley, the dissenters "were jealous and immediately torpedoed the [port] deal." These were the same "big oil" interests that Will had previously confronted in Mexico. According to the US Embassy representatives in Caracas, the contract with Pantepec "caused untold consternation among American and British interests." Buckley, the upstart, small independent operator and entrepreneur, had the vision of what could and should be done. The large oil companies insisted on control only on their terms. Aware of the fraud and bribes by agents of the large multinational oil firms, Buckley once again faced obstruction from larger competitors. The so-called political experts surrounding President Coolidge advised him to let the objections be heard. The protest included a notice that Buckley was developing the port on land he owned and that the location was a poor construction site. For example, attacks by oil executives from New York were highly personal and bordered on libel, informing the Gómez government that Buckley had been expelled from Mexico and was considered persona non grata by the US government—a false accusation. Following an inquiry in Caracas, all the allegations proved bogus, yet now the heightened attention brought more inquiries and delays from the Venezuelan authorities. Debate and discussion continued with pressure from the major oil companies. In September 1927, Buckley's first major deal in Venezuela, despite the obvious need for a modern commercial terminal to increase oil exports, was placed on hold until further notice. Nearly a century later, the Buckley family and the Cecilio Velasco family maintain business interests in the Paraguaná region.[11]

Pantepec of Venezuela

In October 1926, Buckley incorporated in Delaware the Pantepec Oil Company of Venezuela. The formative days of the Venezuelan oil bonanza closely resembled Mexico's. The dynamics of the strong presidency under Gómez and of his extended family's involvement in all aspects of the country's politics and economics, as was demonstrated in Buckley's visionary efforts to secure an oil terminal, offered both a major challenge and an opportunity. As one observer noted, interest in the oil industry within Gómez's inner circle was motivated primarily by desire for personal gain. This linked Gómez's role as steward of the country's natural resources to his own private interests. University of New Mexico historian Edwin Lieuwen concluded in his *Petroleum in Venezuela* (1954), "There is no clearer case of open and shameless fraud than Gómez' disposal of [Venezuela's] national reserves." Contracts and concessions were to be handled and processed by a shell firm created by Gómez, the Compañía Venezolana de Petróleo (CVP). From the very beginning, confusion reigned as the inexperienced CVP was little more than a conduit to funnel money to the president's *gómecista* family network. The potential for intrigue, disputes, and

exploration allowed him to become an important part of the flood of New York and foreign capital entering Venezuela for oil concessions.[12]

Always proud to be identified among the cadre of entrepreneurial independent oil men, Buckley was expert at leveraging his business to deal with the large global oil firms, such as Shell, Texaco, Standard Oil, and the British Oil Syndicate. Risk was always present because the only measure of results was to survive long enough to raise ample investment capital for exploration to bring in new producing oil wells—nothing ventured, nothing gained. Never afraid of bold investments, Buckley acquired the subsoil and surface leasing rights to more than 3 million acres in the Lake Maracaibo region of western Venezuela in 1926, an amount far beyond what his small company could profitably develop in a timely manner.[13] This acquisition would prove to be the most significant Buckley venture, the springboard for the balance of his career in the oil industry. His bold actions were not lost on the big oil companies attempting to get a foothold in Venezuela. Buckley's key to development was to establish "participations" to "farm out" exploration sites to well-capitalized larger firms. These were many of the same companies that blocked the Salinas Bay port project. In 1927, Will executed two contracts. The first was with Union Oil Company of California, which initiated the exploration of 878,000 acres, investing $3.5 million over a period of six years. The second similar joint-venture contract with the Texas Company of Houston and the California Petroleum Company resulted in the exploration of 757,130 acres. Additional land and leasing rights were sold by a Pantepec Oil Company subsidiary, American-Venezuelan Oilfield Company, to a group of investors that included Standard Oil of New Jersey (now Exxon).[14]

Looking to expand his financing sources beyond New York City, Buckley obtained investor funding from Paris and executed a long-term lease agreement with Compagnie Française des Petroles. He succeeded in further diversification when one of his prime competitors in Mexico, Edward Doheny, was also labeled by the Mexican government persona non grata. Doheny decided to direct his investments to new oil field opportunities in Colombia and to a proposal to plan and construct a pipeline between Colombia and Venezuela to reduce the high cost of shipping his Colombian oil. Such competition raised both the awareness of the potential oil fields in both countries and the ongoing demand for new investment capital. These were two ingredients for success in the oil industry that Will Buckley thrived on.[15]

It is doubtful that in 1923 either Buckley or President Gómez foresaw the phenomenal growth of the oil industry in Venezuela. Always pursuing opportunities, Buckley's exit from Mexico and his entrepreneurial hunch to pursue the next chapter of his career in Venezuela proved fortuitous. His conversations with the president about the boom times in Mexico, coupled with his hard-earned experience, established a relationship that resulted in a nexus of oil and land ventures that would in time make Buckley a wealthy man. His difficulties in early exploration and failure to develop a transshipment oil terminal resulted in detractors calling him "Dry-Hole Bill." However, interestingly, every year from 1923 to 1929, Pantepec's oil production and leasing revenue doubled. This clearly demonstrates that had Buckley's seaport terminal proposal been implemented, Venezuela's sensational growth and exports would have moved even higher. Thus, there was indeed a synergism between Buckley's hard work, luck, and good fortune. Furthermore, there was a direct correlation between the decline of the petroleum industry in Mexico and its phenomenal rise in Venezuela. From 1921 to 1929, Mexican oil production steadily declined from a peak of 193,397,587 barrels annually to fewer than 45 million. During the same period, production in Venezuela rose from below 1,433,000 to more than 137 million barrels per year. Clearly there was a series of major changes in the dynamics of exploration technology, new field discoveries and development, as well as expanding global markets all increasing the demand for oil products. Meanwhile, Mexico declined from 25 percent of the world's oil output, a market share never again to be regained, to less than 3 percent by 1930. Venezuela absorbed and dominated Mexico's export markets, supplanting her as the leading foreign oil supplier for the United States.[16]

Frederick C. Chabot

Will Buckley was well versed in developing strategic friendships with local

good books, very dry white wine, and chamber music. Following in the steps of his grandfather who served in the British Foreign Service, Chabot applied to and was accepted by the State Department in 1917. After postings in Paris, Athens, and Sofia, he spent the rest of his career in the Latin American countries of El Salvador, Costa Rica, and Brazil. His final assignment was as a commercial officer with chargé rank in Caracas in early 1923. During his two-year tenure at the embassy in Venezuela, he became a critical contact and close friend of Buckley. Their relationship was not limited to Caracas but also involved business and diplomatic contacts in Europe. Given the sudden boom in oil exploration and influx of US and foreign operators, Chabot's prime job, with detailed instructions from the US secretary of state's office, was to review Venezuela's government-granted concessions and agreements to ensure they were in the best interests of American investors. Former Venezuelan president Romulo Betancourt would later note in his landmark book *Venezuela: Oil and Politics* (1979) that the purpose for the strict review process dictated by Washington was to ensure the concessions granted by the Caracas government did not allow any "measure or suggestion of confiscation" like what had happened in Mexico. In his role of assisting American companies, Chabot worked closely with Buckley and Pantepec Oil Company representatives Warren Smith, Henry O. Flipper, and Cecilio Velasco in reviewing subsoil leases with the numerous foreign and local exploration partnerships. During the early years of Venezuela's oil industry development, American investors and drillers, many with experience in Mexico, dominated the burgeoning business. This was most evident from 1923 to 1927.[17]

Having the proverbial stamp of approval by the US Embassy, a procedure lacking in Mexico, proved to be critical for the protection of agreements, leases, and recourse in the event of a contract dispute. Many such disputes arose between American parent companies that wanted to push out the independent oilmen once a field was discovered. Buckley's personal relationship with President Gómez, whose policy was to make money while being friendly to business, would prove to be most valuable in protecting the long-term investments of Pantepec, along with the initial success structuring concessions between his independent firm and the large oil companies.[18]

Political pressure from the US State Department resulted in Chabot's forced resignation in December 1924, a victim of what he labeled "Republican politics." He was replaced in the US Embassy by military attaché Capt.

Charles A. Willoughby. However, before Chabot departed Caracas, Buckley and Pantepec had established solid credentials and well-crafted agreements with the American Embassy, the State Department in Washington, and President Gómez. Willoughby described Buckley's actions in Venezuela as "reasonable and plausible. He is a most gentlemanly type. His personality is magnetic." A freebooter at heart, Chabot realized the potential of the coming Venezuelan oil boom, and prior to leaving the country he privately purchased stock options in Pantepec and shares in oil field suppliers recommended by Buckley. Furthermore, before returning to San Antonio, he was able to put Buckley in contact with private investors, bankers, and diplomatic friends in London, Madrid, and Paris. Upon returning to Texas, Chabot invested in real estate, traveled, and began a career of historical research, going on to publish several books, including *The Alamo: Altar of Texas Liberty* (1931), along with numerous articles and translations of historical works dealing with the early history of San Antonio, the Spanish Bexar Archives, and the American Indians in Texas.[19]

For the next two decades, and until Chabot's untimely death during a research trip to Mexico, the two remained in constant contact. Their letters provide a window into the growth and diversification of Pantepec and its many subsidiaries. Investor income from Pantepec Oil Company flowed from either lease revenue or producing wells. Buckley's primary aim was to always maintain enough capital for any new land leases or new wells. When a lessee drilled a new producing well, Pantepec profited and the stockholders were paid through dividends. To better address the production growth and to attract more investment capital, Pantepec became a company comprised of two separate but complementary units: production and exploration. Will informed Chabot, "Everybody here seems to be bullish on Pantepec. A well came in the last few weeks in west Urdaneta and there have been good oil showings in Mara. In addition the actual starting of the well at Calcano 'A' seems to have impressed the skeptical. Banker sent a well-known geologist to Venezuela and I understand his report is very bullish on both Venezuela and Pantepec." Excited at the income

to the death of President Gómez in 1935, government regulations, royalties, and fees remained consistent. This allowed the oil companies to invest in more permanent infrastructure and to sustain stable operational costs even amid fluctuating oil prices. While sometimes dry holes were dug and subsoil leases expired or were sold below market, it is important to recognize the dynamic nature of oil exploration. While annual reports from the 1920s are hard to locate and generally were written to impress potential investors, Will's confidential letters give a contemporary perspective seldom uncovered: "Pantepec looks very good. Nearly every development in Venezuela has helped us. The California or rather the Gulf Company got a well in Mara, and within the last few days Atlantic Refining has a good showing in Mara, all of which helps our property. The California Petroleum and the Union Oil are starting to drill a joint well in the northern part of Calcano 'A,' just south of the Mene Grande field of Dutch Shell. This well should be concluded in December."[21]

Chabot did, in fact, provide timely introductions for Buckley in Europe. By the late 1920s, most of the prime areas in Venezuela had been leased or remained in the hands of the government. Clearly, the objective was to begin exploration where there was high production potential. Yet, even then engineers realized that geological formations varied from location to location, thus making drilling a risky endeavor until a new oil field was proven. For those new to the region, one of the best courses of action was to buy existing leases or partner with a current producer to share expenses, royalty payments, and potential production. French and Spanish oil firms, both sponsored by their governments (i.e. state-owned monopolies), were looking to invest and establish footholds in the Venezuelan oil market. Industrial demand worldwide was growing along with the expanding automobile market. Six years of work in Venezuela by Pantepec, given the large tracts of land it controlled and the proven success of the property, served to make the company very marketable. Buckley outlined his plans in what he called a "confidential (very confidential)" letter to Chabot in early 1929:

> I am first going to Madrid, and go a little later to Paris, for the purpose of collaborating with F. J. Lisman & Company [investment bankers] in their efforts to sell a control of Pantepec Petroleum Companies, Inc, to the Spanish Oil Monopoly or the French Oil Monopoly. I expect to sign a six-month option to sell 501,000 shares of the

common stock of the holding company to Lisman & Company for net $6,000,000.00 to the stockholders. Of the $6,000,000.00, $1,000,000.00 will be used to pay past dividends on Preferred "A" stock and the indebtednesses of the company, and the $5,000,000.00 will be distributed among the various stockholders of the holding company in proportion to their stock holdings. It is the plan to give every stockholder the opportunity to sell a little over 50% of his common stock. While the deal will be a good one for the stockholders it is equally good for whoever the purchaser may be.[22]

Chabot was excited at the prospect of the Pantepec transaction. He wrote to Will, "I am negotiating the sale of some of my Oriental rugs and hope to get about twelve hundred dollars out of them. . . . If it is not too late, I will certainly appreciate your permitting me to purchase more of your inside stock with this money." By "inside stock" he was referring to preferred stock. The interest by Chabot was well founded as the Pantepec stock trading at $10–12 a share was expected to go above $20 following an American geologist's report that "we would be taking oil out of this pool 15 or 20 years from now."[23]

Further confirmation of the success and activities of Pantepec and its many partners is found in a fascinating series of letters in 1928–29 between Will and former ambassador Henry Lane Wilson. Wilson retired to California in marginal health, where he was involved in real estate and stock investing. Like Chabot, he held a large portfolio of stock in Pantepec. Furthermore, Wilson was considering a second book on the history of Mexico following his memoirs, *Diplomatic Episodes in Mexico, Belgium, and Chile* (1927). The interest in writing a new book was spurred on most likely by a wave of new books and articles on the situation in Mexico.[24] He urged Buckley to coauthor or fully author his new book to keep his name off the project, noting that given his vocal and active role in the Republican Party denouncing President Wilson's failed diplomacy in Mexico, "It would probably involve me in an unpleasant controversy at a time of life when I ought

Al Smith. Wilson, in spirited letters to Will after the election, concluded, "The real religious opposition to Smith was not that he was Catholic but that he was a New York Tammany Political Catholic." And on the subject of Obregón, Wilson wrote Will, "Mexican history is being repeated, and power and rule seem always to be preceded by the elimination of obstacles. Madero exiled Diaz; Huerta or someone else disposed of Madero; [President] Wilson ousted exiled Huerta; Calles and Obregón disposed of Carranza and later of de la Huerta, Villa, [Arnulfo] Gomez and [Francisco] Serrano. The question now is did Calles dispose of Obregón, and how." The final fate of Ambassador Wilson's book on Mexico is unknown, yet in one of his last notes to Buckley, he wrote, "Have you read Francis McCullagh's '*Red Mexico*' (1928)? It has created quite a stir." Henry Lane Wilson died in December 1932 at the age of seventy-five and was interred in Indianapolis, Indiana.[25]

Mexico Redux

The long-overdue success of Pantepec in the Venezuelan oil business was the result of Will's career of challenges and experiences being expertly applied to manage a company. After an invitation from President Plutarco Calles to return to Mexico, Will and Aloise returned in the fall of 1927 for the first time since the 1921 expulsion. Visits with brothers Claude and Edmund, along with longtime friends, painted a mixed picture of life in Mexico. Buckley wrote Chabot after his return to Austin, "We had a very interesting trip there and found conditions to be the worst imaginable." The country had not yet recovered economically from the destruction of the revolution. As Henry Wilson noted, its major leaders—Madero, Villa, Zapata, Carranza, and Obregón—had all met their deaths at the hands of assassins, and Porfirio Díaz and Huerta died ignoble deaths in exile. Thousands of Mexicans were without jobs, many schools remained closed, oil production dropped monthly (annual production was down drastically from 193 million barrels in 1921 to 50 million in 1928), agrarian reform stalled due to outdated programs, and only the faintest hint of law and order had returned. US recognition of Calles was contingent on the continued protection of American lives and property—yet, very little was said about the Catholic Church. However, tensions in Mexico were once again high as a radical element of the Church rebelled against Calles and the government's harsh anti-Church policies.[26]

The grassroots Catholic Church rebellion against the government during 1926–29, known as *la Guerra Cristera* (the Cristero War), was made up largely of militant parish priests, lay organizations, and rural campesinos who supported the embattled hierarchy of the Church.[27] Calles perceived this as a major threat to his government and moved to crush any opposition:

This Government is not against religion nor against any one religion— for us all religions are good. What we have been opposed to here is not religion but the high dignitaries of the Roman Catholics who have not wanted to submit themselves to our law; laws which do not in the least affect dogma or beliefs. The clergy of the Church in all Latin American countries has constituted itself as a power superior to the State and has always aimed at temporal power. It has invaded the spheres of politics, it has organized and conducted internal wars. In sober truth it has been the greatest handicap and incubus of these countries.[28]

The Church overestimated its influence and command of its "special privileges" and, therefore, lost credibility and support following the assassination of General Obregón by a lone assailant, José de León Toral. Buckley's return visit gave him a firsthand look at the Catholic uprising. He came to agree with those who branded Calles, Obregón, and their officials as "Bolsheviks," and quietly set out to support the Church movement. Accusations of a communist movement were rampant, driven by the design of the revolutionaries to confiscate foreign companies. Much of the political disruption was fueled by the anarchist-led Industrial Workers of the World (IWW), which supported the Communist Federation of the Mexican Proletariat, which tried unsuccessfully to gain a foothold in the Mexican labor movement. The AAM monthly *Bulletin* was quick to point out the evils of this "dangerous Bolshevist movement," and Buckley had explained in detail to the Fall Senate hearing that the communists advocated three objectives: the crippling of the Catholic Church, the abolition of private

ridiculous propaganda" to support the Mexican Catholics. Opposition to the Obregón administration turned violent during the presidency of his successor, Calles. Bitterness erupted in violent militancy in 1926 after the archbishop of Mexico, José Mora y del Río, published an article in *El Universal* critical of the anticlerical provisions of the 1917 constitution. He called on the faithful to ignore the new laws, and his actions were deemed a hostile challenge to the government. The new revolutionary opposition, known as the "Cristeros," or "Cristiada," would last for over three years. Official Washington during the presidency of Calvin Coolidge—still deeply involved in the oil question and demands over the legality of Article 27—wanted no part of this "upstart" Catholic revolution. When Calles pushed back, Catholic authorities in mid-1926 countered by closing all the churches in Mexico. The Catholic clergy in the United States issued "pastoral letters" urging lay support in hopes that the standoff would bring private-sector and religious organization aid from the United States.[30]

Leaders of the Liga Nacional Defensora de la Libertad Religiosa (LNDLR) movement in Mexico sent representatives to Texas and New York to attempt to raise money for the fight. Historian Julia Young confirms that while the Cristero rebellion is regarded as an event that existed only within Mexico, in fact "the war also involved participation from beyond the Mexican border." The LNDLR was one group that sought external support. Will Buckley met with Capistran Garza in San Antonio to review a plan to raise between $350,000 and $500,000 (US), of which Buckley was prepared to pay half, to aid the Cristeros. Buckley offered his support by introducing Garza to industrialist Nicholas Brady, president of New York Edison Company. Brady was also trustee of more than a score of other prominent corporations and was the most influential Catholic layman in America at the time. Some have surmised that Buckley, having lost many of his investment properties in Mexico after he was expelled, saw a possible opportunity to recoup some of his lost fortune by financing the Catholics in their attempt to overthrow the Calles regime. Garza went to New York City to meet with Brady, but confusion as to who was authorized to represent the LNDLR Mexican Catholics, coupled with opposition from Bishop Pascual Díaz, scuttled the proposal by Buckley, foreclosing any hopes of a donation by Brady.[31]

It became obvious, after months of bloodshed, that neither side in this postrevolutionary struggle could dominate absolutely. In 1929, the government and the Church, through the mediation efforts of the United States and Ambassador Dwight Morrow, reluctantly agreed to an uneasy truce. Ill feelings and recriminations lingered for another decade. Concerned with the plight of the Church in Mexico, Buckley continued to support efforts to calm the ongoing dispute while maintaining his full business focus and interest on Venezuela.[32]

Wildcat

By 1928, the investment in Venezuela by Pantepec was beginning to pay off. Cash flow from the leases and land deals provided a solid base for

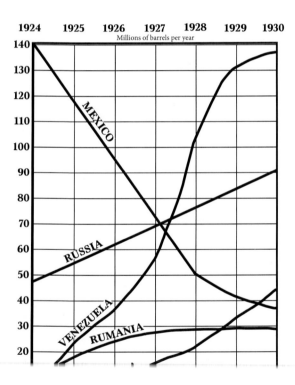

Buckley's negotiations with new potential investors from Madrid and Paris. The national companies in both countries were slow to act and very pretentious. Their clear expectations were for Buckley to pay or subsidize their entry into the oil business in Venezuela. The lack of resolve by the companies did not prevent Buckley from opening new investor contacts with local banks and suppliers. The US stock market crash in late 1929 did not affect the oil markets until mid-1930. Pantepec maintained its major contracts in Venezuela, yet gradually income was reduced as the "Big Three" oil companies led the way in curtailing production. A critical French loan for Pantepec, agreed to and approved in mid-1928 by a Paris investment firm, that would expand operations along Lake Maracaibo was canceled in the economic panic that swept Europe.

To shore up Pantepec's financial position, Buckley was able, in the harshest economic climate, to secure a $1 million loan from a Parisian bank. By agreement, Pantepec reduced its dividends. Like most of the wealthy during the Great Depression, Buckley did incur debt collection problems, recalling one such individual was "*muy sin verguenza*" (very shameless); "he is the kind of debtor that makes it a point to get angry with the creditor and then not pay because he is angry!" The impact of the Depression soon hit the Caracas treasury with a 26 percent drop in petroleum tax revenues. The Venezuelan government responded by raising tariffs and taxes to make up for the shortfall. Buckley used the early 1930s as a time to maintain and cultivate his relationships with the big oil firms since most still held large cash reserves. The most significant contract he signed was with Creole Petroleum, a subsidiary of Standard Oil of New Jersey. Still holding a large portion of the 3 million–acre Pantepec investments from 1926, Creole had access to cash but not to any proven or potential properties. In the sublease, Creole agreed to pay all exploration and drilling expenses, and in return pay a share of the profits to Pantepec, provided Buckley would maintain government relations and assist with the oil shipping firms.[33]

After observing the success of the Creole-Pantepec discoveries, the Atlantic Refining Company acquired a half interest in the remaining Pantepec concessions and within four months found two new producing oil fields. However, by mid-1935 Buckley concluded, given his good fortune in the early 1930s, that it was time to forgo his unsound, risky investment policy—the "all-eggs-in-one-basket" approach—especially in view of its dependence on depleting natural resources at the mercy of political

uncertainty, new tax laws, and always looming labor problems. He therefore crafted a new strategy based on diversification. The death in December 1935 of President Juan Gómez, Buckley's friend and the godfather of
the emerging Venezuelan petroleum boom, was a watershed. Gómez's
death had a major impact on Buckley's future course of operations. The
wildcat approach that proved successful in the early days of Mexico and
Venezuela had now changed due to the varying economic and geopolitical
conditions worldwide.[34]

Will Buckley's intent to diversify Pantepec proved to be a good decision.
However, it was met with harsh opposition from stockholders, investment
bankers, and brokers who wanted to continue to rely on what they believed
were the proven profits of Pantepec through dividends. Buckley was concerned with the American price-setting strategy called "market demand
prorationing," which maintained import quotas while artificially holding
the domestic oil price at $1–1.50 per barrel above the imported price. The
biggest winners of prorationing and quotas were the big US oil companies.
Thus, unaware of the full ramifications in the oil markets' dynamics, stockholders took action to block Buckley's planned changes; the opposition
launched a proxy fight to limit the company's new venture investment outside of Venezuela. How much Buckley informed the stockholders of his
planned future ventures is unknown. The new area of identified exploration-
oriented opportunities was Florida, where Buckley had quietly inked
leases on a large area of offshore claims. The strategic move entrenched
Pantepec in the new project and captured the opportunity before the larger
oil companies could. News of the proxy challenge in the financial markets
of New York City was followed by a request by *Fortune* magazine to do a
feature story on Pantepec, which Buckley declined by admitting, "I have a
temperamental dislike for publicity." And at the same time, he secretly dispatched his team of oil scouts to Canada to determine the best options to
pursue. W.F.B. won the proxy fight, and in the spirit of compromise and
diversification, he agreed to split Pantepec's operations to address stockholder concerns.[35]

Refining contract that had just hit two wells, plus the new Florida lease. To guard against future stockholder meddling, Pancoastal was structured under a voting trust, controlled by Buckley, for a period of ten years. James Buckley notes:

> The logic of the reorganization was for Pantepec to retain the proven, producing properties while assigning the exploratory "wildcat" holdings (including the Venezuelan holdings currently being tested by Atlantic Refining and the Florida lease, which was held by a subsidiary called Coastal Caribbean) to a new company Pancoastal Petroleum, which was spun off to Pantepec's shareholders. Soon thereafter, Pancoastal in turn spun off Coastal to its shareholders with the result that Pantepec's original holdings were now held by three independent companies, all operating under Will's direction.[36]

After President Gómez's death, Pantepec worked to protect its investments in Venezuela. An uncertain business environment developed due to growing resentment of the autocratic actions of the former president and the large foreign oil companies. The petroleum sector in Venezuela in the mid-1930s dominated all political, social, and economic actions in the country like no other nation in Latin America. In 1935, Venezuelan oil production was the largest to date at 148 million barrels, representing 9 percent of world production. However, in the wake of the transition to the new leader, Gen. Eleazar López Contreras, unrest spread and troops were used to quell an uprising by mobs of protesters, who threatened to set fire to wells and storage facilities. Much like the backlash in Mexico in 1914–18, concerns and disagreements on the future course of the oil industry were further supported by an antibusiness Congress in Caracas. News of the nationalization of the oil industry in Mexico in March 1938 was followed in Venezuela by the announcement that the granting of any new concessions to multinational oil companies would be suspended. Other than having to adapt to new laws and pay more taxes, Pantepec's productive operations remained relatively safe. Buckley's strategic redirection of Pantepec away from a concentration in Venezuela was, without a doubt, strongly influenced by his past experiences in Mexico.[37]

Also, looking to escape the cold winters and stodgy social life in Connecticut—Reid said his mother "detested being condescended to by Yankee dowagers"—Buckley purchased a summer estate in Camden, South

Carolina, known for decades as Kamschatka. One observer noted, "One parent had a Texas accent modified by years in Mexico, the other had a Southern accent, and there was a fair amount of French and Spanish being spoken around the house." Aloise heartily approved.[38]

The Last Oil Stunt

The expropriation by the Mexican government of all foreign oil properties in the country by decree of President Lazaro Cardenas (1934–40) had a marked and lasting impact on all petroleum operations worldwide. His dramatic speech was an attack on the leading sector of his nation's economy, and it was received by the Mexican public with wild enthusiasm. Cardenas railed, "The [foreign] oil companies have enjoyed great privileges that favor their development and expansion—often against Mexico's will and against public interest." The companies' intervention was a "persistent and wrongful intervention in our national politics," he declared. The action was met with a mixed reaction in official circles in Washington. The failure of the Roosevelt administration to advocate for the protection of the extensive American investments in Mexico was generally due to the depressed global economic conditions. FDR was "in a very precarious situation," noted Buckley; "the depression here is a very serious one." Like oilmen worldwide, Buckley understood the implications of Mexico's action for any foreign operation: "It naturally would be a great temptation to other Latin American countries to find that they could with impunity take over for nothing mineral resources developed by American capital." The fragile political and social conditions as well as the uncertain regulatory and taxation climate in Venezuela following the death of President Gómez was not lost on the Texas oilman. The sweeping actions in Mexico were in fact viewed as "confiscation," or as Mexican historian Lorenzo Meyer noted, it was "more of a nationalization," without recourse:

Cardenas' last oil stunt is extremely interesting. I see that [Secretary

over by the government not on the basis of the value of the property, but on the basis of the cost of the one well. This is also new international law."[39]

Buckley expressed great concern with the reaction of the Roosevelt administration and its Good Neighbor policy, which he and other oil company executives were told would protect their vast investments in Mexico. "All the countries to the south of us are welcoming Mr. Roosevelt's enthusiastic approval of the confiscation of American property," he worried. While there were rumors that the United States and Britain might send troops, in fact no military action was planned or expected. Yet, just in case, the Mexican military commander in the oil region was told to set fire to the wells if any foreign forces landed in Tampico or Veracruz. This was Mexico's boldest postrevolutionary move from an international standpoint. "Article 27 of the Constitution had finally been fulfilled," noted Mexican historian Enrique Krauze, "in both letter and spirit." One byproduct of tensions in Mexico created by the continuous disruption of the revolution and by expropriation was the ongoing response by detractors to challenge the sitting government. Grassroots rebel uprisings solicited support from anyone that would help. Years after Buckley had abruptly departed from Mexico, he continued to receive unsolicited calls for assistance. For example, Fred A. Dato from Los Angeles sent Buckley a Western Union telegram in 1938 requesting an urgent meeting. He informed Buckley he had been to Mexico City and conferred with "our mutual friend, General Peláez. . . . I have friends [most likely conservative Mexican exile groups conspiring against Cardenas] in San Francisco and there is certain information that you alone can advise me on." Sensing the purpose of Dato's request, Buckley was not surprised because he routinely received inquiries from those interested in the situation in Mexico. He sent an immediate letter, clearly noting that he had moved on: "I am really not having anything to do with the Mexican situation, and have not for a number of years. *We have all given this up as a bad job a long time ago.*"[40]

An Uneasy Peace

Soon after the excitement of the Mexican petroleum-sector expropriation, Buckley sailed from New York with Aloise and four children for France. Before departing, he conferred with Claude, who had moved from

Tampico to San Antonio, Texas, and formed Cabildo Oil Properties, Inc. to handle oil and gas clients.[41] The trip to Europe was for the purpose of settling the children in boarding schools there and reviewing business opportunities. The possibility of war in Europe was much more apparent to those on the Continent, and only distant news for most Americans thousands of miles away. Buckley's prime objective was to obtain new sources of financing for his projects in Florida and Canada, and failing this, to sell Pantepec stock. Given the war jitters, Buckley estimated that "several hundred thousand shares of weak stock will be taken out of the open market" if needed, but "we really have no desire to sell stock and give options" unless market conditions improve. Much like the demand for oil during World War I, an outbreak of war in Europe would require the immediate need for new sources of petroleum and the shipping capacity to move bulk crude to refineries and then to markets.

With the war confined to Europe, Buckley reasoned, American companies should be able to profit from the conflict. Buckley was against US involvement in any new European war, but he was eagerly preparing to be a supplier of oil. War clouds on the horizon were confirmed by Pantepec's legal counsel in Paris, Richard Cronan. Following the September 1938 appeasement meeting in Munich between Germany, France, and Great Britain, at which Hitler stated he had no additional territorial aspirations in Europe, Buckley pondered:

Things have quieted down considerably and everybody is now figuring up the cost of the game of strip poker played with Mr. Hitler, in which the latter gentleman left Mr. [Edouard] Daladier and Mr. [Neville] Chamberlain with hardly their underwear. In the meantime, Hitler and his hold-up has received the sanctimonious blessing of the democracies, and all is very regular. He openly seized Austria—the *Anschluss*—by force. The major powers gave him Czechoslovakia. It is not clear whether Mr. Hitler is getting more civilized, has developed a certain *finesse*, or whether democracy is pretty nearly

contract with Standard Oil to "farm out" or sublease unexplored Pantepec property in Venezuela. After years of delays and minor successes in
oil production, major wells were being discovered. As the oil field expanded,
Pantepec received a half interest in all the production. Concentration on
production in Venezuela over a highly productive two-year period together
with Allied demand for oil and gas sealed a solid financial position for
Buckley. Pantepec's lease holdings in 1938 totaled more than $25 million,
and once developed, they provided Buckley much needed funding to follow through with his diversification plans, now being delayed by war.[43]
Longtime close friend and confidant Douglas Reed noted: "A serene self-
confidence that nothing ruffled was either native to him or was acquired
in the years of matching wits with protagonists of a stature ranging from
bandits and squatters to attorneys, revolutionary generalissimos, great oil
companies, cold-eyed bankers and government. Without the gift of imper-
turbability he might not have weathered those years."[44]

World War II

William F. Buckley Sr., a lifelong conservative and now a staunch nonin-
terventionist, was a backer of the America First Committee's isolationist
movement and was concerned with the prospect of the United States being
forced—again—into a war in Europe. Unlike most Americans who only
received news on the brewing European war via the newspapers and the
radio (which he saw as biased), he had traveled across the Continent during the months following Hitler's overwhelming September 1939 invasion
of Poland. Furthermore, a small group of American private business leaders and government officials were disturbed by the German and Japanese
economic connections in Latin America—specifically the demands of the
Axis powers for oil reserves.[45] Notwithstanding, Buckley in the late 1930s
was a fervent isolationist, mostly owing to his disgust with Woodrow Wilson's bungling of foreign policy toward Mexico, and he was against US
involvement in another war of Europe's making—yet he had been a vocal
interventionist on behalf of Huerta in Mexico. Buckley expressed his
concerns and strong biases in a confidential letter to his old University of
Texas classmate Burke Baker, only a few weeks before the attack at Pearl
Harbor:

I had dinner last night with a Boston lawer [sic] . . . my friend reminded him [me] that Roosevelt had promised to keep us out of war, to which he rejoined that he believed Willkie but did not believe Roosevelt. It is a sad thing to think that in our wonderful democracy the leaders of both parties at the last election were deliberately deceiving the people. Roosevelt is considered a more unscrupulous man than Woodrow Wilson, and I don't suppose his fondest followers expected the man to tell the truth.

I hope you are heartily ashamed of the policy of your co-religionists in preventing a free discussion of this question and the nasty propaganda of the patriotic Americans running Hollywood and the radio.

I see that the widely advertised proposed gift by our friends in Texas of 2,000,000 barrels of oil to England has simmered down to 11,000 barrels. I think our war effort, if we get into the war, will be a great fiasco. I don't believe that we have the unity necessary to fight the kind of war that we will have to fight to defeat Germany and keep her in subjection. In my judgment—and I have felt this for 10 years— that France and England are old and decadent; their star is setting, and we haven't the strength to keep them going. England has not the vitality, after two years of war, to land a force on the Continent at a time when Germany's army is occupied in Russia. I don't think they have any intention of *landing any army on the Continent except an American army.*

I hope for your own sake and mine, and the sake of our country, that we fail to get into this war. I find that pacifists are a very bellicose lot. In times of peace they insist on not preparing for war and then when the slightest opportunity to fight comes, they insist on plunging in unprepared.[46]

During the late 1930s and 1940–41, as war raged across much of Europe and Asia, Buckley continued to expand his commercial operations and visits to Europe, Venezuela, Florida, and Canada. The interest in Florida may

discovered wells around Lake Maracaibo. However, there was much concern over the looming war clouds. A vocal supporter of the America First movement, Buckley expressed some relief that Hitler had met with his first major military disaster in Russia, which he thought possibly would end the war in Europe. In the meantime, there were growing apprehensions on the part of the US War Department Planning Division about whether the logistical operations of strategic fuel could supply the demands of a war in Europe. Planning for a two-ocean war had not, as yet, been fully considered.[47]

Pantepec oil production in Venezuela was bolstered by an independent engineering evaluation that documented company reserves in excess of 247 million barrels. Little did Buckley realize that the US entry into the Second World War would commence in the Pacific on December 7, 1941. Despite the uncertainty of what the American response in Europe would be, the Japanese attack on Pearl Harbor would bring a "unity" to the nation that has seldom been known. The oil business in the late 1930s, thanks in large part to Standard Oil's new discoveries, was solid in Venezuela, and Pantepec was once again in good financial shape—to the benefit of its thousands of shareholders, including Buckley. While opposed to the war, and likely more opposed to Roosevelt, all notions of remaining an isolationist ended with Pearl Harbor. Buckley's long-term plans included expectations for his sons to join the growing oil business, but Buckley was a patriot at heart and fully supported the three oldest boys enlisting in the military. John was commissioned in the army in late 1942 after graduating from Yale and served as an intelligence officer in North Africa and France. James was commissioned in the navy in 1942 as an LST (landing ship tank) commander and served in the Pacific for the duration of the war. William Jr., following enrollment in Universidad Nacional Autónoma de México, or UNAM, in Mexico City to polish his Spanish in 1943, joined the army in 1944 for two years before returning to Yale. (In 1946, John joined their father's firm Pantepec-Catawba Corporation, followed by James, fresh out of law school, in 1950. William "Bill" Jr. graduated from Yale in 1950 and went to work for the Central Intelligence Agency at the US Embassy in Mexico City, serving under station chief E. Howard Hunt—of Watergate fame. Bill was profoundly influenced by his father, writing his first conservative book, *God and Man at Yale*, his senior year at the university; he then worked briefly as associate editor of the *American Mercury*, then established the monthly periodical *National Review* in November 1955.) Being concerned with the course of US foreign policy in Europe, Will Buckley was proud of his sons' military service, and he volunteered to support the military's logistical operations in Washington. And it was indeed, as he had written Burke Baker, an "American army" that landed "on the Continent" at Normandy in June 1944 and would eventually lead to the defeat of the Germans.[48]

Preclusive Operations

Buckley was contacted by the Preclusive Operations Division of the Board of Economic Warfare (BEW) in Washington to consider assisting the petroleum procurement process. The board of the BEW solicited the assistance of American business executives who had established contacts and experience in foreign countries that possessed resources and materials critical to the Allied war effort. After being considered for work as an agent in Mexico or Argentina, Buckley was offered a position to coordinate commercial activities in Spain. With the Allied victories in North Africa and the Mediterranean, the war planners realized the most effective avenue to resupply the army in Europe was to establish a strong logistical link through Spain. Negotiations with the BEW on his assignment continued until September, when it was mutually agreed that Buckley could best assist the war effort as a principal member of the Caribbean Area Petroleum Committee to coordinate the increase of oil production and refining in Trinidad, Venezuela, and Colombia. The War Department was concerned with the supply of fuel due to Germany's increased submarine activities in the Atlantic. Few are aware that Nazi U-boats in 1942–43 stalked shipping in the Gulf of Mexico, sinking a score of ships and shelling oil refining installations on the Dutch island of Aruba, off the northwest coast of Venezuela, and facilities in the harbor of Curaçao.[49] Security of oil production facilities and safety for oil convoys became a major strategic priority. To meet demand, Venezuela was encouraged to increase petroleum production from 700,000 to 1 million barrels per day by employing "intense drilling

company's development contract with Creole Petroleum Corporation and can move at once to develop these properties."[50]

The demand for more fuel had a major positive impact on Pantepec. Daily production in Venezuela on company leases increased from 8,000 to 20,000 barrels within a few weeks and was projected to exceed 70,000 barrels by the end of 1943. Price controls and quotas established during the depressed economy in the United States during the 1930s were lifted. The dramatic increase in production was the result of a new drilling operations arrangement with the Atlantic Refining Company, in exchange for a 50 percent undivided interest in the concessions. This was a small, but critical, portion (7 percent) of the million-barrel target agreed to by Buckley, and was very profitable to Pantepec. The Venezuelan government cooperated with the Allied drive to increase petroleum production by maintaining existing taxes at a stable level and minimum royalties at 16 2/3 percent. Concessions and contract-granting programs were expanded along with approval to promote domestic refining. This regulatory consistency and increased production enhanced Venezuela's oil revenue projections to record levels, an increase of 72 percent by 1945, when Venezuelan production reached 323 million barrels. These seemingly positive events did not diminish Buckley's concerns with behind-the-scenes government diplomatic dealings between Caracas and Washington that could bring a disruption to operations and/or the threat of Venezuelan confiscation. Abrupt actions could, as he wrote Governor Thomas E. Dewey of New York, "impose unjustifiably heavy burdens on all American oil companies as a part of a settlement with certain large oil companies who had been guilty of misconduct."[51]

To escape the cold New England winter, and with the business in Venezuela in good hands following the promotion of Warren W. Smith as president of Pantepec operations in Venezuela (and especially after a windfall following a cash purchase from Pantepec of 1.6 million barrels of reserve oil by Standard Oil), in 1943 Buckley traveled with Aloise and four children to Mexico City. There seem to have been no repercussions from his expulsion twenty-two years earlier. While intending to vacation and enjoy social visits, Will took time to obtain information about and gauge the state of the Mexican petroleum industry, which was now his direct competition. Former law partner Emilio Rabasa and his associates were eager to learn of the current attitude in the United States and the status of the war.[52]

Déjà Vu

When he returned full-time to the operation of Pantepec in early 1944, it was clear to Will he had correctly judged the future course of political and industrial transformation in Venezuela. Postwar Venezuela was soon to be a repeat of the post–World War I experience in Mexico. Social unrest, a void of political leadership, and various revolutionary movements were positioning themselves to take control in Caracas. Strongman Romulo Betancourt, a democratic reformer, captured power. Hoping to calm dissent, Betancourt immediately mandated a wage increase and arbitrarily enacted a retroactive 50 percent tax on profits, on top of the 16 2/3 percent royalty excise on foreign operations. David Reed recalled, "These were heavy blows to a company dedicated to dividend-paying. After thirty years W.F.B. again found himself between a revolutionary regime, on the one hand, and, on the other, a home government and big oil companies which both had acquired the habit of capitulation." Buckley, as an independent producer, protested to both President Betancourt and the US State Department (which feared a rising communist movement in Latin America) for redress, to no avail. Pantepec, in fact, was soon to find itself in a strategic position with available undeveloped land just as the government declared there would be no more new contracts (concessions) to foreign companies. Buckley's solid contracts, dating from the time of Chargé d'affaires Chabot in the US Embassy and the Gómez presidency, proved a binding and solid bulwark against the existing political unrest. Nonetheless, the time for diversification of operations was at hand.[53]

After World War II

With the conclusion of the war in 1945, it was evident that the oil and gas industry was truly a global enterprise. Buckley fully rejected prognostications that the demand for petroleum products would collapse after the war. One observer noted, "He was an incisive and incessant student of every

Buckley family reunion at Great Elm, Sharon, Connecticut, in 1946.
Buckley Family Collection.

profitable to Buckley's expanding network of potential exploration sites. In the increasingly capital-intense industry, Pantepec's cash reserves were estimated to exceed $40 million. Because it was still considered a small-medium oil and gas producer, Pantepec's strategy to diversify operations versus the growing multinational companies would prove important. Buckley did not abruptly exit Venezuela, but instead he executed an extensive strategy to lease open tracts of land held in the original concession dating from 1926 and to sell participations in the company's producing fields.[54]

The announcement that Buckley was opening new operations on a lease of 4.6 million acres in Florida at a cost of $1,111,111 became headline news in the financial markets worldwide. The Pantepec contract was subject to a royalty of 1/8 percent to the state of Florida, 1/24 percent to former stockholders of Arnold Oil Explorations, and 1/48 percent to "certain individuals." While much of the new exploration attention by large oil companies shifted to the Middle East, Buckley executed an agreement with Compagnie Française des Petroles (CFP) to sell the full production of the Pantepec Oil Company in Venezuela for three years based on the market price (averaging between $.90 and $1.50 per barrel) set on the Gulf Coast of Texas. In a separate contract, CFP agreed to pay Pantepec half of the cost of seventy-five producing wells in the El Roble and Mulata fields for $4,375,000.[55]

The rise of production in the Middle East (primarily in Iran and Saudi Arabia) began to concern, and in some quarters threaten, the progress of the Venezuelan oil industry. With his deal complete and buyers confirmed for near-term production and delivery with CFP, Buckley announced that the expansion of the major oil companies in the Middle East "will tend to lessen the market for Venezuelan petroleum," much to the irritation of government officials in Caracas. "Upon the completion of the proposed pipe lines in the Middle East," Buckley noted, "the oil production of Venezuela can be cut down and oil kept as a reserve in the ground while oil in the Middle East is used to supply the market heretofore supplied by Venezuela . . . which will relegate Venezuela to a reserve status." Concerned with operations and the government response in Venezuela, Warren Smith, manager of Pantepec in Caracas, tempered his boss's proclamations noting, "There is no danger production will be relegated to a reserve status." Notwithstanding, within a week of Buckley's declaration promoting the Middle East, Juan Pérez Alfonso, minister of development, proclaimed the Venezuelan government would raise taxes and take 50 percent of the profits from foreign oil operations instead of the existing 16 2/3 percent. Alonzo criticized Buckley, since Pantepec was the only company to formally object to the 1945 excess profits tax, "as the head of a small company and his viewpoint is of no importance."[56]

Following the war, the expansion of Pantepec into Florida and Canada was further enhanced by the two eldest sons, John and James, who joined the management of the company in 1953. Assisting the younger Buckleys along with their father were close associates Dean Reasoner, a Washington lawyer; Warren Smith, president of Pantepec-Venezuela; Joseph H.

deep-well test by Pancoastal Petroleum Company was six miles north of St. Petersburg. And in early 1952, Pancoastal signed a lease with US Sugar for 100,000 acres on the southern shore of Lake Okeechobee.[57]

With his eyes set on additional international markets, Buckley established Catawba in April 1948 as the service group to coordinate and advise many functions common to all the spinoff operational companies, now numbering nearly a dozen. James Buckley noted the new corporation's principal task was to keep the various companies adequately financed, and "Catawba also negotiated 'farm out' agreements on their behalf and investigated new opportunities for expansion. And always, when entering a new petroleum frontier, these companies would follow the same basic pattern: the securing of exploration rights on reasonable terms over sufficiently large

William F. Buckley Sr. and Bill Jr. in 1950 at the latter's wedding shortly before Will secretly and liberally funded the start-up of the conservative opinion magazine *National Review*, with William Jr. as editor and publisher and sister Priscilla soon as managing editor. Buckley Family Collection.

lantic Refining Co.	Pantepec Oil Company, C.A. Mexico: 1911–1923 transferred to Venezuela, 1924	Standard Oil Co. of N. J. lease—sub: Creole Petroleum
se		
ion Oil Co. of California		California Petroleum Company lease
se		
	Compagnie Française des Petroles (CFP) lease	
ntepec duction	Pantepec International Holding Company, 1928–1947 Pancoastal exploration	Coastal Caribbean Oil production and refining
nso Oil Producers	Catawba Corporation 1948	Canada Southern Oil
nso Natural Gas	Pan-Israel Oil Co.	General American
rger	Israel-Mediterranean Petro merger	concessions and holdings
ited Canso Oil & Gas, Ltd.	Magellan Petroleum Corp.	Venezuela Guatemala
Jose Petroleum	American Grecian Oil Co. Isle of Zakynthos	Australia and Philippines Italy and Ecuador

areas to make sure that the potential of the new hunting ground was adequately tested and that the company owning the rights could survive initial failures." These functions included assistance with personnel requirements, interfacing with foreign government regulatory agencies, public relations, as well as expertise in acquisition, exploration, and operation of properties. John Buckley was primarily focused on the Venezuelan and Canadian companies; James handled the concessions negotiations in the Philippines, Ecuador, South Africa, Libya, Guatemala, and Italy; and Benjamin Heath handled the Israel and Australia companies as well as Pancoastal in Florida.[58]

This new structure would grow into a global oil exploration organization with operations in more than a dozen countries. *Oil and Gas Journal* in 1949 noted that of the ten most carefully watched exploration wells, three—in the Canadian arctic, central Australia, and offshore South Africa—were clients of Catawba. It was estimated in the mid-1950s that the companies under the guidance of Will Buckley in Venezuela, Canada, Israel, Ecuador, Australia, the Philippines, and Guatemala, as well as Florida had an estimated eighty thousand shareholders and a stock market value of over $110 million, an amount that would today exceed $1 billion.[59]

Grelmschatka

The postwar period was a significant time of transition for Buckley's oil concerns as operations expanded globally. It was also the years when the Buckley children came of age—college graduations, new marriages, new jobs, growing families. At the encouragement of their father, the children wrote and edited a family newsletter beginning in late 1947. Named the *Grelmschatka*, a contraction of the two homes at Great Elm in Sharon and Kamschatka in Camden, was published six times until the death of Will Buckley in 1958. Aloise "Allie" Heath authored the feature column, "The Buckleyana," chronicling the family "doings."[60]

Epilogue
Legacy of an Adventurous Texan

WILLIAM F. BUCKLEY SR. had come a long way from San Diego, Texas. Following a spartan upbringing, Will finished at the University of Texas and at age twenty-seven, law degree in hand, then journeyed to Mexico City in 1908 to open his fledgling law practice. In the last years of President Porfirio Díaz's three-decade-long regime, the capital was a festive cosmopolitan location and the center of business, social, and political power in the country. The dictatorial administration invited millions of dollars in foreign investment that was intended to improve the domestic economy, expand the nation's infrastructure, and raise Mexicans' standard of living. Major economic steps were taken but at the cost of alienating the majority of the population who were not benefiting from the promised progress. Uneasiness about the eventual passing of the aging Díaz emerged in competing rebellious factions outside the capital by 1910. These groups grew rapidly to challenge the old order and succeeded in ending the Porfiriato, ushering in a decade of destructive and deadly revolution.

William Buckley soon had a front-row seat to the violent revolution that swept Mexico. This experience shaped his political views, sharpened his business acumen, and bolstered his religious convictions, while setting the future course of his dynamic business career. After establishing law offices in Mexico City and Tampico, he relinquished the practice to his brothers

revolutionary Mexican leaders that worked to dominate and discredit foreign industry, on the other.

By 1920, more than 150 oil companies worked in Mexico, many of which were small independent operators. As an indication of his impact, Buckley, with his Pantepec Oil Company, was one of the only independent oilmen singled out in Daniel Yergin's 1992 Pulitzer Prize–winning chronicle of the global oil industry, *The Prize: The Epic Quest for Oil, Money and Power.* Ironically, perhaps, Will was among the first Texas oilmen *who did not find oil in Texas.* His first million was made in Mexico, and following his expulsion as a "pernicious foreigner" in 1921, he ventured to pioneer and expand oil operations in Venezuela and locations worldwide for the next three decades.

Buckley's hallmark was a great familiarity with the oil industry and a keen ability to negotiate with local politicians and industry operators. As an independent oilman, he moved effectively in Mexico and Venezuela, due primarily to his extensive knowledge of Spanish, but also to his skill at identifying new areas of oil exploration and his tact relating to local private and public authorities in their language and culture. He was the first Texan to operate in a dozen countries on four continents—in time he had control over and/or options on more than 10 million acres. This accomplishment, coupled with his ease and expertise doing business in foreign lands, placed him among the early pioneers of global oil exploration. The thrill of the job was the hunt for and control of new exploration sites and the resulting "game" of negotiating both control and working agreements to sublease or "farm out" to the big oil firms. One irony of the global exploration of oil is that after the departure of Buckley from Mexico in 1921 and the eventual nationalization of land and petroleum rights, the Mexican oil sector struggled for decades to recover the golden days of the early Tampico-Tuxpan and Veracruz oil fields. Government-controlled exploration and production languished and by the early 1990s there were new calls to open the oil sector to foreign investment. Economic pressures slowly rolled back the restrictions of Article 27 in the Constitution of 1917, and the dominant government-owned PEMEX once again encouraged foreign oil concessions. One only wonders what independent oilman Will Buckley would do to stake a new field in the dormant Burgos region of northern Mexico, just south of the Rio Grande. In Venezuela, where Buckley was highly successful, the socialist political disaster in 1998 crippled oil production, triggered a mass exodus of people and capital, and wrecked the

William F. Buckley at Great Elm in Sharon with his favorite dog, Beau.
Author's Collection.

economy for decades, a clear example of the need for economic diversity in the face of such upheaval.

As William F. "Bill" Buckley Jr. noted about his father, after years raising a family in Sharon, Connecticut, "The call of the South was strong." Will and Aloise's southern roots made them very much at ease in later years at their Camden, South Carolina, home surrounded by family and friends. Their ten children would each find success in their chosen endeavors—all very well versed in their father's devout Catholicism, conservative-patriotic views, and independent flair that ever since has been the hallmark of media

daughters to be absolutely perfect." To this end, his children were, at one time or another, given professional instruction in "apologetics, art, ballroom dancing, banjo, bird-watching, building boats in bottles, calligraphy, canoeing, carpentry, cooking, driving trotting horses, French, fold dancing, golf, guitar, harmony, herb-gardening, horsemanship, history of architecture, ice-skating, mandolin, marimba, music appreciation, organ, painting, piano, playing popular music, rumba, sailing, skiing, Spanish, speech, stenography, swimming, tap-dancing, tennis, typing and woodcarving."

The excellent social and business skills and eclectic learning William Buckley obtained in his youth and through his many experiences led him to desire the same for his children: to be fully prepared, versatile, reverent, and politically savvy. His challenging South Texas upbringing in a small conservative Catholic community of ranchers in the brushlands scratching out a living, followed by formal training in the law, proved to be a complementary combination. In his lifetime, he became one of the most successful and wealthy independent oilmen in the history of the industry, an industry that would dominate the world economic and geopolitical future for decades to follow. Lifelong boyhood friend William Coley observed, "Will Buckley seems to have found out early in life that money and power, while very enjoyable, were means, not ends."

William F. Buckley Sr. suffered a stroke in 1955, and thereafter he and Aloise split most of his time between their two homes in Connecticut and South Carolina. After a couple of trips to milder weather in Bad Gastein, Austria, to escape the New England hay fever season, he died of a stroke at age seventy-seven following his return voyage to New York City on October 5, 1958. By his request, Will Buckley was interred in Camden. Aloise remained in South Carolina with family and dozens of grandchildren until her death in 1985.

Chronological Statement of Events in Mexico City

February 9 to February 18, 1913
William F. Buckley

Sunday, February 9, 1913—The two artillery regiments in Mexico City and the cadets of the Tlalpam Military School "declare" for general Felix Díaz and liberate him and General Reyes from prison in Mexico City.

General Reyes is killed in an attempt to capture the National Palace. In the shooting over five hundred innocent people and church-goers lose their lives in the park in front of the Palace and Cathedral.

President Madero arrives at the Palace from Chapultepec, three miles to the west. Goes to Palace on horseback with small guard. Twelve hundred soldiers, cavalry and infantry follow later, and take up position in the Palace.

The rebelling troops under Felix Díaz take the arsenal or citadel, containing all the large cannon and all reserve arms and ammunition of the nation. It is a low building and constructed for defense, with only broken streets leading to it.

At night President Madero goes to Cuernavaca for reinforcements. Nobody in city expects bombardment.

Monday, February 10, 1913—A day of uncertainty, with a little rifle fighting between outpost. Felix Díaz makes no move other than to secure

No notice of impending bombardment given by either party.

American Ambassador publishes notice to Americans to keep in safe places, and request Government to protect foreign colonies. Police force entirely disappears. Patrols of American and other foreigners established in streets.

Tuesday, February 11, 1913—Bombardment of the citadel begins without warning to the people of the city. Over four hundred soldiers killed in assaults on the citadel in narrow streets. Shells fire in many angles from the citadel. Two American women killed in their homes. Reinforcements to the Government arrive from Zapata country, and ammunition for the Government arrives from Veracruz.

American Ambassador asks Government and revolutionists to respect non-combatants. Re-publishes warning to Americans.

Midnight: All patients of English Hospital ordered out. Battery set up nearby.

Wednesday, February 12, 1913—Bombardment and assaults continue. Battery of 12 guns set up about a quarter of a mile from the Embassy but out of line. Its shells begin to destroy homes of American and others. The firing temporarily stopped at request of Embassy, and over twelve hundred people in danger removed to houses in the Embassy district where they are cared for by Embassy service organized since beginning of bombardment to meet the emergency. Cable office, post office, and hospital established at Embassy. Messenger service to cable office started.

Ambassador [US] and German and Spanish Ministers go through the firing line to Palace, where they request President to have more regards for foreign lives and property. Go later with British Minister to citadel where they make the same request of General Díaz.

Replies not entirely satisfactory. Apparent that bombardment must continue. Many non-combatants killed. Bodies burned in streets and in piles outside of town. Red Cross and White Cross services abolished. Surgeons subsequently protected by American flag.

Thursday, February 13, 1913—Bombardment continues. News of sailing of American warships arrives and makes good impression. Bombardment subsides in the evening.

Friday, February 14, 1913—Bombardment renewed in morning. Senate convenes and appoints a committee to wait on the president to request his resignation as only method to end the fierce battle in the City. President Madero refused to receive them. Spanish Minister, member of the cabinet and other delegations reported to be making the same request. Former president de la Barra tries to mediate the matter. His attendant killed at his side.

General Blanquet is expected to arrive from Toluca, but does not appear. Troops brought in from as far north as Monterrey.

Infantry and cavalry assaults on citadel becoming rarer. Embassy automobile held up by men in army uniforms, and robbed of $300.

Saturday, February 15, 1913—Bombardment continued. Shells striking new points in town. Government soldiers reported to be going over to Felix Díaz.

Ambassador makes another automobile trip to palace and returns with promise of President to respect Embassy district as neutral zone; to remove soldiers stationed on roof on a school to which American women refugees had been sent; to give proper notice in case of opening fire in localities occupied by foreigners; to cooperate in establishment of centers for distribution of bread to the poor; and to grant an armistice of 24 hours for the removal of all those in the danger zone.

Messenger (Capt. Burnside) sent to notify General Díaz of agreement. He orally consents to armistice, asking Government to fix the time.

Americans and foreigners notified of arrangement. More optimistic feeling produced.

Pay-day—Practically no workman paid off. This is a serious phase.

Sunday, February 16, 1913—Fast work done removing families, some of which were marooned without food or water for days. Armistice broken at 10:30 and fire resumed. Government accuses revolutionists of opening fire. Revolutionists accuse government of placing

Rurales in district refusing request for passage through lines issued by Embassy for humanitarian purposes.

Monday, February 17, 1913—Bombardment continues, but government soldiers, many of them drunk, broken into small bands all over town, from either fatigue, unwillingness to join the storming parties, or by order from superiors for fear of detection in masses. Evident that soldiers are not enthusiastic about attacking. Outpost from citadel fighting all day near Embassy, with rural police in streets. Bodies burning all over town.

General Blanquet, with 1,800 men, known to have arrived from Toluca, but does not go into action, . . . as he is an aggressive soldier, and his men are fresh.

Secretary of relations comes to Embassy to say that a battery must be planted nearby, and offering Ambassador a temporary embassy in the suburb, and transportation thereto with army wagons. Ambassador asks if the many refugees in the district will also be removed and cared for. As the Secretary cannot assure him of this, the Ambassador refuses to go and leave his people to their fate, and protest against the proposed violation of the neutral zone. Result, no battery is placed there, and refugees are saved, This act of Mr. Wilson saved the lives of hundreds of people.

General feeling in all quarters since morning is that the affair is nearly ended. Government ammunition reported nearly exhausted. Soldiers unpaid and unfed.

At night sharpshooters firing on American patrols. Drunkenness and looting among many bands of detached soldiers increasing. Smell of burning bodies pervading city. Disintegration manifest.

Tuesday, February 18, 1913—Bombardment continues, but much slackened. More infantry fire extending from the citadel. Late in the day a messenger comes from the Palace with a letter from General Huerta to the diplomatic corps reporting that he has arrested the President in the interest of humanity, and states that he desires to end the battles. Also requests diplomatic corps to notify General Díaz that he desires a conference.

Jubilation in center of town, but rifle fighting continues around the citadel and in residential district.

Ambassador send messenger to citadel reporting arrest of Madero and conveying Huerta's request for a conference. Díaz thanks messenger for this notice, and says he will meet Huerta only at the Embassy. Suspicion naturally then existed between the leaders in the ten-day battle. Messenger goes to Palace and notifies General Huerta, who agrees to meet General Díaz in the Embassy.

At about 9:00 P.M. Huerta arrives at Embassy. A messenger is sent to citadel to notify Díaz who returns to the Embassy with him.

Negotiations continue until early morning, when, after three failures to agree smoothed out by diplomacy of the Ambassador, whom both requested to remain with them, they come to terms; written memorandum of agreement read before witnesses in the Embassy and left with Mr. Wilson.

Police service immediately restored. Looting stopped and dead collected from streets.

Wednesday, February 19, 1913—City at peace and assuming normal conditions for first time in ten days. Ambassador cheered in the streets and Americans thanked for their part in amelioration of conditions.

Ambassador, the Diplomatic Corps, requests Government assurance that the life of Madero will be spared. Assurance given.

Mrs. Madero and Mrs. Pino Suarez come to Embassy and ask Ambassador to intercede for the lives of their husbands. Government assurance communicate to them, and at their request another appeal for protection for the men made to the officers of the Government.

Laborers in the city return to work. Relief committee of the Embassy begins distribution of funds and food.

Source: Buckley Papers

Embassy and Consul Staff, 1911–1919

US Embassy, Mexico City

Henry Lane Wilson, ambassador (appt. Nov 1909; ret. Dec 1913)

Nelson O'Shaughnessy, chargé d'affaires

Montgomery Schuyler, first secretary

Henry F. Tennant, second secretary

Capt. W. A. Burnside, military attaché

Luis d'Antin, clerk and interpreter

Charles B. Parker, second clerk

Dr. Ryan, embassy physician

Arnold Shanklin, consul general

George A. Chamberlain, consul general

Henry B. Fletcher, ambassador (March 1917)

US Consular General Officers, Mexico, 1911–1919

City	Consul officer	Comments
Nuevo Laredo	Alonzo B. Garrett	investigates Vergara murder
Tampico	Henry Miller	leads evacuation from Tampico
	Claude I. Dawson	
	& Thomas H. Bevan	
Veracruz	William W. C___	

& Phillip E. Holland

San Luis Potosí	Wilbert L. Bonney	arrested April 21, 1914
Piedras Negras	William P. Blocker	San Antonio rancher
Puebla	William O. Jenkins	kidnapped for ransom
Guadalajara	John R. Silliman	Carranza contact
	Will B. Davis	
Torreón	George C. Carothers	Villa contact
Durango	Theodore C. Hamm	Villa contact
Matamoros	Jesse H. Johnson	border agent
Mazatlán	William E. Alger	seaport
Chihuahua	Marion Letcher	Benton investigator
Hermosillo	Louis Hostetter	commercial
	Robert Gutman	
Monterrey	Philip Hanna	arrested April 21, 1914
Ciudad Porfirio	Luther T. Ellsworth	assassination threats
Nogales	Thomas Bowman	border
	Frederick Simpich	
Aguascalientes	Gaston Schmutz	agricultural region
	George Donald	
Ensenada	Claude E. Guyant	Baja seaport
	Frederick Sawdat	
Manzanillo	Richard M. Stadden	seaport
Guymas	Charles D. Taylor	
Tuxpan	Arthur C. Payne	1916 only
Cananea	Charles L. Montague	1916 only
Topia	Thomas J. Lawrence	1911 only

Source: Buckley Papers

Pacto de la Ciudadela

I N THE CITY OF MEXICO, at 9:30 p.m. of February 18, 1913, General Felix Díaz and Victoriano Huerta met together, the former being assisted by attorneys Fidencio Hernandez and Rodolfo Reyes and the latter by Lieutenant Colonel Joaquin Mass and Engineer Enrique Zepeda.

General Huerta stated that, inasmuch as the situation of Mr. Madero's government was unsustainable and in order to prevent further bloodshed and out of feelings of national fraternity, he had made prisoners of Mr. Madero, his cabinet, and other persons; and that he desires to express his good wished to General Díaz to the effect that the elements represented by him might fraternize and, all united, save the present distressful situation.

General Díaz stated that his movements have had no other object than to serve the national welfare, and that accordingly he is ready to make any sacrifice which might rebound to the benefit of the country.

After discussions had taken place on the subject among all those present as mentioned above, the following was agreed on:

First. From this time on, the Executive Power which has held sway is deemed not to exist and is not recognized, all elements represented by Generals Díaz and Huerta pledging themselves to prevent by all means any attempt to restore said power.

There shall be created a new ministry, to be charged specially with solving the agrarian problem and matters connected therewith, being called the ministry of Agriculture, and the portfolio thereof being entrusted to Lic. Manuel Garza Aldape.

Any modifications which may for any reason be decided upon in this Cabinet slate shall take place in the same manner in which the slate itself was made up.

Third. While the legal situation is being determined and settled, Generals Huerta and Díaz are placed in charge of all elements and authorities of every kind the exercise whereof may be necessary in order to afford guaranties.

Fourth. General Felix Díaz declines the offer to form part of the Provisional Cabinet in case General Huerta assumes the Provisional presidency, in order that he may remain at liberty to undertake his work along the lines of his promises to his party at the coming election, which purpose he wishes be expressed clearly and which is fully understood by the signers.

Fifth. Official notice shall immediately be given to the foreign representatives, it being confined to stating to them that the Executive Power has ceased; that provision is being made for a legal substitute thereof; that meantime the full authority thereof is vested in Generals Díaz and Huerta; and that all proper guaranties will be afforded to their respective countrymen.

Sixth. All revolutionists shall at once be invited to cease their hostile movements, endeavor being made to reach the necessary settlements.

General Victoriano Huerta   General Felix Díaz

Joaquin Mass

Rodolfo Reyes

Fidencio Hernandez

Dr. F. L. Collantes

E. Zepeda

Buckley Family Tree

William Frank Buckley Sr.

John Buckley   Mary Langford Buckley
1851–1903   1851–1930

John Charles   Priscilla   Claude Herbert   Eleanor Claire   Edmund Langford
1872–1890   1879–1956   1884–1975   1886–1965   1888–1951
William F. Buckley Sr.   Aloise Steiner Buckley
July 11, 1881–October 5, 1958   1895–1985

Aloise Buckley Heath (1918–1967)
John William Buckley (1920–1984)
James Lane Buckley (1923–)
Priscilla Langford Buckley (1921–2012)
Jane Buckley Smith (1924–2007)
William Frank Buckley Jr. (1925–2008)
Patricia Buckley Bozell (1927–2008)
Mary Ann Buckley (1928–1928)
Fergus Reid Buckley (1930–2014)
Maureen Buckley O'Reilly (1933–1964)

Notes

Introduction

1. Buckley, *American Family*, 29–30, 154.

Chapter 1

1. C. F. I. Madero, "Al Ejercito Mexicano," San Luis Potosi, October 5, 1910, and "Partido Constitucional Progresista," September 1911, Garcia Collection, Benson Latin American History Collection, University of Texas at Austin.

2. V. Carranza in Saltillo to Francisco Madero in Mexico City, February 4, 1913, File 122.1, William F. Buckley Sr. Papers, Benson Latin American History Collection, University of Texas at Austin (hereafter cited as Buckley Papers); Gen. Emiliano Zapata to Trinidad Sanchez Santos, August 20, 1911, Garcia Collection, Benson Latin American History Collection, University of Texas at Austin; Butterfield, "Conspiracy against Madero," 474; Krauze, *Mexico*, 240–42. See also Madero, *La sucesión presidencial en 1910*; and Raat, *Revoltosos*, 243–45.

3. "Chronological Statement of Events in Mexico City: February 9–13, 1913, Exhibit 'A,'" Buckley Papers (see appendix A); Henry L. Wilson to Knox, 812.00/6056, February 9, 1913, and 812.00/6091, February 11, 1913, Department of State, *Papers Relating to the Foreign Relations of the United States* (Washington: GPO, 1922–36) [hereafter cited as FRUS], 1913.

4. Wilson to Knox, 312.11/1073, February 12, 1913; and Knox to Wilson, February 12, 1913—in FRUS 1913. Secretary Knox quickly approved $10,000 in funds to succor Americans needing assistance.

Díaz; and Brayer, "Cananea Incident," 387–415; Singelmann, "Sugar Industry in Postrevolutionary Mexico," 64–65.

7. Remarks delivered by Henry L. Wilson at Knights of Columbus Chapter of Mass. Dinner in Boston, April 19, 1923, Buckley Papers. See also Ross, *Francisco I. Madero*; and Wilson to Knox, 812.00/6394, February 26, 1913, FRUS 1913.

8. Governor O. Colquitt to M. A. Jennings, August 26, 1912, File 151; and V. Carranza to Francisco I. Madero, February 3, 1913, File 122.1—Buckley Papers; "Colquitt's Activity Exciting Jealousy," *Austin American*, August 29, 1912; "Letters Reveal Carranza Plot against Madero," *New York Herald* (hereafter cited as *Herald*), December 6, 1919; Sterling, *Los últimos días del presidente Madero*, 4–17; Katz, *Secret War in Mexico*, 45–49; Wilkinson, *Laredo and the Rio Grande Frontier*, 382–83; Ivey, *Ranger Ideal*, 2:442–48; Fehrenbach, *Fire and Blood*, 488–92.

9. Beals, *Porfirio Díaz*, 447–52; Womack, *Zapata*, 86. See also Slattery, *Felipe Angeles*, 43–57.

10. Memo, H. L. Wilson to Canada, February 18, 1913, and Canada to Secretary of State, February 23, 1913, File 167, Buckley Papers; Wilson to Knox, 812.00/6244, February 18, 1913, FRUS 1913; Testimony of Henry Lane Wilson, "Investigation of Mexican Affairs," Committee on Foreign Relations, 66th Cong., 2nd sess., Senate Doc. 285, 1919–1920 [hereafter cited as Mexican Affairs], 2:2261–64; Wilson, *Diplomatic Episodes*, 252–88; Meyer, *Huerta*, 57–63; Winton, *Mexico, Past and Present*, 180–81. For the German diplomatic perspective of events, see Schuler, *Murder and Counterrevolution in Mexico*, 15–60.

11. Knox to Wilson, 812.00/6058, February 10, 1918, FRUS 1913. See also Testimony of Lucille Wetherell, Mexican Affairs, 1:1700–1703; Testimony of George C. Carothers, Mexican Affairs, 1:1760–62; and de Zayas Enriquez, *Mexico and the Policy of President Wilson*, 35–59.

12. Knox to Wilson, February 10, 1913, and Wilson to Knox, February 19, 1913, 812.00/6264, and February 17, 1913, 812.00/6225 and 6223A—all in FRUS 1913; Wilson, *Diplomatic Episodes*, 280–88; Blaisdell, "Henry Lane Wilson," 126–35. See also Prida, *La Culpa de Lane Wilson*; and Davids, "American Political and Economic Penetration," 308–11. For a detailed account by Amb. Henry Lane Wilson, see Wilson, Mexican Affairs, 2:2259–2302.

13. V. Huerta to President Taft, 812.00/6250, February 18, 1913, FRUS 1913; Meyer, *Huerta*, 66–69, 235–36. See also Blaisdell, "Henry Lane Wilson," 126–35; Meyer and Beezley, *Mexico*, 445; and Callcott, *Liberalism in Mexico*, 228. At the formal opening of Congress on April 15, 1917, President-elect Carranza, in a long rambling report, confirmed the process of transition used by Huerta for the "appearance of legality"; see Carranza opening presentation to Congress, April 15, 1917, FRUS 1917, 984.

14. W. W. Canada to Secretary of State, February 23, 1913, No. 797, Buckley Papers; Adams, *Murder and Intrigue*, 13; O'Shaughnessy, *Diplomatic Days*, 217. US Consul Canada, posted in Veracruz, noted that Madero and the vice president were arrested by both General Huerta and Aureliano Blanquet.

15. Victoriano Huerta, "Huerta on Madero Deaths," *New York Times*, March 8, 1913; Wilson, *Diplomatic Episodes*, 283–88; Meyer, *Huerta*, 82. See also Weber, *Heroic Mexico*, 119–28. Nemesio Garcia Naranjo, a close Buckley friend and distinguished Mexican journalist and lawyer, noted, "No sensible or moral human being can justify the murder . . . it will always stand out as the most stupid crime committed in Mexico." Quoted in Garcia Naranjo, "A Friend of Mexico," Buckley and Buckley, *W.F.B.: An Appreciation by His Family and Friends* (hereafter cited as *W.F.B. Appreciation*), 42.

16. Consul Canada to State, "Political Conditions," February 23, 1913, No. 797, Buckley Papers; Knox to Wilson, February 24, 1913, 735; and Wilson to Knox, February 26, 1913, 742—in FRUS 1913; Wilson, *Diplomatic Episodes*, 296–99; Morris, *Our Mexican Muddle*, 96–100; Womack, *Zapata*, 160.

17. Wilson to Knox, 812.00/6321, February 23, 1913, FRUS 1913; Womack, *Zapata*, 160; "Says H. L. Wilson Guilty [of Madero murder] with Huerta," *New York Times*, January 10, 1914; Quirk, *Mexican Revolution*, 7; O'Shaughnessy, *Diplomat's Wife in Mexico*, 121, 215. Shortly after the events, the March 8, 1913, issue of the widely read *Literary Digest* reported, in an article titled "The Iron Hand in Mexico," that in Mexico it seemed there was "quiet acceptance of the deed [the murder of Madero] in Mexico City."

18. Buckley to H. L. Wilson, March 24, 1928, Buckley Papers. Buckley made the same comments at the December 6, 1919, US congressional hearing; see Testimony of William F. Buckley, Mexican Affairs, 1:770. It has never been proven who ordered the assassination; perhaps it was Huerta, or Felix Díaz, or Aureliano Blanquet. Mexican historian Enrique Krauze, in his grand history of Mexico, has insightful observations on the "memorable death, an ironic legacy for future generations" (*Mexico*, 363). Furthermore, in November 1940, in response to concerns expressed by Jack and Warden Wilson, Buckley responded to a *Time* magazine article that once again impugned Ambassador Wilson's role in Madero's death, advising the editor that "the assassination of Madero was not political but an act of revenge carried out by members of the families of Colonels Riverol and Izquierdo, members of Madero's staff whom he shot in one of his almost maniacal frenzies when they tried to persuade him to resign after the report was confirmed that General Blanquet['s] troops had trained his guns on Madero's palace." Buckley to Editor, *Time*, November 12, 1940, Box 32, Buckley Papers.

19. "Mad Dog," *Brenham (TX) Weekly Banner*, May 14, 1880; Interview with James L. Buckley, August 14, 1995, by Wendy S. White, Oral History Project, Historical Society of the District of Columbia Circuit, 2–5 [hereafter James Buckley

Willie—never Billy. His wife called him Will. In Mexico, he routinely was introduced as Guillermo. Also, his five youngest children first spoke Spanish before they learned English.

21. James Buckley Circuit Interview, 6–10; Claude quoted in Buckley, *American Family*, 8–9. See also Buckley, *Gleanings from an Unplanned Life*, 11–12; and Castillo Crimm and Massey, *Turn-of-the-Century Photographs*, 26–34.

22. *L. L. Wright vs. The State of Texas and John Buckley*, Supreme Court of Texas, Austin Term, 1890; Uncle Claude Buckley to Edmund, n.d., Buckley Family Files; Wayne Slater, "The Buckley Clan's Roots," *Dallas Morning News*, September 20, 1987.

23. "Stepped Down and Out," *Austin Statesman*, August 2, 1890; "A Gang of Horse Thieves," *Austin Statesman*, August 16, 1891; "Wouldn't Work Twice," *Fort Worth Daily Gazette*, September 20, 1891; "San Diego," *Fort Worth Daily Gazette*, September 13, 1894; "A Gray Horse: What Jack Evans Thinks," *Fort Worth Daily Gazette*, February 4, 1892; "Killing at a Quarry," *Galveston Daily News*, August 20, 1895; "Death of John Buckley," *Corpus Christi Weekly Caller*, August 14, 1903; Young, *Catarino Garza's Revolution*; Weeks, "Texas-Mexican," 625–26; W.F.B. *Appreciation*, 11–14; Buckley, *American Family*, 57, 242; Buckley, *Gleanings from an Unplanned Life*, 12.

24. James Buckley Circuit Interview, 8–10, 17; Heath, *Will Mrs. Major Go to Hell?*, 30–31; *City Directory of Austin*, 106; W.F.B. *Appreciation*, 13–19; *The Cactus*; Buckley, *American Family*, 50–51.

25. Buckley, *American Family*, 136; Cecilio Velasco, in W.F.B. *Appreciation*, 19, 25–31; Beals, *Porfirio Díaz*, 389; Creelman, "Thrilling Story of President Diaz," 1; Curley, *Citizens and Believers*, 59; Crowell, "What's Wrong with Mexico?" 262. See also Harris and Sadler, "1911 Reyes Conspiracy," 325–48; and Cumberland, "Mexican Revolutionary Movements from Texas," 285–303.

26. Adams, *Murder and Intrigue*, 159–60; Pletcher, *Rails, Mines, and Progress*, 313–15; Hart, *Empire and Revolution*, 123; Klein, *Jay Gould*, 274; Callahan, *American Foreign Policy*, 475–533; W.F.B. Sr. to Pope, May 17, 1914 quoted in Buckley, *American Family*, 111; "Mexico amenazado por los Estados O[U]nidos," *Mexico City Nueva Era*, August 11, 1911. See also Coatsworth, *Growth against Development*. Grenville M. Dodge, a leading railroad competitor, was very impressed with the Mexican Oriental Interoceanic & International Railroad, calling it "the best line in the republic, both in an engineering and a commercial point of view." The railroad's success allowed the movement of people and material into the heart of Mexico, while further linking Mexico to the US economy.

27. Jennings, "Pres. Díaz interview,," n.p., n.d., Buckley Papers; "Society," *Mexican Herald*, January 27, 1911, August 30, 1911, September 11, 1911; Wilson to Sec. Bryan, 812.00/7999, July 9, 1913, FRUS 1913; interview with Amy Hopkins, 1974, Houston Public Library, Houston Oral History Project; Buckley, "Madero's Downfall"; Johns, *City of Mexico*, 50–51. Interestingly, the number of Chinese estimated to be residing in Mexico in early 1914, of which twenty thousand were

in Mexico City, was the same as the number of Americans: thirty thousand. Minister Reinsch, American Legation, Peking, to Secretary of State, 312.03/70, April 25, 1914, FRUS 1914.

28. Díaz, "To the American People," México, DF, March 14, 1911, Buckley Papers; Schoonover, *Dollars over Dominion*, 257, notes letters encouraging Porfirio Díaz in February 1867 to seek the active cooperation of the United States to enhance economic and industrial development; [?] to Porfirio Díaz, February 27 and May 20, 1867, in Mexico City, Biblioteca Nacional, Archivo Benito Pablo Juárez. See also Pletcher, "Mexico Opens the Door," 1–14; and *Album Conmemorativo, Visita a Chihuahua del Sr. Presidente General Don Porfirio Díaz*, Chihuahua, October 1909, 25–28; and Schell, *Integral Outsiders*, 134–49. Díaz worked to attract new investment through early 1911, mainly from Europe to offset concerns over the growing American concessions; see Katz, *Secret War in Mexico*, 60–84.

29. Creelman, *Díaz*, 381–95; Beatty, "Impact of Foreign Trade," 399–433; Turner, *Barbarous Mexico*, 259; Memo, "The Visit of W. J. Bryan to the City of Mexico," n.d., File 167, Buckley Papers; Smith, *United States and Revolutionary Nationalism*, x. For example, railway mileage during the Porfiriato grew from 407 miles in 1876 to more than 15,000 miles in 1910; and the total length of telegraph and telephone lines grew from 4,200 miles to more than 20 million miles over the same period.

30. Wilson, Mexican Affairs, 2:2256; "The Man Who Made Mexico," *New York Sun* (hereafter cited as *Sun*), July 4, 1915. See also Johnson, *Madero in Texas*. Between November 1910 and February 1911, the date Madero issued the Plan de San Luis Potosí and began taking an active role in the revolution, the US State Department received thirty-one cables from the ambassador in Mexico City and the Mexican ambassador in Washington protesting and identifying cross-border rebel activities against the Díaz government; see FRUS 1911, 358–406.

31. "Victoriano Huerta," *New York Times*, May 31, 1914; Meyer, *Huerta*, 3–16; H. L. Wilson, April 19, 1923, Buckley Papers; Wilson, *Diplomatic Episodes*, 295; O'Shaughnessy, *Diplomat's Wife in Mexico*, 60; Beals, *Porfirio Díaz*, 450. See also Lieuwen, *Mexican Militarism*, 3–17.

32. V. Carranza to Taft, 812.00/6425, February 26, 1913; US Consul Hostetter (Hermosillo, Sonora) to Knox, 812.00/ 6434, February 28, 1913; and Wilson to Bryan, 812.00/6503, March 5, 1913—all in FRUS 1913; "Huerta as a Dictator," *Literary Digest*, October 25, 1913, 737–38.

33. Woodrow Wilson to E. G. Conklin, in Baker, *Woodrow Wilson*, 4:55; Smith,

wealthy and powerful Liberal with extensive oil holdings; and (2) the British navy had a long-term contract with Cowdray's company for fuel oil, "which was rapidly becoming indispensable as the fuel for warships." See also Heindel, *American Impact on Great Britain*, 111–12.

35. James Bryce to Bryan, 812.00/6985, March 31, 1913; Letcher to Knox, September 15, 1912, 812.00/5056; and Steever to Knox, September 15, 1912, 812.00/5031—all in FRUS 1913; Sir Edward Grey to Sir C. Spring Rice, July 14, 1914, in Bourne, *British Documents on Foreign Affairs* (hereafter cited as BFA); Meyer, *Huerta*, 19–44; Maurer, *Power and the Money*, 141–45; Meyer and Deeds, *Course of Mexican History*, 501, 509; *New York World* (hereafter cited as *World*), March 7–13, 1913; Cumberland, *Mexican Revolution*, 90. Formal recognition of Huerta was extended, for example, by China, Italy, Germany, Spain, Portugal, Belgium, Italy, Japan, Great Britain, Austria-Hungary, Norway, and Russia. The term "dollar diplomacy," well known in diplomatic circles, was used by the State Department; see Memo, Pierreport, 817.75/5424, May 22, 1913, FRUS 1913.

36. H. L. Wilson, April 19, 1923, Buckley Papers. See also O'Shaughnessy, *Diplomat's Wife in Mexico*, 88.

37. Spring Rice to Grey, Doc. 129, August 15, 1913, BFA; "Idealism as a Mexican Policy," *Literary Digest*, November 8, 1913; Clements, "Woodrow Wilson's Mexican Policy," 115–17. See also Link, *Wilson the Diplomatist*, 15–16.

38. Bogus, *Buckley*, 49; Notter, *Foreign Policy of Woodrow Wilson*, 274; Meyer and Beezley, *Mexico*, 446–47; Williams, *Tragedy of American Diplomacy*, 64. Williams notes that many historians have characterized Wilson's diplomacy as "moral imperialism" or "missionary diplomacy."

39. Garcia Naranjo, "A Friend of Mexico," *W.F.B. Appreciation*, 36–50; Markmann, *Buckleys*, 12–14; Buckley to House, November 3, 1913, Box 20, Yale University Archives; "Foreign Comments on Wilson's Policy," Lima, Peru, *La Prensa*, quoted in *Literary Digest*, October 18, 1913, File 114, Buckley Papers.

40. "Huerta Worries British," *New York Times*, November 7, 1913; Lodge to Spring Rice, March 10, 1913, in Gwynn, *Letters and Friendships*, 1:189; Adams, *Murder and Intrigue*, 51–52.

41. "Mexican Foothold Sought for Japan," *New York Times*, July 20, 1913.

42. Gerald to Bryan, 812.00/9259, October 17, 1913, FRUS 1913; "Germans Denounce Our Mexican Policy," *New York Times*, November 5, 1913; Spring Rice to Grey, Doc. 131, August 19, 1913, BFA; Maurer, *Power and the Money*, 141–53. See also Gwynn, *Letters and Friendships*, 178–208, on the British perspective of the Mexico crisis.

43. Seymour, *Intimate Papers of Colonel House*, 1:194–95, 204–6; Buckley, *American Family*, 142; Markmann, *Buckleys*, 12; Diamond, *Economic Thought of Woodrow Wilson*, 152. See also "Huerta's Pacific Message," *Literary Digest*, September 27, 1913. The British government committed the Royal Navy to petroleum and laid the keel of the battleship HMS *Queen Elizabeth* in 1912 to use nothing but fuel oil.

44. "Mexico and Mobilization," *New York Times*, November 6, 1913; Lt. Col. M. F. Gates, "Report on the United States Army. 1912–1913," April 29, 1914, 311–12, BFA; John Lind to the President, Veracruz, January 10, 1914, in Link, *Papers of Woodrow Wilson*, 29:111, 118–27, 328; Admiral Cradock to Admiralty, Doc. 190, March 8, 1914, BFA; and Spring Rice to Grey, Doc. 167, January 23, 1914, BFA; "Mexico and Mobilization," *New York Times*, November 6, 1913. The regular US Army in mid-1913 had a strength on paper of 46,000 in combat arms, and a stationary 30,150 troops manning coastal artillery defenses. Also, in his January 10, 1914, telegram to the president, Lind took the opportunity to attack Catholics: "The aristocratic element in the past has used the Church as its principal instrumentality for keeping the people in subjugation and slavery."

45. Memo, "Carranza's Treason against Pres. Madero," from No. 16 to Buckley, December 9, 1919, Buckley Papers; "Letters Reveal Carranza Plot against Madero," *Herald*, December 8, 1919.

46. "Plan de Guadalupe," Publicado en el numero I de 'el Constitucionalista' organo oficial de la Primera Jefetura, en Hermosillo, Sonora, el 2 de Diciembre de 1913, Buckley Papers; "The Plan of Guadalupe Which Rebels Insist Upon," *Sun*, July 18, 1914.

47. "The Plan of Guadalupe Which Rebels Insist Upon," *Sun*, July 18, 1914; "Carranza Pledges Mexico Neutrality," *Sun*, April 17, 1917; Memo No. 18, Source: F. Sommerfeld, Subject: Henry Lane Wilson, January 19, 1920, Buckley Papers; Consul Holland to Bryan, 812.00/6968, March 11, 1913, FRUS 1913; "Affairs in Mexico," 64th Cong., 1st sess., Senate, Doc. 324, 1916, 24; Beals, *Brimstone and Chili*, 324–28. The telegram was sent by Ambassador Wilson to the consul on March 3, 1913. Also, John Reed, in *Insurgent Mexico*, 249, noted that in his in-person meeting with Carranza, the First Chief "wore smoked [colored] glasses."

48. Memo, "The Mexican Constitution of 1917: The Effect on Property Rights and Americans," n.d., Buckley Papers. See also "Letters Reveal Carranza Plot against Madero," *Herald*, December 8, 1919; and Beals, *Brimstone and Chili*, 324–28, 330–33.

49. Ignacio Bonillas, "The Character and Progress of the Revolution," draft paper for the American Academy of Political and Social Science, January 1917, File 122.5, Buckley Papers; Buckley, Mexican Affairs, 1:768–70; Holland to Knox, 812.00/6472, February 21, 1913, FRUS 1913; Adams, *Murder and Intrigue*, 59–63.

50. "Diagnosing Mexico's Case," *Literary Digest*, May 17, 1913, 1147–52; "Mexico: A Review," *Outlook*, November 22, 1913, 611–15; Katz, *Secret War in Mexico*, 20. Executions by Carrancistas by order of the First Chief continued through

Doheny's oil company, and he was succeeded at the State Department by New York lawyer Robert Lansing.

52. Spring Rice to Grey, Doc. 139, October 29, 1913, BFA; Houston, *Eight Years with Wilson's Cabinet*, 69; Hill, *Emissaries to a Revolution*, 49–62; Hart, *Empire and Revolution*, 162–63, 306; "Lind Sent for Final Effort," *New York Times*, November 8, 1913.

53. "Henry Lane Wilson Sues," *New York Times*, May 11, 1916. Wilson filed a suit against *Harper's* for $350,000.

54. Sommerfeld memo, January 19, 1920, and "Excerpts from articles entitled 'Huerta and the Two Wilsons,'" *Harper's Weekly*, Buckley Papers; Wilson, *Diplomatic Episodes*, 176–77; Stephenson, *John Lind of Minnesota*, 230–31; Katz, *Secret War in Mexico*, 89; Hill, *Emissaries to a Revolution*, 26, 892. Luis d'Antin was employed as a clerk and legal counselor at the US Embassy in 1911. Born in Texas of a French father and Mexican mother, he spoke fluent Spanish. In addition to providing intel to Mexico, he provided inside data to Lind.

55. Jennings to William R. Hearst, March 23, 1914, Buckley Papers.

56. Hill, *Emissaries to a Revolution*, 30–37, 92; Cumberland, *Mexican Revolution*, 89–93; Villalpando and Rosas, "Venustiano Carranza," in *Historia de México a través de sus Gobernantes*, 186–87. See also Central Intelligence Agency, Benbow, "All the Brains"; and Cline, *United States and Mexico*, 141–42.

57. Bryan to O'Shaughnessy, 812.00/8061, August 4, 1913, FRUS 1913; Buckley, Mexican Affairs, 1:774–78; "Mr. Lind's Mission to Mexico," *Literary Digest*, August 16, 1913, 235; Testimony of John Lind, Mexican Affairs, 2:2219. See also Starr, *Mexico and the United States*; Society of the American Colony of Mexico City, "Facts Submitted . . ."

58. Buckley, Mexican Affairs, 1:774–75.

59. "A Plea for Justice," Ester Lobato Uda de Barreiro to Senate and House Representatives, August 27, 1913, Buckley Papers; "Mr. Lind Should Be Cautious," *New York Times*, November 8, 1913; and "Say Lind Upset Situation," *New York Times*, November 9, 1913; O'Shaughnessy to Bryan, 123.W931, July 17, 1913, FRUS 1913; Hill, "Progressive Politician as a Diplomat," 360; Stephenson, *John Lind of Minnesota*, 208–29; Sweetman, *Landing at Veracruz*, 4–5; Smith, *Benighted Mexico*, 13–14; O'Shaughnessy, *Diplomat's Wife in Mexico*, 217; Testimony of Sloan W. Emery, Mexican Affairs, 2:2216–20. US Consul W. W. Canada, concerned for Lind's safety, requested and received a detachment of six marines from the USS *Minnesota* for twenty-four-hour security duty at the American Consulate in Veracruz.

60. Testimony of M. J. Slattery, April 1, 1920, Mexican Affairs, 2:2007; Hill, "Progressive Politician as a Diplomat," 360–68; "Mr. John Lind," *Nation*, August 7, 1913, 112; Smith, *Benighted Mexico*, 226–30. See also Lara Pardo, "Tragic Farce of John Lind," 57.

61. Woodrow Wilson, "Wilson's Special Message on Mexico," Joint Session of Congress, August 27, 1913, File 223, Buckley Papers. This presidential proclamation

was transcribed and remained in Buckley's files for more than a decade, and it served as a key reference document in preparations for congressional hearings.

62. "Buckley Back to Mexico," *Austin Statesman*, September 2, 1913; "President Wilson and Mexico," *American Review of Reviews*, September 1913, 280–83; "The Key to President Wilson's Mexican Policy," *Literary Digest*, May 30, 1914, 1297–99; Buckley to House, November 29, 1913, Box 20, Yale University Archives. See also "Address of Mexican Affairs at Joint Session of Congress, August 27, 1913," in Scott, *President Wilson's Foreign Policy*, 1–9; and "American Exodus from Mexico," *Literary Digest*, September 13, 1913, 405–6.

63. Buckley, *American Family*, 162–64. See also "The Rise of Villa's Star," *Literary Digest*, April 18, 1914, 899; Katz, *Life and Times of Pancho Villa*; and McLynn, *Villa and Zapata*; Brandt, "Pancho Villa," 146–62. Representatives of the National Association for the Protection of American Rights in Mexico testified to the Fall Committee in November 1919 that from April 10 to July 31, 1919, 317 train robberies, rebel incidents, murders, looting of ranches, and/or battles took place. Mexican Affairs, 1:715.

Chapter 2

1. V. Carranza to President Wilson, 812.00/7298, April 21, 1913, FRUS 1913; "Arms to Huerta Indirectly," *New York Times*, December 24, 1913.

2. Buckley Timeline, Mexico 1914–15, Buckley Papers; Bryan to O'Shaughnessy, November 24, 1913, FRUS 1914, 443–44; President's Address to Congress, December 2, 1913, FRUS 1913, 864. See also Small, *Forgotten Peace*, 22, 29–30.

3. Gov. O. B. Colquitt to Bryan, 812.00/7578, May 19, 1913, FRUS 1913; Raat, *Revoltosos*, 170, 231–32, 247; Kerig, *Luther T. Ellsworth*, 59; Harris and Sadler, "1911 Reyes Conspiracy," 325–48; Kurzman, *Democracy Denied*, 128–33, 233–34. The neutrality statutes only prohibited the organizing of a military expedition on US soil to be carried out against a noncombatant foreign nation.

4. Bryan to Colquitt, 812.00/7743, May 13, 1913; and Mexican Embassy to State, 812.00/10023, November 26, 1913—in FRUS 1913; "Stop Rifles at Laredo," *New York Times*, April 10, 1911; "100,00 Militia Are Concentrating for Service on the Mexico Border," *Laredo Weekly Times*, June 25, 1916; "Border Smuggling Totals $20,000,000 Yearly," September 7, 1919, Mexican Affairs, 1:466–68; Raat, *Revoltosos*, 254; George Diaz, "Smugglers in Dangerous Times," in De Leon, *War along the Border*, 276–83; Ivey, *Ranger Ideal*, 491–92. The 1898 Arms Embargo statute was thus strengthened; the original act only prohibited arms exports from

Plain Sight, 351–53. For a detailed review of arms smuggling, see FRUS 1913, 867–84. Also, the loss of the Ojinaga federal garrison and evacuation of some four thousand troops interned to El Paso, Texas, was a major blow to Huerta's hold on to, and strategic control of, northern Mexico; see O'Shaughnessy, *Diplomat's Wife in Mexico*, 148.

7. W. Buckley, "Villa report," ca. fall 1915, Buckley Papers. See also Inman, *Intervention in Mexico*, 130–31. The Mutual Film Company, headquartered in New York City, produced with Villa's paid permission three short films of the Ojinaga battle; see "The Villa Movies Shock Aged Madero," *New York Times*, January 23, 1914. Historian John Mason Hart notes that given the increased pressure from Dodge, Stillman, Hearst, Fall, and New York financiers, and the advice of Texas members of the president's cabinets, "The preparation for the U.S. intervention at Veracruz began in November 1913 and in January 1914 the cabinet secretly agreed to prepare the army for invasion of Mexico to protect American interest in oil, rubber, copper, and zinc." Hart, *Revolutionary Mexico*, 289, 307.

8. Turner, *Barbarous Mexico*; O'Shaughnessy, *Diplomat's Wife in Mexico*, 64; "Diagnosing Mexico's Case," *Literary Digest*, May 17, 1913, 1147.

9. Memo, Larry Hill, "Famous Action Photograph(s)," December 1980, Cushing Archives, Texas A&M University. See also John D. Wheelan Collection, Cushing Archives.

10. "Villa, Bandit and Brute," *New York Times*, December 14, 1913.

11. Wilson, *Diplomatic Episodes*, 304; "Dollarless Diplomacy for Mexico," *Literary Digest*, November 22, 1913, 987–89; Baker, *Woodrow Wilson*, 4:252; Hanighen, *Secret War*, 64; Notter, *Foreign Policy of Woodrow Wilson*, 227–28; Buehrig, *Wilson's Foreign Policy in Perspective*, 172. See also Nearing and Freeman, *Dollar Diplomacy*, 84–120.

12. Buckley to House, November 3, 1913, Folder 664, Box 20, Yale University Archives.

13. Buckley, Mexican Affairs, 1:770, and Testimony of W. A. Thompson, Mexican Affairs, 2:1943–44; "Mexican Railways Are in a Bad Way," *New York Times*, December 11, 1913; "Germans Denounce Our Mexico Policy," *New York Times*, November 5, 1913; *Cologne Gazette*, quoted in "German Praise for Huerta," *New York Times*, January 31, 1914; McCaleb, *Banking in Mexico*, 208–24; Meyer, "Militarization of Mexico," 293–306; Turlington, *Mexico and Her Foreign Creditors*, 250–62; Skirius, "Railroads, Oil and Other Foreign Interests," 25–51. See also Palacios Roji, *La Mano de Alemania en México*. Wilson recognized tumultuous Peru in February, stating that Lima's new violent government differed from Mexico's.

14. "Dollarless Diplomacy for Mexico," *Literary Digest*, November 22, 1913, 987; Cecil Spring Rice to Sir Edward Grey, August 26, 1913, Doc. 131, 234–36; and Memorandum by Sir L. Carden, September 12, 1913, Doc. 132, 236–38—in BFA; Ruiz, *Great Rebellion*, 122–25. The drop in the price of silver ultimately compelled

Mexico to adopt the gold standard. Mexico was the world's third leading producer of cooper.

15. C. Spring Rice to Grey, *British Annual Report from Washington, DC, to London for the Year 1914*, June 1, 1914, Doc. 147, 270–79, BFA; Notter, *Foreign Policy of Woodrow Wilson*, 246–55; Atl, *Mexican Revolution*, 9; Seymour, *Intimate Papers of Colonel House*, 201–6; Delaisi, *Oil*, 23–25. To block any British canal-building activity in Nicaragua, the United States signed the Bryan-Chamorro Treaty in 1914, with an option to build an "interoceanic canal" up the Río San Juan and across Lake Nicaragua; this treaty was abrogated in 1970.

16. W. W. to Mrs. Hulbert, February 1, 1914 (emphasis added); unless otherwise noted, all emphases in quoted material are in the original sources. See also "History of Revolt," *Sun*, August 15, 1914.

17. W. J. Bryan to Secretary of Labor, August 26, 1913, and Supervising Inspector, El Paso, to Commissioner of Immigration, December 13, 16, 1913, US Bureau of Immigration, Records of the Immigration and Naturalization Service, Mexican Immigration, 1906–1930, Record Group 85, NARA; "Rebels Drop Back and Are Now Fifteen Miles Down the River," *Laredo Daily Times*, January 3, 1914.

18. Statement of Dolores Vergara, March 11, 1914, Aldrich Papers, Briscoe Center for American History, University of Texas at Austin; O. B. Colquitt to President, White House, February 26, 1914, Colquitt Papers, Texas State Archives, Austin; "Colquitt Insistent in Plea to Wilson," *New York Times*, February 26, 1914; "The Vergara Case," *Laredo Daily Times*, March 1, 1914; "Huerta Promises to Punish Slayers," *New York Times*, February 28, 1914; "Affairs in Mexico," 64th Cong., 1st sess., Senate Doc. 324, January 6, 1916, 48–50; O'Shaughnessy, *Diplomat's Wife in Mexico*, 204, 208, 216. See also "An Exciting Border Incident," *Frontier Times*, August 1919, 441–43.

19. Colquitt to W. J. Bryan, March 5, 1914; Colquitt to V. Huerta, March 12, 1914; and V. Huerta to Colquitt, March 13, 1914—all in Colquitt Papers, Texas State Archives; "Benton Executed by General Villa," *Houston Daily Post*, February 21, 1914; "British Subject Is Executed by Villa: Indignation Great," *Austin Statesman*, February 21, 1914; "Threat of Texas to Send Rangers into Mexico," *New York Times*, February 27, 1914; "Vengeance for Vergara," *New York Times*, February 28, 1914; "El Gobierno de Washington y La Muerte del Americano Clemete Vergara," *El Imparcial*, February 28, 1914. See also Feilitzsch, *In Plain Sight*, 361–65, 377; Carothers, Mexican Affairs, 1:1784–86; and Hendrick, *Walter H. Page*, 1:285. In his epic monograph *Insurgent Mexico* (1914), John Reed, who was in Mexico in

postrevolution claims. See, for example, A. B. Lyon Claim, in Department of State, *Special Mexican Claims Commission*, Doc. 814, 567.

21. Knox to H. L. Wilson, 812.00/6102, February 13, 1913, FRUS 1913; O'Shaughnessy, *Diplomat's Wife in Mexico*, 199–200; "Villa's Defense Is Attack by Benson," *Laredo Daily Times*, February 21, 1914. The State Department assigned US Consul Marion Letcher in Chihuahua to secure a satisfactory settlement following Benton's death and the yearlong occupation of and damages to his ranch, Los Remedies, only to be advised in mid-March 1915 by Villa's representative, General Avila, to pay Mrs. Benton the sum of 300 pesos (approximately $30 US). Letcher to State, 312.41/369, March 25, 1915, FRUS 1915.

22. "Delicate Crisis Seems Near at Hand," *Austin American*, February 24, 1914 "Colquitt Insistent in Plea to Wilson," *New York Times*, February 27, 1914; "Wilson Accused of British Deal," *New York Times*, March 29, 1914; W. H. Page to Woodrow Wilson, February 28, 1914, in Baker, *Woodrow Wilson*, 4:308; Hanighen, *Secret War*, 65. In *Insurgent Mexico*, Reed notes: "During the two weeks that I was in Chihuahua, Fierro killed fifteen inoffensive citizens in cold blood" (144).

23. O'Shaughnessy Confidential memo, No. 778, February 22, 8 p.m., 1914, Buckley Papers.

24. Hart, *Empire and Revolution*, 306–7.

25. Buckley Timeline, Mexico 1914–15; and Wilson to Colonel House, February 25, 1914—Buckley Papers; "Villa Declares That Benton Was Armed and Wanted to Kill Him," *Austin American*, February 22, 1914; "British Protest Direct to London," *New York Times*, March 1, 1914; Gov. Colquitt to Secretary of State, 812.00/7577, May 19, 1913, FRUS 1913; "Carranza's Agent in Benton Case Missing," *Sun*, June 29, 1914. See also Cox, "Enemy Closer to Us," 59–62; and Clements, "Woodrow Wilson's Mexican Policy," 122.

26. Buckley Timeline, and Ed Williams, "The Tampico Incident," Agent No. 16, January 2, 1920, Box 32, Buckley Papers. See also Admiral Mayo to General Zaragoza, 812.00/11988, April 9, 1914, FRUS 1914; and Buckley, Mexican Affairs, 1:778–81. Quirk makes clear the troops were "escorted," not "paraded," from the dock to the military HQ. *Affair of Honor*, 115.

27. Buckley Timeline; Admiral Fletcher to Secretary of Navy, 812.00/11988, April 11, 1914, FRUS 1914; *New York Times*, April 10, 1914; Buckley, Mexican Affairs, 1:780. For a detailed review of the Tampico Incident, see Sweetman, *Landing at Veracruz*, 27–40.

28. W. W. Canada to Governor Lind, April 15, 1914; and Memo, Flag Dolphin to Flag Florida from Mayo, April 1914, File 167—Buckley Papers; Clements, "Woodrow Wilson's Mexican Policy," 123; Quirk, *Affair of Honor*, 3, 49, 115; Feilitzsch, *In Plain Sight*, 383. Clearly there is reason to believe the US admiral should have accepted the apologies made by the Mexican commander at Tampico. In September 1916, Secretary Daniels changed official navy regulations to require the commanding officer in such a similar event to communicate directly with the Navy

Department first before making demands on a foreign government. Furthermore, in correspondence between Buckley and Henry Wilson in 1928, Buckley expressed extreme disgust with Mayo's actions at Tampico.

29. Quirk, *Affair of Honor*, 29. See also "General Huerta Defends His Acts as Dictator," *Sun*, July 5, 1915, quoted in Buckley Papers.

30. Nelson O'Shaughnessy to USS FLORIDA, Flagship, April 12, 1914 (8:00 PM) and Daniels cablegram to Flag Officer, Florida, Veracruz, April 12, 1914 (11:00 AM), Buckley Papers; O'Shaughnessy to Bryan, 812.00/11514 and 11522, April 14 and 15, 1914, FRUS 1914; Hinckley, "Wilson, Huerta," 197–206; Meyer, *Huerta*, 192–202.

31. President Wilson Congressional Address, April 20, 1914, FRUS 1914, 474–76; [Secretary] Daniels cipher radiogram to consulates, "Warn all American merchant vessels," April 20, 1914, Buckley Papers. The leadership of both the US Army and US Navy had held meetings as early as 1910 at the Army War College to prepare contingency plans for an invasion of Mexico, code name "War Plan Green"; however, the plan was not used for the Veracruz landing. See Gole, *Road to Rainbow*, 25, 82. The *New York Times* as of early January 1914 reported the prepositioning of US marines in ships off shore at Veracruz; see "Marines for Veracruz," *New York Times*, January 11, 1914.

32. Canada to Bryan, 812.00/ 11547, Veracruz, April 20, 1914, and 812.00/11594, April 21, 1914, FRUS 1914; "The Mediation," *Outlook* 107 (May 23, 1914): 140; Buckley, Mexican Affairs, 1:767, 790–91.

33. Telegram, Canada to State, April 20, 1914, File 226, Buckley Papers. See also Daniels, *Life of Woodrow Wilson*, 181–83.

34. Daniels to Veracruz, Cipher radiogram, April 20, 1914, 1:00 a.m., File 226, Buckley Papers; *Atlas of the Mexican Conflict*, 7–8. Daniels ordered the navy to stop the steamer *Mexico* and "buy the stores of war in her" if necessary. In addition to the fourteen warships anchored off of the Port of Veracruz, the US Navy had dispatched an additional twenty warships to be "available in case needed." Only three Mexican warships were on station at Tampico—the *Veracruz*, the *Bravo*, and the *Zaragosa*—and none were at the Port of Veracruz. Additionally, eight warships patrolled the Pacific off the coast of the Port of Mazatlán, for a grand total in April 1914 of more than forty US warships.

35. Hart, *Empire and Revolution*, 307; *Atlas of the Mexican Conflict*, 15–16. Secretary Daniels announced incorrectly that arms on "1333 boxes had been shipped from Hamburg." Daniels, *Life of Woodrow Wilson*, 183.

36. Buckley, "Outline of Some Topics," n.d., Buckley Papers; Buckley, Mexican

Secret War in Mexico, 234–40. Consul Miller resigned from the State Department in April and joined the Texas Company in Tampico; see "Consul Miller Goes with the Texas Company," *Oil Trade Journal*, February 1914, 10.

37. Albert B. Fall, "Affairs in Mexico," April 21, 1914, 1–12, Albert Fall Papers, New Mexico Commission of Public Records, New Mexico State Archives, Santa Fe.

38. W. F. Buckley, Veracruz, to R. H. Baker, Houston, April 27, 1914, and May 5, 1914, Buckley Family Files; Admiral Badger to General Maass, Commandant Mexican Forces, Veracruz, April 21, 1914 (1:00 PM), Buckley Papers; "Marines Ready to Seize Mexico City," *New York Times*, April 21, 1914.

39. Buckley, *American Family*, 158, 141–42; *W.F.B. Appreciation*, 141–42; Quirk, *Affair of Honor*, 95–96.

40. L. C. Christian, Houston, to Buckley, April 29, 1914; Walter S. Pope, Dallas, to Buckley, April 30, 1914; and President Mezes, University of Texas, Austin, to Buckley, May 1, 1914—all in Box 32, Buckley Papers; Buckley, *Gleanings from an Unplanned Life*, 32–33.

41. Buckley, Mexican Affairs, 1:778; W. F. Buckley, Veracruz, to Baker, April 27, 1914, Box 32, Buckley Papers; W. F. Buckley to Walter Pope, May 17, 1914, quoted in Buckley, *American Family*, 36, 53, 109–11, 114; "W. F. Buckley Inspector of Ports and Justice," *Fuel Oil Journal*, May 1914, 14; Sweetman, *Landing at Veracruz*, 151; Daniels, *Wilson Era*, 192. Robert Kerr, an attorney with offices in Chicago and Mexico City and known as the author of the definitive English translation of the Mexican civil code, was selected as acting governor, while Charles H. Stewart and William Buckley were named advisers to oversee the treasury and justice system (they declined), and J. F. Luby was named postmaster. Kerr, because of some anti-Wilson comments he made in the United States before arriving in Veracruz, was relieved on May 1 and replaced by an army officer.

42. Buckley to L. M. Garrison, July 21 and 29, 1914, Box 32, Buckley Papers; Buckley, *American Family*, 151, 161. The views and themes of William Buckley closely parallel those of Luis Cabrera, the secretary of finance and public credit in 1919–20, in his draft paper, "The Mexican Revolution—Its Causes, Progress and Results," File 122.5, Buckley Papers; this paper was submitted to the Academy of Political and Social Sciences in the fall of 1916 (in the midst of the revolution) and edited under the same title for the January 1917 edition of the organization's *Annals*. Buckley, a contemporary of Cabrera, possibly had a hand in preparing and editing the original draft.

43. Buckley to Sec. L. M. Garrison, December 29, 1914, William F. Buckley Letters, DeGolyer Library, SMU, Dallas [hereafter cited as Buckley SMU]; O'Shaughnessy, *Diplomat's Wife in Mexico*, 290, 304; Testimony of Nelson O'Shaughnessy, Mexican Affairs, 2:2708. See also Inman, *Intervention in Mexico*.

44. *Mexican Herald*, April 24, 25, 1914; Testimony of Dr. Samuel G. Inman, Mexican Affairs, 1:138; Quirk, *Affair of Honor*, 108; "Our War on Huerta," *Literary Digest*, May 2, 1914, 1029–32. See also Stewart, *Woodrow Wilson*, 16–17.

45. "Fight at Embassy?" April 26, 1914; and "Still Holds the Embassy," May 8, 1914—in *Kansas City Star*; Schuler, *Murder and Counterrevolution in Mexico*, 116–17.

46. O'Shaughnessy, *Diplomat's Wife in Mexico*, 329; Buckley, Mexican Affairs, 1:778.

47. Hanna to Bryan, 812.00/11719, April 24, 1914; and File 123B641/23, May 6, 1914—in FRUS 1914; Quirk, *Affair of Honor*, 109; Hill, *Emissaries to a Revolution*, 211.

48. Quirk, *Affair of Honor*, 23, 107–9; Davis, *Experiences and Observations*, 19, 25; "U.S. Gunboat Sent to Tuxpan," *Sun*, June 20, 1914; Thompson, Mexican Affairs, 2:1931–32. See also Rosenbaum, *Mexicano Resistance in the Southwest*, 49–51. Ordered to leave the country on April 23, by Nelson O'Shaughnessy, Davis had to bribe Mexican customs officers to exit Manzanillo on a German ship.

49. Carothers to Bryan, 812.00/11654, April 23, 1914, FRUS 1914; Feilitzsch, *In Plain Sight*, 405–7. The German ambassador in Mexico City, Adm. Paul von Hintze, agreed with Villa "that the United States was not prepared for war: "You can't make soldiers overnight." Adams, *Murder and Intrigue*, 62.

50. V. Carranza to Wilson, 812.00/11618, April 22, 1914, FRUS 1914; Baker, *Woodrow Wilson*, 4:331; "Carranza Resented Seizure Which He Calls Hostile," *Laredo Daily Times*, April 23, 1914; Quirk, *Affair of Honor*, 116; Meyer, *Huerta*, 203–4; Richard N. Smith, "The High and Rocky Road," *Wall Street Journal*, April 21, 2018, C5. The Medal of Honor was awarded to thirty-seven officers and eighteen enlisted men for their participation at Veracruz, the largest awarding ever made for a single engagement.

51. Hill, *Emissaries to a Revolution*, 177, 182–87. See also "The Solution in Mexico," *Sun*, June 22, 1914.

52. Hill, *Emissaries to a Revolution*, 136; Quirk, *Affair of Honor*, 31, 68, 73, 77, 92; Testimony of Joseph P. Chamberlain, Mexican Affairs, 2:2863; Department of State, *Register*, Mexico Consular Officers, 54–56; McCullagh, *Red Mexico*, 88. See also Davis, *Experiences and Observations*.

53. O'Shaughnessy, *Diplomat's Wife in Mexico*, 296–97; "Huerta Offers Protection to the Americans," *New York Times*, April 21, 1914.

54. Buckley, Mexican Affairs, 1:781; Bemis, *Latin American Policy*, 179.

55. Quirk, *Affair of Honor*, 98, 151. Only one US naval warship, the USS *Nashville*, had been assigned to patrol Puerto Mexico, yet it had been recalled, thus allowing the *Ypiranga* to land its cargo of arms unopposed!

56. Lodge, *Senate and League of Nations*, 17–18; "Arms for Huerta on German
Ship," *New York Times*, ...

Times, May 31 1914; Feilitzsch, *In Plain Sight,* 386–90; "Hoy Saldran Para Niagara Falls los Delegados a la Conf. De Paz," *El Imparcial,* May 9, 1914.

58. Buckley, Mexican Affairs, 1:775, 787–90; Hale, *Emilio Rabasa,* 69–70; Hart, *Empire and Revolution,* 306.

59. Buckley, "Outline of some Topics," n.d.; and Emilio Rabasa to Buckley, June 21 and 29, 1914—in Box 32, Buckley Papers. See also Meyer, *Huerta,* 205–6; Buckley, *American Family,* 114; and Small, *Forgotten Peace,* 62.

60. Buckley, "Outline of some Topics," n.d.; and Buckley to Senator Boise Penrose, October 29, 1915, Box 32, Buckley Papers. See also Buckley, Mexican Affairs, 1:788–92.

61. "Extract from Speech by Representative Rogers in the House of Representatives on July 29, 1916," File 110, Buckley Papers, provides a detailed timeline of shipments and embargo status during 1914.

62. Buckley, Mexican Affairs, 1:792–94, 2413–14; *New York Times,* June 4, 1914 [re: arms embargo]. See also "W. J. Bryan Time Line," File 224.3, Buckley Papers.

63. Arms correspondence and proposals with F. Uruidi, Box 1, July–September 1915, Buckley Papers; Bryan to Silliman, 812.00/14052, July 23, 1914, FRUS 1914; Buckley, Mexican Affairs, 1:787–88, 792–94; Cradock to Admiralty, March 8, 1914, Doc. 190, 354–55, BFA; and Colville Barclay to Sir Edward Gray, July 2, 1914, Doc. 232, BFA, 407–8. During Adm. Cradock's port of call to Galveston, he dispatched men to recon the border, reporting, "The Rio Grande is fordable anywhere up to within 100 miles of the sea, which probably accounts for the many depredations now going on."

64. Testimony of Sherburne G. Hopkins [legal counsel for Carranza], Mexican Affairs, 2:2413–15; Quirk, *Affair of Honor,* 118; Brenner, *Wind That Swept,* 48–49; Skaggs, *German Conspiracies in America,* 78–81. Some reports indicate that Huerta departed Mexico from the Puerto Mexico on the *Ypiranga,* whose registry had been changed from commercial to the Imperial German Navy. Teitelbaum, *Wilson and the Mexican Revolution.*

65. Buckley to Secretary L. M. Garrison, July 29, 1914, Buckley SMU; "For President, Pancho Villa," *Sun,* July 20, 1914; "Villa Imprisons Obregon, Carranza's Chief General," *Sun,* July 21, 1914.

66. Oliveira to Bryan, 812.00/12497, July 15, 1914; and Statement by the President, 812.00/15122b, June 2, 1914—in FRUS 1914; Small, *Forgotten Peace,* 118–224; Buckley, Mexican Affairs, 1:808; Hill, *Emissaries to a Revolution,* 223; "U.S. Declares Huerta Loans Invalid," *New York Times,* July 21, 1914, transcript, File 111.2, Buckley Papers.

67. Buckley to Garrison, July 21, 1914, Buckley SMU; Douglas Reed, "Odyssey of an Oil Man," *W.F.B. Appreciation,* 154–55; Memoranda, Mexico Update, October 17, 1914, November 10 and 14, 1914, and December 30, 1914, File 122.2, Buckley Papers; "Carranza Is Using Iron Hand in Mexico," *Sun,* September 12, 1914.

68. "Mexico City," File 145, Buckley Papers; Buckley, Mexican Affairs, 1:800–804; W. F. Buckley, President of the American Association of Mexico, "Some

Aspects of the Problem of Recognizing the Present Government of Mexico," May 12, 1922, 4, Box 1, Buckley Papers; Lind, Mexican Affairs, 2:2346–47, and Sidney S. Conger, 1737–41.

69. Buckley to Mr. McReynolds, September 2, 1914, File 145, and Buckley to Secretary L. M. Garrison, September 1, 1914, Box 32, Buckley Papers; "Sacking of Mexico City Described by Eyewitness," Sun, December 23, 1914; "Women Refugee Says Anarchy, Famine, Death Ravage Mexico City," Sun, March 3, 1915. See also statement of "American Residents in Mexico City in Mass Meeting," March 20, 1915, Buckley Papers, which concluded: "The present struggle does not represent the efforts of a people to secure liberty and civil rights so much so as a clash of personal ambition and revenge." See also Whitney, *What's the Matter with Mexico?*, 28.

70. Silliman to Bryan, 812.00/13278, September 23, 1914; and Secretary of War to General Funston, 812.00/13974, November 20, 1914—in FRUS 1914; Buckley, Mexican Affairs, 1:798–801; "Loot, Dirt, Graft All Reign in Fair Mexican Capital," *World*, October 4, 1914, transcript, File 122.5, and Canada Villa memo, "14 December 1914" chronology—in Buckley Papers; "Three Capitals in Mexico Now as War Begins," Sun, November 5, 1914; and "Gen. Gonzales President No. 3 for Mexico," Sun, November 30, 1914; Quirk, *Mexican Revolution*, 61–63; Sweetman, *Landing at Veracruz*, 163; Kandell, *La Capital*, 428–30. On September 15, 1914, Wilson ordered Secretary of War Garrison to "make preparation for immediate withdrawal of the troops."

71. Canova to State, 812.00/14048, December 8, 1914, FRUS 1914; "Villa and Zapata Confer on Control of Mexico City," Sun, December 3, 1914; "Wilson Advises Mexican Chiefs to End Executions, Grudge Killings Daily," Sun, December 30, 1914; Hill, *Emissaries to a Revolution*, 282–84; Womack, *Zapata*, 219–21; McLynn, *Villa and Zapata*, 276–78.

72. Buckley, *American Family*, 166–68. See also Priscilla Buckley's account in *The Light-Hearted Years*.

Chapter 3

1. Callahan, *American Foreign Policy*, 503–5; W. F. Buckley contra C. F. Davis, Tribunal Superior del Distrito, *Diário de Jurisprudencia*, December 1, 1911; Dunn, *Diplomatic Protection of Americans*, 274–305; Brown, *Oil and Revolution*, 90–93; Bulnes, *Whole Truth about Mexico*, 123–27; Wilson, Mexican Affairs, 2:2252–55.

3. Edgington, *Monroe Doctrine*, 218–21; Krauze, *Mexico*, 355, 360; Meyer, *Mexico and the United States*, 46–49; McConnell, *Mexico at the Bar*, 254–56; Dunn, *Diplomatic Protection of Americans*, 392–93; "Cabrera Fears Our Egotism," *New York Times*, December 16, 1919, transcript, File 224.24, Buckley Papers.

4. Whitney, *What's the Matter with Mexico?*, 157.

5. Buckley to Garrison, August 29, 1914, Buckley SMU. Secretary Daniels expressed concern, stating that Carranza "left much to be desired as a chief magistrate." Daniels, *Life of Woodrow Wilson*, 185.

6. W. F. Buckley to Walter Pope, May 17, 1914, quoted in Buckley, *American Family*, 109–11; "Buckley and Buckley," *Oil Trade Journal*, February 1914, 4.

7. Buckley, quoted in Brown, *Revolution and Oil*, 211; "Buckley and Buckley," *Fuel Oil Journal*, October 1914, 8.

8. Testimony of Edward L. Doheny, Mexican Affairs, 1:219; Santiago, *Ecology of Oil*, 78, 118–22; DeGolyer, "Mexican Petroleum Industry during 1912," 560; Hamilton, *Early Day Oil Tales*, 79–81, 139–42; Brown, *Oil and Revolution*, 309–13. See also Harper, *Journey in Southeastern Mexico*.

9. Ocasio Melendez, *Capitalism and Development*, 194–203, 259; Lozano, *El Puerto del Oro Negro*; Buckley, *American Family*, 120–21, 134; Hanighen, *Secret War*, 57, 121. See also London, "Our Adventure in Tampico," 5–7.

10. Buckley, "Summery of the Oil Controversy," n.d., Buckley Papers.

11. Adams, *Murder and Intrigue*, 29, 159–60; Marion Letcher, "Wealth of Mexico," [US] Department of Commerce and Labor, Bureau of Foreign and Domestic Commerce, *Daily Consular and Trade Reports*, 15th year, III, no. 168, July 18, 1912; "Concessions in Mexico," *New York Times*, November 10, 1913. See also Hall and Coerver, "Oil and the Mexican Revolution," 229–44.

12. "Rival Oil Giants in Mexican Broils," *New York Times*, November 9, 1913; Hall and Coerver, "Oil and the Mexican Revolution," 231; Quirk, *Affair of Honor*, 5–8; Adams, *Murder and Intrigue*, 26–32, 40; Foster, *Texaco*, 5–15.

13. Hart, *Revolutionary Mexico*, 147–52. See also Feilitzsch, *In Plain Sight*, 326; and Hart, *Empire and Revolution*, 157–63.

14. Hart, *Empire and Revolution*, 154–56, 159–61; Ruiz, *Great Rebellion*, 120–21.

15. W. F. Buckley to Walter Pope, May 17, 1914, in Buckley, *American Family*, 51–52, 109–17, 136–37, 160, See also Meyer, *Mexico and the United States*, 30–32.

16. Hart, *Empire and Revolution*, 161, 306.

17. *W.F.B. Appreciation*, 29.

18. Buckley to Pope, May 17, 1914, in Buckley, *American Family*, xi, 120.

19. John W. Buckley, "Love Affair with Oil," *W.F.B. Appreciation*, 187; Buckley, *American Family*, 132, 166.

20. Wilson, *Diplomatic Episodes*, 238; Meyer, *Mexico and the United States*, 34–38; Brown, *Oil and Revolution*, 179.

21. Buckley, Mexican Affairs, 1:873–90.

22. Buckley, "Summery of the Oil Controversy," n.d., Buckley Papers; Cleland, Mexican Year Book, 1920–21, 290–92, 301; Government of Mexico, True

Facts about the Expropriation, 22–26; Hamilton, Early Day Oil Tales, 19–20; Ocasio Melendez, Capitalism and Development, 97–100. See also Dunn, Diplomatic Protection of Americans, 332–37; O'Shaughnessy, Intimate Pages of Mexican History, 295–97; and Callcott, Liberalism in Mexico, 279; Santiago, "Culture Clash," 64–65.

23. "Rival Oil Giants in Mexican Broils," New York Times, November 9, 1913; Doheny, Mexican Affairs, 1:209–12, 226–33; Cleland, Mexican Year Book, 1920–21, 293–96; Doheny, Mexican Affairs, 1:215; Ocasio Melendez, Capitalism and Development, 128–45; Hall and Coerver, "Oil and the Mexican Revolution," 234–35; Brown, Oil and Revolution, 7–46; Turner, Barbarous Mexico, 208; Callahan, American Foreign Policy, 516–20. See also Foote, "Oil Fuel vs. Coal," 61–62; and "Oil Operations in Mexico Described by a Pioneer Developer," Fuel Oil Journal, August 1914, 10–12.

24. Miller to State, Tampico, May 14, 1913, File 148, Buckley Papers; "Mexican Oil Down," New York Times, November 4, 1913; "Mexico's Oil Field Menaced," Fuel Oil Journal, May 1914, 3–8; "Mexicans Loot Oil Fields," Sun, November 28, 1914; Santiago, "Culture Clash," 65–68; Brown, Oil and Revolution, 136–62.

25. Parliament, "Oil Properties and Mining Rights in Mexico," Exchanged Notes, No. 1 (1914); and "Oil Properties in Mexico," Exchanged Notes, No. 7 (1914).

26. Bryan to Carothers, 812.6363/29a, April 28, 1913; Bryan to British Ambassador, 812.6363/60a, April 29, 1913; and Carothers to Bryan, 812.6363/ 32, May 1, 1913—all in FRUS 1913; Brown, Oil and Revolution, 190–203.

27. Rear Adm. C. Cradock to British Ambassador, 812.6363/110, May 7, 1914, FRUS 1914; Adams, Murder and Intrigue, 41.

28. Miller to Secretary of State, 812.6363/69, May 17, 1914, FRUS 1914; Bryan to Sir C. Spring Rice, June 2, 1914, Doc. 217, 397, BFA.

29. Buckley to Garrison, July 29, 1914, Buckley SMU; "Resuming Work in Mexico's Oil Field," Fuel Oil Journal, June 1914, 3–6; "A Stiff Raise in Tax on Mexican Oil," Fuel Oil Journal, August 1916, 6; Hill, Emissaries to a Revolution, 222; Feilitzsch, In Plain Sight, 421–26; W.F.B. Appreciation, 32–33. For a review of the pending land policy, see Buckley to Garrison, September 1, 1914, Buckley SMU.

30. Hill, Emissaries to a Revolution, 211–14.

31. Silliman to State, 812.00/12469, July 10, 1914, FRUS 1914; Buckley to Garrison, July 29, 1914, Buckley SMU; Buckley, Mexican Affairs, 1:813; Davis, Experiences and Observations, 214–16. Davis noted Silliman was "too much a partisan for Senor Carranza—he was thoroughly hypnotized by Carranza."

32. Carothers to State, 812.00/12472, July 5, 1914; and Canova to State,

Petrolero Maritima, 812.6363/219, March 4, 8, 1916—all in FRUS 1916. Among the eighty-four signatures was Will's brother E. L. Buckley.

34. Garrison to Buckley, January 5, 1915, Box 32, Buckley Papers. See also "Villa Recognition by U.S. Improbable," Sun, March 22, 1915.

35. Carranza Oil Decree, January 7, 1915, File 153.4, Buckley Papers; "Carranza Warned by Bryan to Let Tampico Ship Oil," World, January 16, 1915.

36. James Rodgers to Secretary of State, 812.00/1218, May 20, 1916, FRUS 1916; Meyer, Mexico and the United States, 54–60. For a sampling of mining and petroleum decrees, see FRUS 1916, 765–71. See also "Mexico Badly in Need of a Juarez or a Diaz," Sun, January 1, 1916.

37. Rodgers to State, 812.00/18332, June 6, 1916, FRUS 1916.

38. "Mexico in New Oil Decree," Sun, September 10, 1916; "Heavy Tax on Exports," New York Times, February 26, 1917; De Bekker, Plot against Mexico, 6–16; Ansell, Oil Baron of the Southwest, 171–77; Brown, Oil and Revolution, 238–42.

39. "Mexico's Neutrality," New York Times, January 9, 1919, transcript, File 154.3; and confidential transcript of "Secret Session of the Convention Held in Mexico City," June 5, 1915, File 122.2—in Buckley Papers; Meyer, "Mexican-German Conspiracy of 1915," 76–89. See also Rausch, "Exile and Death of Huerta," 133–51.

40. "Dr. Zimmermann's Defense of the Mexican Plan," New York Times, transcript, June 1917, File 154.3, Buckley Papers; MacAdam, "German Intrigue in Mexico," 495–500. See also Herbert Kraus, "The Monroe Doctrine as Germans See It," File 154.4, Buckley Papers; and "The Spy Is Generally a Man of Ability and Modern Facilities Enable Him to Do Tremendous Damage," Houston Daily Post, February 24, 1918.

41. Carranza statement, April 16, 1917, File 154.1; "Carranza's Attitude during World War," February 15, 1917, File 122.6; "Dr. [Arthur] Zimmermann's [secretary of foreign affairs] Defense of His Mexican Plan," April 1917, File 154.1; "The Alliance with Mexico and Japan Proposed by Germany," April 1917, File 154.1; and "Cabrera Fears Our Egotism," File 154.3—all in Buckley Papers; "German Hand Seen in Move on Tampico," Sun, November 16, 1917; Seymour, Intimate Papers of Colonel House, 2:452; Testimony of John A. Valls, Mexican Affairs, 1:1224–25; Meyer and Beezley, Mexico, 506–9; Phillips, Ventures in Diplomacy, 79–81; Skaggs, German Conspiracies in America, 78–79. See also Herman, 1917, 111–14, Strother, Fighting Germany's Spies; and "Carranza's Message to the National Congress, September 1, 1919," 812.032/63, September 3, 1919, FRUS 1919, 542.

42. Tuchman, Zimmermann Telegram; Von zur Gathen, "Zimmermann Telegram: The Original Draft," 2–37. The German diplomatic term for the telegram was Mexiko Depesche (Mexico dispatch). In a note in the margin of the draft of the original dispatch was "California should be reserved for Japan." It is not known if this was conveyed to the Japanese.

43. E. DeGolyer, "The Importance of Mexican Petroleum to the United States and Allies," Box 115, File 5352, Buckley SMU; I. Witake statement taken by Capt. Hanson,

ca. 1919, Box 154.3, Buckley Papers; Cunningham, "New British Oil Industry," 110–21; Hanighen, *Secret War*, 76; MacAdam, "German Intrigue in Mexico," 495–500. There were seven commercially viable sources of petroleum during World War I: the United States, Russia, Mexico, the Dutch East Indies, Romania, India, and Spain—and the oil fields of Russia and Romania were in the hands of America's enemies.

44. Doheny, Mexican Affairs, 1:248–50; "Fuel Oil Requirements of British Navy," *Fuel Oil Journal*, June 1914, 9; La Botz, *Edward L. Doheny*, 71–75; Ansell, *Oil Baron of the Southwest*, 152–60.

45. La Botz, *Edward L. Doheny*, 74–75; Baruch, *My Own Story*, 213; Fletcher to State, Petroleum Decree, 812.6363/275, April 19, 1917, FRUS 1917.

46. Dawson to State, 812.6363 and 344, February 19, 1918; Summerlin to State, 812.6363/351, February 20, 1918; and "Decree on Oil February 19, 1918" from Mexico City *Diário Oficial* of February 27, 1918, 713–14—all in FRUS 1918. See also Ansell, *Oil Baron of the Southwest*, 164–65, 177–79.

47. Lansing to Fletcher, 812.512/1885, February 27, 1918; and Polk to Summerlin, 812.6363/328, January 23, 1918—in FRUS 1918.

48. Fletcher to Lansing, 812.512/1888 and 1894, March 1, 1918, FRUS 1918.

49. "Provisions Regulating Article 14 of the Decree of February 19, 1918, with Amendments Dated August 18, 1918," Mexican Affairs, 1:259–67; Fletcher to State, 812.512/1983, May 22, 1918; newspaper headlines, and Fletcher to State, 812.512/1993 and 2047, June 13, 1918, and July 19, 1918—all in FRUS 1918. See also "Band of 15 Mexicans Killed by Rangers," *Houston Daily Post*, February 8, 1918.

50. "Hughes Rotary Disc Bit," *Fuel Oil Journal*, June 1914, 70; "U.S. Backs Britain's Mexican Oil Action," *Sun*, August 16, 1918; Doheny, Mexican Affairs, 1:248, 289–90; Brown, *Oil and Revolution*, 146–49; Delaisi, *Oil*, 86–87. See also Tinkle, *Mr. De*, 84–140; Curzon quoted in Foster, *Texaco*, 20; and Wilson, "Oil Legislation in Latin America," 108–19.

51. W. F. Buckley to Mrs. Steiner, October 21, 1917; and marriage record of December 29, 1917, filed in Parish of Orleans, January 7, 1918—Buckley Family Files; *W.F.B. Appreciation*, 41–46; Markmann, *Buckleys*, 20; Bogus, *Buckley*, 60–62; Buckley, *Gleanings from an Unplanned Life*, 19–20; Buckley Jr., "Aloise Steiner Buckley, RIP." See also Irene C. Kuhn, "Our Five Enduring Women: Smith, Kennedy, Buckley, Luce, Mesta," *Family Weekly*, August 1, 1971; Ted Knap, "Mrs. Buckley: Serving a Life-style," *Evansville (IN) Press*, November 27, 1970; and Charlotte Wyndham, "A Famous Mother Loyal to Family and to the South," *Columbia (SC) State*, April 18, 1971.

52. "Ometusco Bound Party Forced to Return to City," *Mexican Herald*,

55. Secretary of Sate to Alvey A. Adee, 812.6363/522, September 9, 1919, FRUS 1919; MacAdam, "German Intrigue in Mexico," 495–97; "Mexican Field Notes," *Oil Trade Journal*, August 1920, 124; De Bekker, *Plot against Mexico*, 26, 40; Velasco, *W.F.B. Appreciation*, 32–35; Hall and Coerver, "Oil and the Mexican Revolution," 239–40. See also Ansell, *Oil Baron of the Southwest*, 168–70, 177–79. General Peláez, whom *Oil Trade Journal* in 1920 deemed to be "in charge of the oil fields of Mexico," would become a strong supporter of Obregón and surely vouched for his friend Buckley when he was being expelled from Mexico. See Hall, *Obregón*, 241.

56. Buckley, Mexican Affairs, 1:839–40; "Peláez Driven from Tampico Oil District," *Houston Daily Post*, February 24, 1918; Brown, *Oil and Revolution*, 253–54, 284–85; Tinkle, *Mr. De*, 133–40.

57. Interview with James Buckley, November 11, 2019; Buckley, *American Family*, 28–29, 128–33. There is no mention or reference in the Buckley Papers of the kidnapping incidents.

58. Doheny, Mexican Affairs, 1:252; "Oil Producers Organize," *Sun*, August 8, 1918; "Oil Producers Will Quit Mexico," *Sun*, December 10, 1918. See also Davenport and Cooke, *Oil Trusts*, 165, 222–26, 264.

59. Hale, *Rabasa*, 68–70; Claude Buckley, legal counsel, "Mexican-Pánuco Oil Company," *New York Tribune* (hereafter cited as *Tribune*), May 28, 1919; Hull, "Tampico and Vicinity," 7–15.

60. Buckley to Garrison, August 29, 1914, and December 29, 1914, Buckley SMU.

61. "Agent reports," File 112.9, Buckley Papers; Hall and Coerver, "Oil and the Mexican Revolution," 233.

62. Buckley to Rabasa, September 27, 1915, Box 32, Buckley Papers; Hale, *Rabasa*, 33, 68–74.

Chapter 4

1. O'Shaughnessy, Mexican Affairs, 2:2714–16; Quirk, *Mexican Revolution*, 22, 248; Hanson, *Politics of Mexican Development*, 39–40, 142–44; "The Mexican Tangle," *Sun*, March 29, 1915; Redinger, *American Catholics*, 4–6; Markmann, *Buckleys*, 13. See also Fyfe, *Real Mexico*, 175–83, and Michael Tangeman, *Mexico at the Crossroads*, 26–35.

2. Decorme, "Catholic Education in Mexico," 168–81; Quirk, *Mexican Revolution*, 6–7; Brandenburg, *Making of Modern Mexico*, 23–25, 166–204; Redinger, *American Catholics*, 3–4; Hodges and Gandy, *Mexico*, 7, 33–34; Krauze, *Mexico*, 80–81. See also Ruiz, *Great Rebellion*, 67–68, 412–20; Redinger, "To Arouse and Inform," 491; and Winter, *Mexico and Her People Today*, 313. For a historical overview of Church wealth in Mexico, see Catholic historian Don Lucas Alaman's "A Calumny Shattered," which notes, "By purchase, by gift, and by legacy, not less

than half of all the real estate in Mexico at the beginning of the nineteenth century belonged to ecclesiastical orders" (753–54).

3. Quirk, *Mexican Revolution*, 11–12, 17; Portes Gil, *Conflict*, 86–87, 91–93; Cabrera, *Religious Question in Mexico*, 15; Brandenburg, *Making of Modern Mexico*, 42–43. See also Callcott, *Liberalism in Mexico*, 142–44.

4. Niemeyer, *Revolution at Querétaro*, 4–11; Redinger, "To Arouse and Inform," 492. Monsignor Francis Kelley, appearing before the Fall Committee in 1919, argued that the Catholic Church in Mexico was not wealthy, and that any such charges "usually hark back to Spanish times," yet he went on to detail its properties and facilities. See Testimony of Father Kelley, Mexican Affairs, 2:2671–76.

5. Cabrera, *Religious Question in Mexico*, 4–9; Quirk, *Mexican Revolution*, 38–41; Krauze, *Mexico*, 356; Mecham, *Church and State*, 380–82; Niemeyer, *Revolution at Querétaro*, 61; Molina Enríquez, *Los grandes problemas nacionales*; Madero, *La sucesión presidencial en 1910*; Creelman, "Thrilling Story of President Diaz," 241; Curley, *Citizens and Believers*, 92–99.

6. Silliman to State, 812.00/12634, July 27, 1914, FRUS 1914; Paganel, *What the Church Has Done*, 13; O'Shaughnessy, *Diplomat's Wife in Mexico*, 10; O'Shaughnessy, *Intimate Pages of Mexican History*, 280–81; Curley, *Citizens and Believers*, 93; Hill, *Emissaries to a Revolution*, 74, 221; Callcott, *Liberalism in Mexico*, 229–31; Cumberland, *Mexican Revolution*, 216; McCullagh, *Red Mexico*, 86–92.

7. Hodges and Gandy, *Mexico*, 14–18; Curley, *Citizens and Believers*, 114–17. See also Cleven, "Religious Aspects of Mexico's Constitution," 8–16. For a detailed response to the "many groundless accusations against the Constitutionalists" concerning the Catholic Church, see Enriquez, *Religious Question in Mexico*.

8. Vice Consul William P. Blocker to State, February 23, 1915, File 152, Buckley Papers. Consul Canada in Veracruz submitted a similar detailed report to the State Department based on his years of experience in Mexico and a close assessment of the impact of events on Mexico, stating that "the officers of the Constitutionalist army, the politicians who surround Mr. Carranza and other leaders are nearly all men of no moral strength whatsoever and most of them are shameless grafters fattening on money and property wrung from the suffering people of their land." Canada to State, June 18, 1915, No. 1232, File 113, Buckley Papers.

9. "Mistreatment and Expulsion of Mexican Clergy by Carrancistas," Statement by Eber C. Byam, September 21, 1914, File 145, Buckley Papers; "Priests and Nuns Expelled by Villa," *Sun*, May 31, 1914; Guzmán, *Memoirs of Pancho Villa*, 202, 284–85; Crowell, "What's Wrong with Mexico?" 262; Slattery, Mexican Affairs, 2:2034–35; Curley, *Citizens and Believers*, 112–17. See also Curley, "Anti-

majority rule the Indian will rule in Mexico—the rule of a population 80 percent of which is unable to read or write."

10. Bryan to Hanna, 312.51/45a, June 26, 1914; Hanna to State, 312.51/48, June 29, 1914; Clause, French chargé d'affaires, to Bryan, 312.51/69 and 312.51/76, July 18 and 27, 1914; Silliman to State, 312.51/68, July 24, 1914; and Ambassador Jusserand, France, to Secretary of State, 312.51/44, June 20, 1914—all in FRUS 1914; W. L. Bonney, consul, "San Luis Potosi," August 20, 1914, File 145, Buckley Papers; Archives of the Catholic Church Extension Society, "Mistreatment and Expulsion of Mexican Clergy by Carrancistas," File 145, 114, 144, 170; Buckley Papers; "French Envoy to Protest to Wilson against the Rebels," *Sun*, July 21, 1914; McLynn, *Villa and Zapata*, 197, 239–40, 318, 321; Testimony of Mother Elias, Mexican Affairs, 2:2652; Callcott, *Liberalism in Mexico*, 245. Consul Bonney said, "All the pianos of this place have been shipped to the North, is not known to what point." The Extension Society document is a key primary source covering more than two hundred pages of first-person accounts and responses concerning attacks on the Catholic Church and clerics during 1914–15.

11. Buckley, Mexican Affairs, 1:874–9; "Loot, Dirt, Graft All Reign in Mexican Capital," *New York Times*, October 4, 1914, transcript, File 173, Buckley Papers.

12. Buckley, "Some Aspects of the Problem," 4, Buckley Papers. See also Fallaw, "Seduction of Revolution," 91–100; and Curley, "Anticlericalism and Public Space," 511–33.

13. Spring Rice to Grey, Doc. 147, February 7, 1914, and June 1, 1914, BFA; "Catholics Lash Wilson for Backing Carranza," *Sun*, October 17, 1915; Testimony of Father Joyce, Mexican Affairs, 2:2661–62. See also "Priests in Jail, Nuns Homeless in Mexico City," *Sun*, March 8, 1915; and Krauze, *Mexico*, 356–62.

14. Minister de Oliveira to State, 312.12/20, June 26, 1914; and Bryan to Hanna, 312.12/20, June 30, 1914—in FRUS 1914; "Jail for all Native Priests in Mexico," *Sun*, February 21, 1915. See also Buckley, Mexican Affairs, 1:815.

15. Gibbons to President, 812.404/8, August 18, 1914; Tierney to State, 812.404/22, October 17, 1914; and President to Gibbons, 812.404/134, August 21, 1914—all in FRUS 1914; Bryan to American Consuls in Mexico, 812.404/31a, January 14, 1915, FRUS 1915; Kelley to President Wilson, February 23, 1915, and Wilson to Kelley, March 18, 1915—quoted in "Mistreatment and Expulsion of Mexican Clergy by Carrancistas," 181–202; "Cardinal Gibbons Scores U.S. Policy," *Sun*, January 14, 1916; "Mexico Is 'Plain Hell,' Says Father Tierney," *Sun*, December 9, 1915. Some have challenged the accuracy of Tierney's report and claims; see Cumberland, *Mexican Revolution*, 214–16.

16. Redinger, *American Catholics*, 48–52; Batzell, *Protestant Establishment*, 73–76; La Botz, *Edward L. Doheny*, 114–15.

17. Davis, *Experiences and Observations*, 40–42, 116–18; Theodore Roosevelt, "Our Responsibility in Mexico," *New York Times*, December 6, 1914; Quirk, *Mexican Revolution*, 60–66; Theodore Roosevelt, "Criticism of the President's Message," Oyster Bay, December 7, 1914, transcript, File 224.1, Buckley Papers;

Roosevelt to Cabot Lodge, December 8, 1914, in Morison, *Letters of Theodore Roosevelt*, 861–63. US Consul Davis confirmed that Archbishop Jimenez smuggled out over $2.5 million in jewelry.

18. While there did not seem to be an extensive response to conditions in Mexico in the United States except among Catholics, there were articles in newspapers nationwide with stories. See, for example: "Catholics Are Driven Out by General Villa," *Fort Worth Star-Telegram*, May 31, 1914; "Five Priests Are Murdered; Hotel Looted," *Albuquerque Morning Journal*, March, 16, 1914; "Priests and Nuns Ousted by Villa," *Las Cruces La Estrella*, June 6, 1914; "Insult Catholic Priests," *Tulsa Daily World*, August 22, 1914; "Wants Brutality to Catholics Stopped," *Duluth News Tribune*, September 28, 1914; "Horses Stabled in Churches in Mexico," *San Jose Mercury Herald*, November 7, 1914; "Mexican 'Holy War' Rumored," *Portland Morning Oregonian*, October 27, 1914.

19. Memo, Msgr. Francis C. Kelley, "The Catholic Church and the Solution of the Mexican Problem," December 2, 1919, File 145; and Kelley, "European Attitude toward Intervention," December 5, 1919, File 224.23—Buckley Papers; Kelley, *El Libro de Rojo y Amarillo*. A sampling of pamphlets includes *A Nation in Bondage* and Knights of Columbus, *Red Mexico*.

20. Post Aguascalientes Conference presentation by Antonio I. Villarreal and attack of the Catholic Church and bases for his anticlerical decree in Nuevo León, "Mistreatment and Expulsion of Mexican Clergy by Carrancistas," File 145, 113–14, 137, Buckley Papers. See also US Consul to General Carranza, February 21, 1915, File 147, Buckley Papers.

21. Doc. 2, "Antonio I. Villareal," File 145, Buckley Papers. The personal library of rare documents, collected by the archbishop, an authority on the antiquities of Mexico, over a forty-year period, contained some twenty-five thousand books and more than seven hundred irreplaceable manuscripts of great historical and archaeological value dating from the sixteenth century.

22. Silliman to State, 812.00/12634 and 812.404/3, July 26 and 27, 1914, FRUS 1914; Gen. Candido Aguilar Handbill of Rules, August 28, 1914, File 145; and Canada to State, No. 1232, File 113, June 18, 1915—Buckley Papers; Quirk, *Mexican Revolution*, 54–56; Mecham, *Church and State*, 382–83.

23. Canova to State, 312.51/80, August 2, 1914; and Canada to State, 812.404/16, September 25, 1914—in FRUS 1914; "Appeal to Cardinal Gibbons," *Sun*, June 28, 1914; "Accuses Mexicans of Killing Priests," *World*, March 15, 1915; Mecham, *Church and State*, 382; Reed, *Insurgent Mexico*, 103.

24. American Consul Canada to Gen. V. Carranza, February 21, 1915, File 145;

25. Gamboa to Lind, August 26, 1913, File 167, Buckley Papers.

26. Lind, Mexican Affairs, 2:2360–62; Buckley, Mexican Affairs, 1:790–94.

27. Lind, Mexican Affairs, 2:2361. See also Stephenson, *John Lind of Minnesota*, 284.

28. Lind, 2:2362–68; Buckley, 1:812–25; and Nelson O'Shaughnessy, 2:2716—all in Mexican Affairs. See also "Says Carranza Pay Goes to Americans," *Sun*, January 22, 1920; and "Messages Reveal Carranza Intrigue," *Sun*, January 25, 1920; Capt. Sherburne Hopkins memo, October 4, 1919, File 223, Buckley Papers. Payments were made from customhouse revenue and deposited in the Milmo National Bank in downtown Laredo or the German Bank in San Antonio.

29. Buckley, 1:804–5; and O'Shaughnessy, 2:2710—Mexican Affairs; "Bryan Defends Wilson on the Mexican Policy," *Sun*, April 22, 1915; Clements, "Woodrow Wilson's Mexican Policy," 128, 134; Redinger, *American Catholics*, 49–50; Teitelbaum, *Wilson and the Mexican Revolution*, 141; Curley, *Citizens and Believers*, 138–39.

30. Belt to State, 812.00/16534, October 19, 1915; Lansing to Arredondo, 812.00/16532b, October 19, 1915; and Arredondo to Lansing, 812.00/16533, October 19, 1915—all in FRUS 1915; "Los Catolicos y su Participacion en la Politica Actual," *El Universal*, November 25, 1919; E. B. Ledvina, secretary Extension Society, to Wilson, October 5, 1915, in "Mistreatment and Expulsion of Mexican Clergy by Carrancistas," 203–4. A looming issue was the access and control of Mexican oil; Buckley concluded in his assessment that both the American and British navies "were absolutely dependent upon a steady flow of oil from Mexico." See Buckley, "Summary of the Oil Controversy," n.d., Buckley Papers; and Smith, *United States and Revolutionary Nationalism*, 42.

De facto recognition, a first stage in advance of full de jure status, is predicated on a subjective political and diplomatic evaluation after a government demonstrates "good behavior."

31. "Treatment of Catholics," *New York Times*, November 29, 1915, transcript, File 121.5; and Bryan to Carranza, "Translation of Ciphered Message," July 14, 1914, File 224.3—Buckley Papers; Cumberland, *Mexican Revolution*, 296–97.

32. "Protest to Wilson," *Sun*, October 18, 1915; "Attacks Wilson Policy," *Sun*, November 18, 1915; "Carranza Pledges Safety of Catholics in Mexico," *Sun*, October 20, 1915; "Mr. Tumulty as an Apologist for Carranza," *Sun*, November 20, 1915; "Mexican Bishops Deny Charges of Inciting Revolts," *Sun*, November 10, 1915. Former ambassador Wilson, Brazilian minister de Oliveira, and presidential special agent Paul Fuller advised against recognition of Carranza.

33. Buckley to Reverend Richard Tierney, September 23, 1915, Box 32, Buckley Papers; "Gen. Carranza Invades Guatemala; Graft Rules Mexico City Government," *Sun*, October 15, 1915.

34. Carothers to State, 812.00/16653, October 31, 1915, FRUS 1915; "Villa Insults Wilson, Threatens Reprisals," *Sun*, January 20, 1915; Raymond Carroll, "Villa Found Market in U.S. for Stolen Cattle," *Sun*, August 17, 1915; Meyer, *Mexico*

and the United States, 44–46; Hall, *Obregón*, 127, 131; Redinger, *American Catholics*, 5–6.

35. "Wilson Stands against Intervention: The Bodies of Eighteen Victims of Santa Ysabel Massacre Found," *New York Times*, January 14, 1916; Letcher to State, 812.00/17268, February 9, 1916; and Cobb to State, 812.00/17377, March 9, 1916—in FRUS 1916; Testimony of Mrs. Laura Ritchie, Mexican Affairs, 1:1599–1605; Levario, *Militarizing the Border*, 38–52; Gibbon, *Mexico under Carranza*, 72–92.

36. Carranza Note, May 22, 1916, File 180; White House "Statement to Press" [re: expedition into Mexico], *New York Times*, March 26, 1915; and Luis Cabrera, alias Blas Urrea, "Regarding the Pershing Expedition," *New York Times*, n.d., transcript, File 112.3—all in Buckley Papers; Adams, *Murder and Intrigue*, 137; Funston to Secretary of War, 812.00/18067 and 20044, May 4, 1916, and December 2, 1916, FRUS 1916; Buckley, Mexican Affairs, 1:810; "Checking Mexican Outlawry," *New York Times*, January 26, 1916; Simpson, *Many Mexicos*, 305–7; Katz, "Alemania y Francisco Villa," 96–97; Vandiver, *Blackjack*, 2:640–48; Hall, *Obregón*, 146. See also Foulois, "Operations of the First Aero Squadron." Braddy, *Pershing's Mission in Mexico*; and Valle, *La no intervención*, 8.

37. Charles Hilles to Buckley, October 23, 1915, and Buckley to Hilles, November 23, 1915, Box 32, Buckley Papers; Redinger, *American Catholics*, 51.

38. Buckley to Thomas Streeter, July 15, 1916, and August 17, 1917; and Buckley to Hilles, November 15, 1915, Box 32—Buckley Papers.

39. Hendrick, *Walter H. Page*, 1:362; Quirk, *Mexican Revolution*, 101, 78; Leary, "Woodrow Wilson," 57–59; Krauze, *Mexico*, 357. See also Clendenen, *Blood on the Border*.

40. Canada to Secstate, September 10, 1916, File 113, Buckley Papers; "Obregón, Who Defeated Villa, Is Dead at Leon," *Sun*, June 14, 1915; "Obregón Is Loyal," *Sun*, September [?,] 1915. Obregón was severely wounded at Leon and lost his right arm. Canada also reported, "New paper money rapidly depreciating, now 33 pesos for 1 dollar; old paper bills 330 for 1."

41. "American Military Intelligence Agent Describes Destruction of Mexico's Industry," *New York Times*, August 31, 1919; "Have the Germans Captured Carranza?," *Sun*, February 13, 1917.

42. Lansing to Rodgers, 812.00/18355, June 10, 1916; Lansing to Secretary of Foreign Relations of Mexico, 812.00/18450, June 20, 1916; and Garrett to State, 812.00/18392 and 18430, June 12 and 15, 1916—all in FRUS 1916; Secretary of State to Ambassador Fletcher, 811.0144/86, June 15, 1918, FRUS 1918; Testimonies of Grover Webb, 1:1529–31; Capt. Frederick J. Herman, 2:1811–28; O. C. Dowe,

"Pershing's Story of Villa Chase," *New York Times*, November 11, 1921; Buckley, Mexican Affairs, 1:810; Beezley, *Insurgent Governor*, 96–97.

44. Cablegram, Canada to Secstate, September 10, 1916, File 113, Buckley Papers.

45. Parker to State, 812.00/20080, December 15, 1916, FRUS 1916; Quirk, *Mexican Revolution*, 79–112; "Pope Aids Mexicans," *Sun*, November 7, 1914; "The Mexican Tangle," *Sun*, March 29, 1915; "Carranza's Vision," *Sun*, August 9, 1916; Kelley, Mexican Affairs, 2:2669–2670; Krauze, *Mexico*, 359–61; Cleven, "Religious Aspects of Mexico's Constitution," 16; Hall, *Obregón*, 174–75; Quirk, *Mexican Revolution*, 81.

46. "Extracts from Constitution Bearing on Religious Questions," File 145, Buckley Papers; "Mexican Delegates Sign Constitution," *Sun*, February 1, 1917; "Lansing Protests Laws Mexico Plans," *Sun*, January 26, 1917; Hall, *Obregón*, 167–74; Buckley, Mexican Affairs, 1:825–29. See complete text of Constitution of 1917 published in *Diário Oficial* on February 5, 1917 (copy at Mexican Affairs, 812.011/31, February 7, 1917, FRUS 1917, 950–81).

47. Díaz, "State vs. Church in Mexico," 401; Portes Gil, *Conflict*, 49, 93–96, 99–100; Quirk, *Mexican Revolution*, 96–100; Simpson, *Many Mexicos*, 306–7; Callcott, *Liberalism in Mexico*, 268–88; Young, *Ordeal in Mexico*, 25–28; See also Sec. Frank B. Kellogg to Rep. Stephen G. Porter, 812.404/306, March 3, 1926, FRUS 1926; Brown, *Protestants and the Mexican Revolution*; Niemeyer, "Anti-clericalism in the Mexican Constitutional Convention," 31–49; Curley, "Anticlericalism and Public Space," 518; Testimony of Edwin R. Brown, Mexican Affairs, 2:2071–81; and Woods, *Finding Refuge in El Paso*, 8–34.

48. Redinger, *American Catholics*, 179–82.

49. Briefing document: The New Anti-American Constitution of Mexico, n.d., Buckley Papers.

50. "Carranza Elected to the Presidency," *Sun*, March 12, 1917; Niemeyer, *Revolution at Querétaro*, 31–209; Quirk, *Mexican Revolution*, 101–3; Curley, *Citizens and Believers*, 149; Cline, *United States and Mexico*, 168. See also Carpizo, *Constitución Mexicana de 1917*.

51. Fletcher and Long to Secretary Lansing, 712.12/229, December 12, 1919, FRUS 1919.

52. Silliman to State, February 13, 1918, FRUS 1918. See also Curley, *Citizens and Believers*, 115–30.

53. Interview with James Buckley, April 7 2019; Curley, *Citizens and Believers*, 151.

54. Cabrera, "The Mexican Revolution—Its Causes, Purposes, and Results," draft for the *Annals of the American Academy of Political and Social Science*, January 1917, File 122.5, Buckley Papers; Niemeyer, *Revolution at Querétaro*, 62–78; Decorme, "Catholic Education in Mexico," 176–81; Richmond, *Venustiano Carranza's Nationalist Struggle*, 220; Brandenburg, *Making of Modern Mexico*, 179–82; "Mexico Schools, Shut 5 Years, Open March 6," *Sun*, February 19, 1916;

"Tells Carranza Plans for Schools in Mexico," *Sun*, February 29, 1916; Quirk, *Mexican Revolution*, 90–94, 99; Cumberland, *Mexican Revolution*, 225–27.

55. "Memorandum of notes on an interview with a leading educator of Mexico," ca. 1919, File 111.1, Buckley Papers; Whitney, *What's the Matter with Mexico?*, 98–102, 168; Curley, *Citizens and Believers*, 115. For a regional perspective see "Public Instruction in Yucatan" [unpublished], ca. 1917, File 111.1, Buckley Papers. The archdiocese of Guadalajara estimated the interruption of education affected twenty thousand children.

56. "Failure of the Authorities," File 111.1, Buckley Papers; Quirk, *Mexican Revolution*, 104; "New Minister of Education Tells of His Plan for War on Illiteracy," *Herald*, November 7, 1921.

57. "Wilson Address to Visiting Mexican Editors on the Policy of the United States toward Mexico and Latin America," June 7, 1918, FRUS 1918, 577–80; "Says Bolshevism Hit Mexico First," *Sun*, September 12, 1919; Daniels, *Life of Woodrow Wilson*, 188.

58. Rice, "Diplomatic Relations," 15.

Chapter 5

1. Sugar Industry Report, July 1919, File 123.1; and Wallace Thompson, "Bankrupt Mexico"—Buckley Papers; "American Military Intelligence Agent Describes Destruction," *New York Times*, August 31, 1919; Trow, "Woodrow Wilson," 51–52; Powell, *Railroads of Mexico*, 56–60; Bernstein, *Mexican Mining Industry*, 106–23; Forrest, "Significance of Mexican Oil Fields." See also Aguirre, *Cananea*; "Revolution's Blight on Mexico's Industries," *Sun*, August 24, 1915; and "Mexican Railways Hard Hit by Revolt," *New York Times*, December 15, 1917. A decade of chronic instability and loss during revolutionary upheaval has been estimated at some 2 million lost due to disease, lost births, combat deaths, and outmigration; see McCaa, "Missing Millions," 367–400.

2. Buckley, "Some Aspects of the Problem," Buckley Papers.

3. Polk to Wilson, 711.12/187, March 1, 1919; and Wilson to Lansing, 711.12/187, August 4, 1919—in FRUS 1919; "Mr. Fletcher's Career," *New York Times*, June 26, 1929; "Henry Fletcher, Diplomat, 86, Dies: Envoy for Almost 30 Years," *New York Times*, July 11, 1959; "Mr. Wilson's Judgment in Foreign Affairs Is Not Often Right," *New York American*, August 25, 1919.

4. Consul Stewart, Chihuahua, to State, 812.00/22516, February 8, 1919; Acting Secretary of State to President Wilson, "Embargo of July 12, 1919," 612.110/2623a,

Activities in Yucatán," Agent No. 16 report, December 19, 1919, File 154.3, Box 35; and Agent No. 16 report, "Carrancista Propaganda in the U.S.," December 31, 1919, File 154.3—all in Buckley Papers; Brown, "Why Foreign Oil Companies Shifted Production," 372; Cline, *United States and Mexico*, 9; Domeratsky, "American Industry Abroad," 569–82. The Marazan Plan, named for Francisco Marazan, a heroic soldier, patriot, and statesman of the early 1800s, called for the unification of the Central American nations under one president with the capital located at San Salvador.

6. "Extract from the Presidential Message of Venustiano Carranza to the Mexican Congress," September 1, 1919, File 154.4, Buckley Papers; "Preliminary Analysis of Article 27 of the Constitution," Association of Foreign Oil Producers in Mexico, September 20, 1921, Box 32, Buckley Papers; "Mexican Catholics Oppose U.S. Entry," *Sun*, August 30, 1919; De Bekker, *Plot against Mexico*, 6–16; Ansell, *Oil Baron of the Southwest*, 175–77.

7. Buckley, Mexican Affairs, 1:825–26; Trow, "Woodrow Wilson," 50; Ansell, *Oil Baron of the Southwest*, 174–76; La Botz, *Edward L. Doheny*, 76–78; W. F. Buckley to Capt. Hanson, May 9, 1921, Box 32, Buckley Papers.

8. Spring Rice to Grey, July 12, 1913, Doc. 125, BFA; "Fall Wants 500,000 in Army for Mexico," *New York Times*, November 5, 1916; "Location of Border Troops," *New York Times*, June 29, 1916. In August 1916, there were 34,592 troops stationed on the US-Mexico border.

9. "Senators Ready to Take Up Mexico," *New York Times*, September 3, 1919; Senate, *Preliminary Report and Hearings*, 3; Trow, "Woodrow Wilson," 46–48. See also "Committee Investigation," *New York Times*, July 17, 1919, and August 9, 1919.

10. *New York Times* article, July 17, 1919, in Buckley Papers.

11. Hart, *Empire and Revolution*, 334–35. See also Nelson O'Shaughnessy, former chargé d'affaires, "What Is Wrong in Mexico?," n.d. [ca. 1919]; and Msgr. Francis C. Kelley, "The Catholic Church and the Solution of the Mexican Problem," Agent No. 16, December 5, 1919—in Box 32, Buckley Papers.

12. "Outline of some topics that could be covered and brought out in the Congressional Investigation," n.d., Buckley Papers; C. W. Robinson to W. F. Buckley, November 8, 1919; Statement of John B. Crawford (Mr. R), November 22, 1919; Statement of J. W. MacDonald (Mr. Q), January 2, 1920; Statement of H. George Zoeller (Mr. P), November 1919; Statement of D. W. Davis (Mr. O), November 1919; Statement of William B. King (Mr. L), October 25, 1919; Statement of Hiram Catron (Mr. G), October 25, 1919; Statement of Louis Holmberg (Mr. K), November 1919; and James & Cowan (Mr. N)—all in Buckley Papers; Buckley, Mexican Affairs, 1:768. To protect the identity of those in Mexico that provided statements and exhibited a willingness to appear before the committee, they were given code names: "Mr." followed by a letter.

13. "Joaquin Armedaiz reasons for refusing to testify," memo by No. 16, December 1919; and F. Sommerfeld, re: Henry Lane Wilson testimony, January 19,

1920—in Box 32, Buckley Papers; Testimony of Capt. George Hyde, Mexican Affairs, 1:1194–96; Testimony of Henry Forrest, Mexican Affairs, 1:1241, 2965; "Mexico to Bar Witnesses at Fall Hearing," *San Antonio Light*, January, 20, 1920; "To Expel Fall Witnesses," *New York Times*, February 6, 1920. For an overview of the proceedings, see Dennis W. Lou, "Fall Committee: An Investigation of Mexican Affairs" (PhD diss., Indiana University, 1963). See also "The Threat to Mexico," *Nation*, August 23, 1919, 234.

14. Summerlin to State, 125.61383/118 and 139, October 21 and 26, 1919, FRUS 1919. See also Testimony of Wilber Forrest, Mexican Affairs, 2:2047–45; and Brown, Mexican Affairs, 2:2082–84. The Buckley Papers include a broad cross-section of documents on the Jenkins affair, including a report by W.F.B., presumably sent to the US State Department: "Brief Account of the Jenkins Kidnapping and Subsequent Developments."

15. "American Consul Is Kidnapped by Mexican Bandits," *New York American*, October 23, 1919; "Jenkins Case—Cordoba Statement," *New York Times*, December 2, 1919, transcript, File 121.3, Buckley Papers. For the best overall reviews of this incident, see Paxman, *Jenkins of Mexico*, 104–35; Cumberland, "Jenkins Case," 586–607; and Glaser, "1919," 337–50.

16. Summerlin to State, 125.61383/158, November 3, 1919, FRUS 1919; "Mexican Government Refuses to Pay Ransom of Consular Agent," *Excelsior*, November 4, 1919; "No Hay Razon para Acusar a W. O. Jenkins," *La Prensa*, November 3, 1919; "Carranza Refuses to Repay Jenkins $150,000 Ransom," *New York American*, November 6, 1919; Myer Resolution, 66th Cong., 1st sess., vol. 58, pt. 8, October 25, 1919, 7477.

17. "Translation: Statement of Justice Mitchell Regarding the Arrest of Consul Jenkins," Puebla, November 15, 1919, File 152, Buckley Papers; "The Case of Mr. Jenkins," *New York Times*, November 8, 1919; Cumberland, "Jenkins Case," 597. The book by Paxman, *Jenkins of Mexico*, incorrectly identifies Buckley in the single mention in the text as only a "temporary or occasional visitor" (135).

18. "Mexico Sends Note on Jenkins Case," *Sun*, November 24, 1919; "El Caso de Mr. Jenkins," *El Heraldo de México*, November 24, 1919; "Carranza Trickery Back of Charges That Caused Second Arrest of Jenkins," *New York American*, November 24, 1919.

19. Lansing to Chargé Summerlin, 812.6363/582, November 18, 1919, FRUS 1919; Smith, "Robert Lansing," 135–42; Editorial: "The Case of Mr. Jenkins," *New York Times*, November 8, 1919.

20. Forrest, Mexican Affairs, 2:2049; "Bandit Describes Jenkins' Capture,"

Are Near Break," *New York Evening Mail*, November 21, 1919; "Stop Molesting Jenkins, Mexico Is Told by U.S.," *Herald*, November 21, 1919; "La Actitud de Casa Blanca es Inexplicable," *Excelsior*, November 25, 1919; "Jenkins' Release Eases High Strain in Mexican Crisis," *World*, December 7, 1919; Meyer, *Mexico and the United States*, 71; Wilson, *My Memoirs*, 298–99; Viereck, *Strangest Friendship in History*, 306–13; Daniels, *Cabinet Diaries of Josephus Daniels*, entry December 4, 1919, 467. A feature article in the *Sun*, "Rebels for Invasion," on November 22, 1919, speculated that the War Department more than once estimated it would take 450,000 men and three years of occupation to "pacify" Mexico. See also Kraig, *Woodrow Wilson*, 168–76.

23. "Summary of Points Brought Out in Attached Material and Counter Accusations Made by Carranza," Shoreham Papers, December 8, 1919, File 152, Buckley Papers; Jones, Mexican Affairs, 2:2928. See also "Documentos Oficiales Sobre el Plagio de Mr. W. Jenkins," *El Monitor*, November 4, 1919.

24. "War Not Necessary," *New York Times*, August 22, 1919; "The Mexican Dilemma," *New York Globe*, August 15, 1919.

25. Emiliano Lopez Figueroa, "Carrancista Propaganda in the U.S. (Jenkins Case)," No. 16, December 1919, Buckley Papers; "American Government Will Not Ask Mexico to Pay Ransom of Consular Agent Jenkins," *Excelsior*, November 7, 1919. See also US Senate, "Investigation of Mexican Affairs: Partial and Ad Interim Report," December 9, 1919.

26. "William Jenkins Case," No. 16, November 28, 1919, File 123.2, Buckley Papers. This memo outlines the legal reasons supporting referral of the Jenkins case to federal court, citing the new Mexican Constitution of 1917, Section 104, paragraph 6.

27. "Consul Jenkins' Own Story of His Abduction," *World*, December 1, 1919; "Mexican Trick Seen in Jenkins' Release on Bail," *Herald*, December 7, 1919. Insisting on complete vindication of all charges, Jenkins tried to refuse all bail until his case was dismissed, to the extent that after being released he returned to the Puebla Penitentiary and demanded to be locked up again until his case was over! He was sent home.

28. "Aids Anti-American Campaign in Mexico," *New York Times*, April 29, 1921; Paxman, *Jenkins of Mexico*, 117; Erby E. Swift, Tampico, to D. D. Lester, November 1, 1919, Box 131, Buckley Papers.

29. Testimony of Gerald Brandon, Mexican Affairs, 2:2040–45. See also Paxman, *Jenkins of Mexico*, 386–87; and LaFrance, "Revision del caso Jenkins," 911–57.

30. Summerlin to State, 125.61383/251, December 5, 1919, FRUS 1919; W. O. Jenkins to Summerlin, 125.61383J41/48, February 1, 1920; and Summerlin to State, 125.61383J41/75, December 4, 1920—in FRUS 1920; "High Mexican Court Gets Jenkins Case," *Sun*, December 12, 1919; "Mexican Leader Has No Fear of U.S. Intervention," *World*, December 19, 1919; "Mexicans Here Charged with Jenkins Plot," *Wall Street Journal*, December 30, 1919; "Mexico to Cancel Jenkins Exequatur," *New York Evening Mail*, February 4, 1920; Stephen Bonsal, "Corrupt Courts,

Poisoning Nation, Say Mexican Papers," *Washington Post*, March 3, 1920; Paxman, *Jenkins of Mexico*, 119–27, Cumberland, "Jenkins Case," 603–7. The $500 bond for Jenkins was paid by J. Salter Hanson of Chicago.

31. Intervention documents in the Buckley Papers include "American Intervention in Mexico," November 20, 1919, File 123.2; "Constitution of 1917 and Political Rights," December 9, 1919, File 123.2; and "[US] Army Plans for Possible Intervention in Mexico," File 123.3, August 14, 1919. Of those attacked in January 1920, Joseph E. Askew of the Tlahualilo Cotton Company was abducted, and Gabriel Porter and James Wallace of the Penn-Mex Oil Company and Earl Bowles and P. J. Roney of the International Oil Company were murdered. See "Prominent American in Mexico Abducted," *Journal of Commerce*, February 5, 1920; "American[s] Killed by a Carranzista," *World*, January 8, 1920; and "American Oilmen Slain," *Excelsior*, January 9, 1920.

32. Memo from No. 16 re: Henry Lane Wilson, January 19, 1920, Buckley Papers. See also Memo, "Excerpts from Articles Entitled 'Huerta and the Two Wilsons' by Herbert Murray," *Harper's*, 1916, Buckley Papers; Feilitzsch, *In Plain Sight*, 153–300; and Katz, *Secret War in Mexico*, 92–115.

33. Jones, Mexican Affairs, 2:2889–2958, 2905, 2956. See also "Murray Hill Material: Jones Letter," June 19, 1922, Buckley Papers.

34. Jones, Mexican Affairs, 2:2892–98, 2945–46, 2951–52, 3003, 3114–16. Adam Leckie's close connection with officials in Mexico was owing to his Washington firm's handling of all American claims stemming from the revolution against the Mexican government. He died in December 1919 under very mysterious circumstances; Jones commented that "he was possibly bumped off."

35. Ibid., 2:2924–25, 2928. See also Ramón de Negri to Flavio Berquees, the Senate, Mexico City, October 23, 1919, File 114, Buckley Papers.

36. Jones, Mexican Affairs, 2:2894, 2912–14, 2917, 2927. See also La Botz, *Edward L. Doheny*, 105–9. General Alvarado, while visiting New York City, was subpoenaed to testify before the Fall Committee but did not appear.

37. "Luis D'Antin Zuloaga Dead," *Washington Post*, January 9, 1917; "Begins D'Antin Inquiry," *Washington Post*, January 11, 1917; "Ayer Salio Arredondo de Nuevo Laredo para la Capital," *San Antonio La Prensa*, January 7, 1917; "D'Antin Sent Note Warning a Friend [he was in danger]," *Sun*, January 11, 1917. The *Post* article noted: "It was said that D'Antin knew more of the inside secrets of Mexican-American relations than any other living American."

38. Jones, Mexican Affairs, 2:2954–57, 3007–8.

39. Ibid., 2:2958–62.

40. Ibid.

and Meyer, *Mexico Frente a Estados Unidos*, 141; La Botz, *Edward L. Doheny*, 89–97; Meyer, *Mexico and the United States*, 58, 81–84, 93.

43. "Says Oil Men Won't Pay, *Sun*, January 9, 1920; "Es Enemigo de E. U. el Sr. Cabrera," *Excelsior*, January 8, 1920.

44. "Britain Denies It Opposed U.S. on Mexican Oil," *Sun*, April 18, 1921; "Mexico's Oil Secrets Told by Oil Expert," *Houston Telegram*, April 25, 1921; "Break in Concord of Oil Interests," *New York Times*, December 14, 1920; Hart, *Empire and Revolution*, 320–21; Sprout and Sprout, *Toward a New Order of Sea Power*, 75–77.

45. W. F. Buckley, "Memorandum on the Mexican Situation for Hon. Bainbridge Colby, Secretary of State," May 12, 1920, Buckley Papers.

46. William F. Buckley to Ireland Graves, May 6, 1920, author's collection.

47. The White House, "Wilson' Statement of Recognition of de la Huerta," August 10, 1920, File 110, Buckley Papers; Summerlin to Secretary of State, 712.00/3, April 7, 1921, and 711.1211/17, June 3, 1921, FRUS 1921; "Mexican President [Huerta] Promises Oil Settlement," *Oil Trade Journal*, August 1920, 20; Maurer, *Power and the Money*, 166–67. See also Memorandum by Hanna on conference with de la Huerta, 711.12/526, July 21, 1922, FRUS 1922, in which Huerta defends Obregón and asserts Carranza "killed himself as a brave man might be expected to do."

48. President Harding to General Obregon, 812.00/25114, July 21, 1921, FRUS 1921, 42–43; "Three Large Wells Completed in South Mexico," *Oil Trade Journal*, August 1920, 22; E. L. Doheny, "Mexican Oil Alarms Ridiculed by Doheny," *New York American*, May 4, 1921; Meyer and Beezley, *Mexico*, 472–75; Capt. W. M. Hanson to W. F. Buckley, September 7, 1921, Box 32, Buckley Papers; John K. Turner, "Why the Obregón Government Has Not Been Recognized," *Nation*, June 1, 1921, 783–85; "Obregón Outdoing Carranza in Methods of Confiscation," *Sun*, June 17, 1921; Department of State, press release, June 7, 1921, File 380, Buckley Papers; La Botz, *Edward L. Doheny*, 100–103. During this period the United States maintained "protector-ships" off the coasts of Nicaragua, Honduras, Haiti, and Santo Domingo.

49. Buckley to Senator Fall, November 4, 1920; and Buckley to Capt. W. M. Hanson, May 7, 1921—in Box 32, Buckley Papers; La Botz, *Edward L. Doheny*, 110n40; Perlstein, *Before the Storm*, 70–71. See also Secretary of State Charles Hughes to Summerlin, 711.211/31, April 15, 1922, FRUS 1922, 651; and Smith, *United States and Revolutionary Nationalism*, 194–96. The Obregón hard-liners did not accept US provisions of the Treaty of Amity and Commerce to honor religious rights in Mexico.

50. W. C. Teagle, President of the Standard Oil Company of New Jersey, to Secretary of State, 611.127/394, August 18, 1921, FRUS 1921; "Oil Men Endorse Fall on Mexico," *New York Times*, March 3, 1921; "Ask That Obregon Be Not Recognized," *New York Times*, April 12, 1921; Ansell, *Oil Baron of the Southwest*, 206; Hart, *Empire and Revolution*, 344–45; Smith, *United States and Revolutionary*

Nationalism, 194–98. See also British Protect, Geddes to Secretary of State, 841.6363/143, April 20, 1921, FRUS 1921.

51. Bureau of Investigation report in La Botz, *Edward L. Doheny*, 104.

52. W. F. Buckley, "State's Attitude on Mexican Affairs Is Criticized by Texan," *Austin Statesman*, August 10, 1921. See also Smith, *United States and Revolutionary Nationalism*, 194–97, 202.

53. C. E. Castaneda, "The Truth Concerning Mexico," *Austin Statesman*, August 17, 1921; Buckley to Editor, *El Heraldo de México*, September 13, 1912; Buckley to Editor, *Austin Statesman*, August 25, 1921; and draft response to the *Austin Statesman* on Castaneda article, August 25, 1921—all in Box 32, Buckley Papers; Meyer, *Mexico and the United States*, 81–84, 91–95; Clark, "Oil Settlement with Mexico," 606–10. A detailed twenty-five-page brief on the Texas Company decision can be seen in Box 32, File 124: Edward Schustor to Frederic Watrise, "Decision of the Mexican Supreme Court in the "amparo" Legal Action Brought by the Texas Company of Mexico," October 13, 1921.

54. Buckley, Mexican Affairs, 1:798–802; "Mexican Govt. Proposes 100% Oil Tax Increase," *Wall Street Journal*, June 10, 1921.

55. "Mexico Banishes Head of American Association," *Tribune*, November 27, 1921; "Se Aplicara el Articulo 33 al Sr. William F. Buckley," *Excelsior*, November 27, 1921; *W.F.B. Appreciation*, 48, 139–40, 147; Buckley, *American Family*, 28, 258.

56. "Rebels Headed by Cantu Start Mexican Revolt," *Sun*, November 14, 1921; "U.S. Should Recognize Obregón Government, Asserts Mr. Hearst," *New York American*, November 13, 1921; "Hobby Endorses Obregón's Stand on Recognition," *San Antonio Express-News*, June 15, 1921; "Mexican Protective Association Forces Sec'y Hughes' Policy," *New York American*, June 9, 1921. See also "Fall Tells How Mexico Can Win Recognition," *Tribune*, March 2, 1921; "Senator Fall and Mexico," *New York Globe*, March 8, 1921, and June 9, 1921; Harry Chandler, editorial, *Los Angeles Times*, October 23, 1921; and William Randolph Hearst, *It Is Time to Accord Recognition to President Obregón and Mexico*, August 24, 1921, n.p., as presented to the US Senate, "Recognition of President Obregón," *Congressional Record*, 67th Cong., 2nd sess., March 25, 1922, 4532–42. In a letter to President Obregón, dated October 19, 1921, Hearst proposed an extensive promotional campaign in the United States to encourage diplomatic recognition through articles aimed at reaching 3.4 million newspaper readers across the country. See also F. E. Monteverde to Ramón F. de Negri, June 21, 1921, Buckley Papers.

57. Buckley, Mexican Affairs, 1:797; "Obregón and His Propaganda for Recognition," American Association of Mexico, Bulletin No. 8, November 1, 1921. In the wake of the failure of the

League of Nations, attention in late 1921 in Washington, DC, turned to the nego-
tiations of the Naval Power Conference. See "Arms and the Men," *New York
Times*, November 20, 1919; and "Fear Failure Means Biggest Naval Race," *New
York Times*, November 25, 1921.

59. "Sent in Code from Buckley to Friend [code name: Furman] in New York,"
Mexico City, November 24, 1921, Buckley Papers.

60. "Mexico Expels Buckley," *New York Post*, November 29, 1921; "Sale de la
Republica el Sr. William F. Buckley," *Excelsior*, November 29, 1921; "Expelled
American Back from Mexico," *New York Times*, November 30, 1921; "Mexico
Agitated over Rumor about Fletcher," *New York Times*, November 21, 1921; "Mex-
ico Still Unyielding," *New York Times*, November 25, 1921; "From Mexico for His
'Own Safety,'" *Tribune*, November 30, 1921; *W.F.B. Appreciation*, 34.

61. "Buckley," *Excelsior*, December 1, 1921.

(Mexico City November 27, 1921

Hereby advises the civil and military authorities on the Mexico City–Laredo
route, not to obstruct the American citizen William F. Buckley who is heading
to the American border.

NO REENTRY.

Chief of Protocol

Office of the Secretary)

62. "Austin Man Draws Wrath of Obregón," *Austin American*, November 27,
1921; "Article 33 Is Applied to W. Buckley: Refused in the American Embassy,"
Excelsior, November 27, 1921; *W.F.B. Appreciation*, 146. Buckley had very little to
say publicly about the expulsion, and family memoirs mention are generally
silent about these events—except for a detailed presentation against Obregón in
May: Buckley, "Some Aspects of the Problem," Buckley Papers.

63. James Buckley, interview by phone, April 7 and November 11, 2019.

64. Buckley to D. Basil O'Conner, July 23, 1927, Box 32, Buckley Papers.

65. Buckley to The Honorable Secretary of State, January 20, 1922, Buckley
Papers.

66. Benito Perez, "Un Error de Politica que de Diplomacia," *Excelsior*,
November 30, 1921; "William F. Buckley Lanza Cargos a Nuestro Gobierno,"
Excelsior, December 1, 1921; "Un Error Del General Obregón," *San Antonio La
Prensa*, December 5, 1921; "Los Verdaderos Intervencionistas," *San Antonio
La Prensa*, December 1, 1921; "Expelled American Back from Mexico," *New
York Times*, November 30, 1921; Meyer, *Mexico and the United States*, 99; *W.F.B.
Appreciation*, 144–45.

Chapter 6

1. Mexican Minister of Foreign Affairs Pani to Chargé Summerlin, 711.1211/61,
March 31, 1923, FRUS 1923, 523–26; "Salt Water Confined to Deep Mexican Oil
Wells," *Wall Street Journal*, August 24, 1921; "Big Oil Fields in Mexico Giving

Out," *Herald*, February 20, 1921; "New Mexican Oil Rules Endanger American Firms," *Herald*, February 14, 1919; "A Bit of Advice [on reduced Mexico oil production]," *Oil Trade Journal*, January 1922, 74; Adams, "Black Gold: Energy Dynamics of Mexico," in *Bordering the Future*, 61–76; Rubio, "Role of Mexico"; Meyer, *Mexico and the United States*, 6, 7, 66, 88, 117, 137; Haber, Maurer, and Razo, "When Institutions Don't Matter," 2–3; *New York Times*, June 30 and July 8, 1922. See also "Water Encroaches in More Mexican Wells," October 27, 1920; and "Shows Water Ravages in Mexican Field," February 2, 1921—*National Petroleum News*.

2. Buckley, *American Family*, 206–17; *W.F.B. Appreciation*, 174; Markmann, *Buckleys*, 20–21; Bedford, "World Oil Situation," 96–107.

3. H. A. Ellis to Buckley, March 13, 1922; and W. F. Buckley to J. L. Martin, May 25, 1922—File 442.121, Buckley Papers; "Big Tampico Bank Closes for Business," *Excelsior*, May 24, 1922; Buckley to Cecilio Velasco, May 25, 1922; Emilio Rabasa to Buckley, November 10, 1922; and Edmund L. Buckley to Charles Cope, May 25, 1922—all in Box 32, Buckley Papers; "Mexico Imposed Still Another Tax as American Oil Men Reach Capital," *National Petroleum News*, August 31, 1921, 28; *W.F.B. Appreciation*, 181; Woodhouse, "New Understanding with Mexico," 1010–21. The Big Five oil companies (with their company representatives) included Texaco (Amos L. Beaty), Standard Oil of New Jersey (Walter C. Teagle), Atlantic Refining Company (J. W. Van Dyke), Sinclair Consolidated Oil (Harry F. Sinclair), and Mexican Petroleum Company (Edward L. Doheny).

4. W.F.B. to Thomas F. Lee, National Association for the Protection of American Rights in Mexico, September 8, 1921, Buckley Papers; *W.F.B. Appreciation*, 150; Betancourt, *Venezuela*, 22. Betancourt, twice president of Venezuela (1945–47 and 1959–64), provides a detailed insider's look at the rise of the petroleum industry in Venezuela and its impact on the economic, political, and social fabric of the country. In addition to exploration in Venezuela, Royal Dutch Shell and Standard Oil constructed and controlled two gigantic refineries in Curaçao and Aruba.

5. Brokaw, "Oil," 89–100; Betancourt, *Venezuela*, 26–33. See also Cover, *Law of Hydrocarbons*.

6. "More Americans Attracted to Venezuelan Fields," *Oil Trade Journal*, May 1923, 28; McBeth, *Juan Vicente Gómez*, 1–12, 23–35; "Henry O. Flipper Is in Venezuela on Big Mining Job," *Cleveland Gazette*, May 26, 1923. See also Lieuwen, *Petroleum in Venezuela*, 18–32, 38, 116; and Salas, *Enduring Legacy*, 55–57, 71.

7. Stephen Bonsal, "Taxation to Stifle Petroleum Industry," *Boston Evening Transcript*, April 19, 1921; "Crude Production in Mexico Grows Steadily," *Oil Trade Journal, October* . . .

fishing town of Maracaibo at the north end of the lake grew from forty-five thousand in 1920 to more than eighty thousand by 1926.

9. *W.F.B. Appreciation*, 156, 173, 190–91; interview with James Buckley, December 31, 2018; Duarte-Vivas, "First Venezuelan Geological Oil Map"; "Colored Man Appointed Ass't. Secretary of Interior," *Chicago Broad Ax*, August 27, 1921; Fleming, *West Point*, 231. See also Brown, "Why Foreign Oil Companies Shifted Production," 363–85.

10. Memo for dispatch 1657 Mil., Attaché Captain Willoughby, June 17, 1925, Buckley Family Files; *W.F.B. Appreciation*, 156–58, 173; "Oil Producers May Abandon Mexico," *Journal of Commerce*, August 29, 1924; Lieuwen, *Petroleum in Venezuela*, 47–48; Yergin, *Prize*, 233–36; Salas, *Enduring Legacy*, 60–63.

11. James Buckley, interview by phone, April 7, 2019; Ansliner to State, 831.6363/73/4, March 7, 1924, FRUS 1924; McBeth, *Juan Vicente Gómez*, 165–68. James Buckley recalled that the royalty, if the port had been completed, was estimated to be a "penny per barrel"; therefore, given the amount of oil exported over the next three decades, "that would have been quite some investment and payment."

12. "Texas Men Operating in Venezuela Oil," *Dallas Morning News*, October 10, 1926; Lieuwen, *Petroleum in Venezuela*, 30–38; Arnold, Macready, and Barrington, *First Big Oil Hunt*; McBeth, *Juan Vicente Gómez*, 19; Betancourt, *Venezuela*, 27–34; Yergin, *Prize*, 235–36.

13. "Pantepec Oil Company of Venezuela," Authorization of 2,000,000 shares of stock, Transfer Agent: National Bank of Commerce, New York, n.p., n. d., underwriting operations based on 3,044,074 acres throughout Venezuela, and an agreed contract with Union Oil Co. of California "to expend $3.5 million over a period of six years" (author's collection). See also "Venezuela Magnet for Big Companies," *Oil Trade Journal*, April 1923, 13.

14. "Activities of American Commercial Interests," 831.6363/324, January 6, 1926, in Skinner, *Oil and Petroleum Manual*; "Gets Pantepec Oil Option," *New York Times*, April 18, 1928.

15. "Venezuelan Oil Contract," *Christian Science Monitor*, September 26, 1926; *W.F.B. Appreciation*, 175–76; McBeth, *Juan Vicente Gómez*, 95–96, 102, 211; Veatch, "Oil, Great Britain, and United States," 666.

16. American Petroleum Institute, *Petroleum Facts and Figures*, 19–23, 33–38, 65–66; Brown, "Why Foreign Oil Companies Shifted Production," 379–81; Lieuwen, *Petroleum in Venezuela*, 39, 47; "Venezuela Out Ranks Mexico," *New York Times*, March 29, 1928; Haber, Maurer, and Razo, "When Institutions Don't Matter," 2–3; Rubio, "Role of Mexico," 69–93; *W.F.B. Appreciation*, 157. Mexico did not regain its 1921 production levels until 1974.

17. Frederick C. Chabot to Secretary of State, 831.6363/206 and 211, June 7, 1924, and July 14, 1924, FRUS 1924; Flipper, *Colored Cadet at West Point*, xxxix–xli; Betancourt, *Venezuela*, 31; McConnell, *Mexico at the Bar*, 288; Martinez, *Venezuelan*

Oil, 43, 48; Department of State, *Register*, 101. See also "Wine in the Blood," *Wine Enthusiast*, June 1998, quoted in Buckley, *Torch Kept Lit*, 74–77.

18. Chabot to State, 831.6363/233, July 10, 1924, and 813.6363/196 and 198, May 9 and 17, 1924, FRUS 1924.

19. Fredrick Chabot to Buckley, March 12, 1928; and May 15, 1928, Box 32, Buckley Papers; Government Accountability Office, *Decisions of the Comptroller General*, 4:825–27; Memo for dispatch 1657 Mil., Attaché Captain Willoughby, US Embassy, June 17, 1925, Buckley Family Files.

20. Buckley to Chabot, May 10 and 28, 1928; and Chabot to Buckley, May 15, 1928—in Box 32, Buckley Papers.

21. Buckley to Chabot, February 20, 1928, Box 32, Buckley Papers. See also McConnell, *Mexico at the Bar*, 286–89.

22. Buckley to Chabot, March 2, 1929, Box 32, Buckley Papers. See also confidential memo, G.S.M. Jr. to J.W.B, February 10, 1961, Buckley Family Files.

23. Chabot to Buckley, March 22, 1929; and Buckley to Henry Lane Wilson, March 29, 1929—Buckley Family Files; "Gets Pantepec Oil Option: F. J. Lisman & Co. Expected to Buy Control in Venezuela," *New York Times*, April 18, 1928.

24. Examples of contemporary publications include Stevens, "Protecting the Rights of Americans," 164–75; McCullagh, *Red Mexico*; Rippy, Vasconcelos, and Stevens, *Mexico*; and Clark, "Oil Settlement with Mexico"; in addition, an English translation of Father Mariano Cuevas's *Historia de la Iglesia en Mexico* was published in 1928 (*History of the Church in Mexico*).

25. Buckley to Wilson, February 29, 1928, August 2 and 10, 1928, and March 28, 1929; and Wilson to Buckley, May 7, 1928, August 7, 1928, November 1 and 7, 1928, and March 8, 1929—all in Box 32, Buckley Papers; Shoemaker, "Henry Lane Wilson," 103–22. McCullagh in *Red Mexico* reviews in detail the assassinations of political opposition—de la Huerta, Gómez, and Serrano—to clear Obregón's path to the presidency.

26. Buckley to D. Basil O'Conner, July 23, 1927; Buckley to Chabot, February 20, 1928; and Buckley to Claude Buckley, November 12, 1928—in Box 32, Buckley Papers; *W.F.B. Appreciation*, 156–57; McCullagh, *Red Mexico*, 53–70; Hart, *Empire and Revolution*, 364–81; Meyer, *Mexico and the United States*, 9, 132–44; Williams, *Tragedy of American Diplomacy*, 150.

27. Young, *Mexican Exodus*, 5–17; Bailey, *¡Viva Cristo Rey!*, 76–118; Jeff McLemore, ed., "Conditions in Mexico," *Hebbronville (TX) News*, April 13, 1927.

28. Calles, quoted in Walling, *Mexican Question*, 199–200.

29. Buckley to Nemesio Garcia Naranjo, August 7, 1928, Box 32; American

Mexico, 420–24; Bailey, *¡Viva Cristo Rey!*, 216–21; Hart, *Empire and Revolution*, 361–64; Camargo and Grubb, *Religion in Mexico*, 76–81. A political opposition document acquired from Felicista sympathizers by Agent No. 16 reported their concerns: "The Constitution is 'Bolsheviki' because it empowers (in Article 27) the nation to define private property in the interest of the public good, thus the legal definition of public property shall always be at the mercy of the Government or public power." See also Charles Wood, "Radicals in Mexican Cabinet," *World*, September 11, 1921, transcript, File 421, Box 32, Buckley Papers.

30. Buckley to Father Mariano Cuevas, February 8, 1929, Box 32, Buckley Papers; Curley, *Mexican Tyranny*; American Hierarchy, *Pastoral Letter*; Redinger, *American Catholics*, 116–45; Butler, "Church in 'Red Mexico,'" 520–42. See also George Farias, "Exiled Archbishop of Mexico Was Buried in S.A.," *San Antonio Express-News*, April 26, 2015. The archbishop, along with six bishops, was deported by President Calles to Texas on April 21, 1927, where he died the next year. His remains were repatriated to the Cathedral of Mexico in 1947. The leader of the Knights of Columbus in Laredo was Dr. F. R. Canseco.

31. Young, *Mexican Exodus*, 6, 107–10; Bailey, *¡Viva Cristo Rey!*, 119–34; Quirk, *Mexican Revolution*, 197–203. See also Lippmann, "Church and State in Mexico," 186–207; Hart, *Revolutionary Mexico*, 346–47; McCullagh, "United States and Mexico," 869; and Andes, *Vatican and Catholic Activism*, 94–98.

32. Bailey, *¡Viva Cristo Rey!*, 134, 259–310; Redinger, *American Catholics*, 170–92; Lippmann, "Church and State in Mexico," 186–207; Brown, "Mexican Church–State Relations," 205–15.

33. Buckley to Claude I. Dawson, February 16, 1933; and Buckley to Velasco, July 13, 1934—in Box 32, Buckley Papers; "Standard Oil of Venezuela," *Christian Science Monitor*, July 3, 1934.

34. Lieuwen, *Petroleum in Venezuela*, 56–64; *W.F.B. Appreciation*, 158–60, 175–79; Salas, *Enduring Legacy*, 192–93, 207–8. The diversification of Pantepec holdings had actually begun in early 1933, by the establishment of Inversiones Espanolas in Madrid under the direction of longtime Buckley partner Cecilio Velasco, to develop oil and potash properties in Caraluna.

35. Buckley to Jose Vasconcelos, March 16, 1936; and Buckley to Naranjo, April 13, 1936—in Box 32, Buckley Papers; *W.F.B. Appreciation*, 160–61; Lieuwen, *Petroleum in Venezuela*, 63; Markmann, *Buckleys*, 35–36; Alan R. Plotnick, "American Government Oil Price Policies: 1930–1984," Faculty Working Papers, University of New Haven, November 14, 1984, 2–4.

36. Interview with James Buckley, November 11, 2019.

37. Lieuwen, *Petroleum in Venezuela*, 71–80; Hanson, *Politics of Mexican Development*, 30–31. See also Government of Mexico, *True Facts about the Expropriation*.

38. Buckley, *American Family*, 258; Bogus, *Buckley*, 65.

39. Buckley to Garcia Naranjo, April 4, 1938; Burke Baker to Buckley, May 19, 1938; and Buckley to Baker, May 20, 1938—in Box 32, Buckley Papers; Meyer,

Mexico and the United States, 169; Prewett, *Reportage on Mexico,* 110–11. See also Wild, "International Law and Mexican Oil."

40. Buckley to Baker, May 12, 1938; Buckley to Fred A. Dato, May 31, 1938; telegram, Dato to Buckley, May 29, 1938—in Box 32, Buckley Papers; Meyer, *Mexico and the United States,* 170–74; Krauze, *Mexico,* 476; Adams, *Bordering the Future,* 62–63. See also Meyer and Beezley, *Mexico,* 527–29. Buckley was well aware of Peláez's activities, which did not seem to involve any new or future counterrevolutionary actions. The two had met in New York City during late summer 1938. The general was under media and political attack for his past activities and solicited Buckley's assistance to extend his visa, noting that "it would really be dangerous for General Peláez to go back [now]." Buckley to Judge George Clifton, July 26, 1938, Box 32, Buckley Papers.

41. Claude Buckley to W. F. Buckley, April 13, 1937, Box 32, Buckley Papers. Claude informed Will that he had disinterred "Papa and John from their graves at San Diego" and moved them to the family plot in Austin.

42. Buckley to Richard J. Cronan, September 28, 1938; and Cronan to Buckley, September 30, 1938, and October 26, 1938—in Box 32, Buckley Papers; Hanson, *Second World Wars,* 28–33; House of Representatives, "Events Leading Up to World War II," 160–67.

43. Buckley to Naranjo, December 8, 1945, Box 32, Buckley Papers; *W.F.B. Appreciation,* 153–60.

44. *W.F.B. Appreciation,* 158.

45. Williams, *Tragedy of American Diplomacy,* 176–78.

46. Buckley to Burke Baker, September 3, 1941, Box 32, Buckley Papers; Markmann, *Buckleys,* 27–28. For those concerned with the prospect of American involvement, Buckley recommended they read a book by Sargent, *Getting Us into War* (1941). See also Holland, *Rise of Germany.*

47. Buckley to Micheline Bryden, December 19, 1941, Box 32, Buckley Papers; "Pantepec Oil Head Discusses Transfer of Surplus Funds," *Wall Street Journal,* April 5, 1940; Senate, Committee on Foreign Relations, "Multinational Oil Corporations," 1–10; "Search for Oil Renewed in Florida," *Barron's Financial Weekly,* July 26, 1948; Yergin, *Prize,* 434–37.

48. James Buckley, interview by phone, December 19 and 31, 2018, and January 11, 2019; "Pantepec Oil Reports El Roble Reserves of 247 Million Barrels," *Wall Street Journal,* July 3, 1941; Buckley to Max Clanc, February 26, 1942; and Buckley to Raymond Dickman, November 10, 1942—in Box 32, Buckley Papers; Elaine Sciolino, "John W. Buckley, Petroleum Executive Dies," *New York Times,* December 9, 1984; Buckley, *Truth Kept Us Free,* Hoath, *Will McCoy's Son.* Garonzik, "El Roble field" sat atop a large salt dome. Although it was regarded as one of the largest wells in the Western Hemisphere, it resembled a floating shoe box and earned the wartime sobriquet "Large Slow Target."

49. Wiggins, *Torpedoes in the Gulf*, 17–18; Baptiste, *War, Cooperation, and Conflict*, 148–50; Kieshell, *U-Boat War in the Caribbean*; "Sunken German U-Boat Found in Gulf of Mexico," *New York Times*, June 10, 2001; "The Night World War II Came to the Texas Coast," *Victoria Advocate*, July 25, 2012; Hanson, *Second World Wars*, 452–57.

50. William S. Wasserman to Buckley, April 12, 1943; Buckley to Wasserman, April 19, 1943; Ben H. Reese to Buckley, July 21, 1943; Buckley to Reese, October 14, 1943; and Buckley to Joseph Himes, October 15, 1943—in Box 32, Buckley Papers; "Pantepec Oil Co." *Wall Street Journal*, April 30, 1942; "Pantepec Oil Negotiating Deal to Exploit in Venezuela," *Wall Street Journal*, October 17, 1942; Office of War Coordination, *History of the Petroleum Administration*; Betancourt, *Venezuela Oil and Politics*, 64. See also Seddon, "Incorporating Corporations," 134–49; and Geological Survey, Attanasi and Root, "Statistics of Petroleum Exploration." In the Pacific War, a Japanese submarine shelled an oil refinery near Santa Barbara, California, on February 23, 1942.

51. Buckley to Reese, October 14, 1943; and Buckley to Gov. Thomas Dewey, "Memorandum on Latin American Relations," July 19, 1944—Box 32, Buckley Papers; *W.F.B. Appreciation*, 178; Betancourt, *Venezuela Oil and Politics*, 64–72, 129–30; Lieuwen, *Petroleum in Venezuela*, 96–102; Salas, *Enduring Legacy*, 209–13. See also Yergin, *Prize*, 368–77, 391–406.

52. "Pantepec Oil Head Quits; Buckley Succeeded by W. W. Smith," *New York Times*, July 2, 1943; Buckley, *At the Still Point*, 33–34; "New Oil Operating Plan Set Up in Venezuela," *Wall Street Journal*, February 15, 1043.

53. Buckley to Henry Cooper, January 21, 1946; and Buckley to Nemesio García Naranjo, December 8, 1945—Box 32, Buckley Papers; *W.F.B. Appreciation*, 161–63. Buckley had worked to ensure the word "contracts" is a more accurate description of the relation between the government and the oil companies than "concession," which carries the implication of a gift—thus, "a concession in Venezuela is a contract"; see "Oil Firms Will Cooperate in Revising Venezuelan Laws, Buckley Says," *Wall Street Journal*, November 20, 1941.

54. "Pantepec Oil Plan Contract with Compagnie Française," *Wall Street Journal*, October 7, 1946; "Pantepec Oil Co. Buys Florida Leases, First Outside of Venezuela," *Wall Street Journal*, November 8, 1946.

55. "Pantepec Co. of Venezuela Acquires Rights to Huge Potential Oil Acreage in Florida," *New York Times*, November 8, 1946; "Pantepec Oil to Sell Output for 3 Years to French Company," *Christian Science Monitor*, October 8, 1946; *W.F.B. Appreciation*, 160–62; Betancourt, *Venezuela Oil and Politics*, 128–34; Yergin, *Prize*, 409–27.

56. Lieuwen, *Petroleum in Venezuela*, 103–15; Markmann, *Buckleys*, 34; "Pantepec Director Says Middle East Deals to Hit Venezuelan Oil," *Wall Street Journal*, December 31, 1946; "Venezuela Wants 50% of Profits Made by Foreign Oil Companies," *Wall Street Journal*, January 10, 1947; Salas, *Enduring Legacy*, 211–12.

57. Interview with James Buckley, December 19 and 31, 2018, and November 11, 2019; Last Will and Testament, William F. Buckley, August 5, 1958, Buckley Family Files; Buckley, *Gleanings from an Unplanned Life*, 96, 100; "Search for Oil Renewed in Florida," *Baron's Financial Weekly*, July 26, 1948.

58. "Pantepec Oil Puts Earnings at 93 Cents a Share," *Wall Street Journal*, August 17, 1949; "Pancoastal Oil Plans to Separate Venezuelan and Florida Operations, *Wall Street Journal*, November 10, 1952; "Pancoastal Oil Unit Signs Lease for Florida Tract of US Sugar Corp.," *Wall Street Journal*, March 3, 1952.

59. "Another Buckley," *New York Times*, December 19, 1971; *W.F.B. Appreciation*, 36–37, 153–71. Operations in Israel, Ecuador, and Australia were all the province of essentially one venture. When the wells drilled in Israel by Pan Israel and Israel Mediterranean proved dry, they merged and became Magellan Petroleum, which acquired a controlling interest in Manabi Oil Company, which held properties in Ecuador. Magellan subsequently disposed of Manabi and moved to Australia, where it succeeded in discovering oil and natural gas.

60. *Grelmschatka*, October 1, 1949, February 1, 1958, and May 20, 1963, in Buckley Family Files; Heath, *Will Mrs. Major Go To Hell?*, 59–81.

Bibliography

Archival Sources

Benson Latin American History Collection, University of Texas at Austin
   William F. Buckley Sr. Papers (1910–1920)
   Ferrocarril Noreste de Mexico Papers
   Lázaro de la Garza Papers
   General Claims Commission—Mexico and the United States
   George Lister Papers (1887–2004)
   Papeles Varios Sobre la Revolución, 1910–1915, Garza 1917
   Emilio Rabasa Papers
Briscoe [Barker] Center for American History, University of Texas at Austin
   Roy Wilkinson Aldrich Papers
   Albert S. Burleson Papers
   Charles Chabot Papers
   Oscar B. Colquitt Papers
   Edward M. House Papers, 1896–1938
Buckley Family Files, Sharon, CT
Huntington Library, San Marino, CA
   Albert B. Fall Papers
Minnesota Historical Society Library and Archives, M208, St. Paul, MN
   Mexico in Transition: The Diplomatic Papers of John Lind 1913–1931.
National Archives and Records Administration, College Park, MD
   Bureau of Immigration, *Records of the Immigration and Naturalization Service, Mexican Immigration, 1906–1930*, Record Group 85

Mexican Revolution Oral History
Taft Papers, Letter Book
J. D. Wheelan Mexican Revolution Photographs (1913–14)
Texas State Archives, Austin, TX
Oscar B. Colquitt Papers
Proceedings of the Joint Committee of the Senate and House in the Investi-
gation of the Texas State Ranger Force, January 13, 1919.
Texas Rangers Papers
United States Military Academy, West Point, NY
Henry O. Flipper Papers
Yale University Archives, Sterling Library, New Haven, CT
William F. Buckley Sr. Papers
William F. Buckley Jr. Papers
Edward Mandell House Papers
John Lind Papers

Government Documents

Great Britain—United Kingdom

Bourne, Kenneth, ed. *British Documents on Foreign Affairs: Reports and Papers
from the Foreign Office Confidential Print.* Pt. 1, ser. C, vol. 15, *North American
Affairs, 1911–1914.* [Bethesda, MD]: University Publications of America, 1987.
Parliament. "Oil Properties and Mining Rights in Mexico." Exchanged Notes with
US Government, No. 1 (1914), London: July 1914.
———. "Oil Properties in Mexico." Exchanged Notes with the Netherlands Min-
ister, No. 7 (1914), London: August 1914.

Mexico

Chihuahua. *Album Conmemorativo, Visita a Chihuahua eel Sr. Presidente General
Don Porfirio Díaz.* N.p., October 1909.
Government of Mexico. *The True Facts about the Expropriation of the Oil Compa-
nies' Properties in Mexico.* Mexico City, 1940.
Obregón, Alvaro. *Ocho mil kilometros en compana.* Mexico City: Fondo de Cultura
Economica, 1959.
Secretaria de Agricultura y Recursos Hidraulicos. *Reformas al Articulo 27 Con-
stitucional.* Mexico City: SARH, November 1991.
Secretaria de Relaciones Exteriores. *Correspondencia Oficial: Mexico y Los Estados
Unidos.* Mexico City: Secretaria de Ralaciones Exteriores, 1926.
———. *Labor Internacional de la Revolucion Consitutionalista de Mexico.* Mexico
City: Imprenta de la Secretaria de Governacion, 1918.

United States

Burton, Senator Theodore E. "Panama Canal Tolls: The Traditional Policy of the United States in Relation to Waterways." Speech in the Senate of the United States, May 19, 1914. Washington: GPO, 1914.

Central Intelligence Agency. Mark E. Benbow. "All the Brains I Can Borrow: Woodrow Wilson and Intelligence Gathering in Mexico, 1913–1915." *Studies in Intelligence* 51, no. 4 (2007). http://www.cia.gov/library/CIS.

Department of the Navy. *Annual Reports of the Navy Department for the Fiscal Year 1913.* Washington: GPO, 1914.

Department of State. *American Mexican Claims Commission: Report of the Secretary of State, with Decisions Showing the Reasons for Allowance or Disallowance of the Claims.* Washington: GPO, 1948.

———. *Commercial Relations of the United States with Foreign Countries: Year 1902.* Washington: GPO, 1903.

———. *General Claims Commission between the United States and Mexico.* Washington: GPO, 1927.

———. Moore, John Basset. *A Digest of International Law.* Vol. 2. Washington: GPO, 1906.

———. *Papers Relating to the Foreign Relations of the United States, 1913–1921.* Washington: GPO, 1922–1936.

———. *Records . . . Relating to the Internal Affairs of Mexico, 1910–1929,* vol. 70.

———. *Register of the Department of State.* Washington: GPO, 1918, 1922.

———. *Special Mexican Claims Commission.* Washington: GPO, 1940.

Department of War. *War Department Annual Reports, 1911.* Washington: GPO, 1911–16.

Fuel Administration. *Final Report of the United States Fuel Administration, 1917–1919.* Washington: GPO, 1921.

Geological Survey. Attanasi, Emil, and David Root, eds. "Statistics of Petroleum Exploration in the Caribbean, Latin America, Western Europe, and the Middle East." Circular 1096. Washington: GPO, 1993.

Government Accountability Office. *Decisions of the Comptroller General.* Washington: GPO, 1925.

House of Representatives. "Events Leading Up to World War II: Chronological History—1931–1944." 78th Cong., 2nd sess., House Doc. 541. Washington: GPO, 1945.

Office of War Coordination. John W. Frey and H. Chandler Ide, eds. *A History of the Petroleum Administration for War, 1941–1945.* Washington: GPO, 1946.

Senate. "Affairs in Mexico." Message from the President of the United States. 66th Cong., 1st sess., Senate Doc. 67, 1919.

———. Committee on Foreign Relations, Subcommittee on Multinational Corporations. "Multinational Oil Corporations and U.S. Foreign Policy." January 2, 1975, Washington: GPO, 1975.

———. "Investigation of Mexican Affairs." Committee on Foreign Relations, 66th Cong., 2nd sess., Senate Doc. 285. Washington: GPO, 1920.

———. "Investigation of Mexican Affairs: Partial and Ad Interim Report." 66th Cong., 2nd sess., December 9, 1919.

———.Nimmo, Joseph. "Commercial Trade between the United States and Mexico." US Bureau of Statistics, 48th Cong., 1st sess., Ex Doc. 86, 1884.

———. *Preliminary Report and Hearings of the Committee on Foreign Relations*, 66th Cong., 1st sess., Doc. 185, 1920, I.

———. "Recognition of President Obregón." *Congressional Record*, 67th Cong., 2nd sess., March 25, 1922, 4532–42.

———. "Revolutions in Mexico." Subcommittee of the Committee on Foreign Relations, 62nd Cong., 2nd sess., S. Res. 335, 1913.

Venezuela

Ministerio de Fomento. *Ley de Minas.* Caracas: Tipografia Americana, 1920.

———. *Ley Sobre Hidrocarburos.* Caracas: Tipografia Cultura Venezolana, 1922.

Court Cases and Actions

W. F. Buckley, contra C. F. Davis. Tribunal Superior de Justicia del Distrito. *Diário de Jurisprudencia.* Mexico City. December 1, 1911.

Pedro R. Palting v. San Jose Petroleum. G. R. No. L-14441, Supreme Court of the Republic of Philippines. December 17, 1966.

United Canso Oil & Gas Ltd. v. Catawba Corp., 566 F. Supp. 232 (D. Conn. 1983), US District Court for the District of Connecticut. June 17, 1983.

L. L. Wright, vs. The State of Texas and John Buckley. Supreme Court of Texas, Austin Term, 1890. June 28, 1890.

Newspapers, Periodicals, and Serials

Albuquerque Morning Journal
The American Magazine
Austin American
Austin American-Statesman
Austin Statesman
Boston Evening Transcript
Brenham (TX) Weekly Banner
Camden (SC) News
Chicago Broad Ax
Cleveland Petroleum News

Cleveland Gazette
Cologne Gazette
Columbia (SC) State
Corpus Christi Weekly Caller
Dallas Morning News
Duluth News Tribune
The Economist
El Paso Herald
El Paso Morning Times
Evansville (IN) Press
Excelsior
Fort Worth Daily Gazette
Fort Worth Star-Telegram
Frontier Times
Fuel Oil Trade Journal
Galveston Daily News
Hebbronville (TX) News
El Heraldo de México
Houston Daily Post
El Imparcial
Journal of Commerce
Kansas City Star
Laredo (Daily) Morning Times
Laredo Weekly Times
Las Cruces La Estrella
Literary Digest
Los Angeles Times
Mexico City Nueva Era
El Monitor
El Monitor Republicano
New York American
New York Evening Mail
New York Globe
New York Herald
New York Sun
New York Times
New York Tribune
New York World

La Prensa
Revolucion

San Antonio Express News
San Antonio Light
San Jose Mercury Herald
Time Magazine
The Times (London)
Tulsa Daily World
El Universal
Victoria Advocate
Wall Street Journal
Washington Post
Washington Times

Books, Book Chapters, and Articles

Adams, John A. *Bordering the Future: The Impact of Mexico on the United States.* Westport, CT: Praeger, 2006.

———. *Conflict and Commerce on the Rio Grande.* College Station: Texas A&M University Press, 2008.

———. *Mexican Banking and Investment in Transition.* Westport, CT: Quorum Books, 1997.

———. *Murder and Intrigue on the Mexican Border.* College Station: Texas A&M University Press, 2018.

Aguirre, Manuel J. *Cananea: Las garras del Imperialismo en las entrañas de México.* Mexico City: Libro Mex Editores, 1958.

Alaman, Don Lucas. "A Calumny Shattered." *Catholic Historical Review,* January 1927.

Albro, Ward S. *Always a Rebel: Ricardo Flores Magón and the Mexican Revolution.* Fort Worth: Texas Christian University Press, 1992.

American Association of Mexico. *Bulletin.* New York: AAM, 1921–22.

———. *Condiciones de los Americanos en México.* New York: AAM, 1921.

———. *Mexico's Denial of the Right of Americans to Purchase Land in Mexico.* New York: AAM, 1921.

American Hierarchy. *Pastoral Letter of the Catholic Episcopate of the United States on the Religious Situation in Mexico.* New York: Paulist Press, 1926.

American Petroleum Institute. Division of Public Relations. *Petroleum Facts and Figures.* New York: J. J. Little & Ives, 1928.

Andes, Stephen J. *The Vatican and Catholic Activism in Mexico and Chile.* New York: Oxford University Press, 2014.

Angle, Paul M. *Crossroads;1913.* Chicago: Rand McNally, 1963.

Ansell, Martin R. *Oil Baron of the Southwest: Edward L. Doheny and the Development of the Petroleum Industry in California and Mexico.* Columbus: Ohio State University Press, 1998.

Aram, Bethany. "Exporting Rhetoric, Importing Oil: United States Relations with Venezuela, 1945–1948." *World Affairs,* Winter 1992, 94–106.

Arnold, Ralph, George A. Macready, and Thomas W. Barrington. *The First Big Oil Hunt: Venezuela 1911–1916*. New York: Vantage Press, 1960.

Atl, Doctor. *The Mexican Revolution and the Nationalization of the Land*. New York, 1915.

Atlas of the Mexican Conflict. Chicago: Rand McNally, 1914.

Baerlein, Henry. *Mexico, Land of Unrest: Being Chiefly an Account of What Produced the Outbreak in 1910, Together with the Story of the Revolution Down to This Day*. Philadelphia: J. B. Lippincott, 1912.

Baez Camargo, Pedro G., and Kenneth G. Grubb. *Religion in the Republic of Mexico*. New York: World Dominion Press, 1935.

Bailey, David C. "Alvaro Obregón and Anti-clericalism in the 1910 Revolution." *Americas* 26, 1969, 183–98.

———. *¡Viva Cristo Rey!: The Cristero Rebellion and the Church-State Conflict in Mexico*. Austin: University of Texas Press, 1974.

Baker, Ray S. *Woodrow Wilson: Life and Letters*. Vol. 4. New York: Doubleday, Doran, 1931.

Baldwin, Deborah J. *Protestants and the Mexican Revolution: Missionaries, Ministers, and Social Change*. Urbana: University of Illinois Press, 1990.

Baptiste, Fitzroy A. *War, Cooperation, and Conflict: The European Possessions in the Caribbean, 1939–1940*. New York: Greenwood Press, 1988.

———. "The Exploration of Caribbean Bauxite and Petroleum, 1914–1945." *Social and Economic Studies*, June 1988, 107–42.

Barker, Frederick F. "New Laws and Nationalism in Mexico." *Foreign Affairs*, July 1927, 589–604.

Barrera Fuentes, Florencio. *Historia de la Revolución Mexicana*. Mexico City: Biblioteca del Instituto Nacional de Estudio, 1970.

Baruch, Bernard. *My Own Story*. New York: Henry Holt, 1957.

Batzell, E. Digby. *The Protestant Establishment: Aristocracy and Caste in America*. New York: Random House, 1964.

Beals, Carleton. *Brimstone and Chili*. New York: Alfred A. Knopf, 1927.

———. *Porfirio Díaz, Dictator of Mexico*. Philadelphia: J. B. Lippincott, 1932.

Beatty, Edward. "The Impact of Foreign Trade on the Mexican Economy: Terms of Trade and the Rise of Industry, 1880–1923." *Journal of Latin American Studies*, May 2000, 399–433.

Bedford, A. C. "The World Oil Situation." *Foreign Affairs*, March 1923, 96–107.

Beelen, George D. " The Harding Administration and Mexico: Diplomacy of Economic Persuasion." *Americas* 41 (1984): 177–90.

Beezley, William H. *Insurgent Governor: Abraham Gonzalez and the Mexican Rev*

Dennis, Samuel F. *The Latin American Policy of the United States*. New York: W. W. Norton, 1942.

Berbusse, Edward J. "Neutrality-Diplomacy of the United States and Mexico, 1910–1911." *Americas*, January 1956, 265–83.

Bernstein, Marvin D. *The Mexican Mining Industry, 1890–1950: A Study of the Interaction of Politics, Economics, and Technology*. Albany: State University of New York, 1964.

Betancourt, Romulo. *Venezuela: Oil and Politics*. Boston: Houghton Mifflin, 1979.

Blaisdell, Lowell. L. "Henry Lane Wilson and the Overthrow of Madero." *Southwestern Social Science Quarterly*, 1962, 126–35

"Blundering into Mexico." *New Republic*, February 13, 1915, 32–33.

Bogus, Carlos T. *Buckley: William F. Buckley Jr. and the Rise of American Conservatism*. New York: Bloomsbury, 2011.

Boue, Juan Carlos. *Venezuela: The Political Economy of Oil*. New York: Oxford University Press, 1993.

Braddy, Haldeen. *Pershing's Mission in Mexico*. El Paso: Texas Western Press, 1966.

Brading, D. A. *Caudillos y Campesinos en la Revolución Mexicana*. Mexico City: Fondo de Cultura Economica, 1985.

Brandenburg, Frank. *The Making of Modern Mexico*. Englewood Cliffs, NY: Prentice-Hall, 1964.

Brandt, Nancy. "Pancho Villa: The Making of a Modern Legend." *Americas*, October 1964, 146–62.

Brayer, Herbert O. "The Cananea Incident." *New Mexico Historical Review* 13, no. 4 (1938): 387–415.

Brenner, Anita. *The Wind That Swept Mexico*. Austin: University of Texas Press, 1976.

Brokaw, Albert D. "Oil." *Foreign Affairs*, October 1927, 89–105.

Brown, Jonathan. *Oil and Revolution in Mexico*. Berkeley: University of California Press, 1993.

———. "Why Foreign Oil Companies Shifted Their Production from Mexico to Venezuela during the 1920s." *American Historical Review*, April 1985, 362–85.

Brown, Lyle C. "Mexican Church–State Relations, 1933–1940." *Journal of Church and State*, Spring 1964, 205–10.

Brown, R. C., ed. *Oil and Gas Field Development in United States—1948*. Austin: National Oil Scouts & Landmen's Association, vol. 19, 1949.

Buchenau, Jurgen. *The Last Caudillo: Alvaro Obregón and the Mexican Revolution*. Malden, MA: Wiley-Blackwell, 2011.

Buckley, Carol. *At the Still Point*. New York: Simon & Schuster, 1996.

Buckley, Christopher. *Bit Enough about You*. New York: Simon & Schuster, 2014.

———. *Losing Mum and Pup: A Memoir*. New York: Twelve, 2009.

Buckley, James. *Freedom at Risk: Reflections of Politics, Liberty, and the State*. New York: Encounter Books, 2010.

———. *Gleanings from an Unplanned Life: An Annotated Oral History*. Wilmington, DE: Intercollegiate Studies Institute, 2006.

———. *If Men Were Angels: A View from the Senate*. New York: Putman, 1975.

———. *Saving Congress from Itself: Emancipating the States and Empowering Their People.* New York: Encounter Books, 2014.

Buckley, Priscilla. *The Light-Hearted Years: Early Recollections, at Home and Abroad.* N.p., n.d.

Buckley, Priscilla L., and William F. Buckley Jr., eds. *W.F.B.: An Appreciation by His Family and Friends.* New York: privately published, 1959.

Buckley, Reid. *An American Family: The Buckleys.* New York: Threshold, 2008.

Buckley, William F., Jr. "Aloise Steiner Buckley, RIP." *National Review*, April 19, 1985.

———. *Cruising Speed: A Documentary.* New York: G. P. Putnam's Sons, 1971.

———. *God and Man at Yale.* 1951. Reprint, Washington, DC: Regnery, 1986.

———. *Gratitude: Reflections on What We Owe Our Country.* New York: Random House, 1990.

———. *In Search of Anti-Semitism.* New York: Continuum, 1992.

———. *Miles Gone By: A Literary Biography.* Washington, DC: Regnery, 2004.

———. *A Torch Kept Lit: Great lives of the Twentieth Century.* Edited by James Rosen. New York: Crown Forum, 2016.

Buckley, William F., Sr. "Madero's Downfall." *Time*, December 9, 1940.

"The Buckleys: Extraordinary Family." *Newsweek*, November 16, 1970, 38.

Buehrig, Edward H. *Wilson's Foreign Policy in Perspective.* Bloomington: Indiana University Press, 1957.

Bulnes, Francisco. *Charges against the Diaz Administration.* New York: M. Bulnes, 1916.

———. *The Whole Truth about Mexico: President Wilson's Responsibility.* New York: M. Bulnes, 1916.

Butler, Matthew. "The Church in 'Red Mexico': Michoacan Catholics and the Mexican Revolution." *Journal of Ecclesiastical History*, July 2004, 520–42.

Butterfield, Dolores. "The Conspiracy against Madero." *Forum*, September 1913, 454–82.

Cabrera, Luis. *The Religious Question in Mexico.* New York: Las Novedades, 1915.

The Cactus. Austin, 1906.

Cahill, Kevin J. "The U.S. Bank Panic of 1907 and the Mexican Depression of 1908–1909." *Historian* 60, no. 4 (1998).

Calero, Manuel. *The Mexican Policy of President Woodrow Wilson as It Appears to a Mexican.* New York: Smith & Thomson, 1916.

Callahan, James M. *American Foreign Policy in Mexican Relations.* New York: Macmillan, 1932.

Callcott, Wilford H. *Liberalism in Mexico 1857–1929.* Hamden, CT: Archon Books,

American Conflict. Cambridge: Cambridge University Press, 1968.

Camargo, G. Baez. *Religion in the Republic of Mexico.* London: World Dominion Press, 1935.

Camp, Roderic. *Mexican Political Biographies, 1884–1935.* Austin: University of Texas Press, 1991.

Carpizo, Jorge. *La Constitución Mexicana de 1917.* Mexico City: Editorial Porrua, S.A., 1983.

"The Case against Mexico." *North American Review,* November 1914, 641–52.

Castillo Crimm, Ana C., and Sara R. Massey. *Turn-of-the-Century Photographs from San Diego, Texas.* Austin: University of Texas Press, 2003.

Chamberlain, George A. *Is Mexico Worth Saving.* Indianapolis: Bobbs-Merrill, 1920.

Charterins, Stewart. "The Petroleum Industry in Mexico." *Engineering and Mining Journal,* October 9, 1920, 725–26.

City Directory of Austin with Street Directory of Residents: 1906–7. Austin: J. B. Stephenson, 1907.

Clark, J. Reuben. "The Oil Settlement with Mexico." *Foreign Affairs,* July 1928, 600–614.

Clark, James A., and Michel T. Halbouty. *Spindletop.* New York: Random House, 1952.

Cleland, Robert G., ed. *The Mexican Year Book: The Standard Authority on Mexico, 1920–21.* Los Angeles: Mexican Year Book, 1922.

Clements, Kendrick A. "Woodrow Wilson's Mexican Policy, 1913–1915." *Journal of Diplomatic History,* Spring 1980, 113–36.

Clendenen, Clarence C. *Blood on the Border: The United States Army and Mexican Irregulars.* Toronto: Macmillan, 1969.

———. *The United States and Pancho Villa: A Study in Unconventional Diplomacy.* Ithaca, NY: Cornell University Press, 1962.

Cleven, Andrew N. "Religious Aspects of Mexico's Constitution." *Current History,* April 1922, 12–16.

Cline, Howard F. *The United States and Mexico.* Cambridge, MA: Harvard University Press, 1953.

Coatsworth, John H. *Growth against Development: The Economic Impact of Railroads in Porfirian Mexico.* DeKalb: North Illinois University Press, 1981.

Coerver, Don M., and Linda B. Hall. *Texas and the Mexican Revolution: A Study in State and National Birder Policy, 1910–1920.* San Antonio: Trinity University Press, 1984.

Cooke, Catherine N. *The Thistle and the Rose.* Bloomington: iUniverse, 2013.

Cosío Villegas, Daniel. *Historia moderna de México.* Vol. 2. Mexico, DF: Editorial Hermes, 1973.

Cover, Gilbert G. *Law of Hydrocarbons and Other Combustible Minerals.* Caracas: Tipografia Garrido, 1940.

Cox, Patrick L. "'An Enemy Closer to Us Than Any European Power': The Impact of Mexico on Texan Public Opinion before World War I." *Southwestern Historical Quarterly,* July 2001, 41–80.

Creelman, James. *Díaz: Master of Mexico.* New York: Appleton, 1916.

———. "The Thrilling Story of President Diaz: The Greatest Man on the Continent." *Pearson's Magazine,* March 1908.

Crowell, Chester T. "What's Wrong with Mexico?" *North American Review,* February 1928, 261–68.

Cuevas, Mariano. *Historia de la Iglesia en Mexico.* Tlalpam, DF: Imprenta del Asilo, 1922.

Cumberland, Charles C. "Border Raids in the Lower Rio Grande Valley—1915." *Southwestern Historical Quarterly,* January 1954, 285–311.

———. "The Jenkins Case and Mexican-American Relations." *Hispanic American Historical Review,* November 1951, 586–607.

———. *The Meaning of the Mexican Revolution.* Lexington, MA: D. C. Heath, 1967.

———. *Mexican Revolution: Genesis under Madero.* Austin: University of Texas Press, 1952.

———. *Mexican Revolution: The Constitutionalist Years.* Austin: University of Texas Press, 1972.

———. "Mexican Revolutionary Movements from Texas, 1906–1912." *Southwestern Historical Quarterly,* January 1949, 301–324.

———. "The Sonora Chinese and the Mexican Revolution." *Hispanic American Historical Review,* May 1960, 191–211.

Cunningham, E. H. "A New British Oil Industry." *Journal of the Institution of Petroleum Technologists,* October 1917, 110–21.

Curley, Michael J. *Mexican Tyranny and the Catholic Church.* Brooklyn, NY: International Catholic Truth Society, 1926.

Curley, Robert. "Anticlericalism and Public Space in Revolutionary Jalisco." *Americas,* April 2009, 511–33.

———. *Citizens and Believers: Religion and Politics in Revolutionary Jalisco, 1900–1930.* Albuquerque: University of New Mexico Press, 2018.

Daniels, Josephus. *The Cabinet Diaries of Josephus Daniels: 1913–1921.* Edited by David Cronon. Lincoln: University of Nebraska Press, 1963.

———. *The Life of Woodrow Wilson, 1856–1924.* Chicago: John C. Winston, 1924.

———. *The Wilson Era: Years of Peace, 1910–1917.* Chapel Hill: University of North Carolina Press, 1944.

Davenport, E. H., and Sydney R. Cook. *The Oil Trusts and Anglo-American Relations.* New York: Macmillan, 1924.

Davis, Harold E. "Mexican Petroleum Taxes." *Hispanic American Historical*

ing the Recent Mexican Revolution. Los Angeles: privately published, 1920.

De Bekker, L. J. *The Plot against Mexico.* New York: Alfred A. Knopf, 1919.

Decorme, Gerardo. "Catholic Education in Mexico: 1525–1912." *Catholic Historical Review*, April 1916, 168–84.

DeGolyer, Everette L. "The Mexican Petroleum Industry during 1912." *Petroleum Review*, November 22, 1913.

Delaisi, Francis. *Oil: Its Influence on Politics*. London: Labour, 1922.

De Leon, Arnoldo, ed. *War along the Border: The Mexican Revolution and Tejano Communities*. College Station: Texas A&M University Press, 2012.

Denny, H. S. "The Oil Excitement in Mexico." *Mining Journal*, June 1910, 4.

Denny, Ludwell. *We Fight for Oil*. New York: Alfred A. Knopf, 1928.

de Zayas Enriquez, Rafael. *The Case of Mexico and the Policy of President Wilson*. New York: Albert and Charles Boni, 1914.

Diamond, William. *The Economic Thought of Woodrow Wilson*. Baltimore: Johns Hopkins Press, 1943.

Díaz, Pascual. "State vs. Church in Mexico." *North American Review*, April 1928, 401–8.

Dickens, Paul D. "Argentine Arbitrations and Mediations with Reference to United States Participation Therein." *Hispanic American Historical Review* 11 (December 1931): 464–84.

Domeratsky, Louis. "American Industry Abroad." *Foreign Affairs*, July 1930.

Dunn, Frederick S. *Diplomatic Protection of Americans in Mexico*. New York: Columbia University Press, 1933.

Edgington, Thomas B. *The Monroe Doctrine*. Boston: Little, Brown, 1904.

Edwards, Lee. "Catholic Maverick: A Profile of William F. Buckley, Jr." *Crisis Magazine*, February 1995, at www.crisismagazine.com/1995.

Eisenhower, John S. D. *Intervention! The United States and the Mexican Revolution, 1813–1917*. New York: W. W. Norton, 1993.

Enriquez, I. C. *The Religious Question in Mexico—by a Mexican Catholic*. New York: n.p., 1915.

Espinosa, David. "Restoring Christian Social Order: The Mexican Catholic Youth Association, 1913–1932." *Americas*, April 2003, 451–74.

Fabela, Isidro. *Historia Diplomática de la Revolución Mexicana, 1912–1917*. 2 vols. Mexico City: Fondo de Cultura Economica, 1959.

Fallaw, Ben. "The Seduction of Revolution: Anticlerical Campaigns against Confession in Mexico, 1914–1935." *Journal of Latin American Studies* 45 (2013).

Fanning, Leonard M. *Foreign Oil and the Free World*. New York: McGraw-Hill, 1954.

"Fast Freight Service: Mexico." *Traffic World*, December 22, 1928, 1435.

Fehrenbach, T. R. *Fire and Blood*. New York: Collier Books, 1973.

Feilitzsch, Heribert von. *In Plain Sight: Felix A. Sommerfeld, Spymaster in Mexico, 1908–1914*. New York: Henselstone Verlag, 2012.

Felzenberg, Alvin S. *A Man and His Presidents: The Political Odyssey of William F. Buckley Jr*. New Haven, CT: Yale University Press, 2017.

Fenwick, Charles G. *The Neutrality Laws of the United States.* Washington, DC: Carnegie Endowment for International Peace, 1913.

FitzGerald, E. V. K. "Oil and Mexico's Industrial Development Plan." *Texas Business Review,* May 1980, 133–37.

Fleming, Thomas J. *West Point.* New York: William Morrow, 1969.

Flipper, Henry O. *The Colored Cadet at West Point.* Lincoln: University of Nebraska Press, 1998. Originally published in 1878.

———, trans. *Law Governing Hydrocarbons and other Combustible Minerals of the Republic of Venezuela.* New York: Evening Post Job Printing, 1922.

Foote, Frederick. "Oil Fuel vs. Coal Freight Steamers." *Fuel Oil Journal,* March 1914.

Forrest, William. "Significance of Mexican Oil Fields to the United States." *Evening Post Foreign Trade Review,* September 1919.

Foster, Virginia, ed. *Texaco: A Century of Energy.* Harrison, TX: Texaco Inc., 2001.

Foulois, Benjamin D. "Report of Operations of the First Aero Squadron, Signal Corps, with the Mexican Punitive Expedition, for Period March 15 to August 15, 1916." www.earlyaviators.com/esquadro.htm.

Fyfe, H. Hamilton. *The Real Mexico: Study on the Spot.* New York: McBride, Nast, 1914.

Garner, Paul. *British Lions and Mexican Eagles: Business, Politics, and Empire in the Career of Weetman Pearson in Mexico, 1889–1919.* Stanford, CA: Stanford University Press, 2011.

Gibbon, Thomas E. *Mexico under Carranza.* New York: Doubleday, Page, 1919.

Gibler, John. *Mexico Unconquered: Chronicles of Power and Revolt.* San Francisco: City Light Books, 2004.

Gilderhus, Mark. *Diplomacy and Revolution: US-Mexico Relations under Wilson and Carranza.* Tucson: University of Arizona Press, 1977.

———. "Senator Albert Bacon Fall and 'The Plot against Mexico.'" *New Mexico Historical Review* 48 (1973): 299–311.

Glaser, David. "1919: William Jenkins, Robert Lansing, and the Mexican Interlude." *Southwestern Historical Quarterly,* January 1971, 337–56.

Godley, Andrew. "Weetman Pearson in Mexico and the Emergence of a British Oil Major, 1901–1919." Reading, UK: Henley Business School, 2007.

Gole, Henry G. *The Road to Rainbow: Army Planning for Global War.* Annapolis, MD: Naval Institute Press, 2003.

Gonzales, Michael. "U.S. Copper Companies, the Mine Workers' Movement, and the Mexican Revolution, 1910–1920." *Hispanic American Historical Review* 76 (1996): 503–34.

Goodrich, Luke. "Mexico's Separation of Church and State." *New York Times*

———. *The United States and Mexico*. Lincoln: University of Nebraska Press, 1969.

Guzmán, Martin Luis. *The Eagle and the Serpent*. Gloucester, MA: Peter Smith, 1969.

———. *The Memoirs of Pancho Villa*. Austin: University of Texas Press, 1965.

Gwynn, Stephen. *The Letters and Friendships of Sir Cecil Spring Rice*. Boston: Houghton Mifflin, 1929.

Haber, Stephen, Noel Maurer, and Armando Razo. "When Institutions Don't Matter: The Rise and Decline of the Mexican Oil Industry." https://web.stanford.edu/class/polisci313/papers/Haber-RazoFeb25.pdf.

Hackett, Charles W. *The Mexican Revolution and the United States, 1910–1926*. Boston: World Peace Foundation, 1926. Vol. 9, no. 5.

———. "The New Regime in Mexico." *Southwestern Political Science Quarterly*, June 1921, 51–72.

Hale, Charles A. *Emilio Rabasa and the Survival of Porfirian Liberalism*. Stanford, CA: Stanford University Press, 2008.

Hall, Linda B. *Alvaro Obregón: Power and Revolution in Mexico, 1911–1920*. College Station: Texas A&M University Press, 1981.

———. *Oil, Banks, and Politics: The United States and Postrevolutionary Mexico, 1917–1924*. Austin: University of Texas Press, 1995.

Hall, Linda B., and Don M. Coerver. "Oil and the Mexican Revolution: The Southwestern Connection." *Americas*, October 1984, 229–44.

Hamilton, Charles. *Early Day Oil Tales of Mexico*. Houston: Gulf, 1966.

Hanighen, Frank C. *The Secret War*. New York: John Day, 1934.

Hanson, Roger D. *The Politics of Mexican Development*. Baltimore: Johns Hopkins Press, 1971.

Hanson, Victor D. *The Second World Wars*. New York: Basic Books, 2017.

Harper, Henry H. *A Journey in Southeastern Mexico*. Boston: De Vinne Press, 1910.

Harris, Charles H., and Louis R. Sadler. "The 1911 Reyes Conspiracy: The Texas Side." *Southwestern Historical Quarterly*, April 1980, 325–48.

———. *The Texas Rangers and the Mexican Revolution: The Bloodiest Decade, 1910–1920*. Albuquerque: University of New Mexico Press, 2004.

Hart, John M. *Empire and Revolution: The Americans in Mexico since the Civil War*. Berkeley: University of California Press, 2002.

———. *Revolutionary Mexico: The Coming and Process of the Mexican Revolution*. Berkeley: University of California Press, 1987.

Hearst, William Randolph. *It Is Time to Accord Recognition to President Obregón and Mexico*. N.p., August 24, 1921.

Heath, Aloise Buckley. *Will Mrs. Major Go to Hell?* New Rochelle, NY: Arlington House, 1969.

Heindel, Richard H. *The American Impact on Great Britain 1898–1914*. New York: Octagon Books, 1968.

Henderson, Peter V. N. *Felix Díaz, the Porfirians, and the Mexican Revolution*. Lincoln: University of Nebraska Press, 1981.

———. "Mexican Rebels in the Borderlands, 1910–1912." *Red River Valley Historical Review*, 1975, 207–19.

Hendrick, Burton J. *The Life and Letters of Walter H. Page.* 2 vols. New York: Doubleday, Page, 1923.

Herman, Arthur. *1917: Lenin, Wilson, and the Birth of the New World Disorder.* New York: Harper Collins, 2017.

Herzberg, Bob. *Revolutionary Mexico in Film.* Jefferson, NC: McFarland, 2015.

Hill, Larry D. *Emissaries to a Revolution: Woodrow Wilson's Executive Agents in Mexico.* Baton Rouge: Louisiana State University Press, 1973.

———. "The Progressive Politician as a Diplomat: The Case of John Lind in Mexico." *Americas*, April 1971, 355–72.

Hinckley, Ted C. "Wilson, Huerta, and the Twenty-One Gun Salute." *Historian* 22 (February 1960): 197–206.

Hodges, Donald, and Ross Gandy. *Mexico 1910–1976: Reform or Revolution?* London: Zed Press, 1979.

Hoffman, Fritz L. "Edward L. Doheny and the Beginnings of Petroleum Development in Mexico." *Mid-America*, April 1942.

Holland, James. *The Rise of Germany.* New York: Atlantic Monthly, 2015.

Holt, Hamilton. "The Niagara Falls Mediation Conference." *Independent*, June 22, 1914, 518–21.

House, Edward M. *The Intimate Papers of Colonel House.* New York: Houghton Mifflin, 1928.

Houston, David. *Eight Years with Wilson's Cabinet.* New York: Doubleday, Page, 1926.

Hull, B. E. "Tampico and Vicinity and Recent Development of Property of the Texas Company of Mexico, S.A." *Texas Star*, November 1918, 7–15.

Inman, Samuel G. *Intervention in Mexico.* New York: Association Press, 1919.

Ivey, Darren L. *The Ranger Ideal.* Vol. 2. College Station: Texas A&M University Press, 2018.

Jacobs, Ian. *Ranchero Revolt: The Mexican Revolution in Guerrero.* Austin: University of Texas Press, 1982.

James, Marquis. *The Texaco Story: The First Fifty Years, 1902–1952.* N.p., 1953.

Jayes, Janic L. *The Illusion of Ignorance: Constructing the American Encounter with Mexico, 1877–1920.* Lanham, MD: University Press of America, 2011.

Johns, Michael. *The City of Mexico in the Age of Díaz.* Austin: University of Texas Press, 1997.

Johnson, David N. *Madero in Texas.* Edited by Felix D. Almaraz Jr. San Antonio: Corona, 1988.

Simon & Schuster, 1988.

Kahle, Louis G. "Robert Lansing and the Recognition of Venustiano Carranza." *Hispanic American Historical Review*, August 1958, 353–72.

Kandell, Jonathan. *La Capital: The Biography of Mexico City*. New York: Random House, 1988.

Katz, Friedrich. "Alemania y Francisco Villa." *Historia Mexicana*, July 1962.

———. *The Life and Times of Pancho Villa*. Stanford, CA: Stanford University Press, 1998.

———. *The Secret War in Mexico: Europe, the United States, and the Mexican Revolution*. Chicago: University of Chicago Press, 1981.

Kelley, Francis C. *The Book of Red and Yellow: Being a Story of Blood and a Yellow Streak*. Chicago: Catholic Extension Society, 1916.

———. *Blood-Drenched Altars: A Catholic Commentary on the History of Mexico*. Milwaukee, WI: The Bruce Publishing, 1935.

Kelley, Francisco C. *El Libro de Rojo y Amarillo: Una Historia de Sangre y Cobardía*. Chicago: Extension de la Iglesia Católica, 1915.

Kellogg, Frederic R. "The Mexican Oil Situation." *Journal of International Relations*, October 1920, 206–8.

———. "The World Petroleum Problem—Mexico." *American Petroleum Institute Bulletin* 132 (December 10, 1920): 13–28.

Kemmerer, Edwin W. *Inflation and Revolution: Mexico's Experience of 1912–1917*. Princeton, NJ: Princeton University Press, 1940.

Kenny, Michael. *The Mexican Crisis: Its Causes and Consequences*. Brooklyn, NY: International Catholic Truth Society, 1927.

Kerig, Dorothy P. *Luther T. Ellsworth: U.S. Consul on the Border during the Mexican Revolution*. El Paso: Texas Western Press, 1975.

Kieshell, Gaylord T. M. *The U-Boat War in the Caribbean*. Annapolis, MD: Naval Institute Press, 1994.

"Killing Foreigners in Mexico." *Literary Digest*, March 27, 1915, 674–75.

Klein, Maury. *The Life and Legend of Jay Gould*. Baltimore: Johns Hopkins University Press, 1986.

Knight, Alan. *Porfirians, Liberals and Peasants: The Mexican Revolution*. Cambridge: Cambridge University Press, 1986.

Knights of Columbus. *Red Mexico: The Facts*. New Haven, CT: Supreme Council, 1926.

Koenig, Louis W. *Bryan: A Political Biography of William Jennings Bryan*. New York: G. P. Putnam's Sons, 1971.

Kraig, Robert A. *Woodrow Wilson and the Lost World of the Oratorical Statesman*. College Station: Texas A&M University Press, 2004.

Krauze, Enrique. *Mexico: Biography of Power*. New York: Harper Collins, 1997.

Kurzman, Charles. *Democracy Denied, 1905–1915*. Cambridge, MA: Harvard University Press, 2008.

La Botz, Dan. *Edward L. Doheny: Petroleum, Power, and Politics in the United States and Mexico*. New York: Praeger, 1991.

LaFrance, David. "Revisión del caso Jenkins: La confrontación del mito." *Historia Mexicana*, 2004, 911–59.

Lara Pardo, Luis. "La Nueva Aurora: Las Riquezas Petroliferas de Mexico." *Revista Universal*, December 1917, 10–12.

———. "The Tragic Farce of John Lind." In *Matchs de Dictadores*. Mexico City: A. P. Marquez, 1942.

Lear, John. *Workers, Neighbors, and Citizens: The Revolution in Mexico City*. Lincoln: University of Nebraska Press, 2001.

Leary, William M. "Woodrow Wilson, Irish Americans, and the Election of 1916." *Journal of American History*, June 1967, 57–72.

"Letting the Guns into Mexico." *Literary Digest*, February 14, 1914, 303–5.

Levario, Miguel A. *Militarizing the Border: When Mexicans Became the Enemy*. College Station: Texas A&M University Press, 2012.

Lieuwen, Edwin. *Mexican Militarism: The Political Rise and Fall of the Revolutionary Army, 1910–1940*. Westport, CT: Greenwood Press, 1968.

———. *Petroleum in Venezuela: A History*. Berkeley: University of California Press, 1954.

Lind, John. "The Mexican People." *Bellman*, December 5, 1914.

Link. Arthur S., ed. *The Papers of Woodrow Wilson*. Vol. 29. Princeton, NJ: Princeton University Press, 1979.

———. *Wilson: Confusions and Crises, 1915–1916*. Princeton, NJ: Princeton University Press, 1964.

———. *Wilson the Diplomatist: A Look at His Major Foreign Policies*. Baltimore: Johns Hopkins Press, 1957.

———. *Wilson: The Struggle for Neutrality, 1914–1915*. Princeton, NJ: Princeton University Press, 1960.

———. *Woodrow Wilson and the Progressive Era, 1910–1917*. New York: Harper & Brothers, 1954.

Lippmann, Walter. "The Church and State in Mexico: American Mediation." *Foreign Affairs*, January 1930, 186–207.

Lodge, Henry C. *The Senate and the League of Nations*. New York: Scribner's Sons, 1925.

London, Jack. "Our Adventure in Tampico." *Collier's*, June 27, 1914, 5–7.

Lozano, Samuel. *El Puerto del Oro Negro: O Tampico en su sueno*. Mexico City: Imprenta Guerrero, n.d.

Lyon, Jessie S. "Huerta and Adachi: An Interpretation of Japanese-Mexican Relations, 1913–1914." *Academy of American Franciscan History*, April 1978, 176–80.

democrático. San Pedro, Coahuila: n.p., 1908.

Markmann, Charles L. *The Buckleys: A Family Examined*. New York: William Morrow, 1973.

Martinez, Anibal. *Venezuelan Oil: Development and Chronology*. London: Elsevier Applied Science, 1989.

Matloff, Maurice, ed. *American Military History*. Washington: GPO, 1969.

Matovino, Timothy. *Latino Catholicism*. Princeton, NJ: Princeton University Press, 2012.

Maurer, Noel. *The Power and the Money: The Mexican Financial System, 1876–1932*. Stanford, CA: Stanford University Press, 2002.

McBeth, Brain S. *British Oil Policy 1919–1939*. London: Frank Cass, 1985.

———. *Juan Vicente Gómez and the Oil Companies in Venezuela, 1908–1935*. Cambridge: Cambridge University Press, 1983.

McBride, Annetta. "The Buckleys of Texas." *Texas Parade*, April 1969, 20–24.

McCaa, Robert. "Missing Millions: The Demographic Cost of the Mexican Revolution." *Mexican Studies*, Summer 2003.

McCaleb, Walter F. *History of Present and Past Banking in Mexico*. New York: Harper & Brothers, 1920.

McCann, Irving G. *With the National Guard on the Border*. St. Louis, MO: C. V. Mosby, 1917.

McConnell, Burt M. *Mexico at the Bar of Public Opinion*. New York: Mail and Express, 1939.

McCullagh, Francis. *Red Mexico: A Reign of Terror*. New York: Louis Carrier, 1928.

———. "The United States and Mexico." *Living Age*, November 15, 1927, 864–71.

McLaren, Alice D. "The Tragic Ten Days of Mexico." *Scribner's Magazine*, January 1914, 97–111.

McLaughlin, R. P. "Regularity of Decline of Oil Wells in California." *Bulletin: American Association of Petroleum Geologists*, March 1921, 178–85.

McLean, Robert N. *That Mexican!* New York: Fleming H. Revell, 1971.

McLynn, Frank. *Villa and Zapata*. New York: Carroll & Graf, 2000.

Mecham, J. Lloyd. *Church and State in Latin America*. Rev. ed. Chapel Hill: University of North Carolina Press, 1966.

"The Mediation." *Outlook* 107 (May 23, 1914).

———. "The Militarization of Mexico, 1913–1914." *Americas*, January 1971, 293–306.

Mena Brito, Bernardino. *Carranza Sus Amigos Sus Enemigos*. Mexico City: Ediciones Botas, 1935.

Mexican Petroleum Company. *Los impustos sobre la industria de petroleo*. Mexico City: PEMEX, 1912.

Meyer, Jean. *The Cristero Rebellion: The Mexican People between Church and State, 1926–1929*. Translated by Richard Southern. Cambridge: Cambridge University Press, 1976.

Meyer, Lorenzo. *Mexico and the United States in the Oil Controversy, 1917–1942*. Austin: University of Texas Press, 1972.

Meyer, Michael C. "Albert Bacon Fall's Mexican Papers: A Preliminary Investigation." *New Mexico Historical Review* 40 (1965): 165–74.

———. *Huerta: A Political Portrait.* Lincoln: University of Nebraska Press, 1972.

———. "The Mexican-German Conspiracy of 1915." *Americas*, July 1966.

———. *Mexican Rebel: Pascual Orozco and the Mexico Revolution, 1910–1915.* Lincoln: University of Nebraska Press, 1967.

Meyer, Michael C., and Susan M. Deeds. *The Course of Mexican History.* 6th ed. New York: Oxford University Press, 1999.

Middleton, Harvey. *Industrial Mexico: 1919 Facts and Figures.* New York: Dodd, Mead, 1919.

Molina Enríquez, Andrés. *Los grandes problemas nacionales.* Mexico City, 1909.

Moreno, Julio. *Yankee Don't Go Home! Mexican Nationalism, American Business Culture, and the Shaping of Modern Mexico, 1920–1950.* Chapel Hill: University of North Carolina Press, 2003.

Morison, Elting E. *The Letters of Theodore Roosevelt.* Cambridge, MA: Harvard University Press, 1954.

Morris, Henry. *Our Mexican Muddle.* Chicago: Laird & Lee, 1916.

"Mr. Lind's Mission to Mexico." *Literary Digest*, August 16, 1913.

Munoz, Rafael F. *Memorias de Pancho Villa.* N.p.: El Universal Grafico, 1923.

Murray, Robert H. "Huerta and the Two Wilsons." *Harper's Weekly*, March 25–April 29, 1916.

A Nation in Bondage. New York: Latin American News Association, 1916.

Nearing, Scott, and Joseph Freeman. *Dollar Diplomacy: A Study in American Imperialism.* New York: B. W. Huebsch, 1925.

Neu, Charles E. *Colonel House.* New York: Oxford University Press, 2015.

The New Handbook of Texas. 6 vols. Austin: TSHA, 1996.

Niemeyer, E. V. "Anti-clericalism in the Mexican Constitutional Convention, 1916–1917." *Americas*, July 1954.

———. *Revolution in Querétaro: The Mexican Constitutional Convention of 1916–1917.* Austin: University of Texas Press, 2014.

Notter, Harley. *The Origins of the Foreign Policy of Woodrow Wilson.* Baltimore: Johns Hopkins Press, 1937.

Ocasio Meléndez, Marcial E. *Capitalism and Development: Tampico Mexico 1876–1924.* New York: P. Lang, 1998.

O'Shaughnessy, Edith. *Diplomatic Days.* New York: Harper & Brothers, 1917.

———. *A Diplomat's Wife in Mexico.* New York: Harper & Brothers, 1916.

———. *Intimate Pages of Mexican History.* New York: George H. Doran, 1920.

O'Toole, Patricia. *The Moralist: Woodrow Wilson and the World He Made.* New

Chavez y Hno., 1919.

Patrick, Jeff, ed. *Guarding the Border*. College Station: Texas A&M University Press, 2009.

Paxman, Andrew. *Jenkins of Mexico: How a Southern Farm Boy Became a Mexican Magnate*. New York: Oxford University Press, 2017.

Perlstein, Rick. *Before the Storm: Barry Goldwater and the Unmaking of the American Consensus*. New York: Hill & Wang, 2001.

Philip, George. *Oil and Politics in Latin America*. Cambridge: Cambridge University Press, 1982.

Phillips, William, *Ventures in Diplomacy*. Boston: Beacon Press, 1952.

Pletcher, David M. "Mexico Opens the Door to American Capital, 1877–1990." *Americas*, July 1959, 1–14.

———. *Rails, Mines, and Progress: Seven American Promoters in Mexico, 1867–1911*. Port Washington, NY: Kennikat Press, 1972.

Poole, David. *Land and Liberty*. Montreal: Black Rose Books, 1977.

Porter Gil, Emilio. *The Conflict between the Civil Power and the Clergy*. Mexico City: Press of the Ministry of Foreign Affairs, 1935.

Powell, Fred W. *The Railroads of Mexico*. Boston: Stratford, 1921.

Prewett, Virginia. *Reportage on Mexico*. New York: E. P. Dutton, 1941.

Prida, Ramón. *La Culpa de Lane Wilson, Embajador de los E.U.A. en la Trajedía Mexicana*. Mexico City: Ediciones Botas, 1962.

Quirk, Robert E. *An Affair of Honor*. Lexington: University Press of Kentucky, 1962.

———. *The Mexican Revolution, 1914–1915: The Convention of Aguascalientes*. New York: Citadel Press, 1963.

———. *The Mexican Revolution and the Catholic Church 1910–1929*. Bloomington: Indiana University Press, 1973.

Raat, W. Dirk. *Revoltosos: Mexico's Rebels in the United States, 1903–1923*. College Station: Texas A&M University Press, 1981.

———, and William H. Beezley, eds. *Twentieth-Century Mexico*. Lincoln: University of Nebraska Press, 1986.

Rabasa, Emilio. *La Constitución y la Dictadura: Estudio Sobre la Organización Política de México*. Mexico City: Tip. de Revista de Revistas, 1912.

———. *La evolución histórica de México*. Mexico City: Librería de la Viuda de Ch. Bouret, 1920.

Rausch, George J. "The Exile and Death of Victoriano Huerta." *Hispanic American Historical Review*, May 1962, 133–51.

Redinger, Matthew A. *American Catholics and the Mexican Revolution, 1924–1936*. Notre Dame, IN: University of Notre Dame Press, 2005.

———. "'To Arouse and Inform': The Knights of Columbus and the United States–Mexican Relations, 1924–1937." *Catholic Historical Review*, July 2002, 489–518.

Reed, John. *Insurgent Mexico*. 1914. Reprint, New York: International Publishers, 1969.

Richmond, Douglas W. *Venustiano Carranza's Nationalist Struggle, 1893–1920*. Lincoln: University of Nebraska Press, 1963.

——, and Sam W. Haynes, eds. *The Mexican Revolution: Conflict and Consolidation, 1910–1940*. College Station: Texas A&M University Press, 2013.

Rippy, J. Fred. *The United States and Mexico*. New York: Alfred A. Knopf, 1926.

Rippy, J. Fred, Jose Vasconcelos, and Guy Stevens. *Mexico: American Politics Abroad*. Chicago: University of Chicago Press, 1928.

"Rival Oil Giants in Mexican Broils." *New York Times*, November 9, 1913.

Ronfeldt, David F. *Mexico's Petroleum and U.S. Policy: Implications for the 1980s*. Santa Monica: Rand Corp., June 1980.

Rosenbaum, Robert J. *Mexicano Resistance in the Southwest*. Dallas: Southern Methodist University Press, 1998.

Ross, John. *The Annexation of Mexico: From the Aztecs to the IMF*. Monroe, ME: Common Courage Press, 1998.

Ross, Stanley R. *Francisco I. Madero, Apostle of Mexican Democracy*. New York: Columbia University Press, 1955.

Rubio, Maria del Mar. "The Role of Mexico in the First World Oil Shortage: 1918–1922: An International Perspective." http://core.ac.uk/pdf.

Ruiz, Ramón E. *The Great Rebellion: Mexico 1905–1924*. New York: W. W. Norton, 1980.

Russell, Thomas H. *Mexico in Peace and War*. Chicago: Reilly & Britton, 1914.

Salas, Miguel T. *The Enduring Legacy: Oil, Culture, and Society in Venezuela*. Durham, NC: Duke University Press, 2009.

Samponaro, Frank N., and Paul J. Vanderwood. *War Scare on the Rio Grande: Robert Runyon's Photographs of the Border Conflict, 1913–1916*. Austin: Texas State Historical Association, 1992.

Sanders, Sol W. *Mexico: Chaos on Our Doorstep*. Lanham, MD: Madison Books, 1986.

Sandos, James. "German Involvement in Northern Mexico, 1915–1916: A New Look at the Columbus Raid." *Hispanic American Historical Review* 50 (1970): 70–88.

Santiago, Myrna I. *The Ecology of Oil: Environment, Labor, and the Mexican Revolution, 1900–1938*. Cambridge: Cambridge University Press, 2006.

——. "Culture Clash: Foreign Oil and Indigenous People in Northern Veracruz, Mexico, 1900–1921." *Journal of American History*, June 2012, 62–71.

Saragoza, Alex. *The Monterrey Elite and the Mexican State, 1880–1940*. Austin: University of Texas Press, 1988.

Schell, William. *Integral Outsiders: The American Colony in Mexico City, 1876–1911*. Wilmington, DE: Scholarly Resources Inc., 2001.

Schurman, Jacob G. "Wilson's Mexican Failure." *Independent*, October 16, 1916, 103.

Scott, Hugh L. *Some Memories of a Soldier.* New York: Century, 1928.

Scott, James B., ed. *President Wilson's Foreign Policy.* New York: Oxford University Press, 1918.

Seddon, Mark. "Incorporating Corporations: Anglo-US Oil Diplomacy and Conflict over Venezuela, 1941–1943." *Journal of Transatlantic Studies*, May 2012, 139–49.

Severance, Frank H. "The Peace Conference at Niagara Falls in 1914." *Buffalo Historical Society* 18 (1914).

Seymour, Charles. *The Intimate Papers of Colonel House.* 2 vols. Boston: Houghton Mifflin, 1926.

Sherman, William L., and Richard E. Greenleaf. *Victoriano Huerta: A Reappraisal.* Mexico City: Mexico City College Press, 1960.

Sherrill, Charles H. "Practical Mediation and International Peace." *North American Review*, December 1914, 887–92.

Shoemaker, Raymond L. "Henry Lane Wilson and Republican Policy toward Mexico, 1913–1920." *Indiana Magazine of History*, June 1980, 103–22.

Schuler, Friedrich E., ed. *Murder and Counterrevolution in Mexico: The Eyewitness Account of German Ambassador Paul Von Hintze, 1912–1914.* Lincoln: University of Nebraska Press, 2015.

Simpson, Lesley B. *Many Mexicos.* 4th ed. Berkeley: University of California Press, 1967.

Singelmann, Peter. "The Sugar Industry in Postrevolutionary Mexico: State Intervention and Private Capital." *Latin American Research Review* 28, no. 1 (1993): 61–87.

Skaggs, William H. *German Conspiracies in America.* London: T. Fisher Unwin, n.d. [ca. 1917]

Skinner, Walter R. *The Oil and Petroleum Manual.* London: Eigenverlag, 1928.

Skirius, John. "Railroads, Oil and Other Foreign Interests in the Mexican Revolution, 1911 to 1914." *Journal of Latin American Studies*, February 2003.

Slattery, Matthew T. *Felipe Angeles and the Mexican Revolution.* Dublin, IN: Prinit Press, 1982.

Small, Michael. *The Forgotten Peace: Mediation at Niagara Falls, 1914.* Ottawa: University of Ottawa Press, 2009.

Smith, Arthur D. H. *The Real Colonel House.* New York: George H. Doran, 1918.

Smith, Daniel. "Robert Lansing and the Wilson Interregnum, 1919–1920." *Historian*, November 1959, 135–42.

Smith, Randolph W. *Benighted Mexico.* New York: John Lane, 1916.

Smith, Robert F. *The United States and Revolutionary Nationalism in Mexico, 1916–1932.* Chicago: University of Chicago Press, 1972.

Society of the American Colony of Mexico City. "Facts Submitted by the Committee of the American Colony to President Wilson and Secretary of State

Bryan Relative to the Mexican Situation and the Record of the Honorable Henry Lane Wilson . . ." Mexico City: March 4, 1913.

Spender, J. A. *Weetman Pearson: First Viscount Cowdray, 1856–1927.* London: Cassell, 1930.

Sprout, Howard, and Margaret Sprout. *Toward a New Order of Sea Power: American Naval Policy and the World Scene.* Princeton, NJ: Princeton University Press, 1940.

Starr, Frederick. *Mexico and the United States: A Story of Revolution, Intervention, and War.* Chicago: Bible House, 1914.

Startt, James D. *Woodrow Wilson, the Great War, and the Fourth Estate.* College Station: Texas A&M University Press, 2017

Stephenson, George. *John Lind of Minnesota.* Port Washington, NY: Kennikat Press, 1935.

Sterling, Manuel Márquez. *Los últimos días del presidente Madero.* 1960. Reprint, Mexico City: Miguel A. Porrua, 2013.

Stevens, Guy. "Protecting the Rights of Americans in Mexico." *Annals of the American Academy of Political and Social Science,* July 1927, 164–67.

Stewart, P. Charteris A. "The Petroleum Industry of Mexico." *Journal of the Institution of Petroleum Technology* (London), 1915, 7–37.

Stratton, David H., ed. *The Memoirs of Albert B. Fall.* El Paso: Texas Western Press, 1966.

Strother, French. *Fighting Germany's Spies.* New York: Doubleday, Page, 1918.

Sweetman, Jack. *The landing at Veracruz: 1914.* Annapolis, MD: Naval Institute Press, 1968.

Tangeman, Michael. *Mexico at the Crossroads: Politics, the Church, and the Poor.* Maryknoll, NY: Orbis Books, 1995.

Taracena, Alfonso. *La verdadera Revolución Mexicana, Seguna Etapa 1913–1914.* Mexico City: Editorial Jus, 1960.

Teitelbaum, Louis M. *Woodrow Wilson and the Mexican Revolution, 1913–1916.* New York: Exposition Press, 1967.

Thompson, Wallace. *The People of Mexico.* New York: Harper's, 1920.

Tijerina, Andrés. *Tejano Empire: Life on South Texas Ranchos.* College Station: Texas A&M University Press, 1990.

Tinkle, Lon. *Mr. De: A Biography of Everette Lee DeGolyer.* Boston: Little, Brown, 1970.

Tischendorf, Alfred. *Great Britain and Mexico in the Era of Porfirio Díaz, 1876–1910.* Durham, NC: Duke University Press, 1961.

Tragakiss, Tamara, "Recalling Glory Days," *Passport,* November 17, 2005,

1921.

———. *Woodrow Wilson as I Knew Him.* New York: Doubleday, Page, 1921.

Turlington, Edgar. *Mexico and Her Foreign Creditors.* New York: Columbia University Press, 1930.

Turner, Frederick C. "Anti-Americanism in Mexico, 1910–1913." *Hispanic American Historical Review,* November 1967, 502–18.

———. *The Dynamic of Mexican Nationalism.* Chapel Hill: University of North Carolina Press, 1968.

Turner, John K. *Barbarous Mexico.* 1911. Reprint, Austin: University of Texas Press, 1969.

Usher, Roland G. "The Real Mexican Problem." *North American Review,* July 1914, 45–52.

Valle, Sara Gomez. *La no intervención el los Estados Americanos.* Mexico City: Universidad Nacional Autonomia de Mexico, Escuela de Jurisprudencia, 1949.

Vandiver, Frank E. *Black Jack: The Life and Times of John J. Pershing.* College Station: Texas A&M Press, 1977.

Valecillos, Hector, and Omar Bello Rodriguez. *La Economía Contemporánea de Venezuela.* Caracas: Banco Central de Venezuela, 1990.

Vaughan, Mary Kay. *The State, Education and Social Class in Mexico, 1880–1928.* DeKalb: Northern Illinois University Press, 1982.

Vazquez, Josefina, and Lorenza Meyer. *The United States and Mexico.* Chicago: University of Chicago Press, 1985.

Veatch, Arthur C. "Oil, Great Britain, and the United States." *Foreign Affairs,* July 1931, 665–70.

Vera Estanol, Jose. *Carranza and His Bolshevik Regime.* Los Angeles: Wayside Press, 1920.

Viereck, George S. *The Strangest Friendship in History: Woodrow Wilson and Colonel House.* New York: Liveright, 1932.

Villalpando, Jose Manuel, and Alejandro Rosas. *Historia de México a través de sus Gobernantes.* Mexico City: Planeta, 2003.

Von zur Gathen, Joachim. "Zimmermann Telegram: The Original Draft." *Cryptologia,* 2007.

Walling, William E. *The Mexican Question: Mexico and American-Mexican Relations under Calles and Obregon.* New York: Robins Press, 1927.

Warner, Liam. "The Lion in Winter." *National Review,* August 25, 2018.

Wasserman, Mark. *Pesos and Politics: Business, Elites, Foreigners, and Government in Mexico, 1854–1940.* Stanford, CA: Stanford University Press, 2015.

Webb, Walter P. *The Texas Rangers.* Boston: Houghton Mifflin, 1935.

Weber, William. *Heroic Mexico: The Violent Emergence of a Modern Nation.* Garden City, NY: Doubleday, 1968.

Weeks, O. Douglas. "The Texas-Mexican and the Politics of South Texas." *American Political Science Review,* August 1930, 605–27.

Weinstein, Edwin A. "Woodrow's Wilson's Neurological Illness." *Journal of American History,* September 1970, 324–51.

Welsome, Eileen. *The General and the Jaguar: Pershing's Hunt for Pancho Villa.* New York: Little, Brown, 2006.

Whitney, Caspar. *What's the Matter with Mexico?* New York: Macmillan, 1916.

Wiggins, Melanie. *Torpedoes in the Gulf.* College Station: Texas A&M University Press, 1995.

Wild, Payson S. "International Law and Mexican Oil." *Quarterly Journal of Inter-American Relations,* April 1939.

Wilkinson, Joseph B. *Laredo and the Rio Grande Frontier: A Narrative.* Austin: Jenkins, 1975.

Williams, William Appleman. *The Tragedy of American Diplomacy.* New York: Delta Books, 1959.

Wilson, Arnold. "Oil Legislation in Latin America." *Foreign Affairs,* October 1929, 108–19.

Wilson, Edith B. *My Memoirs.* New York: Bobbs-Merrill, 1938.

Wilson, Henry Lane. *Diplomatic Episodes in Mexico, Belgium, and Chile.* Garden City, NY: Doubleday, Page, 1927.

Winter, Nevin O. *Mexico and Her People Today.* Boston: L. C. Page, 1907.

Winton, George B. *Mexico, Past and Present.* Nashville: 1928.

Womack, John, Jr. *Zapata and the Mexican Revolution.* New York: Vintage Books, 1968.

Woodhouse, Henry. "The New Understanding with Mexico." *Current History,* September 1922, 1010–21.

Woods, Fred E. *Finding Refuge in El Paso: The 1912 Mormon Exodus from Mexico.* Springville, UT: Cedar Fort Inc., 2012.

Woods, Kenneth F. "Samuel Guy Inman and Intervention in Mexico." *Southern California Quarterly,* December 1964, 351–70.

Yergin, Daniel. *The Prize: The Epic Quest for Oil, Money and Power.* New York: Touchstone Books, 1991.

Young, Elliott. *Catarino Garza's Revolution on the Texas-Mexican Border.* Durham, NC: Duke University Press, 2004.

Young, Julia G. *Mexican Exodus: Emigrants, Exiles, and Refugees of the Cristero War.* New York: Oxford University Press, 2015.

Young, Karl E. *Ordeal in Mexico: Tales of Danger and Hardship Collected from Mormon Colonists.* Salt Lake City: Deseret, 1968.

Zoraida, Josefina, and Lorenzo Meyer. *México Frente a Estados Unidos: Un ensayo histórico, 1776–1980.* Mexico City: Colegio de Mexico, 1982.

1919–1923." PhD diss., University of Arizona, 1971.

Buckley, W. F. [Sr.], President, AAM. "Some Aspects of the Problem of Recognizing the Present Government of Mexico." Address to the Annual Meeting of the
Mississippi Valley Historical Association, May 12, 1922.

Calderon, Roberto Ramon. "Mexican Politics in the American Era, 1846–1900:
Laredo Texas." PhD diss., University of California, 1993.

Christie, Thomas W. "Diplomacy of Intervention: The ABC Conference Niagara
Falls 1914." Master's thesis, University of Montana, 1986.

Davids, Jules. "American Political and Economic Penetration of Mexico." PhD
diss., Georgetown University, 1847.

Duarte-Vivas, Andres. "The First Venezuelan Geological Oil Map: The Ralph
Arnold History 1911–1916." Cartagena: AAPG International Conference,
September 2013.

Duke, Travis. "Henry Lane Wilson, Diplomatic Influence, and the Expansion of
the Mexican Revolution." Master's thesis, University of Texas at Dallas,
December 2014.

Edwards, Warrick R. "United States–Mexico Relations, 1913–1916: Revolution, Oil,
and Intervention." PhD diss., Louisiana State University, August 1971.

Giesen, Carlos. "Beginning and Early Stage of the Venezuelan Oil Industry." Master's thesis, University of Calgary, 1982.

Gilderhus, Mark T. "The United States and the Mexican Revolution, 1915–1920: A
Study in Policy and Interest." PhD diss., University of Nebraska, June 1968.

Hindman, Ewell J. "The United States and Alvaro Obregón: Diplomacy by Proxy."
PhD diss., Texas Tech University, 1972.

Holcombe, Harold E. "United States Arms Control and the Mexican Revolution."
PhD diss., University of Alabama, 1968.

Lou, Dennis W. "Fall Committee: An Investigation of Mexican Affairs." PhD diss.,
Indiana University, 1963.

Lyon, Jessie. "Diplomatic Relations between the United States, Mexico, and Japan,
1913–1917." PhD diss., Claremont College, 1975.

Palacio Langer, Ana Julia del. "Agrarian Reform, Oil Expropriation, and the Making of National Property in Post-revolutionary Mexico." PhD diss., Columbia
University, 2015.

Plotnick, Alan R. "American Government Oil Price Policies, 1930–1984." Faculty
Working Papers, University of New Haven, November 14, 1984.

Rice, Elizabeth A. "Diplomatic Relations between the United States and Mexico,
as Affected by the Struggle for Religious Liberty in Mexico, 1925–1929." PhD
diss., Catholic University of America, 1959.

Robertson, O. Zeller. "Mexico and Non-intervention, 1910–1919: The Policy, the
Practice and the Law." PhD diss., University of California, 1969.

Stewart, James E. "The Niagara Falls Conference, 1914: A Study in United States–
Mexico Relations." Master's thesis, University of Arizona, 1970.

Interviews

Buckley, James Lane. December 19 and 31, 2018, by phone; January 11, April 7, and November 11, 2019, from Bethesda, MD, by author.

———. August 14, 1995, thru January 15, 1996, Oral History Project, Historical Society of the District of Columbia Circuit, by Wendy S. White.

Buckley, William H. December 12 and 14, 2018, by phone from Mexico City, by author.

Hopkins, Amy. 1974, Houston Oral History Project, Houston Public Library, No. OH 079.

King, Stuart P. August 1984, Petroleum Industry Oral History Project.

Reasoner, Mel. Canada Southern petroleum geologist, September 1994, Petroleum Industry Oral History Project.

Smith, Cameron O. December 15, 2019, by phone; and February 5, 2020, in Houston, TX—by author.

Index

AAM. *See* American Association of Mexico

ABC (Argentina, Brazil, Chile)/ Niagara Conference (1914), 3, 59–65, 101–3, 123; Buckley as Mexican delegation adviser, 60–65; Carranza opposition, 59–63; Latin America response, 63–64

Aguilar, Cándido, 157

Aguirre, Modesto, 73

Altendorf, Paul Bernardo, 124–25

Alvarado, Salvador, 117, 153; anti-Catholic, 111–12

America First Committee, 196

American Association of Mexico (AAM), 161, 168, 170–71; *Bulletin*, 161, 187

American Chamber of Commerce, Austin, Texas, 162

American Embassy (Mexico City), 6, 8, 10, 12, 19, 24, 30–31, 44, 55–56, 65, 142, 145, 163–69

American Expeditionary Force, 125; failure, 135, 145

American Venezuelan Oilfield Company, 180

amparo (injuctions), 92–93, 162

Angeles, Felipe, 12

Anglo Mexican Petroleum Company, 93

Antilla (schooner), 118

Arms Embargo Law of 1912, 37

Arnold, Ralph, 101–2; Venezuela survey, 177

Arnold Oil Exploration, 202

Arredondo, Eliseo, 120

Association of Foreign Oil Producers of Mexico, 88, 136, 149, 156

Atlantic Refining Company, 190, 192, 200

Baker, Burke, 196, 199

Barker, Eugene C., 3, 20

Bard, John Pierre, 15

barrilero, 15

Baruch, Bernard, 92, 154

Battle of Léon, 124

Bavaria (German ship), 69

Bielaski, A. Bruce, 150–51
Bliss, Tinker, 26
Blocker, John, 76
Bolshevism, 132, 137
Bonillas, Ignacio, 144, 151, 153–54
Bonney, Wilbert, 57
Brady, Nicolas, 188
Braniff, Senora Thomas, 66
British, 2, 83; canal toll dispute, 42–43;
    demands to collect bonds, 42; Foreign
    Office, 30, 105, 113, 126; intelligence,
    62, 113; oil companies, 19, 24, 43;
    protest against murders, 44–47
British Oil Syndicate, 180
Brooks, Richard, 76
Brown, Erwin, 128
Bryan, William Jennings, 20, 23, 29,
    36, 47, 76, 82, 102; Catholic situation
    in Mexico, 113–16; Veracruz landing
    response, 54–55
Buckley, Aloise Steiner (wife), 93–95,
    100, 167, 186, 192, 194, 200, 209;
    death, 210; secret Catholic Mass,
    130; wedding proposal, 94–95
Buckley (Heath), Aloise (daughter),
    206, 209
Buckley, Claude (brother), 15, 16, 33, 77,
    159, 168, 194, 207
Buckley, Edmund (brother), 15, 19,
    74–78, 93, 159, 166, 168, 207
Buckley, Eleanor (sister), 15
Buckley, Elinor Doran (grandmother), 14
Buckley, James L. (son), 3, 4, 14, 17, 93,
    198, 203–4
Buckley, John (grandfather), 14
Buckley, John (father), 14; assassination
    attempts, 17; death, 17; sheriff of
    Duval County, Texas, 15–16
Buckley, John (son), 79, 95, 167, 170,
    173, 177, 203, 206
Buckley, Mary Ann Langford
    (mother), 14, 93
Buckley, Priscilla (sister), 15, 17, 93

Buckley, Priscilla (daughter), 78, 163, 167
Buckley, Reed (son), 2, 4, 33, 54–55, 68,
    77–78, 99, 192
Buckley, William F., Jr. (son), 1, 95, 198,
    209; associate editor, *American
    Mercury*, 198; *God and Man at Yale*,
    198; *National Review*, 1, 199, 204
Buckley, William Frank, Sr.: ABC
    Conference agent Mr. X, 60–66, 165;
    adviser to William Jennings Bryan,
    64; assassination attempts, 99–100,
    150, 154; assassination, use of, 14, 29;
    Benavides, Texas, schoolteacher, 17;
    born Washington-on-the-Brazos,
    Texas, 14; bribery, use of, 74; *The
    Cactus* editor, 17; on Carranza
    Mexico City invasion, 65–67;
    Catholic Church and faith, 1, 15, 24,
    33, 106, 130–32; Compañía Maritima
    Paraguaná, C.A., 178; Constitution
    of 1917, 128; death, 210; Delta Tau
    Delta, 17–18; developed "farm out"
    agreements, 204; early education, 1,
    15–17; Edward House, 41, 61, 145,
    148; encounters with Pancho Villa,
    33–35, 68–69, 99; expelled from
    Mexico, 105, 163–70, 208; Fall
    Committee, 132–69; founder of
    Petroleum Bank and Trust
    Company, 78, 171; intervention in
    Mexico, 61, 145–48; law office in
    Tampico, 27; law school, 6, 17–18;
    meeting with President Gómez,
    177–78; Mexico City, 18–19;
    persecution of Catholic priests, 66;
    return to Mexico City (1927) and
    (1943), 187, 200; sniper incident,
    54; on Tampico incident, 50–51;
    University of Texas, 17–19;
    Venezuela, 173–86; on Veracruz
    landing, 52–55, 58; World War II,
    195–203; post–World War II, 201–3
Buckley, William Hunt, 3

Buckley and Buckley law firm, 38, 70–79, 89, 136
Buckley Port (Venezuela), 178
Bureau of Investigation, 154, 161
Burleson, Albert S., 29, 64
Butler, Smedley D., 51

Caballero, Luis, 152
Cabrera, Alfonso, 143
Cabrera, Luis, 28, 45, 71–73, 103, 121, 145; ABC (Niagara) Conference, 165; anti-American, 72, 143–45; Central America mission, 135–36; escapes assassination, 159; opposition to church, 108, 130–32; opposition to oil companies 79–82; Marazan Plan, 136; professor of law, 72
California Petroleum Company, 180, 184
Calles, P. Elias, 152, 159, 168; anti-Catholic Church, 186–87; president, 186
Camden, S.C., 192–93, 206, 209
Canada, 191, 195, 203
Canada, William, 49, 115–17, 124; Veracruz incident, 52–55
Cananea Consolidated Copper Mines, 8, 80
Canova, Leon, 86
Cantú, Esteban, 152, 160, 164
Carbajal, Francisco, 84
Cárdenas, Lázaro, 159
Catawba Corporation, 203–6
Catholic Extension Society, 114
Chabot, Frederick C., 181–86, 201
Clavo Doctrine, 72
Cardenas, Lazaro, 193
Caribbean Area Petroleum Committee, 190

Army enters Mexico City, 65–67; Catholic Church, 109–12; governor of Coahuila, 27–29; legitimacy questioned, 124; Veracruz landing, 56–58; "war tax," 98
Casasús, Joaquín, 66
Catholic Church, 1, 2, 15, 104–32; Carranza opposition, 109–12; persecution of priests, 66
Central America, intervention, 151
Central Intelligence Agency, 198
Chamberlain, George A., 58
Chapultepec, 5, 7, 22, 46, 66
Chinese refugees, 125
Científicos, 66, 123, 145
Cinco de Mayo, 15
Clayton, Powell, 81
Cobb, Zach, 86
Coolidge, Calvin, 178, 188
Coley, William, 210
Colquitt, Oscar B., 10, 44–47
Compagnie Française des Petroles, 180, 190, 203
Compañía Maritima Paraguaná, C.A., 178
Compañía Venezolana de Petróleo (CVP), 179
Constitution of 1857, 106
Constitution of 1917, 55, 127–28, 132, 137, 208; Article 27, 55, 92, 127, 140, 155, 169, 172, 188; and Bucareli Agreement, 179; expropriation, 193–94
Córdoba, Federico, 142
Corpus Christi, 14
counterrevolutionary groups, 7, 151–53
Cradock, Christopher F., 26, 57
Cradock, Sir Charles, 83

assessment of, 28; Constitutional

cuartelazo (military coup), 141, 150

Culubra Tunnel, 46
Curzon, Lord George, 93

d'Antin, Luis, 10, 30–31; death of, 153;
    Veracruz landing, 56
Damas Católicas, 130
Daniels, Josephus, 49–51, 132, 160
Dato, Fred A., 194
Davis, Will, 85
Decena Trágica (Ten Tragic Days), 7
DeGolyer, Everett, 93, 99, 102
de la Barra, Francisco Léon, 12
de la Huerta, Adolfo, 152, 159, 166
Delta Tau Delta, 17–18
de Negri, Ramón P., 151, 154
de Oliveira, Jose M., 56, 113–14, 117
Department of Interior
    (Gobernación), 128
de Peralta, Pedro Grave, 136
Dewey, Thomas E., 200
Diário Oficial, 92–93
Díaz, Felix, 7, 8, 10, 11
Díaz, Carmen (wife), 107
Díaz, Porfirio (Profiriato), 5, 7, 8, 9, 10,
    17–19, 70, 73, 207; Catholic Church,
    107; exiled to Veracruz, 22; foreign
    direct investment, 19–20, 42, 75–76, 79,
    81–82; overthrow, 21, 42; retirement, 18
Diéguez, Manuel M., 129
Diez y Seis de Septiembre, 15
Doheny, Edward L., 75, 81, 88, 91–92,
    101, 137, 140, 156, 159, 162, 180
Dollar Diplomacy, 23, 40, 42
Dresden (German cruiser), 48, 63
Duval County, Texas, 14–16

education, 111, 130–33
ejidos (communal lands), 8;
    redistribution of, 21
Elguero, Luis, 60
Escuela Nacional de Jurisprudence
    (Mexico City), 17
expropriation, 193

Fabela, Isidro, 45
Fall, Albert B., 4, 28, 33, 47, 102;
    assassination attempt, 154; Senate
    Foreign Relations Committee,
    85–86, 101, 112, 115
Favela, Javier, 154
Fierro, Rodolfo: and Benton murder,
    44; Catholic Church, 111
Fiske, Bradley, 52
Fletcher, Henry P., 54, 92, 134–35, 146,
    165; formal recognition of
    Carranza, 129
Flipper, Henry O., 138, 175, 177, 182
Florida, 197, 202–3
Fraustro, Ramón, 47
Fuller, Paul, 86
Funston, Frederick, 53–55

Gamboa, Francisco, 118
Garrett, Alonzo, 44
Garrison, L. M., 55, 65, 72, 84–85,
    102–3
García, José A., 73
Garza, Catarino, 17
Garza, Capistran, 188
Germany, 2; espionage in Mexico, 37,
    89–91, 120, 124, 132, 150; and *golpe de
    estado* (coup d'état), 7, 107; U-boats, 91
gómecista, 176, 179
Gómez, Emilio Vasquez, 7
Gómez, Juan Vicente, 176, 182, 201;
    death, 191–92; meeting with
    Buckley, 177
González, Pablo, 128
Gould, Jay, 19
Grampus (schooner), 118
Grayson, Cary, 144
Great Elm (Sharon, Conn.), 99, 171,
    202, 206, 209
Greene, William C., 139, 161, 165
Gregory, Thomas W., 29, 64, 76
Grelmschatka, 206
Gurría Urgell, Nicanor, 73, 104

Hale, William B., 30, 31
Hamilton, Charles W., 95
Hanna, Philip, 57, 113, 150
Hanson, W. M., 138, 150; assassination
    attempt, 153–54; Fall hearings, 150–55
Hardaker, William, 144
Harding, Warren, 162, 165
Hearst, William Randolph, 30, 138,
    140, 165
Heath, Aloise (Allie; grand-daughter),
    206
Heath, Benjamin W., 203, 206
henequen, 140
Hicks, Marshall, 17
Hilles, Charles D., 123
Hinds, Henry, 177
Hobby, William P., 165
Hogg, James, 76
Hogg, William, 76
Hoover, Herbert, 185
Hopkins, Sherburne G., 62, 84
House, Edgar, 97
House, Edward, 24, 29, 41, 47, 65, 145;
    concern with Zimmermann cable,
    90
House, Henry, 77, 102
Houston, David, 29–30; ABC
    Conference, 61, 73
Huerta, Victoriano, 7, 10, 11, 12, 31;
    Benton murder, 45–46; Chamber of
    Deputies, 108; coup and Catholic
    Church, 11, 107–12; education, 22;
    moratorium on foreign loans, 25,
    41–42; response to Veracruz
    landing, 53–57; seized presidency,
    22–24; US House vote, 50; White
    House opposition, 27–28, 36
Hughes, Charles Evans, 123, 173
Hull, Cordell, 193
Humble Oil, 197

Hunt, E. Howard, 198
Hyde, George E., 138

Industrial Workers of the World, 187
International and Great Northern
    Railway, 37

Jenkins, William O.: kidnapping,
    141–48; ransom, 147–48
Jones, Charles E. "Cresse," 150–55
Jones, Gus T., 138
Juárez, Benito, 106, 121
Juárez Memorial, 55
Jusserland, Jean Jules, 111

Kamschatka, 193, 206
Kearful, Francis J., 138
Kelley, Francis C., 114–15, 126, 140;
    Paris Peace Conference, 115
Kerr, Robert, 54
Kirby, John H., 76
Knights of Columbus, 187
Knox, Philander, 11, 13

La Compañia Terminal la Isleta,
    S.A., 74
Lake Maracaibo, 173–74, 177, 180, 198
Lake Okeechobee, 197, 204
Lansing, Robert, 92, 134, 143–46, 154
Laredo, 14, 19, 153, 161, 167
Lascuráin, Pedro, 12, 66
League of Nations, 115, 135
Leckie, Adam, 151
ley de fugas, 12, 125
Liga Nacional Defensora de la
    Libertad Religiosa (LNDLR), 188
Limantour, José Yves, 19, 66
Lind, John, 31–32, 36, 49–50, 56, 63, 103,

López Contreras, Eleazar, 192

Los Remédios (ranch), 44
Love, Thomas B., 29
LST (landing ship tank), 198

Madero, Francisco Ignacio, 7, 8, 9, 10, 11, 13, 28; assassination, 12–14, 28; Huerta coup, 11–12; *porra* of, 9
Madero, Gustavo (brother), 9
Marazan Plan, 135–36
Mayo, Henry T., 48–50, 57
Mene Grande (Venezuela Oil Concessions), 173, 184
Mexican Central Railroad, 81
Mexican Eagle Oil Company (Petróleo El Águila), 9, 76; oil production, 93; World War I response, 91–92, 95–98, 192
Mexican Federal Army, 9, 26, 38, 41, 44, 48; at Veracruz, 52–55
Mexican Investment Company, 78
Mexican mining law, 79–81, 86–89
Mexican Petroleum and Liquid Fuel Company, 80–81
Mexico: centennial, 19; killed during Revolution, 2, 133; labor strikes, 8, 130–32; land reform, 9; population, 2, 8; railroad destruction, 133
Miller, Henry, 57–58, 83
Montgomery, George S., 173, 203
Moore, John Bassett, 29
Mora y del Río, José, 188
Morgenthau, Hans, 156
Mormon colonists, 127–28
Morrow, Dwight, 189
Mr. X. *See* Buckley, William F., Sr.
Murray, Robert H., 30
Mutual Film Company, 39
Myers, Henry L., 143

National Association for the Protection of American Rights in Mexico, 88, 136–37, 149; Fall hearings, 148
National City Bank, 76–77

National Palace. *See* Chapultepec
neutrality laws, 16, 62, 161
Newman Club, 17
New York Edison Company, 188
Nicaragua, and proposed canal route, 42

Obregón, Alvaro, 27, 38, 66, 84, 124, 152; assassination, 185, 187; on Catholic Church, 113–14, 117, 160; Marazan Plan, 136; Plan of Agua Prieta, 157–58; plots against, 163; presidency, 159–61
Orozco, Pascual, 7
O'Shaughnessy, Edith, 2, 12, 14, 56, 59, 108
O'Shaughnessy, Nelson, 31, 36, 46; backlash to Veracruz, 56–57; Catholic Church, 105, 119; Tampico incident, 50–51

Pacto de la Ciudadela, 11, 219–20
Page Walter, 26, 46
Palmer, A. Mitchell, 154
Pani, Alberto, 167
Pancoastal Group, 191–92, 204
Pantepec-Catawba Corporation, 198
Pantepec Oil Company of Mexico, 67–69, 78, 81, 93, 168, 172
Pantepec Oil Company of Venezuela, 174, 178–82, 203, 207; "farm out" leases, 180, 196; oil production, 181–83, 189, 201–2; stockholders, 191
Pantepec River, 99
Pánuco River, 74, 76, 78
Paraguaná Peninsula, 178–79
Paris Peace talks, 115, 134
Parr, Archie, 17; Democratic political machine, 16–17
Pearl Harbor, 196, 198
Pearson, Weetman (Lord Cowdray), 76, 91
Peláez, Manuel, 92, 97–99, 194; Buckley relationship with, 167; Carranza

assassination, 159–60; Jenkins kidnapping, 143; "war tax," 98
Pershing, John "Black Jack," 122–23; expedition failure, 135, 145. *See also* US Army
Petroleum Banking and Trust Company, 78
Petroleum Club (Mexico City), 25
Pierce, H. Clay, 82
Pino Suárez, José María, 10; assassination, 12
Plan of Agua Prieta, 157
Plan of Guadalupe, 27
Pope, Walter, 78
porra (political group), 9
Preclusion Operations Division of the Board of Economic Warfare (BEW), 199

Querétaro Convention, 80

Rabasa, Emilio, 60, 73, 103–4, 173, 200
Reed, Douglas, 170, 196, 201
Republican National Committee, 123, 185
Reyes, Bernardo, 144
Rice, Cecil Spring, 25
Rice, J. S., 76, 83, 113
Reyes, Bernardo, 7, 8, 10
Rhodes, Cecil, 80
Rihl, George L., 78
Rodgers, James, 87
Rodriquez, Agustin, 60
Roosevelt, Franklin D. (FDR), 193, 197–98; Good Neighbor Policy, 194
Roosevelt, Theodore, 114
Royal Dutch (Shell), 173, 180, 184,
Ruiz Martin C. 73

Slattery, Michael J., 33
Smith, Al, 186
Smith, Cameron, 3
Smith, Warren W., 177, 182, 200, 203
smuggling, 16, 37–38, 47; Church artifacts, 130
Sommerfeld, Felix, 30, 141; Fall hearings, 149–50
Sophie Newcomb College, 94
Spindletop, Texas, 76
Standard Oil of New Jersey, 76, 81, 88, 91, 140, 173, 180, 190, 196, 198, 200
Stillman, John R., 57, 76, 84–86; Catholic Church, 111
Streeter, Thomas W., 123
Summerlin, George, 143–44; Buckley expulsion, 163–69
Sunshine (schooner), 118
Susan (schooner), 118
Swain, Chester, 88, 140

Taft, William H., 9, 11, 12, 13, 22–23
Tampico, 9, 23, 27, 33, 36, 74; German meddling during World War I, 89–91; incident against "the flag," 48–52; oil field disruption, 82–84, 93, 156
Terrazas, Alberta, 27
Texas Company (Texaco), 76, 88, 102, 180
Texas General Land Office, 17
Texas Mexican Railroad, 14
Texas Rangers, 44–45, 138, 155
Tlaxcalantongo, Mexico, 158
Toral, José de León, 187
Treaty of Guadalupe Hidalgo (1848), 90
Trent Affair (1861), 51
Tumulty, Joseph P., 121, 144

San Juan River (Nicaragua), 42
Sharp, Walter B., 76–77

30, 59, 73, 196

Urguizo, Francisco, 45
Urquidi, Francisco, 62
US Army, 26, 28, 47, 135; landing at
    Veracruz, 52–55; use of hot pursuit,
    135. *See also* American
    Expeditionary Force
US Bureau of Mines, 157
US Customs Service, 38
US Embassy (Mexico City). *See*
    American Embassy (Mexico City)
US Embassy (Caracas, Venezuela), 178,
    181–86, 201
US Marines, 51–54, 65
USS *Chester* (ship), 36
USS *Dalphin* (gunboat), 48
USS *Florida* (battleship), 51
USS *Prairie* (gunboat), 51
US State Department, 3, 13, 22, 29–31,
    37–38, 46, 52–53, 58, 87–89, 102, 111,
    114, 120, 12–16, 134, 144–46, 157,
    164–69, 172, 182, 201
USS *Utah* (battleship), 51
US War Department, Planning
    Division, 198–99

Velasco, Cecilio, 68, 98–100, 159, 177,
    179, 182
Venezuela, 171; investment law, 177–78;
    oil production, 181, 186, 189, 192,
    200; *reglamento*, 175; tax system,
    175–76, 190, 192, 203; World War I
    oil concessions, 176
Veracruz, 2, 10, 33, 50–55
Vergara, Clemente: kidnapping and
    murder, 43–46; Oscar B. Colquitt, 44
Villa, "Pancho" (born José Doroteo
    Arango), 1, 17, 27, 72, 84; Benton
    murder, 44–45; border attacks,
    38–39; Catholic Church, 105, 110;
    encounters with William F.
    Buckley Sr., 33–35, 67–69; *Life of
    General Villa*, 39; movie production,
    39; presidential possibility, 39

Villarreal, Antonio I., 115–16
Villavicencio, R, R., 136

Walker, Harold, 88
Washington-on-the-Brazos, Texas, 14
Waters-Peters Oil Company, 76
Willkie, Wendel, 197
Willoughby, Charles A., 183
Wilson, Henry Lane, 2, 6, 9, 11, 12, 13,
    20–24, 27, 30, 40, 141; Fall hearings,
    149–50; retirement, 185; death, 187.
    See also American Embassy
    (Mexico City)
Wilson, Woodrow, 2, 13, 22–24, 28–29,
    33, 36, 156, 196; Catholic Church
    policy, 105–12; "confidential
    agents," 71; Fall Committee
    hearings, 139; on Huerta, 39, 48–49;
    Paris Peace talks, 134; Tampico
    "flag" incident, 48–52; US dead
    returned from Veracruz, 59; US
    House vote against Huerta, 50;
    Veracruz incident, 50–58, 118;
    "watchful waiting" policy, 47
Wood, Leonard, 52
World War I: armistice, 133–34;
    Mexico response, 80–85; petroleum
    demands, 173
World War II, 196–203; oil demand,
    197–98, 199–200

Xochimilco, 68

Ypiranga (ship), 10, 59–60; Tampico
    incident, 50–53; Veracruz landing,
    57

Zapata, Emiliano, 7, 84; in Mexico
    City, 67–69; 72
Zaragoza, Morelos, 57
Zócalo, 6, 73
Zimmermann, Arthur, 90
Zimmermann Cable, 89–91

Made in United States
North Haven, CT
28 March 2023

34688100R00190